Leoncavallo

Life and Works

Konrad Dryden

THE SCARECROW PRESS, INC.
Lanham, Maryland • Toronto • Plymouth, UK
2007

SCARECROW PRESS, INC.

Published in the United States of America
by Scarecrow Press, Inc.
A wholly owned subsidiary of
The Rowman & Littlefield Publishing Group, Inc.
4501 Forbes Boulevard, Suite 200, Lanham, Maryland 20706
www.scarecrowpress.com

Estover Road
Plymouth PL6 7PY
United Kingdom

British Library Cataloguing in Publication Information Available

Library of Congress Cataloging-in-Publication Data

Dryden, Konrad Claude.
  Leoncavallo : life and works / Konrad Dryden.
      p. cm.
  Includes bibliographical references (p.   ) and index.
  ISBN-13: 978-0-8108-5880-0 (hardcover : alk. paper)
  ISBN-13: 978-0-8108-5873-2 (pbk. : alk. paper)
  ISBN-10: 0-8108-5880-0 (hardcover : alk. paper)
  ISBN-10: 0-8108-5873-8 (pbk. : alk. paper)
    1. Leoncavallo, Ruggiero, 1857–1919. 2. Composers—Italy—Biography.
I. Title.
ML410.L517D78 2007
782.1092—dc22 [B]   2006025255

Contents

Foreword

Plácido Domingo

*I*t has been said by non-well-meaning musicologists that Ruggiero Leoncavallo was a "one opera composer"—namely *Pagliacci*. To this I have two reactions. The first is the exclamation "But what an opera!" and the second is the knowledge that this book about him will set the record straight and perhaps bring about revivals of certain of his works like, for instance, his version of *La bohème*. It premiered almost simultaneously with Puccini's but remained in the shadow of the other's tremendous success and popularity. I have had the good fortune to have seen it and find a great deal of inspired music in it. It never entered my repertoire because I did not have the possibility of convincing a theater to do it. However, I recorded both of Marcello's arias (in this *Bohème* Marcello is the tenor): "Io non ho che una povera stanzetta" and "Testa adorata." I also recorded the great aria from *Chatterton*: "Tu sola a me rimani o poesia."

But getting back to *Pagliacci*. Every *spinto* tenor worth his proverbial salt has wanted to sing Canio, starting with Caruso. As a matter of fact, because of him the work became almost synonymous with the concept of opera because he made the aria "Vesti la giubba," through his recording of it, one of the most popular classical compositions.

I think it is fairly safe to say that without *Pagliacci* and Mascagni's *Cavalleria rusticana*, the operatic style of verismo in its fundamental aspect could never have achieved its continuing hold on the operatic repertoire. What I also find fascinating is that, like Puccini, both Leoncavallo and Mascagni broke away from verismo to compose in a different musical style for librettos of less down-to-earth topics.

Canio is a role that I have performed well over one hundred times and the one for which I have had a wide-ranging number of directorial concepts. Among the directors with whom I have worked on the part have been Frank Corsaro, Franco Zeffirelli, Jean-Pierre Ponnelle, Gian-Carlo del Monaco and

Liliana Cavani—to mention only a few—and each one has stressed a different view of Canio's character. One can interpret him in many different ways, especially regarding his motive for killing Nedda. For me, the most preferred is to portray him almost as a father figure to Nedda and to arrive at the terrifying end by sheer momentary impulse. It is the same way I see the killing of Desdemona by Otello—the emotion of jealousy being so overwhelming at that instant that all reason snaps. I prefer this interpretation rather than one of premeditated murder.

I sang both Canio in *Pagliacci* and Turiddu in *Cavalleria rusticana* on the same evening on almost fifty occasions, which was a challenge that I always enjoyed. Two different characters, both dramatic, both in love, one gets killed, the other kills. During one performance in Barcelona, apart from singing both roles, I also sang Tonio's famous prologue from *Pagliacci,* as the baritone was sick. That was really *the* most exciting of all my *Pagliacci* performances.

Foreword

Piera Leoncavallo

$\mathcal{B}$orn in Alexandria, Egypt, I was raised with the awareness of having the unique privilege of belonging to the family that had produced one of opera's most celebrated composers— Ruggiero Leoncavallo.

My ancestor, Giuseppe Leoncavallo, the composer's uncle, settled in Cairo toward the end of the nineteenth century, where he worked in the Foreign Ministry. After the composer originated the idea of his first opera, *Chatterton*, and studied in Bologna with Giosuè Carducci, he faced the dilemma of what to do next. Following the death of his mother, Virginia D'Auria, he was loath to remain in Potenza, aware that his father, the judge Vincenzo, would insist that he take up the legal career that was customary in our family.

My grandfather may have even succeeded in changing music history, by suggesting that his young artistic nephew join him in Egypt for additional time to contemplate his future and to decide whether he indeed wished to become a composer. Leoncavallo remained in Egypt for some years, writing numerous songs and becoming music instructor to Muhammed Hamid, Khedive Tewfik's brother, before being forced to flee to France, where he settled in Paris, now determined to continue his course as a composer.

I have so many cherished memories associated with Leoncavallo. As a young girl I was of course familiar with parts of *Pagliacci*, but I will never forget the power and passion of Leoncavallo's music and how frightened and impressed I was upon seeing the opera for the first time in Alexandria. Leoncavallo succeeded in bringing raw emotions onto the operatic stage, which was, of course, a great novelty at the time. Other remembrances stem from visiting his luxurious estate, Villa Myriam, on the shores of Lake Maggiore, although by that time the family no longer owned the house. The windows of the enormous rooms offered an enchanting view of the lake, while the ceiling in the composer's bedroom was painted with stars to convey the impression that the maestro was sleeping under an open sky.

Now, finally, Konrad Dryden, following years of intense research, has been able to re-create a detailed account of the composer that was Ruggiero Leoncavallo for the very first time.

I hope that future readers will share the same admiration that I did upon reading this important document of a composer who changed operatic history.

Acknowledgments

This volume would not exist without the work of the contributors, and so we thank them first. We are also grateful for a Dean's Fund at Syracuse University's Maxwell School of Citizenship and Public Affairs, which provided support for conference participation that led to this volume's creation and later helped to refine its contents.

Archive Key

$\mathcal{T}$he following abbreviations are used throughout the book when referring to various Leoncavallo archives:

AMI	Accademia Montaltina degli Inculti
ASC	Archivio di Stato, Cosenza
BAB	Biblioteca dell'Archiginnasio, Bologna
BCB	Biblioteca Carducci, Bologna
BCBMB	Biblioteca Civica Bibliografica e Musicale, Bologna
BCGR	Biblioteca Civica Gambalunga, Rimini
BCL	Biblioteca Cantonale, Locarno
BCP	Biblioteca Comunale, Piacenza
BFA	Bayreuth Festival Archives
BHA	Breitkopf und Härtel, Frankfurt/Main
BL	British Library, London
BNB	Biblioteca Nazionale, Bari
BNO	Bibliothèque de l'Opéra, Paris
BNP	Bibliothèque Nationale de France, Paris
BPP	Biblioteca Palatina, Parma
BRF	Biblioteca Riccardiana, Florence
BSM	Bayerische Staatsbibliothek, Munich
CL	Comune di Locarno
CMS	Casa Musicale Sonzogno di Piero Ostali, Milan
CMU	Comune di Montalto Uffugo
CR	Casa Ricordi, Milan
EC	Editions Choudens, Paris
GH	Gemeentemuseum den Haag
GMA	Gino Marinuzzi Archives, Milan

GSPK	Geheimes Staatsarchiv Preussischer Kulturbesitz, Berlin
HOA	Hungarian State Opera Archives, Budapest
IFMR	Italian Foreign Ministry, Rome
LOC	Library of Congress, Washington, D.C.
MAB	Münchhausen Archives, Brissago
MOA	Metropolitan Opera Archives, New York
MTS	Museo Teatrale alla Scala, Milan
MVHP	Maison Victor Hugo, Paris
NY	New York Public Library for the Performing Arts
PA	Peters Archive, Frankfurt/Main
PML	Pierpont Morgan Library, New York
PUL	Princeton University Library, Princeton, N.J.
RAW	Royal Archives, Windsor Castle
SB	Staatsbibliothek Berlin, Preußischer Kulturbesitz
SIMB	Staatliches Institut für Musikforschung, Berlin
SLD/SLSUD	Sächsische Landes-Staats-und Universitätsbibliothek, Dresden
SUBF	Stadt-und Universitätsbibliothek, Frankfurt/Main
SUL	Stanford University Library
TMP	Teatro Massimo, Palermo
USCM	Ufficio Stato Civile, Milan
USCN	Ufficio Stato Civile, Naples
WSL	Wiener Stadt und Landesbibliothek
Y	The Frederick R. Koch Collection, Beinecke Rare Book and Manuscript Library, Yale University, New Haven, Conn.

Introduction

$\mathscr{R}$uggiero Leoncavallo makes a difficult case for any biographer, and it is not without reason that he is sometimes referred to as "opera's mystery man."[1] Although *Pagliacci* ranks as one of the world's most frequently performed works, relatively little is known about its creator, and what sparse documentation remains—thinly spread throughout the world—is not always factual. What has been written about Leoncavallo in musical encyclopedias mainly pokes fun at the composer's appearance, his failures, his litigious nature, his feuds with colleagues, his opportunism, and Puccini and Mascagni's nicknames for him.[2] Even *The New Grove Dictionary of Music and Musicians'* first edition entry on the composer contained no fewer than nine biographical errors and concluded by quoting Gabriele D'Annunzio's pompous and insulting epitaph written at the time of Leoncavallo's death.[3]

The "mysteries," most of which were promoted by Leoncavallo himself, begin with the uncertain year of his birth, his time spent in Egypt and Paris, his health, his finances, *Pagliacci's* origins, and his relationship with Puccini and other colleagues. Most of his operas (other than *Pagliacci*) remain elusive names in musical dictionaries, and his operettas have difficulty even being listed correctly. In 1958 the world celebrated the hundredth anniversary of his birth, although his actual centenary had already passed unobserved one year earlier.

Why a composer of one of the world's most famous operas has received such little research over the past one hundred years is difficult to comprehend. Although Leoncavallo shares this fate with most of his other colleagues,[4] he is a case apart, since recreating his life is more difficult than one might initially assume.

In 1998 I was asked to participate in the fourth International Leoncavallo Convention held at Locarno's Biblioteca Cantonale, Switzerland. The library also contains the Fondo Leoncavallo, an archive housing a large collection of the composer's letters and scores. At the time, like many, I was familiar only with *Pagliacci*, *Zazà*, and *La bohème*. Leoncavallo's other operas, such as *Chatterton* (based on the life of the mythical British poet) and *Der Roland von Berlin* (commissioned by Kaiser Wilhelm II), were intriguing though unfamiliar titles, as was his grand opera *I Medici*, the first of a planned trilogy (*Crepusculum*) dealing with the Italian renaissance and inspired by Carducci and Wagner, which was never completed. Additional works, such as *Maïa*, *Edipo re*, *Zingari*, and *Mameli*, were only names. I soon discovered that Leoncavallo's compositions were even more extensive, including the operettas *Malbruk*, *La reginetta delle rose*, *La candidata*, *Prestami tua moglie*, and *A chi la giarrettiera?*, in addition to the symphonic poems *Séraphitus-Séraphita* and *La nuit de mai*, based on Balzac and Alfred de Musset respectively.

On closer inspection, photos of Leoncavallo revealed more than just a portly, carefree Neapolitan, intent on creating a *bella figura*. There was another side. Numerous other photos, mostly unpublished, show a suffering and ill composer, after years of futile effort spent trying to recapture his earlier successes. *Pagliacci* brought luxury and wealth, the admiration of crowned heads of state, and household recognition of his name. His life, however, culminated in two decades of incessant frustration, disappointment, and fleeting concentration. Gone was the youthful striving for intellectual epics. Lacking money and inundated by self-generated legal battles, Leoncavallo became a tragic figure desperate for success, whose previous inspiration had by now all but vanished. Ensuing efforts were either short operas, operettas, or adaptations of earlier works under new titles (*Mameli*) that only further succeeded in damaging what little remained of his reputation.

Leoncavallo was a man of enormous paradox. He was warm and gregarious, emotional, childlike, ambitious, idealistic, melancholic, soft-spoken, cosmopolitan, modest, sensitive, dedicated, hardworking, helpful, and humorous. He could also be two-faced, gossipy, opportunistic, litigious, naive, megalomaniacal, and petty. This was a man who frequently lied about himself, who quickly adopted other people's ideas, employed ghostwriters, quarreled with colleagues, played his publishers one against another until they abandoned him, and was hopelessly inadequate in financial matters.

Leoncavallo's life is the narration of an immensely gifted man who was independent and ambitious of nature and who remained true to his artistic vision, regardless of the difficulties that initially beset him. *Pagliacci* was a brilliant work that appeared at precisely the right time, instantly catapulting its creator to renown, while simultaneously creating an enormous shadow under which he would suffer for the remainder of his life. Although *Pagliacci* is arguably Leoncavallo's greatest work, *Zazà*, *La bohème*, *Maïa*, and *La nuit de mai* would most likely be in the current international repertory had he *not* written them.

Writing the first documented critical biography of such a celebrated composer about which so little is known is a daunting task indeed and is bound to contain more errors than an additional monograph on Puccini, Verdi, or Wagner. Although the Fondo Leoncavallo houses an extensive collection, it was not sufficient to serve as the sole source for a fully documented study. An additional two hundred letters were eventually located after an exhaustive search at international archives. Although the addition was minimal, each letter and contract was important, since painfully little material regarding Leoncavallo remains. I was finally able to piece together his early Parisian years during the time he worked as a pianist in various café concerts, as well as his relations with his German publisher Fürstner and the genesis of his opera *Chatterton*. Relatively few of the composer's letters were kept before *Pagliacci* (1892), when he had already lived more than half his life. His letters to Berthe and to his family have yet to be discovered and may still be in private collections. Leoncavallo kept no diaries, and most of his letters are of a professional or legal nature, regarding the publishing and performances of his works. In fact, only one or two letters remain that shed some light on *Pagliacci*. Without any direct offspring, there were no individuals that could have helped to add another, more personal, aspect to his life.

This book sets out to unravel and organize the facts of Leoncavallo's life for the first time. Like my biography of Zandonai, it should be a foundation for future research. It also presents a relatively complete analysis of his works,[5] and it is the first time that the themes and motifs of his operas have been identified, let alone that their synopses explained. This section contains numerous references to his and to other composers' works. Although he frequently (and perhaps sometimes unconsciously) did "borrow," it should be viewed as proof of his awareness of international music development. Leoncavallo's style represents a bridge between bel canto and verismo, mostly influenced by Wagner and Massenet, and many of his earlier colleagues would have found it only natural to make short references to other works in their compositions.

Leoncavallo's wish to both please the public and to earn a living by his pen was no more opportunistic than that of most other composers, even though he was incessantly accused of such. Financial pressures kept him from composing what he desired, and his final string of operettas were but an agonized battle against bankruptcy, while his artistic vision cringed at the mediocrity that later dictated the direction of his musical talent.

He knew poverty and hunger during his Parisian years and obesity and wealth during his Swiss years. He was the archetypical Neapolitan, yet he preferred to live away from his own country, where he felt misunderstood. His was a chameleon nature, and his early works mirrored this psyche. I can't help recalling Virginia Woolf's *Orlando*, in which she writes "Every secret of a writer's soul, every experience of his life, every quality of his mind is written large in his works."

NOTES

1. Julian Budden, "Leoncavallo and *Zazà*," Wexford Festival Opera program notes, 1990.

2. "Cavalloleon"and "Leonbestia," among others.

3. The errors are listed in the following: (1) "His Christian name is properly Ruggero, not, as often given, Ruggiero." (2) "Moving to Bologna University, from which he received a degree in literature in 1878" (3) "For his plot [*Pagliacci*] Leoncavallo drew on memories of one of his father's law cases—a middle-aged actor had murdered his unfaithful young wife." (4) "He took his score [*Pagliacci*] to Ricordi's rival, Sonzogno, who promptly arranged a performance. (5) "Up to this time Leoncavallo had written his own librettos; now he turned to Angelo Nessi for *Maìa*." (6) "In 1907 he conducted *Pagliacci*, also for G & T, the first opera to be recorded in Italy." (7) "In the USA he staged his first operetta, *La jeunesse de Figaro* (1906)." (8) *Goffredo Mameli* is listed as an operetta. (9) *Nuit de mai* is listed as "not performed." From *The New Grove Dictionary of Music and Musicians,*1995. Fortunately, these errors were deleted in the 2001 edition.

4. Alfano, Cilèa, Giordano, Mascagni, Catalani, Wolf-Ferrari, and Respighi have yet to be adequately researched in order to prove that they were more than just "one-opera composers."

5. A complete score of *Are You There?* has yet to be discovered.

1
BIOGRAPHY

• 1 •

Initial Impressions

1857–1877

*L*eoncavallo stated in his unpublished autobiographical reminiscences, the *Appunti* (literally "Notes"), that he was "born into an ambience in which art was an essential part of life."[1] He was no doubt referring to his maternal grandfather, Raffaele D'Auria, a well-established Neapolitan painter and professor at the Reale Istituto di Belle Arti, whose works grace the Royal Palace as well as the villa at Capodimonte.[2] Leoncavallo recounts that, while teaching counterpoint at the Conservatory of Naples, Gaetano Donizetti befriended D'Auria, who named one of his daughters, (Leoncavallo's mother) Virginia, after Donizetti's wife, who died in 1837 at the age of twenty-nine, and whose name was Virginia Vasselli. Following her death and his unsuccessful bid to become director of the Naples conservatory (a post given to Saverio Mercadante), Donizetti left Naples for Paris, thus ending the close relationship the composer had enjoyed with the D'Auria family. Of Raffaele D'Auria's children, two were musicians, while a third, Carolina, had a "stupendous mezzo-soprano voice that brought her great success for two seasons at the Teatro San Carlo."[3] Leoncavallo's mother, Virginia, devoted herself to painting, like her father.

In the *Appunti* Leoncavallo also records the aristocratic heritage of his father, who, he claims, was a descendant of the Dukes of Pomarico, belonging to Apulia's "provincial nobility."[4] The family of Domenico and Gelsomina (née Mastropasqua) Leoncavallo, after leaving Apulia due to the collapse of the agricultural economy, first settled in Bari, where Vincenzo Leoncavallo, the composer's father, was born in 1822, as the third of eight siblings. Of these six sons and two daughters, Giacomo became parish priest at San Giuseppe a Chiaia, where the future composer was later to be baptized, and Giuseppe, the last born, emigrated to Egypt, where he worked for many years as the director of the press department at the Italian Foreign Ministry in Cairo. Vincenzo studied law prior to serving eight years in the Bourbon army and wrote two

3

historical novels entitled *Enrichetta Malorosa* and *L'Ultimo dei Capitani a Bari*. His first wife was Giuseppa Trifaldelli; it is not certain whether they had any children. Later, in June 1854 in Naples, he married the twenty-two-year-old Virginia D'Auria.[5] Leoncavallo never mentioned the fact that his father had been married previously.

For more than a century, Leoncavallo's acknowledged date of birth was 8 March 1858, an error promulgated by the composer, who used 1858 professionally but who sometimes used 1857 privately, for his inscription into the armed forces, or when applying for a pension.[6] Why Leoncavallo went to such pains to conceal the authentic date of his birth remains a mystery. While it was (and still is) not uncommon that children born out of wedlock "legitimized" themselves by conveniently shifting their birthdates by nine months or more, this was certainly not the case with Leoncavallo, whose parents were wed three years prior to his birth. Leoncavallo's official documents state that "Ruggiero Giacomo Maria Giuseppe Emmanuele Raffaele Domenico Vincenzo Francesco Donato Leoncavallo" was born on 23 April 1857 at 4 p.m. at the home of his maternal grandfather, Raffaele D'Auria, at 102 Riviera di Chiaia.[7] The name "Ruggero" was taken from his paternal uncle with the spelling altered to "Ruggiero."[8] Leoncavallo never attached great importance to the various spellings of his name, frequently changing it as necessity dictated, sometimes using the "ie" form, other times opting for the same spelling as in his uncle's name. During his years spent in France, he took on the French equivalent, Roger, and altered his family name depending on the country in which he resided.[9] Giacomo and Giuseppe were in honor of two more of his father's brothers, while Donato referred to Donato Stucci, his paternal aunt Giovanna's husband. Raffaele and Domenico honored both his maternal and paternal grandfathers, and Vincenzo of course was his father's name. Both Emmanuele and Maria were either sacred names or perhaps belonged to godparents.

Shortly after Leoncavallo's birth, the family moved to Eboli, where they lived in a former convent. There, Ruggiero shared a bedroom with his older brother by two years, Leone. The *Appunti* state that Leoncavallo's first memory was of Garibaldi, whom he happened to see at some point on the patriot's way from Calabria to Naples in 1860. Perhaps his parents may have later spoken of Garibaldi's presence, as it seems doubtful that he would have been able to recall the incident, which occurred when he was only three years old. According to the same source, Leoncavallo's father was transferred to Montalto Uffugo in the province of Cosenza (Calabria), and it is from there that Leoncavallo had most of his childhood memories, including hearing his father sing during a mass in celebration of the Madonna. He later recalled, "My first studies were musical, and before I had even reached the age of five I had begun to take piano lessons with a certain Sebastiano Ricci."[10] Because Leoncavallo proved to be "a little demon," it was hardly surprising that Ricci was not particularly kind to his young student.[11] Leoncavallo's father was also "quite worried" by his son's "vivacious and restless nature" and, in particular, by his delight in cutting out figures from engravings contained in his father's prized library. Although Leoncavallo later recalled that his father rarely scolded him, he nevertheless successfully enforced the greatest punishment the youngster could imagine: having to attend school. "School at the time was, more than anything else, aimed at correction. But I was an unbending boy and soon became the torment of my companions and the preoccupation of my instructors."[12]

THE *PAGLIACCI* MURDER

Vincenzo Leoncavallo hired Gaetano Scavello at this time to help with Ruggiero and Leone. Scavello would later serve as the inspiration for *Pagliacci*—albeit in a highly altered form.[13] Gaetano, a twenty-two-year-old man from Carmine (Calabria), was in love with a girl from the village who had also caught the attention of the shoemaker Luigi D'Alessandro. On 4 March 1865, Gaetano was visiting with three of his friends when he noticed Pasquale Esposito, a nineteen-year-old manservant to both Luigi D'Alessandro and his brother Giovanni, entering a dwelling together with the girl.[14] When Pasquale returned alone, Gaetano, assuming a tryst had taken place with Luigi D'Alessandro, confronted him and demanded to know what was happening inside. When Pasquale refused to answer, Gaetano struck him with a mulberry branch, whereupon Pasquale ran away to seek the help of his two employers. Luigi approached carrying a whip. When Giovanni slapped Gaetano, the latter hurled a stone at the brothers in self-defense, after which they chased him with a knife without catching him. At 4 a.m. the following morning, the brothers awaited Gaetano near the entrance to the former convent San Domenico, then used as a theater. Luigi stabbed Gaetano in the left arm with an "English shoemaker's knife," while Giovanni brutally plunged another dagger into Gaetano's abdomen. Gaetano died of this wound on 6 March.[15] Scavello's autopsy papers state, with unintentional irony, that the first wound would have accounted for Gaetano's missing twenty days of work, while the second was indeed "mortally dangerous."[16]

Giovanni D'Alessandro was arrested shortly thereafter at his home, while Luigi presented himself voluntarily at the Ufficio di Pubblica Sicurezza in Cosenza, where he pleaded his innocence. Francesco Marigliano conducted the trial, with Vincenzo Leoncavallo presiding over the case as judge, on the morning of 8 July at the Court of Cosenza. Taking into account that the murder was clearly premeditated, Luigi D'Alessandro was condemned to twenty years' hard labor, while his brother received a lifetime sentence. Both brothers managed to receive a reduction in their sentences when the cases were appealed. A third appeal was rejected in 1869. Vincenzo Leoncavallo harbored strong feelings against the death penalty, as he stated in a publication issued in Potenza in 1878. This may have accounted for the fact that the D'Alessandros were discharged rather lightly. The woman involved, who remained nameless, was referred to in the court papers only as "one who does not merit our concern."[17] Gaetano Scavello's death is not the only crime that is touched upon in the *Appunti*. There can be little doubt that his father's profession significantly influenced Ruggiero.

This period also saw the outbreak of Italy's Third Independence War in 1866. However, it did not directly affect Leoncavallo, who fondly remembered costume balls held at the homes of Calabria's leading families, including the Alimenas, Cananeos, and D'Alessandros, and the "patriotic priest" Don Rossi, who seems to have supervised the youth's studies at some point.[18] Such reminiscences also included many afternoons spent at the beach at Paola.

In 1867, Vincenzo Leoncavallo was offered the position of judge at the District Court of Cava de'Tirreni. This signified a return to Naples, and he immediately grabbed at the chance, keeping in mind that the change of location would greatly benefit the schooling of his two sons. Both Raffaele D'Auria and his wife had died, as well as Leoncavallo's uncles Ruggero and Giacomo, since the time spent at Montalto Uffugo. The future composer "distinctly" recalled the family's voyage from Cosenza to Eboli, which required "five long days."[19] The Leoncavallos, with a tearful farewell to the many friends they had made in the area, finally departed during a storm, which, according to the *Appunti*, caused more than one bridge to collapse. The family, unable to cross the river, was forced to take an alternate route through the mountains, with various stops along the way, including Castrovillari and Lagonegro, finally crossing the bridge at Campostrino on the way to Eboli. After a long and arduous journey, the family finally arrived in Naples, where they made their home at the Palazzo del Principe di San Lorenzo on Via Tribunali 181. This was the residence of another of Leoncavallo's uncles, Nicola (Nieda), who was also a lawyer.

Leoncavallo remained at the Vittorio Emanuele Institute until he graduated.[20] In addition, his education was supplemented by piano lessons provided by a poor maestro from the country.[21] His "vocation for music and the theater asserted itself" once again when his parents accompanied him to a production of *La traviata* in Salerno.[22] Leoncavallo, although the performance was far from good, remembered that the opera nevertheless succeeded in making a "profound impression. . . . It is futile to state that my natural inclinations found more favorable conditions for development in Naples, where everything emanated art."[23] These experiences strengthened upon witnessing a performance of *Rigoletto* at the Teatro San Carlo starring his aunt Carolina as Maddalena and baritone Francesco Pandolfini in the role of the protagonist, Rigoletto. He later commented that "the performance was so perfect" that he was unable to sleep for two nights.[24] Another highlight was seeing Anton Rubinstein perform in Leoncavallo's native Riviera di Chiaia as part of a tour the pianist/composer had undertaken following decades spent as an instructor in St. Petersburg. Leoncavallo later recalled, "No other pianist was capable of producing emotions" in him "as was this giant, especially when interpreting Beethoven and Weber."[25]

The eight year old was then enrolled as an external student at the San Pietro a Majella Conservatory in Naples when instruction with the village maestro was no longer adequate.[26] His teachers included Beniamino Cesi (1845–1907) for piano (he had studied composition with Mercadante) and Michele Ruta for harmony, in addition to Paolo Serrao and Lauro Rossi (1812–1885) for composition.[27] Leoncavallo, intrigued by the psychological and emotional aspects of crime, also found sufficient time to attend trials at the city hall. His "particular fascination" with these brutal passions made a significant impression that would later find expression in the verismo movement.

Leoncavallo's mother nurtured her son's artistic talents at home, making certain that he also attended as many operatic performances as possible. Another impressive production was *Aida* at the San Carlo, sung by Teresa Stolz and conducted by his teacher Serrao, with Verdi himself presiding at rehearsals:

> There were manifestations of authentic delirium on the public's part. The performance has remained a memory apart in my spirit. Never again since then have I experienced such perfect attention to detail, taking into account that Verdi's original markings are no longer respected.[28]

The *Appunti* claim that his mother was most sensitive: "For me she was everything: mother, friend, confidante of my dreams and of my hopes. She was an entire world of poetry and kindness."[29] Rather than leaving home to find amusement elsewhere, Leoncavallo was content to remain at his mother's side during the evening, playing operatic scores on the piano, interpreting all parts, while his mother rejoiced in turning the pages.

This affectionate and important bond was severed when Virginia, after giving birth to her third son, Gastone, died on 23 January 1873. She developed an infection, ostensibly after insisting that she breast-feed the infant herself. The family physician, Professor Morisani, informed the Leoncavallos that Virginia was gravely ill. The composer's initial reaction was one of denial: "I was not able to believe, I did not want to believe."[30] A ray of hope shone temporarily when another doctor consulted suggested Virginia only needed "a change of climate."[31] Vincenzo immediately transferred the entire family to Arezzo, where he searched out new physicians while Ruggiero remained at his mother's bedside:

Death's frenzied rattle could be heard. A priest was summoned for the last rites. It was a holiday, and everything was at contrast to our desperation. Two young women across from us were playing the piano and singing joyful songs until I, in a violent rage, made them stop. Then, without realizing what I was doing, and while in the doctor's presence, I took a phial of ammonia and made the agonized patient smell. She once again opened her beautiful black eyes, said something in a hushed voice to the doctor, and then "poor children!" She closed her eyes and resumed her heavy breathing. A few moments later, our house had lost its guardian angel.[32]

Following Virginia's death, Vincenzo transferred the family to Potenza, where his third wife, Giulia Polsea, later raised the children.[33] During this period Leoncavallo probably graduated from the Vittorio Emanuele Institute at the age of sixteen. It is also possible that he earned a diploma from San Pietro a Majella with a cantata.

Although at first his studies at the conservatory had only been considered a hobby ("supplementing my education"),[34] he soon became interested in drafting a libretto based on the legendary English poet Thomas Chatterton. Chatterton had committed suicide at the age of eighteen in 1770. It was an irresistible subject, complementing Leoncavallo's own sentimental and poetic nature. Chatterton ignited his imagination. He later recalled, "In an essentially romantic age, together with my sentimental nature, I let myself be easily conquered by the personage of Chatterton."[35] It was in this opera that Leoncavallo would seek to reproduce the anguished drama of a poet's soul, or, as Vigny stated, "of a more passionate nature, purer and rarer."[36] Although Chatterton incorporates the perfect ingredients of an operatic character, no other composer showed interest in musically capturing his persona, whereas Vigny, Wordsworth, Coleridge, Shelley, and Rossetti created lasting epitaphs. Leoncavallo's Chatterton is essentially another example of an artist on the rim of society, who created the foundation for Leoncavallo's future operatic personages Canio, Marcello, Rodolfo, Zazà, and Mameli.

In March 1876 Leoncavallo contacted the publishers of the *Gazzetta Musicale di Milano*—mouthpiece of Casa Ricordi. He requested the score of Meyerbeer's *Dinorah* as well as photographs of Beethoven, Mendelssohn, Wagner, and Verdi, offered to entice new subscribers. Leoncavallo wrote again—in reference to Chatterton—inquiring whether they could suggest the name of an impresario at Bologna's Teatro Comunale for the fall season. With his conservatory studies completed, Leoncavallo began toying with the idea of a move to Bologna, a town that could offer him more opportunities than either Potenza or Naples. That same year, aware that Verdi was known for his philanthropy benefiting musicians, Leoncavallo sent the maestro a letter requesting financial aid, which was refused after he appealed several times "on an urgent basis."[37]

Returning to Potenza and his piano students, Leoncavallo informed the Gazzetta Musicale that he had completed a score demanding "great musical resources for the orchestra."[38] Leoncavallo was determined that *Chatterton* should receive its premiere that summer in Parma, Ancona, Cremona, or another city offering adequate singers. He again requested information regarding an "honest theatrical agency,"[39] as well as transcriptions of *La traviata*, Meyerbeer's *Les Huguenots*, and Boito's *Mefistofele*.[40]

BOLOGNA

Still without the huge mustache that would one day be his trademark, Leoncavallo decided to set off for Bologna during late summer/early autumn of 1876 to attend lectures by the great Italian poet, critic, and orator Giosuè Carducci (1835–1907), professor of literature and law at the University of Bologna (1860–1904).

A prolific writer, Carducci, who had won a Nobel Prize for literature in 1906, accepted his post in Bologna in 1860 out of financial necessity. Classes in literature were hardly frequented (approximately twenty pupils), and the university only accounted for some three hundred students at the time. This was in marked contrast to its brilliant past, when twelve thousand students attended the country's oldest university, founded in 1088.[41] With competition from the universities of Ferrara, Modena, Parma, and Florence, Bologna was still sought out, since its courses were less rigorous and daily costs were far less than elsewhere, a factor important to Leoncavallo at the time.

Carducci was devoted to Dante and Petrarch, and, although he taught elevated philosophical material, he never failed to include a good deal of humor. Most of Carducci's photographs portray an elderly man with white hair and hat holding a cane. When Leoncavallo was his student, however, the poet was still a young man. Carducci proved to be a major influence on Leoncavallo, even if he was thoroughly opposed to the new realistic style as incorporated in the works of Zola (realism) and other authors of the time. This genre would soon express itself in the musical form of verismo that Leoncavallo later would help found. Due to Carducci's significant influence, Leoncavallo alternated from veristic subjects to classical ones throughout his career.

Leoncavallo's classmates in Bologna included the extremely slender Gualtiero Belvederi, who would remain a lifelong friend as well as future collaborator for the libretto of *Mameli* in 1916. The *Appunti* state that Belvederi introduced him to the great writer Giovanni Pascoli, then living in Via Pelacani (today Via Giuseppe Petroni). When Pascoli first heard that the composer's name was "Ruggiero," he grew sad, remarking "It is a name which is dear to me: my father's name."[42] Pascoli, having lost both his parents and sister within a short period of time, was grateful for the companionship of someone who had also recently experienced the death of his own mother.

Bologna was an antidote against Leoncavallo's recent tragedy, as well as a chance to experience new frontiers. "The school of that great poet of the new Italy was a fermenting of ideas for us youths. It was also a prodigious incentive."[43] Through the aid of Raffaele Marcovigi (or Marcovingi), another of Pascoli's friends who enjoyed the use of a piano, Leoncavallo rejoiced in being able to spend his free time at the instrument composing music to some of Pascoli's poetry. This included the songs *La morta* and *Sussurrano le mille aure del bosco*, composed in 1877.[44] Later preferring poetry of less refinement and believing that his style required a more unpolished form, he settled for the verses of Ugo Bassini, another acquaintance whose writings were both vigorous and macabre, resembling some of Carducci's works.

This bohemian ensemble of creative young men naturally reveled in spending long hours discussing their new works and future hopes with evenings spent at the Caffè del Rosso. Normally, Leoncavallo only returned to his room at 430 Via Cartoleria Vecchia during the early morning hours. He was extremely popular, providing his poetic friends with a source of piano accompaniment.

Of equal importance was his entrance into Bolognese society, including an acquaintance with the diplomat Marco Minghetti, president of the Cabinet Council, whom Leoncavallo met fairly soon after his move. Leoncavallo appreciated Minghetti's sympathetic concern and his offer of paternal friendship, a kind of home away from home. Minghetti's second wife, Donna Laura, was a great admirer and supporter of the arts, who entertained a fair share of the aristocracy in her salon at Villa Mezzarotta. When the composer, invited for breakfast, met her, he called her "one of the most intellectual women" he had ever met in his life.[45] He later recalled that she combined "prodigious culture" with a "refined soul. . . . Her passion was music, and the times when I joined them for lunch—and they were frequent—we played four-handed piano. . . . I took great pleasure in going to the Minghettis. . . . I was able to absorb a bit of the musical culture that the conservatory had been unable to offer."[46]

As Bologna was an important musical center, Leoncavallo's pianistic abilities were soon in demand by other wealthy families, such as the home of Marchese Camillo Pizzardi and Count Pierfrancesco Albicini. Beginning at 9 p.m., these "musical orgies" lasted until well into the early hours of the following day, with only a short pause for refreshments at midnight. It was in these salons that he also heard stories concerning Rossini and his modus operandi: "I only take applauded pieces of forgotten operas for my new works . . . if they were once successful there is no reason why they should not prove to be so twice."[47]

For some time, Leoncavallo had been planning to create his own version of the *Ring*, inspired by Wagner's tetralogy, which premiered in 1876. This lofty idea, based on the Italian Renaissance, incorporated a triptych of operas including *I Medici, Gerolamo Savonarola*, and *Cesare Borgia*.[48] Although Leoncavallo appreciated Carducci's love of Bellini and Wagner, when the conversation turned to his planned operatic trilogy, Carducci was not enthusiastic. He believed that such historic personages should not be set to music. Leoncavallo's insistence that he would not write cavatinas was hardly consoling, and, in spite of Carducci's warnings, he consulted numerous books on Machiavelli, Savonarola, and Lucrezia and Cesare Borgia.

Having discovered Wagner, Leoncavallo was determined to attend a performance of *Rienzi* given in Wagner and Cosima's presence in Bologna on 4 December 1876. According to the *Appunti*, Leoncavallo was present at the performance and at a reception at Hotel Brun, after which he supposedly also met Wagner, although there remains no documentation to prove the claim.

Der Fliegende Holländer was performed in Bologna the following year (1877), although the staging of the work's final apotheosis curtailed the success it later received at the second performance. It was during that season that Leoncavallo was introduced to the slightly mustached and very portly impresaria Giovanna Lucca. Lucca owned the Italian rights to Wagner's works and successfully directed the firm following her husband's death in 1872.[49] The *Appunti* insist that Leoncavallo made Lucca's acquaintance through Count Brunetti, vice director of Bologna's conservatory. Leoncavallo, sharing a box with Filippo Filippi, critic of the newspaper *La Perseveranza*, was introduced as "a young composer and poet."[50] When Filippi suggested Leoncavallo might turn out to be another Boito, Lucca added, "A small Wagner."[51]

Of greater importance was *Tommaso Chatterton*'s completion, which seems to have taken up a large part of Leoncavallo's Bologna period. He initially played the score at the home of Count Pierfrancesco Albicini, who took an interest in the composition. Albicini contacted a certain Agosti, impresario of Bologna's Teatro del Corso, who promised to premiere the work for three thousand lire during the 1877 season.[52] Although the composer felt that everything was proceeding as it should, he was shocked when *L'Arpa*, the Bolognese music journal, announced that "due to lack of time Leoncavallo's new opera must wait its turn" until the spring.[53] Leoncavallo later stated that the impresario pocketed the three thousand lire Albicini had loaned him and was not heard from again. This was certainly not the case, since Agosti later presented both *Rigoletto* and Meyerbeer's *Robert le Diable* during the 1878 season. *Chatterton* and *Eleonora d'Arborea* (by Carlotta Ferrari da Lodi) were canceled in favor of Donizetti's *Lucrezia Borgia*, probably because of poor box office receipts. Whether out of disinterest or because of a serious financial problem, *Chatterton* was never produced, and the score remained unpublished. The libretto was printed in 1878 by the Società Tipografica dei Compositori in Bologna.

Although Leoncavallo stated throughout his life that he graduated from the University of Bologna with a degree in literature, the institution's archives were unable to lend credence to the assertion. However, his later letters to Carducci prove that he had in fact been his student at the university. The composer had probably been registered as an external student.[54] His time in Bologna had come to a disappointing conclusion. With neither money nor a premiere, the only alternative would be to return to Potenza and admit to his father—who possibly had little understanding of his son's vocation—that he had failed. Desperately poor, he sold *Chatterton* to the Bolognese publisher Trebbi for two hundred lire, hoping that his precarious "hand-to-mouth existence" would thereby be immediately if only sporadically relieved.[55] Ironically, Trebbi had a store directly adjacent to the infamous Teatro del Corso, and, although he was completely uneducated (according to Leoncavallo he thought Chopin was spelled "Copin"!), the composer nevertheless believed Trebbi to be a "sincere and honest man."[56] Leoncavallo, with the money he had received, boarded a train heading south, certain that more disasters lay in store.

NOTES

1. *Appunti Vari delle Autobiografici di R. Leoncavallo.* The *Appunti* is a typed eighty-page manuscript in the archives of Casa Musicale Sonzogno, Milan, that prematurely concludes with the premiere of *I Medici*. Leoncavallo dictated these memoirs to Giuseppe A. Andriulli in 1915. Andriulli was a journalist working for Rome's *Il Secolo* newspaper who hoped to publish a full-length biography. The composer proofread most, if perhaps not all, of the manuscript, a portion of which was lost. Leoncavallo was against the monograph appearing in the first-person singular. Following his death, Berthe unsuccessfully tried to find a publisher. Since the text contains both misspellings and faulty use of the Italian language, we may presume that she tried to type her own version of Andriulli's manuscript, especially since extant letters from Andriulli to Berthe encouraged this. A careful checking of facts proved most of the *Appunti*'s details to be correct. No one other than Leoncavallo would have been able to recount the information, especially the numerous names—not famous—mentioned, such as, for example, Francesco Finelli della Valletta, whose letters from the period verify the *Appunti*'s descriptions. There is hardly any information available concerning the composer's early period, and it was therefore necessary to draw upon details from the *Appunti*, although any facts that appear definitive in this biography were checked against other documents before inclusion in the text.

2. Although it would seem probable, there is no certainty that Raffaele D'Auria was indeed a descendant of the famous Neapolitan family of sculptors of the same

name: Giovanni Domenico D'Auria (1541–1573), Giovanni Tommaso D'Auria (1545–1607 or 1550–1600), Geronimo D'Auria (1573–1619), and Vincenzo D'Auria. Whatever the truth of the case may be, Leoncavallo never made mention of these sixteenth-century artisans.

3. *Appunti*, 5.

4. Ibid., 1.

5. USCN.

6. It has been suggested that Leoncavallo made himself one year younger in order to have the same year of birth as Puccini.

7. This is the information that was presented to the City Hall of Chiaia on 25 April 1857 by Leoncavallo's wet nurse Carolina Artiano.

8. Ruggero Leoncavallo taught literature and published a study of Dante for students in Livorno in 1859 entitled *Manuele Dantesco ad uso della gioventù*. This work can still be located in a number of Italian university libraries.

9. In France he became Léon Cavallo d'Auria.

10. *Appunti*, 6–7.

11. Ibid.

12. Ibid.

13. See chapter describing the composition of *Pagliacci* for Leoncavallo's semi-fictionalized account of the event.

14. Annibale Caruso, Francesco Leonetti, and Vincenzo Cicirello. These three men later proved to be witnesses in the court proceedings following the murder.

15. The complete gruesome details are recorded in the autopsy papers at Cosenza's Archivio di Stato.

16. ASC.

17. Ibid.

18. *Appunti*, 11.

19. Ibid., 12.

20. There is in fact no evidence that Leoncavallo attended this school or that he received a diploma, since the archive at the Istituto Vittorio Emanuele was destroyed in World War II.

21. Possibly Francesco Simonetti.

22. *Appunti*, 12.

23. Ibid.

24. Ibid., 13.

25. Ibid.

26. No documentation was available at the San Pietro a Majella archives that would have provided evidence of Leoncavallo's inscription at the institution as a full-time student. "M. Leoncavallo par lui-même" in *Le Figaro*, 9 June 1899.

27. Rossi composed twenty-eight operas.

28. *Appunti*, 13.

29. Ibid., 14.

30. Ibid.

31. Ibid.

32. Ibid., 14–15.

33. Polsea (or Polosa) was Vincenzo's third wife, since his marriage papers ascertain that he had already been a widower upon his marriage to Virginia, having originally entered into matrimony with a certain Giuseppa Trifaldelli (USCN).

34. *Appunti*, 15.

35. *Appunti*, 27.

36. Ibid.

37. Mary Jane Phillips-Matz, *Verdi, A Biography* (New York: Oxford University Press, 1993), 644.

38. Leoncavallo to *Gazzetta Musicale di Milano,* 5 June 1876 (CR).

39. Ibid., 5 July 1876 (CR).

40. These were scores that would influence *La bohème* and *Chatterton.*

41. In 1890, there were 116 instructors for 1,410 students.

42. Ruggero Pascoli was murdered when the poet was twelve, most likely because of political frictions, although the assassin was never found.

43. *Appunti*, 15

44. The songs *Brindisi, Autunno,* and *La viola* also date from this time.

45. *Appunti*, 20.

46. Ibid., 21.

47. *Appunti*, 22.

48. Only *I Medici* reached completion.

49. Francesco Lucca (1802–1872). Casa Lucca was later owned by Casa Ricordi in 1888.

50. *Appunti*, 25.

51. Ibid.

52. Leoncavallo spent years paying back the three thousand lire he borrowed from Albicini for *Chatterton's* premiere.

53. *L'Arpa*, 8 November 1877 (Anno 24), no. 34: 136.

54. Carducci was also a professor of law, and Leoncavallo may have attended classes and received a diploma in this subject. Since the University of Bologna's law archives have remained closed for some time, I was unable to gain access during research for this biography.

55. *Appunti*, 29.

56. Ibid.

• 2 •

At the Khedive's Court

1878–1888

Leoncavallo, fearing that he would have to serve military duty, returned to Naples during January 1878. (He later stated that he had made a brief stop in Rome to witness the funeral of Vittorio Emanuele II.) He was elated to receive an official statement from the District of Potenza on 18 February 1878 excusing him from military service since his older brother Leone had already served in the armed forces. Leoncavallo, hoping to make up for the food he had been deprived of in Bologna, decided to remain in the "hospitable province" of Potenza for a further year after all.[1] It is not difficult to imagine how futile life must have seemed for him without the friends that he had grown fond of in Bologna and without the mental stimulation of Carducci's lectures.

Once again taking up the unfulfilling task of giving piano instruction, he was "preoccupied with a desire to find a way of escape."[2] While others would have chosen Milan or begun a career in Naples, the composer, with a character as unconventional as Chatterton's, decided on Egypt, where his uncle, the lawyer Giuseppe, had been director of the press department at the Foreign Ministry since 1863.[3] Giuseppe also wrote numerous articles dealing with such varied topics as the question of succession to the throne in the Orient or the education of women in Egypt. It was probably Giuseppe who had originally suggested that Leoncavallo would be a success demonstrating his pianistic abilities in the Egyptian capital.[4] The composer was willing to try anything that might take him out of Potenza; he sailed for Egypt in 1879 filled with hopes of adventure and success.

His arrival coincided with the deposition of Ismail Pasha in 1879, a widely traveled cosmopolite and grandson of Muhammad Ali, often called the "founder of modern Egypt." Ali successfully reorganized the Egyptian army and boosted the economy by nationalizing a great part of the land through a government monopoly and by the cultivation of cotton in the Delta. When

15

Ismail Pasha acceded to power, Abbas I had already ruled the country and Said Pasha before him.[5] Said died in 1863, and Ismail Pasha replaced him. Intent on making Egypt a part of Europe, Ismail Pasha resumed the modernization of the Egyptian economy by building railways, harbors, and canals for irrigation from the Nile. He also contributed large sums of money toward the completion of the Suez Canal, which opened in 1869. Shortly thereafter, he obtained the hereditary title of "Khedive" and established the law of primogeniture for Egypt. At the outset of his rule, the Egyptian foreign debt was estimated to be three million pounds and the domestic debt one million more. Within a short time, Ismail Pasha had succeeded in leading the government into a state of bankruptcy, forcing him to sell his Suez Canal shares, which Great Britain purchased for four million pounds in 1875. The Khedive also had to accept Anglo-French financial control over Egyptian affairs, and, in 1878, he was required to adopt a constitutional ministry. Unable to agree with this edict, Ismail Pasha was deposed in 1879 in favor of his son Tewfik. The *Appunti* state that the new Khedive did not "appreciate the invasion of workers from all parts of Europe who frequently failed to speak the language and, consequently, were rewarded three times as much as the natives,"[6] thereby encouraging the national party.

After giving a few concerts, Leoncavallo was engaged as a pianist and piano instructor to the Khedive's brother, Muhammed Hamid. Leoncavallo felt that living at the whim of someone else made the position both "uncertain and precarious."[7] He tried to find a more secure source of income as director of the Egyptian Band, a position always coveted by Italians, which would have enabled him to earn a "stipend of seventy to eighty pounds per month, combined with six months' leave of absence including full pay."[8] Ultimately unable to secure the post, he found his music lessons provided sufficient earnings to rent a room with a small balcony in Ezbeky, which was "the center of the city and the heart of the European part," although he insisted that a room in the palace was also kept available.[9]

Among the numerous Italians Leoncavallo met and with whom he shared a friendship was Professor Giuseppe Botti (1853–1903), who became curator of Alexandria's Greco-Roman Museum and who later also served as a member of the Egyptian Institute in 1896. Together with Botti and an entire group of Italians, Leoncavallo set off to see the pyramids at Giza. The composer felt hunger upon undertaking the excursion directly following a performance at the theater. Some Bedouins were able to offer the men goat milk cheese, which Leoncavallo loathed but ate, nonetheless.

> The sun appeared above the vast desert, resembling a flaming cannon ball announced by a brief weak glimmer. The sight was one of particular beauty. The Nile was full, and the desert was almost completely submerged in water. As the moon rose, it resembled an immense, fiery lake. The effect was far superior to any description, and the aesthetic impression vividly roused one's imagination.[10]

Another unforgettable experience was a Nile journey accompanied by Muhammed Hamid, which lasted some fifteen days. The composer declared it "an uninterrupted series of amazing impressions."[11] Traveling conditions were not always ideal, and, upon reaching one of the Nile's cataracts, the composer's boat needed to be tugged with ropes due to lack of sufficient water. The return journey was more agreeable, even though it meant crossing part of the desert. These trips were enhanced by Leoncavallo's interest in Arabic music, which he described as gentle lamentations "languishing" like "war songs and hymns."[12]

Another event that he would recall for a lifetime occurred when he fell asleep by candlelight in a bed covered with netting to ward off mosquitoes. He awakened in the midst of a fire, the netting having ignited, after dreaming that his mother had warned him. What astounded Leoncavallo was not the fire but the feeling of supernatural foreboding that he would experience once more, later in life, while traveling from Vienna to Milan in 1893.

Leoncavallo's three-year Egyptian sojourn concluded abruptly during the summer of 1882, with the open revolt in Alexandria, and, later, in Cairo, led by Ahmad Arabi Pasha, who was the military leader of the nationalist movement. The composer claimed he knew of the coup early on, having remained in close contact with numerous journalists who had been well informed. Leoncavallo sought refuge in the Khedival palace in Abdin, prior to the arrival of Admiral Seymour's British fleet on 11 July 1882, which bombarded the Egyptian forts, destroying parts of Cairo. Foreigners living in the capital were threatened and sometimes murdered, including one of Leoncavallo's French acquaintances. Although Tewfik Pasha would later be reinstated to rule, the composer opted to leave the country at the first opportunity. Incredible as it may seem, the *Appunti* relate that he disguised himself as an Arab, leaving Cairo on horseback to ride for twenty-four hours to Al Ismailiyah. From there, he supposedly boarded a ship to Port Said, where he remained with his uncle's son-in-law, a certain Cipollaro. While in Port Said, there is evidence that he wrote the song "Tristesse" to a text by Alfred de Musset as early as 15 May 1882! If we are to believe the discrepancies inherent in the *Appunti*, Leoncavallo was able to organize a concert for the European community at the home of Desavary, one of Ferdinand de Lesseps's representatives, which enabled him to earn "between five and six hundred francs," which would have been sufficient money to board the British ship *Propitious*, which took him to France and safety.[13] Leoncavallo reached Marseilles after taking a train that was "neither luxurious nor fast."[14] He headed for Paris, intent on "finding the fortune that had eluded" him in Egypt.[15] Why he had decided to bypass Italy for France is another matter of conjecture. Then again, there is no proof that Leoncavallo did not remain in Italy for some time. Whatever the truth may be, Leoncavallo reached Paris both exhausted and very, very poor.

PARISIAN PIANIST

Knowing that he would have to exist on the few hundred francs remaining, Leoncavallo found lodging "at the top of Montmartre," at Rue Ménessier in a hotel of the "basest category."[16] Almost destitute, he somehow managed to locate sufficient money for one "last extravagance": a ticket to the Opéra for a performance of Ambroise Thomas's *Françoise de Rimini*.[17] He failed to enjoy the work, although he admired the brilliance of the cast. Leoncavallo felt the orchestra was unable to do justice to the theater's renown. What impressed him most was the Opéra's grand staircase, a reflection of his own—yet to be realized—grand dream.

Leoncavallo immediately announced his arrival in the music journal *Le ménestrel* on 9 July 1883: a young Italian poet-musician, who wishes to introduce himself to artists and French music lovers in order to try to secure any kind of work—as a pianist, accompanist, or librettist. The composer aimed for acceptance in Parisian society by frenchifying his surname while at the same time making use of his deceased mother's aristocratic maiden name.

In the belief that Victor Hugo was the most famous Frenchman alive, Leoncavallo immediately set about contacting the author, requesting permission to use some of his poetry for future songs. He received a letter from Hugo's secretary, Richard Lesclide, on 12 July 1882, saying that Hugo would agree to give his permission on condition that Leoncavallo donate any profits made to the needy. Leoncavallo decided to take the matter one step further, securing a meeting with Hugo at his home at 42 Avenue d'Eylau (presently Rue Victor Hugo).[18] On the appointed day, Leoncavallo was escorted into a waiting room that had a solemn, almost religious feeling to it, by Hugo's secretary Paul Maurice. When Hugo appeared wearing his customary *frac*, Leoncavallo was intrigued by the manner in which it set off the white of his almost feminine-looking hands in contrast to his smoldering black eyes. Hugo greeted some of the other visitors before saying to Leoncavallo: "Ah, you are the Italian maestro who wrote me? Welcome. You are an artist and thus have more right than anyone else to be here. . . . I will gladly concede that you use my verses for your music, but if your compositions are successful I want that the poor benefit, not I."[19]

An agent located in the Faubourg Saint-Denis secured Leoncavallo's first employment as an accompanist for artists of "inferior quality" who performed in Sunday concerts at various venues, mostly cafés.[20] Although these events hardly satisfied Leoncavallo's artistic aims, he realized that the money would save him from starvation. He also agreed to the agent's next proposal, which was to accompany singers at a café-concert sixty kilometers outside Paris in the area of Creil. The pay improved, and Leoncavallo earned eight francs while also receiving dinner and breakfast. The reality was somewhat less than anticipated, however, when the piano turned out to be a harmonium, but the excellent food compensated for both the instrument and the horrendous *artistes chanteurs*.

Not only was Leoncavallo faced with endless accompanying but also with transposing and changing keys to suit the singers, which tested his flexibility, demanding "superhuman effort."[21] Accomplishing all that was asked of him, Leoncavallo soon became prized by this society of artists, and, within a short time, "the great little Italian" was inundated with work,[22] which came to an abrupt halt on 14 July. Spending hours looking for someone who might wish to avail himself of his pianistic abilities, the composer walked through Paris without finding a chance of earning anything. He remained for two and a half days without so much as a slice of bread. About to return home with empty pockets, he realized it was too late for transportation in the city, and, with no money for a ticket, he walked for three and a half hours back to his room. "I returned in a deplorable state and just had enough time to throw myself onto the bed without being able to close an eye, overwhelmed by the torture of hunger."[23] Forced to wait until the next morning, he located a "modest restaurant where one could eat for the sum of two lire."[24] Although Leoncavallo entered the still-closed eatery at 10 a.m. his appearance must have been "terribly persuasive," and he was served.[25] His extreme hunger prevented him from eating much, but things improved later when he located a restaurant behind the Opéra-Comique that offered a bowl of soup and a plate of meat, cheese, and as much bread as one could eat, all for the price of one lira and thirty centesimi.

Finally, news of his talent reached Paul Renard, director of the Eldorado variety theatre on the Boulevard de Strasbourg, "which all foreigners visit."[26] Renard was a great music lover, and, for his simple *varieté*, he contracted a complete orchestra, entrusting its direction to the conductor Charles Malot, who presented operatic overtures and suites by Massenet during intermissions.[27] Renard asked Leoncavallo whether he would be interested in composing songs, and, feeling "capable" of writing what Renard demanded, he now considered himself a composer once again.

The next day Leoncavallo returned with a completed song to the lyrics he had received, even though Renard had granted him seven or eight days for the assignment. (Some of Leoncavallo's songs written for the Eldorado, such as "Jeunesse et Printemps," were also published at this time). Renard then asked Leoncavallo whether he would also be capable of orchestrating the given piece, and, from that day forward, his position at the Eldorado was secured. Suddenly, Leoncavallo had almost too much work, supplying material simultaneously for two female singers and presenting at least four or five of his songs nightly, for which he was paid twenty lire. Leoncavallo continued in this vein for one year.

MAUREL, MASSENET, AND THE *HAUTE SOCIÉTÉ*

Pleased with the success of Leoncavallo's work, Renard asked next whether he would be willing to compose an operetta to a libretto he had in his possession. A few months earlier Leoncavallo would have been delighted at the chance to earn money by composing, but with the pangs of hunger now substantially behind him, the thought of spending a lifetime writing for such a mediocre establishment was frightening. He now aspired to "authentic art, great art."[28]

From that Sunday on, Leoncavallo considered ending his career as an accompanist for vaudeville artists. If his financial situation decreed that he must earn his living as such, he speculated that it would be a much better idea to serve as an accompanist for opera and concert singers. While searching for a change in jobs, the composer also attended some concerts organized by Edouard Colonne at the Théâtre du Châtelet. He thought of his *Crepusculum* trilogy again, of which he had only completed the libretto to the first part, together with his earlier opera *Chatterton*, which had yet to be performed. He wondered how much time had been wasted seeking good fortune, which seemed unattainable. He felt loathing for the world of café-concerts, which he had been forced to accept in order to survive. The work had been tiresome and artistically sterile, and he now sought publishers who could perhaps introduce him to opera singers in need of musical preparation or accompaniment.

Through Colonne, Leoncavallo was introduced to Georges Hartmann in the winter of 1883–1884.[29] The publisher took an interest in the young Italian composer with a certain aim in mind: the baritone Victor Maurel had scheduled a season of opera at the Théâtre Italien. It was planned to present Massenet's *Hérodiade* in its Parisian premiere in an Italian translation to open 1 February 1884, after only eleven days of rehearsals. The cast was nonetheless extraordinary, including Jean and Edouard de Reszke as Jean and Phanuel, respectively, while Maurel himself would interpret Hérode. Hartmann suggested that Leoncavallo serve as accompanist and "not one of those vocal instructors who ruin voices." Maurel's permission was required before he could offer the composer anything definite. Leoncavallo was then presented to Massenet, who emanated "truly exquisite manners" and "exaggerated courtesy."[30] He also asked whether his Italian colleague was capable of sight-reading. Leoncavallo began to play an unspecified score at the piano when Massenet stopped him on the third page, asking where he had gained such expert musical training. Having been told that he had studied at the Naples conservatory, Massenet was not surprised, as he considered it "a very good school."[31] While Massenet would remain one of Leoncavallo's few supporters, the meeting with Maurel was also of great importance, with the baritone introducing him to new colleagues, while Leoncavallo's reputation as an excellent accompanist and voice teacher spread rapidly in Parisian music circles.

Among the first students Leoncavallo met was Baroness de Vaux, whom he described as "an intellectual woman and a very fine interpreter of songs."[32] She also happened to be the wife of the "well-known journalist" Charles de Vaux of the newspaper *Gil Blas*,[33] who would help Leoncavallo find additional work as a pianist as well as possible concert engagements. Curiously, Leoncavallo met up again with the young nobleman Francesco Finelli Della Valletta, who had been a friend of his family in Arienzo (Caserta) when Leoncavallo's father worked there as a judge. Francesco gave recitals of Tosti and Denza in the French capital when they happened to meet again. Although Leoncavallo felt that Francesco was musically ignorant, he nevertheless appreciated his friend's fine voice and "uncommon artistic temperament."[34] Theirs was a strained relationship, with Leoncavallo using the formal address and frequently being the victim of petty jealousies culminating in a declaration of his innocence and a scolding of Francesco for his coldness. During the same year (1884), Leoncavallo was already defending himself in letters to Francesco, warning his friend not to listen to gossip. Some of these conflicts may have arisen from Leoncavallo's brother Leone, who had come to live with the composer in France. Leoncavallo's letters are similar to many he would write in the future declaring his innocence and honesty: "You know my family, my education, and you must know my heart. I await an explanation . . . my conscience is tranquil."[35] Sometimes Leoncavallo's letters were also "urgent," as when he had injured his arm, but nevertheless wrote with a shaky hand to request twenty francs:

> Forgive me if I have not come personally, but I have spent the night suffering greatly without closing an eye due to my arm. I have no income whatsoever and would like to ask whether it would be possible for you to lend me twenty francs. . . . I will repay you within a few days . . . please send your response by way of your servant . . . to my address at 89 rue de la Victoire (Chaussée d'Antin). I thank you in anticipation for this favor during such a difficult time in my life.[36]

Leoncavallo's correspondence frequently ended with a request for money— usually 120 francs. He often left notes at Francesco's various Parisian domiciles hoping to meet him in the Bois de Boulogne. Sometimes these meetings were canceled because of Leoncavallo's work at the Théâtre Italien, where he also accompanied rehearsals of *Martha*. Francesco now insisted that Leoncavallo serve as his accompanist while also requesting that he compose songs in the manner of Tosti. Leoncavallo was happy to comply, writing "Ne m'oubliez pas," "Le baiser," "La Renouveau," "Tutto tace," "Je ne sais pas ton nom," "Amore," "Madame, avisez-y," and "Berceuse." Many of the songs composed to French verses were by Emile Collet, who was able to have these delightful *liriche* published by such reputable firms as Girod and Choudens. The song "Madame, avisez-y" to the verses of Malherbe was also published by Choudens in 1887, while "Je ne sais pas ton nom" became a favorite of Madame de Rute, who had the song performed at her salon at Rue d'Alma 67 in December of 1886 in honor of the orator Emile Castelar. Wife of the attaché Suiz de Rute, she was an Englishwoman famous for her spicy novels as well as for the scanty costumes she regularly donned for festivities, at which Leoncavallo provided the accompaniment. He later recalled, "Notwithstanding her caprices, Madame de Rute gave elegant and interesting receptions. I remember a gracious minuet I played to which both her daughters danced—two very charming girls in Louis XV costumes with powdered wigs."[37]

These events were interspersed with others of even more glamour, such as the engagement of Don Carlos, Duke of Braganza—later murdered when king of Portugal—to Amelie d'Orléans. Leoncavallo accompanied the actor/ singer Ernest Coquelin at the piano, and it was thanks to the artist that he was able to witness this festive event. Through Constant, Coquelin's brother, he also attended important premieres at the Comédie-Française.[38] Further work became available when Leoncavallo accompanied Ernest Coquelin and the actress Suzanne Reichenberg in musical sketches that made the rounds of the important salons. Reichenberg was a member of the Comédie-Française and frequently recited Proust in the author's presence, after which she would accompany her "men" for an evening out.[39] He also met Alexandre Dumas *fils*, who, as Leoncavallo recalled upon attending a performance of *La Souris* by the playwright Edouard Pailleron in 1887, said: "Pailleron is always fortunate . . . he is able to present two works at the same time: *La Souris* onstage and 'The World of Boredom' in the auditorium," coyly referring to Pailleron's successful play *Le monde où l'on s'ennuie*.[40]

Through Collet, Leoncavallo was introduced to the publisher Georges Charpentier, who welcomed many writers to his home, including Alphonse Daudet, the right-wing journalist Marquis Henri de Rochefort, and Charpentier's client and friend Emile Zola. Leoncavallo described Zola as "gentleness personified . . . a pure and ingenuous soul" as well as "a lover of truth."[41] One cannot help imagining the composer discussing the new literary form *réalisme* with Zola, which he would later recapture in *Pagliacci*, recalling the author when writing the opera's prologue.

Leoncavallo had still not forgotten about his trilogy *Crepusculum*. In 1884 he continued researching information related to Lorenzo de' Medici. He wrote the Bolognese publisher Zanichelli during September from 10, petite rue du Château in Dijon requesting poetry by Poliziano and Lorenzo de'Medici, both with prefaces by Carducci.[42] He was dismayed when informed that the Poliziano was no longer available, being interested in Carducci's preface as much as in Poliziano's poetry. "Since the preface is indispensable for my studies," he wrote back to the publisher, "I would like to enquire whether it would be possible to have a handwritten copy," which he hoped could be located in Bologna.[43] He also ordered Carducci's *Odi Barbare*, Shakespeare's *Julius Caesar* in Italian translation, and *Life of Lorenzo de' Medici* by William Ruscoe.

Having moved to the Hotel du Printemps at 89 Rue de la Victoire in 1885, Leoncavallo also witnessed Victor Hugo's funeral, leading him to remark, "If one was not present at his funeral, one could not realize how popular the great poet had been."[44] Thanks to his acquaintance with members of the Comédie-Française such as Coquelin, he met Hugo's grandson Edouard Lockro. This enabled him to gain access to the body in state, the face of which reminded him of Homer: "I was greatly impressed to find myself in the presence of the body, dignified in the tranquility of its final rest."[45] Leoncavallo was elated to catch sight of such famous personalities as Sully Prudhomme and Lecomte de Lisle, who joined more than four thousand others in a crowd that stretched from the Pantheon to the Champs-Elysées.

The *Appunti* also claim that Leoncavallo met the politician Georges Clemenceau during his Parisian stay.[46] He may have been introduced by the Charpentiers or Zola, although it seems more likely that it was through the Odéon actress Léonide Leblanc, who was more famous for her liaisons with Prince Napoléon, Duc d'Aumale, and Clemenceau than for her talent. The composer dedicated two songs to her, and both the original manuscripts of "Déclaration" and "La Chanson des yeux" bear inscriptions to her. "Déclaration" is a short yet passionate song set to the lyrics of their mutual friend, the humorist Armand Silvestre, while the "Chanson des yeux" is taken from a fragment (*Lydé* of the *Idylles*, VI) of the French revolutionary Poet André Chénier, its melody later used again for Silvio's "Decidi il mio destin" in *Pagliacci*.

Leoncavallo also played piano in the Quartetto dei Mandolinisti, which consisted of Giovanni Pietrapertosa (mandolin), Luigi Emma (guitar), and Pedro Aperte (mandola). Pietrapertosa had organized it, since the mandolin was still considered a novelty in Paris. Leoncavallo toured foreign cities as well, appearing in Brussels (Palais des Académies in the presence of the Queen) and Amsterdam during April 1885. (The composer had previously been in Brussels during 1884, when he completed "Echo," "Scène Idyllique," and a cantata for voice and orchestra that he orchestrated that July.) He continued earning a reasonable income through this undertaking during the summer months, when most aristocrats fled the stifling heat of Paris for their country châteaux.

Leoncavallo wrote Francesco from Brussels that the quartet had "debuted with great success."[47] Their relationship became strained due to a young woman who had lent Leoncavallo the money to travel to Belgium. "It is sufficient to say that if I did not have those few francs from the signorina I would have left without a penny."[48] Whether the signorina was Leoncavallo's future wife, Marie Rose Jean, is uncertain. In the same letter, he also stated that he wished to spend autumn in Italy to enlarge his repertory. His relationship with Francesco improved, however, when Alphonse Daudet and the wife of the music publisher Charpentier wished Francesco to be present at a reception where he could be alone with Leoncavallo.[49] In the summer of 1886, Francesco also contacted influential friends who he hoped would be able to have some of Leoncavallo's songs published.

Leoncavallo visited Italy for a period during 1885. His thoughts regarding *Crepusculum* also initiated a letter to Carducci, reminding him that he had been his student and that he was searching for the poet's edition of Poliziano's poetry, which he had still not located for an opera that he was about to begin (*I Medici*). He failed to understand why such an important work had "not been reprinted."[50] It is likely that he finally received the work from Carducci himself, making certain to remain in contact with the famous man. In 1893 he sent Carducci a copy of the completed *I Medici* libretto.

During March of 1888, Leoncavallo was also present at a reception, which took place in the home of Countess Marie de Guerne—an acquaintance of Proust—in honor of the Brazilian Emperor Don Pedro II. Another social lioness who impressed Leoncavallo was Princess Ruspoli, whose salon was "one of the most brilliant and appreciated in the artistic and literary world" of Paris.[51]

Yet another was Madame Benardaky, "a Russian who sang very well in Italian" and who was "passionately interested in music."[52] Her daughter Marie spurned Proust, supposedly strengthening his attraction for the same gender. He later recalled their "affair" in *Jean Santeuil*, where he immortalized her as Gilberte. The Benardaky home at 65 Rue de Chaillot (west of the Champs-Élysées) was filled with gothic sideboards, painted ceilings, and stained glass windows, sufficient for Proust to try and convince his parents "to change their furniture and their habits."[53] Benardaky was "statuesque and beautiful" and "said to care for nothing but champagne and love."[54] One of her guests remembered, "She had reached such a high position in society that the only person you see in her house who isn't out of the top drawer is herself."[55]

It was there that Leoncavallo encountered Ambroise Thomas, Jean-Baptiste Fauré, and Charles Gounod, who possessed a beautiful singing voice that astounded Leoncavallo. Gounod was greatly taken by Madame Benardaky's beauty and compared her to a Raphael painting. Gounod, at another gathering, had been so impressed by the "proportions" of a singer whom Leoncavallo accompanied, that although she sang dreadfully, her slender figure made up for any shortcomings, and prompted the Frenchman to place his own Légion d'Honneur rosette on her breast. Leoncavallo later remembered Benjamin Godard as the vainest person he had encountered. At a gathering in the chic Faubourg Saint-Germain, Godard finished accompanying his sister, who had performed on the violin and, when told how wonderful it had been, replied: "Do not thank me! Thank God who gave such genius to man!"[56]

BERTHE AND SYBIL SANDERSON

Leoncavallo remembered that he also found time to cultivate the talents of the young Emma Calvé at about the same time that he met his future wife, Marie Rose Jean. He described her as a twenty year old from Marseilles—who soon became his "preferred student"—interested in making a debut at the Opéra-Comique.[57] Official documents give her name as "Marie Rose Jean," although she is known to history as "Berthe Rambaud," and Leoncavallo always addressed her as "Berthe." The *Appunti* state that she became his "companion for life" in 1888.[58] Even if Leoncavallo's correspondence refrains from using the word "wife," their marriage license proves that the ceremony took place not in France, but in Milan during 1895. He also believed she was the daughter of a Napoleonic officer who possessed "a beautiful voice that encountered much favor in various small theaters."[59]

With only scant documentation, we know little of Berthe's origins, or, for that matter, of her entire marriage to the composer. In fact, only one postcard remains from Leoncavallo addressed to his future wife. Although there are numerous hypotheses about who she actually was, it seems probable that her father died young and that she was raised an orphan. Whether her parents were married at all is another matter of conjecture. Her mother was Thérèse Paut, although she might have been called Thérèse Jean.[60] Berthe was born in Carpentras in August of 1863. She was quite attractive in her early years, with dark brown hair and large eyes. Dressed elegantly in photos, she exudes an abundance of youthful charm, and one understands why Leoncavallo felt attracted to her. Not only did Berthe offer romance, but she was a soprano as well. (She had studied with Maurel, and Leoncavallo may have met her through the baritone. Then again, the composer may have sent her to Maurel). Berthe leaves the impression of having been uneducated, judging from the few remaining letters that survived her husband's death, and her decisions regarding Leoncavallo's estate were not always exemplary. Short of stature like the composer and inclined to obesity, she made a matronly impression for most of her life. The couple had no legitimate offspring, although Berthe did bring an eight-year-old girl into the relationship named Jeanne Puel. Leoncavallo would never adopt Jeanne, but she did receive the rights to his estate following Berthe's death. She died in 1957 at the age of seventy-seven. Jeanne is present in numerous photos as a very pale woman who somewhat resembled Berthe, leading one to speculate as to whether she was in fact her daughter.[61]

At the same time, Leoncavallo also met the young American soprano Sybil Sanderson—through Francesco—at a party in Paris. The composer was stunned by her beautiful and proud appearance singing Rosina's aria from *Il barbiere di Siviglia*. Although her talent was extraordinary, he felt that her voice was still in need of further training. This was not the reaction Sanderson expected, and she brusquely walked away. He later met Sanderson again after she had attended the Paris conservatoire for five months before losing interest.[62] When she asked him to help her reach her goal he suggested that she learn the role of Manon for Massenet, knowing that his colleague had been unable to cast the opera since the death of his preferred interpreter, Marie Heilbron. Upon Leoncavallo's lending her the score Massenet had given him, she promised to learn the role within twenty days. Leoncavallo then wrote Massenet that he had found *the* Manon. She later became Massenet's favorite artist, and he also wrote *Esclarmonde* to display her talents. According to Massenet's account in *Mes Souvenirs*, he met Sanderson at a party without Leoncavallo. However, Massenet wrote Leoncavallo a letter from Bordeaux dated 9 January 1892, thanking him for having introduced him to Sanderson.

"LA NUIT DE MAI"

Leoncavallo had always felt drawn to the French Romanticism of the poet Alfred de Musset, whose life, like Chatterton's, embodied the image of the young romantic hero. Known as "Miss Byron" for his effeminate beauty, his tempestuous and frustrated affair with George Sand culminated in the poems "Nuit de mai" (1835), "Nuit de décembre" (an ode to the suffering of love), "Nuit d'août" (1836),[63] and "Nuit d'octobre" (1837). The sensuous malady of the fin de siècle can also be felt in his autobiographical novel *Confession d'un enfant du siècle*, with which Leoncavallo was familiar. According to Musset's brother Paul, "Nuit de mai" had been written in two days; it was published 15 June 1835 in *Revue des Deux Mondes*.

Thus inspired, Leoncavallo set about composing a symphonic poem of "Nuit de mai," containing twelve movements from Musset's ten parts: a philosophical dialogue between a Poet and his Muse. A tenor voice would interpret the Poet's even-numbered verses, while the orchestra (Muse) would respond with the odd-numbered ones in a sumptuous metaphorical idiom. "In my version I composed a kind of dialogue between the Poet and the orchestra, trying, in this manner, to express the ideas that Musset developed from the Muse."[64] The Muse provides inspiration, seeking to release the Poet from his melancholy, while the Poet remains emotionally restrained as the Muse declares that everything can be beautiful—even suffering and pain. This impressive "Grand Poème symphonique," lasting some forty minutes, had a 218-page orchestral score and was completed in Paris in 1886.

La nuit de mai demonstrates Leoncavallo's talent as an orchestrator and an innate gift for dramatic situations that he later used in his operas. It is a hugely inventive, fresh, and fascinating opus, ranking among the best in the composer's canon. Although Leoncavallo also based his 1899 song "Nuit de décembre" on Musset's second poem of the same name, it is only a short extract of Musset's lengthy prose for the Poet without the Muse. It is regrettable that the composer failed to select "La nuit d'août" or "La nuit d'octobre" as the source of another symphonic poem, since the formats (Poet/Muse) are quite similar to those found in "La nuit de mai." Had he consistently upheld the quality inherent in *La nuit de mai* throughout his career, he would doubtless have fulfilled the great expectations this opus justifiably set.

When Mademoiselle Reichenberg of the Comédie-Française was unable to secure him tickets for the premiere of a new play, the composer was delighted, as it meant "the evening free to work on the orchestration of *La nuit de mai*."[65] It is questionable whether Leoncavallo met with Francesco prior to his friend's departure for London, where Leoncavallo bombarded him with letters concerning more gossip involving the two of them, also mentioning an enamored "*signorina*" who "is always crying and who hopes for your return."[66] His letterhead was now "R. Leoncavallo," replacing "Léon Cavallo," perhaps realizing that it was too similar to the director of the Opéra-Comique's "Léon Carvalho."[67]

La nuit de mai premiered at the Salle Kriegelstein in the rue Charras on 3 April 1887, sung by Leoncavallo's tenor friend Portejoie to critical acclaim. Its success must have made many realize that the voice teacher and accompanist Leoncavallo, who for years was forced to earn his living in vaudeville, was in fact a serious composer. The first to take notice was Édouard Colonne, who asked the composer to come to his home to play the score, not having attended the concert. Leoncavallo agreed to perform the opus as part of the Concerts Colonne series at the Théâtre du Châtelet, suggesting the Poet be sung by the Opéra-Comique tenor Jean-Alexandre Talazac, who had created Gerald in Debussy's *Lakmé* in 1883 and who would premiere Des Grieux in Massenet's *Manon* one year later. *Nuit de mai* received its second performance at the Salle Kriegelstein on 10 April combined with a recital including Berthe and a certain "Signor Louvet" of the Opéra. It seems that Berthe's singing lessons with Victor Maurel were paying off.

Leoncavallo's first success remained muted by his father's death on 3 February 1888 at the age of sixty-eight. Curiously, neither the *Appunti* nor his correspondence during the time mentions the loss. One gathers that Vincenzo had difficulty accepting his son's vocation and, like the composer's mother, he was unable to witness the success of *Pagliacci* four years later, dying in the belief that his son was a thirty-year-old failure. The loss of his parents at a relatively early age may have accelerated Leoncavallo's desire to found his own family with Berthe.

A "real disaster" occurred when the "Triple Alliance" was formed, a military treaty between Germany, Austria-Hungary, and Italy. French newspapers unleashed "a barrage of insults against Italy."[68] With increased French-Italian hostilities, Colonne declared that it would not be possible to present the work of an Italian during the coming season.[69]

·   Leoncavallo once again contacted Victor Maurel, who was preparing to create Iago in the world premiere of *Otello*, slated to take place at La Scala during February 1887.[70] (Leoncavallo had accompanied selections from the opera at Maurel's home on 30 March 1887, sung by Portejoie and the Rumanian soprano Marguerite Nuovina. She frequently performed Leoncavallo's songs and introduced him to some Rumanian ones he would later incorporate into *Zingari*.) Leoncavallo complained to Maurel that his career was not progressing, adding that he had finally completed the *Medici* libretto. Surprised that the composer wished to write another opera, considering that *Chatterton* remained unperformed, the baritone suggested Leoncavallo end his French sojourn in order to return to Italy, where he promised to introduce him to Giulio Ricordi. Initially skeptical, Leoncavallo hoped that he and Berthe could survive by giving music lessons. They sold their few belongings and left for Milan, determined to "begin life again for the third time."[71]

NOTES

1. *Appunti*, 29.
2. Ibid.
3. This information was ascertained in a letter from the Italian Foreign Ministry to the author in 2001.
4. In 1855, Giuseppe had founded *Lo Spettatore Egiziano*, the first Italian newspaper in Egypt. Years later Leone, the composer's brother, issued the political newspaper *La Trombetta*. It is not clear why Giuseppe was in Egypt in the first place, although the *Appunti* state that Leoncavallo's uncle was "involved in patriotic conspiracies" against the Bourbons. *Appunti*,1.
5. Said Pasha had granted his friend Ferdinand de Lesseps the concession to construct the Suez Canal only four months following his taking office.
6. *Appunti*, 33.
7. Ibid., 30.
8. Ibid.
9. Ibid., 31.
10. Ibid.
11. Ibid., 30.
12. Ibid., 31.
13. "M. Leoncavallo par lui-même" in *Le Figaro*, 9 June 1899.
14. Ibid.
15. *Appunti*, 36.
16. Ibid.
17. Ibid.

18. The Maison Victor Hugo, Paris, has been unable to locate any documents during the writing of this book that would verify the existence of the letter Leoncavallo received or that he in fact met Hugo (MVHP).

19. *Appunti*, 50.

20. Perhaps Désert or Malteau.

21. *Appunti*, 37.

22. "M. Leoncavallo par lui-même" in *Le Figaro*, 9 June 1899.

23. *Appunti*, 38.

24. Ibid.

25. Ibid.

26. *Almanach du Commerce*, 1886, 962.

27. *Appunti*, 38.

28. Ibid., 40.

29. Massenet's principal publisher until he sold his business to Heugel in 1891, as well as one of *Werther's* librettists.

30. *Appunti*, 41.

31. Ibid.

32. Ibid.

33. Ibid. Leoncavallo wrote the songs *Ne m'oubliez pas* and *Amore* to texts by Charles de Vaux, dedicated to the latter's wife and published by Lemoine & fils.

34. *Appunti*, 42.

35. Leoncavallo to Francesco Finelli della Valletta, 7 November 1884 (NY).

36. Leoncavallo to Francesco Finelli della Valletta, undated (NY).

37. *Appunti*, 44.

38. Leoncavallo dedicated the songs "Gare au loup!" and "Hue! Dia! Mon Grison" to Coquelin.

39. Leoncavallo dedicated the song "C'est le Renouveau, ma Suzon" to Reichenberg. It was titled "Ma Suzon" when Choudens published it. Although this romantic song to the verses of Emile Collet would perhaps signify an amorous interest on the composer's part, he was also prompt to compose another "Suzon" song for Susanne Levysohn in 1893.

40. *Appunti*, 48.

41. Ibid.

42. Leoncavallo to Zanichelli, 27 September 1884 (BAB).

43. Leoncavallo to Zanichelli, 3 October 1884 (BAB).

44. *Appunti*, 52.

45. Ibid.

46. Ibid., 45.

47. Leoncavallo to Francesco Finelli della Valletta, undated (NY).

48. Ibid.

49. Leoncavallo to Francesco Finelli della Valletta, 30 March 1886 (NY).

50. Leoncavallo to Giosuè Carducci, undated (circa 1885) (BCB).

51. *Appunti*, 45.

52. Ibid.

53. George D. Painter, *Marcel Proust, A Biography* (London: Chatto & Windus, 1989), 48.

54. Ibid., 44.
55. Ibid., 48.
56. *Appunti*, 47.
57. Ibid., 53.
58. Some sources state Berthe's birth as 27 June 1869. Although they were not married in 1888, their relationship had probably begun at that time, as photographs of the era attest.
59. *Appunti*, 53.
60. Mario Morini claims that Berthe was illegitimate and that the name "Rambaud" was to lend credence that she was in fact an offspring of her mother's marriage to Pierre Rambaud, who had left her a widow. ("Prospetto cronologico della vita e delle opere di Ruggero Leoncavallo," 41, in program notes to Palermo's Teatro Massimo production of *Zazà*, 1995.)
61. Leoncavallo later referred to Berthe as "Fernande."
62. Demar Irvine writes in his biography of Massenet: "The statement that 'in January 1886 she entered the Paris Conservatory, where she studied under Massenet, Sbriglia, and Marchesi' cannot be confirmed." Demar Irvine, *Massenet, A Chronicle of His Life and Times* (Oregon: Amadeus Press, 1994), 159. It nevertheless seems justified that she did attend the institution for a certain amount of time; otherwise Leoncavallo would certainly not have been aware of her presence.
63. Leoncavallo wrote a song based on this text with the same title in 1900.
64. *Appunti*, 55.
65. Leoncavallo to Francesco Finelli della Valletta, undated, 1887 (NY).
66. Leoncavallo to Francesco Finelli della Valletta, June 1887 (NY).
67. The director's real name was in fact "Léon Carvaille."
68. *Appunti*, 55.
69. The *Appunti* state that Leoncavallo had been offered a position at the Paris Conservatoire at this time, a statement difficult to believe, since he would have doubtless accepted, considering his precarious finances.
70. Leoncavallo considered the baritone's wife to be a "distinguished musician," frequently accompanying her chorus "Les Victorieuses" at the piano when they performed at various benefits.
71. *Appunti*, 57. Other versions insist that Leoncavallo pawned his watch.

· 3 ·

Working as Puccini's Librettist

1889–1892

*R*eturning to Milan and a rented home on Via Cappuccini 17 with Berthe and Jeanne during the winter of 1888, Leoncavallo was introduced to Giulio Ricordi "at the first opportunity."[1] They met, along with Maurel, at the Casa Ricordi offices on Via Omenoni, and Leoncavallo later recalled that Giulio Ricordi could be quite affable when he wished. It seems that was precisely how Ricordi welcomed the young man at their first encounter. Ricordi was aware of the composer's Parisian success, asking to hear portions of *Nuit de mai.* Maurel then mentioned the *I Medici* libretto, which prompted Ricordi to say that they had come to the "practical side of the visit," implying that his interest in Leoncavallo was largely as an accompanist or librettist. Puccini, at that time occupied with the world premiere of his *Edgar*, then entered the room. He was also introduced to Leoncavallo, whose initial impression was favorable, describing it as an "immediate liking."[2]

Leoncavallo read *I Medici* during his second meeting with Ricordi, and it supposedly made a "profound impression."[3] When he repeated the audition "with some trepidation" at the publisher's home in the presence of his wife, Giuditta, and other members of the Ricordi family, including their young son Tito, who would eventually lead the firm, Leoncavallo once again aroused interest.[4] Although Ricordi frequently made approving gestures and comments to his wife, he informed Leoncavallo that no decision could be made until after the premiere of *Edgar*. It must have certainly seemed a strange coincidence to return to Italy following the success of *Nuit de mai* to attend preparations for Puccini's Musset-based opera. Leoncavallo himself had planned to compose an opera based on *La Coupe et les lèvres*, which is evident from remaining sketches in the composer's hand, parts of which were later used for Canio's final scene in *Pagliacci*. However, *Edgar* was not a success, due to a poor libretto and a scenario at odds with Puccini's style; Leoncavallo nevertheless believed that the work contained "beautiful pages" and "youthful boldness."[5] Puccini's failure was Leoncavallo's chance for a second meeting with Ricordi, where he expressed "sincere affection" for his colleague.[6] Leoncavallo, however, felt considerably slighted when Ricordi, certain that *Manon Lescaut* would confirm his hopes on an international level, continued to esteem Puccini while Leoncavallo was treated with "complete indifference," unable to demonstrate his own capabilities.[7] Nevertheless, Ricordi introduced him to the conductor Franco Faccio during a performance of *Edgar* at La Scala as "a new acquisition. He is a good poet and if his music resembles his libretto, Italy will have a lasting work."[8]

In spite of this, Ricordi failed to produce the coveted contract, and Leoncavallo was forced to seek employment through Carlo D'Ormeville, director of the music journal *Gazzetta dei Teatri*. He decided to make a last effort by approaching Tito Ricordi, and this supposedly led to a contract, signed July 1888, stipulating that he relinquish all rights to *I Medici* for 2,400 lire, payable in monthly installments of 200 lire, to be completed within one year. He was also promised a compensation of 30 percent of the future work's rights, though only for one decade. The most damaging clause was when Casa Ricordi further declared that they were not obliged to produce *I Medici*, although they alone could publish all future works. Leoncavallo signed with hesitancy, remarking to Tito, "It is not an ideal contract, but I have faith in being able to compose an opera that will make your father content, thus affording me his support and patronage with, above all, improved conditions."[9] Leoncavallo immediately set about composing *I Medici* while continuing to give music lessons, aware that he needed to remain vigilant regarding Casa Ricordi, since they were known to purchase artists' rights at a price substantially below their actual worth.[10]

Leoncavallo had originally wanted to audition the opera in its entirety for Giulio Ricordi at the piano, but Puccini—who had now become the composer's "close friend"—advised him that the publisher preferred to hear each new installment at regular intervals. Thus, only two months later, Leoncavallo presented *I Medici*'s prologue and acts 1 and 2. Giulio and Tito Ricordi listened in silence, suggesting Leoncavallo should perform the two acts again that Thursday at a private reception in the presence of both family and friends. This second audition went well and was praised by the conductor Marino Mancinelli—brother of conductor Luigi, whom he had met at the D'Ormeville agency—and once again by Giuditta Ricordi, although not by the firm's director, who was still only interested in his client's literary talent. This interest again became painfully apparent when Leoncavallo was asked to help Puccini with his *Manon Lescaut* libretto based on the Prévost novel *Histoire du chevalier des Grieux et de Manon Lescaut*—a project Leoncavallo felt inadvisable following the success of Massenet's *Manon* in 1884. Later, a similar situation would reach grotesque proportions, when Puccini and Leoncavallo both vied for Henry Murger's *Scènes de la vie de bohème*.[11]

Leoncavallo felt that Puccini lacked culture. The latter's difficulty with foreign languages made him dependent on librettists, while Leoncavallo was able to create his own libretti. The *Appunti* relate that Giuseppe Giacosa suggested Puccini consider Victor Hugo's 1843 *Les burgraves* as a possible operatic vehicle following *Edgar's* failure. Giulio Ricordi returned from his library with a copy of the play, and Giacosa began reading. Although all were enthused, Puccini requested that he be given time to think. When Leoncavallo asked why, Puccini admitted that he had not been able to comprehend any of the French. Unable to find an Italian translation of the work, the subject was dropped. As a Francophile who may also have met Hugo, Leoncavallo had little sympathy at the time.

According to the *Appunti*, Marco Praga and Domenico Oliva, "one of Italy's best playwrights and a most worthy journalist," had already worked on the *Manon Lescaut* libretto.[12] When they relinquished their involvement, Luigi Illica and Giuseppe Giacosa took over. It is likely that Leoncavallo was asked by Ricordi to offer his suggestions at this point, as there is no current documentation to disprove that he sought to revise the libretto in the interim between the Praga-Oliva and Illica-Giacosa collaborations. Leoncavallo felt that Praga and Oliva's work remained stilted in its effort to distance itself from Meilhac and Gille's adaptation for Massenet. Leoncavallo explained his own approach to writing libretti:

> When composing libretti I always write an outline of the subject first and then dramatize it, creating almost the entire dialogue in prose, only to write the verses to fit the music. For *Manon* [*Lescaut*] I created a detailed outline to which I probably would have completed the rest had I not been preoccupied with my *Medici*.[13]

The *Appunti* state that Ricordi asked Praga and Oliva to resume work using Leoncavallo's suggestions. They supposedly refused when told that the published score would fail to carry their names. After Puccini dismissed Leoncavallo's input, Luigi Illica was suggested as the next collaborator. Illica was probably recommended by Giulio Ricordi, since the librettist was already working on Catalani's *La Wally*, which would be published by the firm after their takeover of Casa Lucca in 1888.[14] Leoncavallo suggested that Illica continue to build on his outline without, however, making use of his second act, adding, "that is why the libretto of Puccini's *Manon Lescaut* fails to mention an author's name."[15]

RENAISSANCE FLORENCE AND *I MEDICI*

Leoncavallo now concentrated on *I Medici*, presenting the finished opus to Giulio Ricordi a year later. The latter must have demonstrated little enthusiasm, as neither a premiere—let alone a new commission—was mentioned. Ricordi requested that the composer hand over the original partitura, which Leoncavallo fortunately managed to keep in his possession, claiming that he wished to make use of the time until the work's presentation to undertake some editing. Leoncavallo also introduced the opera to one of La Scala's impresarios, Luigi Piontelli, who supposedly expressed interest, although no definite plans were made.

Leoncavallo's financial difficulties were further aggravated when Gastone also joined Berthe and Jeanne Puel at Via Cappuccini. Nothing had changed since Paris, with the composer still regarded as head of the family, although without a child of his own. He was also weakened by a viral influenza, which attacked everyone except Berthe. Christmas was a depressing affair with virtually nothing to eat. He left his bed plagued with fever in order to ask Casa Ricordi for a loan. He was then told clearly by Cesare Blanc that the firm's legal obligations had already been discharged for that month. With no production of *I Medici* planned, Leoncavallo continued earning his living by giving lessons, before embarking on a tour of Romania with the celebrated soprano Hariclea Darclée during April and May of 1891.

Upon his return, Leoncavallo contacted Ricordi, hoping for some news concerning a prospective production of *I Medici*. He was furious to hear that Catalani's *La Wally* would be presented at La Scala instead. In October 1891, after twelve wasted months, Leoncavallo finally realized that any hope of Casa Ricordi producing *I Medici* was futile. Following years of what he felt to be suppression, Leoncavallo's quarrels with the firm finally came to a head. When some impresarios showed interest, Ricordi made it clear that he would prefer Puccini's second version of *Edgar* instead. Leoncavallo now realized he had wasted three years living in false hope. Believing Ricordi would regret his decision, Leoncavallo and Berthe decided that he needed to create a new work that would awaken Ricordi's interest, even asking his landlady whether he could make use of the peace and solitude her garden provided in order to begin working on a libretto. That October, Leoncavallo had also signed a contract that, for nine hundred lire, he, together with Ettore Gentili, would translate Carré's libretto of André Messager's opera *La basoche* into Italian. The agreement stipulated that the amount was only payable if Messager was content with Leoncavallo's work. Leoncavallo completed the libretto on time, together with a four-page introduction, and Casa Ricordi issued the Italian version of the comic opera in three acts in 1892, bound in the pseudo-medieval style fashionable of the time.[16]

IN MASCAGNI'S FOOTSTEPS WITH *PAGLIACCI*

Pietro Mascagni had achieved a sensational success with *Cavalleria rusticana* in 1890, laying the foundation for the verismo movement. Leoncavallo, inspired by the short opera, decided to try his hand at a similar work, in the hope of rescuing his situation. He drafted a libretto initially entitled *Il pagliaccio* (The Clown) within three weeks, partially inspired by the D'Alessandro murder trial of his youth and mostly influenced by Catulle Mendès and Paul Ferrier's 1887 play *La Femme de Tabarin*, in which an actor murders his wife. Mendès later accused Leoncavallo of plagiarism and took the matter to court, although the case was soon dropped, because Mendès had himself been influenced by Don Manuel Tamayo y Baus's (1829-98) Spanish play *Un Drama Nuevo* (1867). A combination of all these literary efforts led to the origins of Leoncavallo's opera.

Although drawn from disparate sources, *Pagliacci* became a concise work enabling Leoncavallo to display his own personal talent in a persuasive manner. He refused to dilute the work by concentrating solely on the form rather than content as he had in *I Medici*. Rather than a drama set in a historical context, *Pagliacci*, like *Carmen* in the case of Don José, showcases the destruction of a man instead of just telling the story of a cuckolded husband. Deriving from verismo, a genre Leoncavallo loathed, it still failed to satisfy his intellectual and aesthetic ideals.[17] However, it is no coincidence that his fame rests on the "intimate" operas *Pagliacci*, *Zazà* and *La bohème*, rather than on the ponderous *I Medici* or *Der Roland von Berlin*. What makes *Pagliacci* greater than Leoncavallo's other works is its wealth of original, memorable music, connected by an intricate web of thematic structures. This is immediately evident when comparing part 1 to the play within the play in part 2, which is nothing more than a repeat of all the actions that have already been touched upon during the first part, only they are now masked behind commedia dell'arte characters.[18]

Maurel insisted on the inclusion of an aria, and the composer later added the prologue after the opera had been completed.[19] He used the opportunity to explain his own efforts of bringing a Verga- or Zola-like quality to his "realistic" opera. Concluding that an aria for Tonio would be inappropriate during the action, Leoncavallo's decision to create a prologue heightened the theatrical feeling anticipating the later commedia dell'arte play.

LEONCAVALLO VS. CASA RICORDI AND A PREMIERE

Leoncavallo considered introducing *Il pagliaccio* to Casa Ricordi's rival firm Sonzogno, primarily because they had published *Cavalleria rusticana*, but Berthe reminded him that his contract with Ricordi stipulated that he offer all future works to the company. Puccini's lawyer, Ferruccio Foà, suggested Leoncavallo read *Il pagliaccio* to Giulio Ricordi: "If he doesn't like it, you are free of the obligations that bind you in your contract . . . but beware that you read the libretto in the presence of others [witnesses]."[20]

"Cordial affection" now "instantly vanished" from Ricordi's face when Leoncavallo announced that he had prepared another libretto.[21] Recalling Foà's advice, the composer asked for more people, who could offer a wider range of opinions, to attend the audition.[22] Leoncavallo read the libretto in Ricordi's home under enormous tension, recalling that he "began and concluded in a few minutes, without any interruptions in the midst of a truly grave silence."[23] No one dared breathe a word until Giulio Ricordi had given his opinion. Having listened with the utmost reserve while finishing some paperwork, he brusquely announced that the libretto was "nice but difficult. . . . How will this man dressed in white be taken seriously by the public? There is too much confusion between tragedy and comedy."[24] The others shared Ricordi's misgivings and, had it not been the result Leoncavallo wished to achieve, it would have been an evening of "great humiliation."[25] The composer finally confronted Ricordi: "I am not here to listen to criticism but for a much more practical reason. I am bound to you by a clause in my contract forcing me to offer you all new works. This is a libretto. You don't like it, but I do, and I am determined to compose music to it."[26] When Ricordi suggested they should take up the subject *after* the music had been composed, Leoncavallo was furious.

> I originally came here when I was unknown to you and did neither more nor less than what I did now: read a libretto on the basis of which you secured the future *I Medici*. Now you suggest that I compose music without even receiving a stipend! If I am forced to look elsewhere for an income on which to exist that takes away from time devoted to composition, it is necessary that I reclaim my freedom.[27]

The publisher remained uninterested, claiming that he already had too many other projects planned requiring his attention. Forgetting that he was bound to Casa Ricordi for all future work regardless of whether they intended to perform it or not, Leoncavallo returned to his lawyer the next morning, thereby initiating a legal battle that lasted for ten years.

Leoncavallo then decided to approach Ricordi's rival Edoardo Sonzogno (1836–1920). Lison Frandin, the mezzo-soprano who would later create Musette in Leoncavallo's *La bohème*, offered the press her account years later. According to an interview she gave to *Piccolo della Sera* in 1905, Casa Sonzogno's representative, Barilati, told her that he had been approached by "a certain Leoncavallo" who had sought an audition with the firm. Sonzogno had supposedly shown scant interest, and Barilati now hoped that Frandin could convince the publisher. The singer then invited Leoncavallo, together with Amintore Galli, the firm's artistic director, the following day. When Frandin first saw the composer, she described him as having a "powerful head, intelligent face" and "two small but expressive eyes," which mirrored both "hope and desperation." Frandin then recounted that Leoncavallo played portions of *Il pagliaccio*, singing all the parts himself with "elegance" and "poetry." Impressed, Frandin arrived at Via Pasquirolo and supposedly secured an appointment for the composer to audition the following day. Sonzogno greeted Leoncavallo in a cold manner, and Frandin tried to lighten the "heavy silence." If one is to believe her account, Leoncavallo then began playing *Il pagliaccio*. (It is more likely that the audition in fact presented *I Medici*, since Barilati stated that the composer's work had been "completely forgotten" in the Ricordi archive.) Frandin concluded by stating that Sonzogno then immediately assigned Leoncavallo a fixed monthly income.

Whatever the truth of the matter may have been, success could no longer be kept waiting. Leoncavallo's romantic and slightly improbable version described in the *Appunti* is similar to Frandin's, albeit with slight variations. Here we are told that both she and Amintore Galli were greatly impressed with *Il pagliaccio*. They then promised to write to Sonzogno, who was in Florence supervising a production at the Teatro Pagliano.

Armed with the *Il pagliaccio* libretto and a third-class train ticket, Leoncavallo arrived in the Tuscan capital to greet Sonzogno, who was ill in bed at Piazza Cavour 10. Given that Leoncavallo arrived with only the libretto, we may assume that, contrary to Frandin's account, the opera had not yet been written. Since the original *Pagliacci* manuscript bears no date it is indeed difficult to make a final assumption.[28]

At 9:45 the following morning he reappeared at Piazza Cavour, preferring to stand upon hearing his "death sentence." Sonzogno liked the libretto, and, although he must have been attracted by the idea of gaining one of Ricordi's clients, he did not want any legal problems with the rival firm. Sonzogno agreed to see Leoncavallo two days later in Milan to discuss a possible contract, resulting in the same price Ricordi had offered for *I Medici*: 2,400 lire spread over one year, followed by 30 percent of royalties for twenty years.[29] With the terms agreed upon, Leoncavallo thanked the publisher profusely, and Sonzogno, eager for a work to complement *Cavalleria rusticana*, prepared a copy of the contract to be drawn up for his new acquisition to sign.[30]

Maurel immediately saw the possibility of a new role in Tonio, confiding to Leoncavallo that he would only honor an upcoming engagement in Thomas's *Hamlet* at the Dal Verme if they also agreed to present the new opus, providing that Leoncavallo alter the title to the plural *Pagliacci* (Clowns), thereby including Tonio rather than placing all the interest on Canio. Not only would he open the opera with the prologue, which eventually became the credo of the verismo movement, but he also closed it with the line "La commedia è finita," written for Tonio *to sing*.

By April, Sonzogno was planning to produce *Pagliacci* at the San Carlo in Naples, asking Leoncavallo to correct proofs of the published score that would be dedicated to the latter's parents.[31] Leoncavallo was satisfied with the completed opus: "The work has turned out well, and all who hear it make the most joyous predictions. God willing that it will indeed be so! It would be time that I also have some artistic satisfaction and a bit of peace in order to dedicate myself completely to my sole ideal!"[32] The "sole ideal" was still *Crepusculum*.

Leoncavallo now became involved in forming an ensemble of singers for the production. He had originally decided on the Bolognese tenor Alfonso Garulli for Canio, although Maurel suggested he contract a younger artist. He was finally introduced to Fiorello Giraud through his vocal teacher, the former tenor Enrico Barbacini. The twenty-year-old Giraud had recently been successful as Lohengrin, and Leoncavallo now began coaching him as Canio. Nedda was assigned to Adelina Stehle, who might have been suggested by Maurel, since she would create Nannetta to his Falstaff in the upcoming world premiere of the Verdi opera. Peppe/Arlecchino (usually mispelled as Beppe) was entrusted to Francesco Daddi.[33] The baritone Mario Ancona was scheduled to create Silvio on account of his aristocratic manner. Maurel also secured the young Arturo Toscanini, who was originally recommended by Verdi, to conduct.

Sonzogno remained in his Parisian home, receiving word in a letter from Leoncavallo on 12 May 1892 that rehearsals were going well:

> Yesterday we had the first piano rehearsal, and both Maurel and Toscanini were very content; the artists already know the opera musically. . . . The cast is excellent, and I am more than satisfied. . . . [Aleardo] Villa has sketched some splendid costumes that everyone admires who has seen them. . . . Maurel, as well as the management, believe they should be exhibited in the gallery before the performance. Today I have a meeting with the set designer . . . everything is proceeding well and I believe we will be able to open by the 20th or the 22nd at the latest.[34]

Rehearsals, in the company of Cesare, the composer's cat, did not proceed as smoothly as Leoncavallo described, since, like *Cavalleria rusticana*, *Pagliacci* made vocal demands to which most singers were unaccustomed, including Maurel. The composer understandably wanted Sonzogno at his side, hoping that he would be in Milan for the premiere. "Maurel believes that your absence may be negatively interpreted as a lack of faith in my work, since you have always demonstrated a paternal sense of care in being present at the debuts of all the new works you have acquired."[35] Believing that Sonzogno was purposefully ignoring the premiere, he also informed the publisher that Maurel was going to spend "1000 lire to have a journalist he knows, who writes for twelve main London newspapers, come from London, since he wants to advertise both the opera and its interpreters. Although it is true that he is doing this for himself, I will largely profit from it."[36] Maurel, according to the composer, also wanted Sonzogno in Milan to discuss taking the entire production to Covent Garden once the contract at the DalVerme had ended, believing it would "launch the opera in a most unique manner!"[37] He concluded by reminding Sonzogno "one can never take too many precautions."[38] The publisher responded to Leoncavallo's four-page letter by saying that his health would not permit a one- or two-day trip to Milan to attend the premiere. He knew the theatrical world was aware that he would remain absent from Italy for three months, and, with Maurel and Amintore Galli at Leoncavallo's side, his own attendance would be superfluous.

Pagliacci premiered at Milan's Teatro DalVerme on 21 May 1892, although Mario Ancona, the Silvio, had dropped out only a few days earlier and was replaced by Mario Roussel. Leoncavallo arrived at the theater with great apprehension, since the dress rehearsal had been "a disaster." In the performance, however, Maurel's rendering of Tonio's prologue was immediately greeted with three curtain calls. Nedda's aria was encored, as was Arlecchino's serenade, prompting Leoncavallo to acknowledge the applause some four or five times. Toscanini had the orchestra repeat the "Vesti la giubba" theme following Canio's aria, allowing for a scene change, later recommending that Leoncavallo compose an intermezzo using music from the prologue. Leoncavallo heeded this advice, and Sonzogno later also chose to publish the work in two acts.[39]

Critics were perplexed, expecting to hear a modern work, instead being reminded of bel canto.

> The first act begins well. The chorus of villagers announcing the arrival of the clowns is vulgar though in character. Canio's invitation to the villagers is spontaneous: the semi-seria manner of speaking is thus also in character, recalling *recitativo* of the older *opere buffe*. However, with Nedda's romanza . . . the music begins to no longer fuse with the drama, and it seems that it is not the clown's wife who sings but a lady with princely mannerisms, and her aria, no matter how melodious and fascinating, lacks originality. Tonio is not dissimilar to the "honest Iago," and Canio, the clown, could just as well wear the jealous Otello's armor.[40]

The work was widely criticized in the music press, despite the public's approval, with the *Corriere della Sera*, for example, writing that the opera's plot was too drawn out and that the conclusion lacked a sense of drama. Although Leoncavallo was felt to possess "serious musical qualities together with uncommon musical culture, in *Pagliacci* he tried to create not an original and inspired work in which artistic passion triumphs but an opera that complements an older style, with melodies both fluent and known—the taste of the masses—an immediate success regardless of however transient."[41] Reviewers wrote that Stehle sang well, although her acting was hindered by Leoncavallo's music, which detracted from Nedda's character. They agreed with Leoncavallo that Maurel was unable to bring Tonio to life, while claiming Giraud sang with a beautiful voice and dramatic intonation, precisely the opposite of the composer's critique. The still unknown Toscanini was "continuously called to the stage, conducting the orchestra in a distinguished manner."[42] Giulio Gatti-Casazza felt the work only later became popular in Vienna, since "the opera had a moderate success and the Dal Verme season ended before the arranged time."[43]

Leoncavallo grew disillusioned with the cast, writing to Sonzogno that Maurel was not "indispensable" as Tonio since his voice now lacked energy and his appearance was inappropriate to the "horrid" character. He also refused to repeat the prologue! Although Leoncavallo felt Giraud to be "full of good will," Canio's character never emerged, and "Vesti la giubba" was performed too nervously, sung by a lyric voice for a role the composer compared to Don José. In Stehle he lacked a verismo singer capable of lending a sense of drama to the vocal line through passion and diction. Grateful that Roussel had learned the part of Silvio in two days, he now felt the Nedda/Silvio duet lacked brevity and debated whether it should be shortened, although he postponed the decision until Sonzogno's return. He also added a "preludietto" incorporating the work's major themes, convinced that dividing the opera into two acts enhanced its effect.

After Massenet, Mascagni, Lison Frandin, and Mario Ancona sent congratulatory telegrams, Sonzogno wrote that he would present *Pagliacci* in Vienna, stipulating that it be shortened by twenty-five minutes to resemble *Cavalleria rusticana*. This the composer refused to do. The orchestral score also remained unpublished, Sonzogno believing it to be the only guarantee against foreign musical piracy. Hoping that *Pagliacci* would be successful, Sonzogno's thoughts turned to Casa Ricordi's decision regarding the rights to *I Medici*.

First, however, Leoncavallo relaxed during part of July and August in the Swiss village of Vacallo, while, nearby, Puccini worked on *Manon Lescaut*. Once again he asked Leoncavallo to contribute text, resulting in "Manon, Manon! Quest'infame ricchezza, tu la rimpiangi? Ohimé, Nell'oscuro futuro . . . dì, che farai di me?" Puccini incorporated the last line for Des Grieux to sing in the act 2 love duet—evidence that Leoncavallo was involved with the libretto longer than is usually surmised.

Leoncavallo joined Sonzogno and colleagues Mascagni, Cilèa, and Giordano that September for the International Music and Theatre Exposition in Vienna. *Pagliacci* served as a curtain raiser for Mascagni's *L'amico Fritz*, since the combination of *Pagliacci/Cavalleria rusticana* had not yet been considered. These guest performances were important for Casa Sonzogno's reputation, since many of Europe's artistic directors would be present. The Italian season opened on 17 September with *L'amico Fritz* interpreted by Fernando De Lucia, followed by *Pagliacci*'s "successo completo," according to the *Corriere della Sera*. Other than Daddi as Peppe, the cast had changed since its premiere, with a dramatic and forceful Canio in Alfonso Garulli, the first tenor to speak Tonio's final "La commedia è finita."[44] The *Wiener Zeitung* referred to the work as "Hanswurste" (The Buffoon) or "Die dorfkomödianten" (The Village Players), before the more appropriate title "*Der bajazzo*" (The Clown) was used. This is similar to the original, by which it is still known in German-speaking countries—the singular in keeping with the work's original title. Sonzogno concluded the visit with an elaborate dinner for fifty people, while newspapers described Leoncavallo's corpulence, large handlebar mustache, tightly combed hair, low forehead, and inelegant deportment, claiming that he was "the complete opposite of Mascagni in that he is in no way noteworthy."[45] Unlike *Cavalleria rusticana*'s, *Pagliacci*'s success had not been immediate, although its impact was soon felt, with Mascagni resenting *Pagliacci*'s obvious similarities to his own work. Leoncavallo was suddenly catapulted to international fame following years of struggle; the wait had been long, and he was more than ready.

After producing *Pagliacci* in Warsaw during October, Sonzogno and Count Bolko von Hochberg planned performances of *Pagliacci*, *Cavalleria rusticana*, and *I Rantzau* in Berlin, opening on 6 December 1892 and attended by the composer. Although Kaiser Wilhelm II requested *Cavalleria rusticana* with Mascagni on the podium, this was to be his initial encounter with Leoncavallo's music, which would eventually result in the German premiere of *I Medici* during December 1893. Staying in the Friedrichstrasse's luxurious Central Hotel, Leoncavallo realized that the publicity he received was more important than the cost of his sojourn.[46] News of *Pagliacci*'s success soon reached Italy, where Alfredo Catalani wondered whether it was worth striving to create serious art when the Germans exchanged Wagner for the "decadence" of Mascagni, Leoncavallo, and Franchetti.[47] In Berlin, Leoncavallo also met the very influential German publisher Adolph Fürstner, who agreed to publish his two songs "C'était un rêve" and "Qu'à jamais le soleil se voile," based on texts by Alexandre Dumas *fils*.[48] Returning to Milan, the composer heard from Fürstner again immediately, congratulating him on the decoration he received from Umberto I in December 1892.[49] Hopeful for a future collaboration with the composer, Fürstner signed his letters "your happy publisher."[50] These successes were temporarily halted when performances of *Pagliacci* in the Piedmontese town of Vercelli failed, with singers unable to satisfy the work's demands or audience expectations. Leoncavallo attended further performances in Naples, Como, (where he was honored by the Teatro Sociale), and Genoa.

Leoncavallo concentrated next on *I Medici*'s orchestration. This was set to premiere in November at the Teatro Dal Verme in a four-act version with the prologue deleted. Sonzogno had planned the production,[51] although Ricordi still held the rights and refused to release the score. Leoncavallo signed a contract with his former publisher on 16 December 1892: "It seems that I am predestined to be stripped and robbed by publishers. . . . Ricordi took 8,500 francs for my having had the pleasure of losing three years waiting for his approval!"[52] Ricordi's contract also stipulated that the scenario for a future opera be presented by August 1893, with completion by December 1896, and the orchestral score be turned in no later than March 1898, for which he would be paid five thousand lire. If Leoncavallo failed to uphold the requirements he would owe twenty thousand lire. Leoncavallo's ensuing legal battle against Casa Ricordi became known as the "Causa Ricordi–Leoncavallo" in Italy following his inability to honor the contract, and would continue for years.

Further legal conflicts arose when *Chatterton* once again reared its unwanted head. Leoncavallo had originally sold the score for two hundred lire to Casa Trebbi, which was later purchased by Achille Tedeschi. After *Pagliacci*'s success, Casa Tedeschi opted to produce *Chatterton*, a decision Leoncavallo opposed, considering the work to be nothing more than a youthful failure, damaging to his new reputation. Tedeschi refused Leoncavallo's suggestion to pay back the two hundred lire and insisted that the composer trade in *I Medici* for *Chatterton*, implicitly threatening to embarrass him with the latter. Thus more legal troubles began. In addition, Tedeschi spread the rumor that Trebbi had financially supported Leoncavallo for a number of years. The composer was furious, seeking to suppress *Chatterton* at all costs.

> I have created a conscientious reputation thanks to a serious work, and now, at the point of performing another important work, I am being forced to allow a performance of this banal rubbish, lacking in originality and revision, an inferior youthful work, solely for the benefit of Signor Tedeschi, who, up until now, has kept it buried, which is a miracle considering that he had not sold it to a sausage maker.[53]

Leoncavallo hoped Count Pierfrancesco Albicini, who had sponsored him in Bologna, would be able to contact Tedeschi and rescue the situation. It was difficult to imagine a way out of this dilemma, considering that he had also agreed to create six operas for Sonzogno.

LEONCAVALLO VS. PUCCINI

It is unfortunate that no letters have yet appeared shedding additional light on the Puccini-Leoncavallo feud that began during March 1893.[54] One can only rely on newspaper articles and public accounts, since Leoncavallo's correspondence for that year fails to mention it. It began when the composers met in Milan's Galleria on 19 March, one of them stating that he was at work on an operatic adaptation of Henry Murger's novel *Scènes de la vie de bohème*. Leoncavallo supposedly replied that he had already signed a contract with Sonzogno for the same work.[55] *Il Secolo* announced the following day that

Leoncavallo was already at work on the opera and that it would be performed the following year. Although this may have reflected the truth, the completion date was preposterous, considering that Leoncavallo's version was only ready to be produced in 1897.[56] On 22 March *Il Secolo* again published an article on Leoncavallo's behalf:

> Maestro Leoncavallo wishes to state that he signed a contract for the new opera and has been working on the music for that subject since last December. . . . Maestro Puccini, to whom Maestro Leoncavallo declared recently that he was writing *Bohème*, confessed that he only had the idea of using *La bohème* a few days ago, upon returning from Turin, and that he spoke of it to Illica and Giacosa, who, he says, have not yet finished the libretto. Thus, Maestro Leoncavallo's priority over this opera is indisputably established.

According to the article, Victor Maurel could testify that since his arrival in Italy for rehearsals of *Falstaff*, Leoncavallo had considered writing the role of Schaunard for him, while Lison Frandin supposedly acknowledged that the composer had already promised her the part of Musette four months earlier. It is doubtful that Leoncavallo had been working on *Bohème* since December, since he would have spent weeks, if not months, drafting the libretto, rather than writing Fürstner on 30 October 1893 that he would begin to work on *Bohème* following the premiere of *I Medici*. Although the "who came first" question remains unresolved, the information contained in Leoncavallo's press release was far from the truth. Giulio Ricordi felt Puccini should not publicly respond. However, the composer believed that to remain silent was to admit defeat. Puccini was therefore elated when Luigi Illica drafted a letter, suggesting Giulio Ricordi review it before publication in the *Corriere della Sera* on 24 March, informing readers that if his "friend" Leoncavallo had told him earlier, he would not have attempted the same subject.

> From Maestro Leoncavallo's declaration in yesterday's *Il Secolo* the public must understand my complete innocence, for, to be sure, if Maestro Leoncavallo, for whom I have long felt great friendship, had confided to me earlier what he suddenly made known to me the other evening, then I would certainly not have thought of Murger's *Bohème*. Now—for reasons easy to understand—I am no longer inclined to be as courteous to him as I might like, whether as friend or musician. Besides, what does it matter to Maestro Leoncavallo? Let him compose, and I will compose, and the public will judge for themselves. Precedence in art does not imply that identical subjects must be interpreted by identical artistic ideas. I only want to make it known that for about two months, namely since the first performances of *Manon Lescaut* in Turin, I have worked earnestly on my idea and made no secret of this to anyone.[57]

Murger's novel had been translated into Italian by Felice Cameroni in 1872 and published by Casa Sonzogno. Edoardo Sonzogno may have thus first suggested it to Leoncavallo, who then told Illica, who brought it to Puccini's attention, or Leoncavallo may have mentioned it to Puccini in Vacallo while helping with the *Manon Lescaut* libretto. Alternately, Leoncavallo might have received news of the work in his regular correspondence with Massenet, who had originally written incidental music for *Vie de bohème*, including "La chanson de Musette," for the reopening of the Odéon theatre in 1875. Massenet wrote in his autobiography that he had once planned his own version of *Bohème*, having known many of the original characters described in the novel. Ricordi immediately began making inquiries regarding rights in order to impede Leoncavallo. He realized that an opera would have to be based on the novel since the play was still copyrighted and of less interest, not to mention the similarities it bore to *La traviata*.

Although Puccini wrote Illica that he admired Leoncavallo's "marvelous" *La bohème* libretto, from then on he would always refer to his colleague as either "Leonasino," "Leonbestia" or "Cavalloleon."[58] Animosity toward Puccini also continued on Leoncavallo's part for the remainder of his life, becoming almost obsessive, while Puccini wrote of his plans to Illica, also mentioning that Leoncavallo had written:

> The telegram about *Bohème* arrived from Paris. However, unfortunately the novel is free and available, since Murger died without heirs. The play is still under copyright of *the authors* (Barrière and Murger). . . . Have you reread the novel? Send for the French version. I urge you: the gauntlet has been thrown down and the challenge taken up. Leoncavallo wrote to me from Venice that he will have to battle against two colossi: you and Giacosa, and that now he is going to study the background of the "Latin Quarter!!!"[59]

Curiously, there is a complete lack of correspondence between Ricordi and Illica from 23 December 1892 until 25 April 1893. It is significant that these letters are missing, considering the frequency of their contact. Also compelling is the complete absence—during precisely the same period—in the *Appunti*, where no less than fifteen pages (230–45) are "missing," resuming in May 1893, after the Puccini-Leoncavallo feud had largely been played out. A possible hypothesis would suggest, as Jürgen Maehder reasons, that all members involved practiced some "self-editing" in the event of a possible court case.

NOTES

1. *Appunti*, 57.
2. Ibid., 58.
3. Ibid.

4. Ibid.

5. Ibid.

6. Ibid.

7. Ibid., 59.

8. Ibid.

9. Ibid., 60.

10. On 17 November 1889, the *Gazzetta Musicale di Milano* wrote that Leoncavallo's "comic opera" *Songe d'une nuit d'été* was being presented to a delighted audience in a villa near Paris, reminding the French audience of Massenet. This is the only information I have come across regarding the work.

11. At the time of *Manon Lescaut*, Puccini had actually also been interested in composing Sardou's *La Tosca*, already assigned to another of Casa Ricordi's clients, Alberto Franchetti. Puccini was only later able to realize his ambition when Franchetti was outsmarted by Ricordi, who finally manipulated him into relinquishing both his rights and interest in the play.

12. *Appunti*, 62.

13. Ibid.

14. Giacosa and Boito had both read and been impressed by Illica's adaptation of Wilhelmine von Hillern's novel *Die Geierwally*, which would serve as the libretto to Catalani's *Wally*.

15. *Appunti*, 63.

16. Leoncavallo also completed the libretto *Vendetta* for Casa Ricordi.

17. Leoncavallo preferred the term "realismo," believing that "verismo" narrowed his talent and aims toward vulgar subjects that distanced him from composers he admired, such as Wagner and Verdi.

18. Part 1 even begins with the same backstage trumpet reveille announcing the upcoming performance as in the *commedia*.

19. The page numbers of the autograph score attest to this.

20. *Appunti*, 65–66.

21. Ibid., 66.

22. Ibid.

23. Ibid.

24. Ibid., 67.

25. Ibid.

26. Ibid.

27. Ibid.

28. The *Appunti* state that the score had been completed in two months, although the orchestration was still missing at this point.

29. The *Appunti* claim that Leoncavallo was presented with the same contract Mascagni received for *Cavalleria rusticana* (three thousand lire), prompting its author to wonder why "a law never existed directed at the exploiters of ignorance." David Stivender, *Mascagni, An Autobiography Compiled, Edited and Translated from Original Sources* (New York: Pro/Am Music Resources, 1988), 90.

30. Edoardo Sonzogno to Leoncavallo 1892 (BCL).

31. "Alla venerata memoria dei miei Genitori, Vincenzo Leoncavallo e Virginia D'Auria, Il figlio sempre memore, R. Leoncavallo."

32. Leoncavallo to unidentified recipient, undated (CMU).

33. Mascagni later also engaged Daddi for Arlecchino in *his* commedia dell'arte opera *Le maschere*.

34. Leoncavallo to Edoardo Sonzogno, 12 May 1892 (BCL).

35. Ibid.

36. Ibid.

37. Ibid.

38. Ibid.

39. *Pagliacci's* autograph score proves that the intermezzo was added later, since there is no interruption in the pagination between the conclusion of "Vesti la giubba" (206) and the beginning of what would become act 2 (207).

40. *Corriere della Sera*, 22 May 1892.

41. Ibid. Verismo *did* appeal to "the masses" and was frequently transient in its popularity, a confirmation of its modern style albeit subconsciously expressed.

42. Ibid.

43. Gatti-Casazza, *Memories of the Opera*, 280.

44. Credit is usually given to Caruso, although it appears that Garulli was the first to inaugurate the habit.

45. Unidentified Austrian newspaper clipping (BCL).

46. Leoncavallo to unidentified recipient, 5 December 1892 (GH).

47. Michelangelo Zurletti, *Catalani* (Turin: E.D.T.,1982), 195.

48. Fürstner would have to flee Hitler's Germany, thereby saving the Leoncavallo correspondence from destruction during World War II.

49. Leoncavallo was made "cavaliere dell'ordine della corona d'Italia" on 25 December 1892.

50. Adolph Fürstner to Leoncavallo, 3 January 1893 (BCL).

51. Leoncavallo returning to both *Medici* and, later, also the revised version of *Chatterton*, is another curious similarity to Mascagni again taking up his first opera, *Guglielmo Ratcliff*, after *Cavalleria rusticana*.

52. Leoncavallo to Count Pierfrancesco Albicini, 18 February 1893 (CMU). Leoncavallo paid 8,500 lire, 5,000 as "compensation" to Casa Ricordi.

53. Ibid.

54. 3 March 1893 saw the Italian premiere (Teatro Regio, Torino) of André Messager's opera *La basoche*, in an Italian translation by Leoncavallo and Ettore Gentili.

55. The *Bohème* contract has yet to turn up in an archive or private collection.

56. There is no mention of such a statement in any of Leoncavallo's correspondence until March 1893.

57. *Corriere della Sera*, 21 March 1893. Reprinted in Gara, *Carteggi Pucciniani*, 81–82.

58. Literally "Leon-donkey," "Leon-beast," and "Horse-Leon."

59. Gara, *Carteggi Pucciniani*, 83.

• 4 •

Epic Italian Music

1893–1894

$\mathcal{L}$eoncavallo worked on *I Medici*'s orchestration while battling Tedeschi and Ricordi and writing charming letters to Sonzogno and Fürstner. Sonzogno also managed to arrange as many performances of *Pagliacci* as possible, including in Vienna, this time at the Court Opera rather than the Exposition Theater. Fürstner wrote the composer on 11 April 1893—less than four weeks after the beginning of the *Bohème* feud—that a German translation of Murger and Barrière's *Vie de bohème* play had already been made. This is the first mention of Murger's work in Leoncavallo's correspondence. Fürstner also hoped the Parisian firm Choudens would publish the French songs "C'etait un rêve" and "Je ne sais pas ton nom." Berthe, aware that the Fürstners wished to visit Leoncavallo during May, cabled Mrs. Fürstner that they had no time, since "everyone goes to the country,"[1] and that the composer would be in England "for a fortnight" anyway. She thanked them for a traveling bag, excusing her dear "Roger" who was too busy to write.[2]

Leoncavallo left for London and the British premiere of *Pagliacci* that May, taking up residence at the Hotel Metropole. Covent Garden's director, Sir Augustus Harris, had also invited Mascagni to conduct *I Rantzau* and *L'amico Fritz*, while the much-loved composer of salon songs, Francesco Paolo Tosti, made certain that his Italian colleagues would feel at home.[3] Leoncavallo liked his fellow Neapolitan very much and soon wrote lyrics for Tosti's song "Canta." When asked what constituted the difference between Leoncavallo and Mascagni, Tosti nevertheless remarked, "Mascagni is the boss, Leoncavallo the servant."[4] But Leoncavallo, spared this knowledge, marveled at Tosti's "exquisite manners."[5] Puccini would have been envious knowing that the social host Lady Gladys de Grey had invited the composer and Mascagni on 27 May. While Mascagni complained that English food was dreadful and the underground not to his liking, Leoncavallo concentrated on the upcoming production, scheduled to open on 19 May 1893, also writing Fürstner of his problems with Tedeschi on account of *Chatterton*:[6]

> I wrote *Tommaso Chatterton* at 16, selling it to a small publishing house in Bologna. . . . The publisher, whose name is Trebbi, kept the music in a box for 16 years. Now that he is dead, his heirs have sold the shop to Signor Tedeschi, who is in the process of becoming a music publisher. When he noticed that he had one of my operas among his old works, he had his lawyer quickly write that he wanted to perform it immediately. I have done everything possible to hinder a performance of my old opera. . . . All that I could obtain from Signor Tedeschi was [the promise] that he could produce the opera one year after the premiere of *I Medici* and, in exchange, I will revise the score a bit, which I have not glanced at in 16 years.[7]

Leoncavallo also planned to inform newspapers before a possible *Chatterton* premiere—which he would refuse to attend—that it was "a youthful work" that he did not really wish to see produced. He now hoped that a careful revision would at least make the opera a "curiosity piece."[8] Fortunately, his problems were temporarily forgotten in London. The *Pagliacci* cast was sumptuous indeed, including Nellie Melba (Nedda), Fernando De Lucia (Canio), and conductor Luigi Mancinelli. The prince of Wales—later King Edward VII—to whom Leoncavallo was also introduced, attended the premiere. Mascagni saw one of the later performances, commenting that Melba's portrayal failed to possess the necessary "*sentimento*" for verismo, resembling a "mummy" or "marionette,"[9] while writing off De Lucia as "a real dog!"[10] Baritone Mario Ancona was the only artist favorably mentioned by Mascagni. Leoncavallo, excusing himself for not saying goodbye, sent Tosti the "Canta" lyrics before leaving Britain. He blamed his "strange disposition of spirit" on the "pathologically morbid" state of his soul, hoping that Tosti—"a modern day troubadour"—would understand.[11] The most amusing account of Leoncavallo's stay came from Vincent Seligman. He recalled how a stranger asking for directions had once stopped the composer, who responded: "Th-th-there are s-s-six m-m-million inhabitants of L-L-London-so w-w-why the h-h-hell did you p-p-pick on me?"[12]

Returning to Italy, Leoncavallo regretted the time "wasted" in London that should have been devoted to *I Medici*. Still busy with the orchestration, he "sacrificed" the prologue, an "archaic" dialogue between Pope Sixtus IV and Giambattista da Montesecco, that would have been interpreted as an anticlerical statement, although its exclusion would make the plot appear somewhat disjointed.[13] Unable to find quiet at Via Vivaio with Berthe, her mother, Jeanne Puel, and Gastone, Leoncavallo left for the mountain resort town of Abetone. However, Sonzogno soon informed him that the designer Aleardo Villa wished to prepare *I Medici*'s premiere by visiting Florence. This forced the composer to join Villa in the Tuscan town, where, in a museum, he became incensed that a statue of Catherine de' Medici had been transported elsewhere.

> I find it tedious the way our art collections are moved about. I have a special manner of visiting galleries, standing in front of works that [particularly] strike me, and, during following visits, I go directly to these works as if the rest did not exist. I am disoriented by these changes, feeling as if I am no longer in the same place, while the artwork that I looked for no longer pleases me.[14]

On his return he managed to spend some time in Bologna with Count Albicini, who told him that the situation with Tedeschi had somewhat relaxed. To follow *Pagliacci*'s success, Sonzogno was determined to present the most lavish production of a new work ever seen at the Dal Verme, with subsequent performances in Berlin. Most of his letters to the composer were sent from Vienna, while Leoncavallo worked on *I Medici*'s orchestration fifteen to sixteen hours a day, suffering from the July heat, aiming for completion by the beginning of September.[15] The composer earnestly hoped Sonzogno would make a special effort to attend "in order to be useful," since he had been absent from the *Pagliacci* premiere.[16] This was not to be the case, however; the publisher infuriated Leoncavallo by returning to Paris, where plans regarding the premiere were proposed by mail. Leoncavallo wanted La Scala and Toscanini, but Sonzogno wrote on 1 July 1893 that if he insisted on the "*antipatico*" Toscanini he would not attend the premiere, preferring a more "modest" conductor. He was still livid that Toscanini had refused to conduct a run of Mascagni's *I Rantzau* in Rome one year earlier, because Mascagni had wished to lead the premiere himself. Sonzogno also proposed the tenor Francesco Tamagno, who had created Otello at La Scala, for the rigorous part of Giuliano. Aware that the artist was performing *La forza del destino* in Fano, Leoncavallo arrived there during a rehearsal to hear him sing the entire role of Don Alvaro to his complete satisfaction. He recalled that the tenor was a "true revelation, thanks to the seriousness and the conscientiousness of his preparation."[17] He was also impressed when Tamagno first insisted on reading the *Medici* libretto to know whether the part would be dramatically viable for him. The tenor then asked Leoncavallo to play the score and mark Giuliano's role since he was unable to read music. Standing behind Leoncavallo, Tamagno sang every note perfectly, explaining that he had only wanted a bit of revenge since many felt that to possess such extraordinary vocal qualities he must lack intellect. He added that when preparing Otello he had played the same jest on Verdi.[18]

Leoncavallo also managed to attend Catalani's funeral in July. Massenet then asked him to supervise a production of *Manon* with Adelina Stehle at Milan's Teatro Carcano soon thereafter. Luigi Illica, who saw the performance, told Ricordi that Puccini's work on *La bohème* was proceeding slowly. The publisher replied that with all the effort of rescuing the piece from Leoncavallo, it was time that Puccini got to work.[19]

"NIGHTS WITHOUT SLEEP AND DAYS WITHOUT BREAD"

Leoncavallo brilliantly succeeded in attracting both the ridicule and wrath of his enemies and colleagues when he sent a formal "letter" to the Milanese newspaper *La Sera* that appeared on 16 October 1893. The letter, addressed to his friend at the newspaper, Francesco Carlo Tonolla, described his new work. The text of the libretto had taken Leoncavallo months to write, and he had already quoted some of it as early as July.[20] This naive letter was written to defend *I Medici*, rather than as a pompous self-portrait, which is how most viewed it. Unfortunately for Leoncavallo, it also succeeded in raising the public's expectation to a level that his opera would be unable to satisfy.

> I spent nights without sleep and days without bread, but my resolve was unshakable to create and achieve. Now mid-way has been reached. The work is finished, and fate wishes it that you and Belvederi[21] are here, in Milan, to write for *La Sera* and to attend the premiere of *Medici!* It is therefore natural that I turn to you, old friend, requesting your hospitality for these few lines in your newspaper, to finally explain the task clearly that I have taken upon myself.
>
> > *On va s'imaginer que c'est une préface*
> > *Moi qui n'en lis jamais! . . .*
>
> Musset said that, and, recalling the spirituous verses of the great French poet, I declare that I prefer to explain my concept here, in four words, rather than burden the reader with a booklet of numerous pages that no one usually reads. I am attempting a style hitherto unused in the theater: I wish to write an *epic poem. . . .* I have therefore decided to create *epic music. . . .* I nevertheless had to reconcile this idea without falling short of my convictions as a verista in art and literature. Since, I confess, music for me is nothing less than *the most poetic and perfect expression of the soul.* For inspiration it was necessary for me to have subjects that were men made of flesh and blood as myself . . . *always human. . . .* It was therefore in history that I would find my epics. . . . It was Macchiavelli's *Istorie fiorentine* that awoke the first concept of this work in my soul. Then I studied and read—what was possible to read—everything that had been published and written dealing with this important historical period. . . . What helped me above all were the works and essays of Villari on Macchiavelli and Savonarola. Also Gregorovius concerning Lucrezia Borgia and Alvisi on Cesare Borgia, in addition to Carducci's splendid foreword to the poetic works of

Poliziano and Lorenzo de' Medici. . . . What a great era for the artist, for the philosopher, and for the historian this grand period in our history, the renaissance! *How much blood and how much filth.* . . .

Studying the era, I decided to use the form of a trilogy, since it was the only way of theatrically rendering my concept. I subdivided the historic periods in the following manner: the first part, *I Medici*, from the accession to the pontification of Sixtus IV and the emergence of the Pazzi conspiracy; the second part, *Gerolamo Savonarola*, from the investiture of Fra Benedetto to Savonarola's death; the third part, *Cesare Borgia*, from the death of the Duke of Candia to the death of Alexander VI.

I scrupulously respected the historic characters and remained faithful to the customs . . . and, to the utmost of my ability, the language of the time. The trilogy's general title came from the last part of Wagner's tetralogy: *Götterdämmerung*.

What I have produced, regarding the music, one will see shortly. I only wish to say that, faithful to the lofty principles of Bayreuth, I wish to create a *national poem*. . . . My task is complete—for the first part—and if I am partially comforted in these moments of fearful anxiety and expectation, it is because I have done *everything I could*. And if I am not successful, regardless of my diligence, it will not have been the fault of bad will, if I may quote Musset's verses, which I have adopted as my motto: *Mon verre n'est pas grand, mais je bois dans mon verre.*[22]

Between Leoncavallo's unparalleled example of naiveté in *La Sera* and the premiere of *I Medici*, he wrote Fürstner that he had "secretly" come to terms with Tedeschi, that *Chatterton* would be presented at the end of 1894 in a commercially more feasible three-act version. Fürstner was interested in the work's German rights, and Leoncavallo suggested that he contact Tedeschi himself, now that he was preparing work on "*Vie de Bohème.*"[23] Details would be discussed in Berlin.[24] The composer was proud that his opera would finally receive a premiere after years of delay, writing Giosuè Carducci a letter similar to the one in *La Sera*, calling his attention to the new work in the disguise of an invitation:

Permit me to send you the libretto of *Medici* and allow me to call you "maestro," since I created this work in the image of your voice, when, as an unknown student seated on the benches at the University of Bologna, I dreamed of music, learning art from you. Since that time many years have passed, I studied—suffered even—but in the meantime I cultivated good seeds that may bear fruit tomorrow. You will be able to see when you read *I Medici* (the first completed part) that my concept was to try and create epic Italian music. . . . Rather than musical romanticism or . . . composers who content themselves with re-evoking old legends and dramas of contrasting emotional and theatrical scenarios that are always the same, is it not preferable to musically influence our heroes, our renaissance? Wagner took his subjects from the Rhine legends, though how more human to have a tragic musical unity [made up] of Giuliano and Lorenzo de' Medici, Gerolamo Savonarola and Duke Valentino (Cesare Borgia), the Italian princes. . . . To artistically conceive and musically execute all this is arduous work. I repeat grand. Have we succeeded? I do not know. If we have, at least in part, it is a sign that the student has known how to learn from you and, perhaps, will be someone tomorrow. May I hope that you will attend the premiere of *Medici*, which will take place the night of the 9th?[25]

I Medici finally premiered at Milan's Teatro dal Verme on 9 November 1893, sung by Francesco Tamagno (Giuliano de' Medici), Ottorino Beltrami (Lorenzo de' Medici), Adelina Stehle (Simonetta Cattanei), Giovanni Scarneo (Giambattista da Montesecco), Gini Pizzorni (Madre di Simonetta), and Ludovico Contini (Francesco Pazzi). Although the composer felt it was a "formidable success,"[26] the performance failed to create the positive impression he had striven so hard to achieve. It began when the horns already sounded flat during the very brief hunting theme that opened the work. Standing in the wings, Tamagno reassured the composer that his first aria, "No! de l'antica Grecia," was certain to be well liked.[27] The public was indeed jubilant, and Leoncavallo presented himself three times before Tamagno's encore. The act 1 Giuliano/Simonetta duet was repeated, as was Lorenzo's serenade, the choral "Ben venga maggio," and the Fioretta/Giuliano duet of act 2. Act 3 was largely successful. The septet received twelve minutes of applause, and it was one of the most moving moments in Leoncavallo's career. He himself felt that act 4 made both a solemn and profound impression.[28]

I Medici impressed both Wilhelm Jahn, director of the Vienna Court Opera, and the Berlin Opera's Pierson; each wished to offer the work following a German translation. With everyone banking on another *Pagliacci*, German reviews were, for the most part, laudatory, but the Italian critics believed Leoncavallo had presented an interesting though unoriginal work, despite the *Corriere della Sera* considering him a "conscientious artist" with "serious aspirations."[29] Leoncavallo's letter to *La Sera* was immediately ridiculed by the critics, who suggested that the composer wanted to "encompass" more than was "embraceable,"[30] agreeing that the opera assimilated Wagner and Meyerbeer rather than presenting its own individual style. Only the septet and final half of act 1 found critical favor. The singers fared markedly better. Regarding Tamagno, critics were in unanimous disbelief that such a jewel of a voice could "possibly be found in a human throat." Beltrami sang well, though he failed to succeed as an actor. The improbable conclusion of act 2—Giuliano leaving one woman for another—produced "smiles on the lips of those male spectators that have faith in their irresistible art of seduction—that is to say 99 percent."[31] While the sets were beautiful, there were minor quibbles concerning the questionable taste of their color. The French press was more complimentary, although they did share the opinion that act 1 and the septet were of greatest interest in "Léoncavallo's" manner of turning "history into music."[32]

Tosti and Massenet were the first to send Leoncavallo their affectionate greetings from London and Paris. Mascagni loathed the work. He wrote his wife Lina after attending the final rehearsal that *I Medici* was both "heavy and boring," without "the shadow of a melody, for the little there is, is not original."[33] According to Mascagni, only Tamagno—"who sings like a god"—was able to create a bit of enthusiasm. When Leoncavallo noticed that two British critics (Nevers and Thompson) shared Mascagni's opinion, he immediately wrote to an English acquaintance that *I Medici* was "twice as successful as *Pagliacci*."[34] He then stated that Mr. Nevers had demanded two thousand francs during his London stay to write a good review of *Pagliacci*.

PLAYING BILLIARDS WITH JOHANN STRAUSS II

Pagliacci received its premiere at Vienna's Court Opera ten days later on 19 November. Budapest's German newspaper *Pester Lloyd* interviewed the composer, concentrating on *I Medici*'s Wagnerian influence rather than on the upcoming production. When asked to comment on the future of Italian opera, Leoncavallo took a stab at Puccini, remarking that composers needed to be not only cultured but also in possession of a "higher literary education beyond their own art."[35] The premiere was a gala occasion, taking place on Empress Elisabeth's name day. The public thronged as if it were "attending an opera by Richard Wagner,"[36] thanks to *Pagliacci*'s success one year earlier. The German-speaking cast included Ernest van Dyck (Canio)[37] and the attractive Paula Mark as Nedda; Hans Richter conducted. The production was directed by the theater's intendant, Wilhelm Jahn, who paid careful attention to the singers' movements. He frequently demonstrated poses himself, with unintentional humor, as when instructing Mark how to perform a death dance prior to her murder—convinced that Nedda knew she would die. Leoncavallo agreed, enchanted by her "ideal" interpretation.[38] Van Dyck occasionally forced his voice, portraying a hysterical Canio, more in keeping with Leoncavallo than what pleased some Viennese critics. Hanslick returned with a nine-page essay detailing what he didn't like about the opera,[39] relieved that da capos were not allowed at the Vienna Court Opera as they had been during performances at the Exposition Theater. He judged Leoncavallo to be a "better musician" than Mascagni, though the latter was more "original."[40] While he detected Wagner's influence, Hanslick felt that Mascagni and Leoncavallo had sprung from Verdi's school in contrast to the "soft and melodic monotony of Bellini and Donizetti."[41] What irritated him most was the opera's passion, a detrimental factor in his eyes, frequently personified in Italian singers. Concluding that German singers were more intelligent, his critique of the evening's Tonio contained his biased credo: "Too much voice and too much emotion!"[42]

The composer left the performance by way of the Court Opera's grand staircase, showered with flowers, while others proceeded to kiss his hand in the "German manner."[43] A formal dinner reception was then held by the "Oberster Hoftheater-Direktor," Prince Constantin zu Hohenlohe-Schillingsfürst at the Augarten Palace, where the guests were able to admire an electrically illuminated ice-skating rink. Leoncavallo also enjoyed a game of billiards with Johann Strauss II. The next morning the composer was present at a reception with Archduke Wilhelm, presenting extracts from *I Medici*, hoping that his lofty host might arrange a production in Austria. Although Wilhelm seemed pleased at the time, Leoncavallo only gained a cigarette case with the archduke's insignia.[44]

His return to Italy, traveling on a train bound for collision, marked another instance of his remarkable precognition:

> A few hours prior [to the crash], I was in the train coming from Vienna. Before arriving in Mestre, I was suddenly engulfed in panic; a strange nervousness took hold of me, making me wonder why I did not remain [for a stopover] in Venice. As if by a sudden impulse, when the train approached the Mestre station, without having had a chance to reason or decide, I threw my luggage onto the sidewalk and got out.[45]

He awoke the following morning at Hotel Bauer, to the headlines of newspapers describing the disaster. Alive and well, he was present at the Roman premiere of *I Medici* on 27 December at the Teatro Costanzi, sung by the Court Opera's cast and attended by Queen Margherita, who welcomed the composer during the interval. He also met with the statesman Francesco Crispi, who offered to introduce Leoncavallo to influential individuals in Naples, where *I Medici* was performed—without the composer—at the Teatro San Carlo.

PAGLIACCI CONQUERS THE WORLD AND THE METROPOLITAN OPERA

Leoncavallo's sparse correspondence for 1893 fails to mention whether he intended to attend the Metropolitan Opera premiere of *Pagliacci* on 11 December. Perhaps he felt his presence to be more essential in Berlin for the German unveiling of *I Medici*, long awaited by his publisher Fürstner.[46] At that time, the Metropolitan Opera's production of *Pagliacci* was paired with Gluck's *Orfeo ed Euridice*. It was only on 22 December that it was finally presented with its "twin," *Cavalleria rusticana*.[47] Nellie Melba, who had recently made her house debut, played Nedda, Mario Ancona, Tonio, and Fernando De Lucia, Canio.[48] American audiences found both *Cavalleria rusticana* and *Pagliacci* to be "lurid melodramas" that combined "adultery with murder." Leoncavallo's offering nevertheless went on to become a staple of the Metropolitan Opera's repertory, with some 121 performances during 1900–1921. It only missed one season.[49]

The opera was also successful in St. Petersburg during January 1894, sung by Marcella Sembrich (Nedda) and Mattia Battistini (Tonio). However, the subject once again turned to *Bohème* when the Canio, Alfonso Garulli, wrote the composer that he had enjoyed reading Murger's *Scènes de la vie de bohème* and understood why Leoncavallo had in fact chosen it. Although the composer had offered that he create the role of Marcello, he was more interested in Rodolfo, in case it would be written for tenor after all. He knew that Leoncavallo had always intended Rodolfo to be a baritone prior to hearing Puccini's version.

A COMMISSION FROM THE KAISER

Leoncavallo arrived in Berlin that January for *I Medici*'s German premiere, while *Pagliacci* was scheduled for Munich later that year.[50] Returning to the Central Hotel, he attended rehearsals that were soon postponed for weeks when the Giuliano (Sylva) became ill. The theater suggested Tamagno as a replacement, in order to accommodate Leoncavallo's tight schedule, but the idea was vetoed since the composer insisted on a German-language performance. During this hiatus, social engagements filled his agenda, including a dinner with the conductor Karl Muck at his Wilhelmstrasse home. Additional invitations followed from Prince George of Prussia[51] and for a reception given by the empress on 30 January.

Sylva eventually recovered, and the delayed premiere took place on 17 February. Wilhelm, wearing a Hussar uniform (Umberto I honorary regiment), impressed Leoncavallo as he entered his box, prompting the composer to remark that the kaiser "could be kind when he wanted to demonstrate his interest in someone."[52] The performance was a public if not critical success. The Court Opera's artistic director, Count Bolko von Hochberg,[53] told Leoncavallo following act 2 that the kaiser was impressed with the work and, more importantly, with the composer's ability to "glorify his country's history."[54] Hochberg then invited Leoncavallo to visit the royal box and expressed interest in having a similar work dedicated to Prussia and the Hohenzollern. Following the performance, Kaiser Wilhelm offered a commission, requesting that Leon-cavallo remain in Berlin a few days longer, until Count Hochberg could find a suitable subject that he would then have delivered to Sanssouci. Wilhelm felt attracted to *I Medici*'s bombastic style and grand format, which illuminated the Italian renaissance and one family in particular. With a simple synopsis and un-demanding melodies, he felt that Leoncavallo, one of the world's most popular composers, would be the perfect choice to create a national German opera. Leoncavallo readily accepted the commission without, however, realizing the enormous difficulties and suffering he would be forced to endure from both his German and Italian colleagues.[55] Count Hochberg sent an official proposal, in French, dated 24 February 1894:

> Following the great success of *Pagliacci* and *Medici* at Berlin's Court Opera, I would like to commission you to compose a work especially for this theater to be premiered here. I will explain any additional details in person, but I will now confide that I have the idea of deriving the subject from Willibald Alexis's novel *Der Roland von Berlin*.[56]

This letter proved the Kaiser's interest in him and was an extremely positive factor in defining the composer's future worth to both his Italian and Ger-man publishers,[57] although Leoncavallo stressed that he never received "un centesimo" from Wilhelm for writing *Der Roland von Berlin*. Peters paid Leon-cavallo ten thousand francs for *Chatterton*'s German rights, and the composer left Berlin boarding a train bound for Vienna on 3 March 1894, stopping in Mannheim.

INSPIRED BY BALZAC AND BATTLING MENDÈS

During the spring of 1894 Leoncavallo completed the symphonic poem *Séraphitus-Séraphita*, taken from Balzac's lengthy philosophical novel *Séraphita* (1835), which would only be given one performance that year at La Scala. Sonzogno thought it a "nice idea" combining music with literature of a philo-sophical nature.[58] Seeking rest at the Villa d'Este on Lake Como, Leoncavallo turned to his love of French literature for this orchestral work in three parts that marks a musical continuation from *I Medici* toward German opera and symphonic music.

He was soon in Milan in order to concentrate on *Chatterton*'s world premiere, hoping to convince Fürstner that St. Petersburg would be an ideal choice, since Mattia Battistini and Fernando De Lucia had engagements in Russia during January 1895. He felt no one to be more likely to bring his romantic poet to life than De Lucia, while Hariclea Darclée could sing

Jenny—all "first class artists."[59] Fürstner disagreed with the proposal of St. Petersburg. However, Leoncavallo's reason for choosing far-off Russia may have had other motives. With Tedeschi and Sonzogno in Milan, he preferred a country distanced from both publishing houses should the premiere be a failure. Originally embarrassed when *Chatterton* resurfaced, Leoncavallo had no choice other than to proceed with a world premiere. After a reworking of the score, intent on generating enthusiasm at all costs, the composer now charmed Fürstner, even speaking poorly of Sonzogno, whose interest in such short-lived works as Mascagni's *Silvano* irritated him. With his Berlin success earlier that year now behind him, Leoncavallo felt Germany could be used advantageously. Leoncavallo wrote letters on Tedeschi's stationary, and it seems that all the antagonism toward a publisher he had originally wanted to take to court was finally resolved. He was delighted to profit from three publishers all vying for his services, even if it meant playing one against the other for *Chatterton's* "commercial success."[60] He continued to edit the opera in the "common interest" of both himself and Fürstner.[61]

Unable to convince Fürstner, Leoncavallo now shrewdly suggested Rome rather than Milan for a *Chatterton* premiere, followed by five additional Italian theaters. Fürstner hoped *La bohème* would be completed by the end of the year, before Puccini's version, while the situation was precisely the same on the opposite front, with Giulio Ricordi asking Puccini whether "Il gran Kaiser Leon-Cavallo" was working on the Murger opus.[62]

Bayreuth was next on Leoncavallo's agenda. On the way, he managed to spend some time in the Bohemian spa Marienbad, where *Pagliacci* received two performances. He also had himself photographed in a light striped suit holding a cane and straw hat. With his "imposing" figure and waxed mustache, he seemed the epitome of a turn-of-the-century *bon vivant*. During this period, it is possible that he also stopped in Prague, where *I Medici* was to be staged during January 1895. It was in Marienbad that he wrote Ernest Van Dyck, hoping that the tenor would perform Giuliano in *I Medici*. In addition, he offered to undertake any alterations that the artist deemed necessary if the opera was performed in Vienna. He then wrote Fürstner, stating that he would not be able to visit him in Berlin following his Bayreuth visit,[63] "greatly regretting" that *I Medici* was not in the German publisher's hands.[64] According to Leoncavallo, Sonzogno had paid him 60,000 francs together with 30 percent of the work's rights for the future *La bohème*. He had also signed a contract for another opera with the same conditions. Leoncavallo attributed this to Sonzogno's shrewdness in minimizing his possibly greater costs for the second opera. Armed with his studio portraits as well as an advance on *Chatterton*, Leoncavallo began his journey to Bayreuth.

He was also on a hopeless mission in Bayreuth in order to obtain an unlikely exception to the copyright of *Parsifal* from Cosima Wagner. Sonzogno had bombarded the composer with a multitude of letters regarding the subject as he traveled between Milan and San Pellegrino, where he had gone to take the waters.[65] Cosima belatedly invited Leoncavallo to Villa Wahnfried. He was unable to accept, having received her note only one hour prior to his planned return to Italy on 28 July.[66] However, he assured her that he would be present for the remainder of the season as a "faithful" devotee.[67] He then spent some time in Munich at the Hotel Vier Jahreszeiten, where he told the conductor Hermann Levi that he had not heard comparable conducting since visiting Bayreuth in 1876. "Such perfection . . . such youth and warmth . . . the honor goes to you, maître, in proving that the ancient ramparts of Wagnerism are the most solid and that God keeps you young in heart and soul in order to transmit his master's voice.[68]

Following a period of rest in Lugano during September, Leoncavallo began renovating the Via Vivaio house in Milan for nine thousand lire.[69] Although his income had certainly improved, he still supported five people,[70] and the expense of traveling to supervise productions took its toll. The trip to Germany alone had cost him 3,000 lire and, as he stated to Albicini, was undertaken "not for fun" but in order to maintain his business contacts.[71]

A new legal conflict arose when Catulle Mendès sent a letter to numerous newspapers during late September declaring that he "opposed performances of Leoncavallo's *Pagliacci* on French stages,"[72] since its unacknowledged inspiration derived from his *La femme de Tabarin*. With performances of *Pagliacci* planned in both Paris and Brussels, Mendès felt it would be "mere stupidity" not to speak out, although he "disliked conflict," complaining that he had tried to form an agreement with both Leoncavallo and Sonzogno to no avail.[73] Mendès also insisted that his name be printed on the opera's score and on the placards announcing the performances. He then threatened to present the case to France's Society of Authors. While most French newspapers sided with Mendès, Leoncavallo officially answered the author in a series of public letters that, to Fürstner's amazement, would reverberate as far as London and Berlin. In November, Leoncavallo requested that *Le Figaro* publish his letter defending himself against Mendès's accusations, certain that the Society of Authors would fail to find him at fault, while Mendès told *Le Soir* that he would take Leoncavallo to court regardless of what the society said. With little support from the Society of Authors, Mendès's claims suddenly came to a halt, and the public antagonism ceased.[74] Leoncavallo proved to be unintentionally humorous when writing Fürstner regarding the matter that, "unlike Mascagni," he was "not very eager to have publicity."[75] When the case was dropped for unspecified reasons, Leoncavallo began sending Fürstner parts of *Chatterton*'s revision, certain that he would be content, while Aleardo Villa was put to work designing the sets and costumes.

The French battle won, a new front now opened in Germany, where numerous newspapers began voicing their opposition to a foreigner's receiving Wilhelm II's commission, rather than one of their own composers. When the tumult continued to increase, the composer requested that Fürstner "make the little bit of black on the horizon disappear" prior to his arrival in Berlin to present *Chatterton*.[76] (The fierce opposition in the German press would continue for more than a decade until *Der Roland von Berlin*'s world premiere in 1904, resulting in a poor critical reception.) Leoncavallo believed frustrated German composers negatively influencing the press had initiated the campaign raging against him. In order for the "little war to stop," Leoncavallo wrote Fürstner that he would be willing to make "a sacrifice" if it were "a question of money" to make the "hostilities cease,"[77] considering "journalists the easiest merchandise to purchase."[78] He felt Wilhelm II had chosen him because he was the only Italian composer who really "understood" Wagner. He also emphasized that he would never have agreed to compose the work had it not been for the kaiser's personal commission. Not wishing to "take the place of any other German composer," Leoncavallo put Fürstner in charge of rounding up and subduing his enemies.[79] Most of Berlin's *I Medici* reviews had been biased, but, in spite of them, the opera was performed twenty-five times. This is an important factor to remember when judging the opera's critical reception. Leoncavallo was correct in surmising that the opera itself would eventually succeed in changing critical opinion. The year ended with an invitation from Italy's Society of Authors for a reception with Emile Zola. Additional guests were Boito, Giuseppe Giacosa, and Puccini. One wonders whether Leoncavallo asked Puccini how his work on *La bohème* was progressing. With Leoncavallo's boisterous personality there can be little doubt that he did just that![80]

NOTES

1. Berthe Leoncavallo to Mrs. Fürstner, 23 April 1893 (Y).
2. She signed the letter "Berthe Leoncavallo," although she did not have a legal wedding until 1895 as "Marie Rose Jean."
3. Tosti also served as music instructor to numerous members of the Royal Family.
4. Pietro Mascagni to Lina Mascagni in Mario Morini, Roberto Iovino, Alberto Paloscia, *Pietro Mascagni: Epistolario* (Lucca: Libreria Musicale Italiana, 1996), 157.
5. *Appunti*, 71.
6. Leoncavallo wrote all of his letters to Fürstner in French.
7. Leoncavallo to Adolph Fürstner, 19 May 1893 (Y).
8. Ibid.
9. Pietro Mascagni to Lina Mascagni in Morini, *Pietro Mascagni: Epistolario*, 157.
10. Ibid., 14 June 1893. Leoncavallo, however, wrote the song "Déclaration" for De Lucia during this time. Other songs originating from the London sojourn are "To-night" and "To-morrow" to the verses of Frederic E. Weatherly.
11. Leoncavallo to Tosti, 6 June 1893 in Franco Di Tizio, *Francesco Paolo Tosti* (Francavilla al Mare, privately published, 1984), 171.

12. Vincent Seligman, *Puccini among Friends* (London: Macmillan, 1938), 32.

13. *Appunti*, 71.

14. Ibid., 72.

15. Leoncavallo to Emilio Usiglio, undated (BPP), and Leoncavallo to unidentified recipient, undated (CMU).

16. Leoncavallo to Count Pierfrancesco Albicini, undated (CMU).

17. *Appunti*, 73.

18. According to Leoncavallo, Boito and Ricordi encouraged Verdi to hire Tamagno to create *Otello*, after the composer had originally been uncertain.

19. Giulio Ricordi to Luigi Illica, 2 November 1893 in Eugenio Gara, *Carteggi Pucciniani* (Milan: Casa Ricordi, 1958), 189.

20. Leoncavallo to unidentified recipient, 20 July 1893 (MTS).

21. Gualtiero Belvederi, a friend of many years since Leoncavallo's Bologna days, was also employed at *La Sera*.

22. Excerpts from Leoncavallo's letter (to Tonolla) in *La Sera*, 14 October 1893.

23. Leoncavallo to Adolph Fürstner, 30 October 1893 (Y).

24. Max Brockhaus was another German publisher interested in his works, who later published some of his songs.

25. Leoncavallo to Carducci, 6 November 1893 (BCB).

26. *Appunti*, 76.

27. Ibid.

28. Sonzogno had invited numerous impresarios, including Sir Augustus Harris. The press wrote that reporters spent twenty thousand lire on telegrams.

29. *Corriere della Sera*, 10/11 November 1893.

30. The press felt the opera should have been called "The Pazzi Conspiracy."

31. *Corriere della Sera*, 10/11 November 1893.

32. *Le Monde Artiste*, 10 November 1893.

33. Pietro Mascagni to Lina Mascagni, 9 November 1893 in Morini, *Pietro Mascagni: Epistolario*, 162.

34. Leoncavallo to Joseph Bennett, 14 November 1893 (PML).

35. Leoncavallo interviewed in *Pester Lloyd*, Budapest, 9 November 1893. Leoncavallo also described his meeting with Wagner in this interview. Had he not met the composer it is doubtful that he would have recalled this episode, since it would be read by Hans Richter, *Pagliacci*'s conductor and Wagner's colleague, who may have been in contact with the composer's widow, Cosima.

36. Marcel Prawy, *Die Wiener Oper* (Vienna: Verlag Fritz Molden, 1969), part 1, 128.

37. Creator of Massenet's *Werther*.

38. *Appunti*, 76.

39. Hanslick preferred Mascagni's *I Rantzau* and *L'amico Fritz* to *Pagliacci*.

40. Eduard Hanslick, *Fünf Jahre Musik (1891–1895)* (Berlin, 1896), 99.

41. Ibid., 100.

42. Ibid., 104.

43. *Appunti*, 77.

44. Archduke Wilhelm was the grandson of Emperor Leopold II and great-grandson of Empress Maria Theresa. He died six months later after falling from his

horse. Although Empress Elisabeth was in Vienna during part of November, it is doubtful that she was present at any of Leoncavallo's appearances.

45. *Appunti*, 32.

46. *Pagliacci*'s U.S. premiere ("The Clowns") had taken place in New York's Grand Opera House on 15 June 1893.

47. Both works are unique in opera, sharing performances for a century, although they originated from different composers. Mascagni would have no doubt preferred to see *Cavalleria rusticana* coupled with *Silvano* or *Zanetto*, while Leoncavallo later penned *Zingari* to serve as a twin.

48. *Pagliacci* was presented on 22 December, conducted by Luigi Mancinelli, *prior* to *Cavalleria rusticana*, which was conducted by Enrico Bevignani.

49. John Dizikes, *Opera in America, A Cultural History* (New Haven: Yale University Press, 1993), 313.

50. It is doubtful that Berthe accompanied him, as none of the invitations mentions her name. She was present in Berlin years later when *Der Roland von Berlin* was unveiled in 1904.

51. His play *Catherine de' Medici* appeared during the same year as *I Medici*.

52. *Appunti*, 79.

53. Count Hochberg abandoned a state career in order to compose under the name of "Franz." His opera *Der Werwolf* (1876) premiered in Hannover, followed by three string quartets and two symphonies, in addition to numerous lieder. Since *Der Werwolf* (the title is symbolic, referring to the atmosphere of religious uncertainty during the sixteenth century) was taken from Willibald Alexis's novel (1848), he no doubt wished to employ the same author's *Der Roland von Berlin* as a literary source.

54. *Appunti*, 79.

55. Leoncavallo accepted the commission without having read the Alexis novel. An Italian translation by Gustavo Macchi was completed in nineteen months.

56. Count Bolko von Hochberg to Leoncavallo, 24 February 1894 (BCL).

57. With Peters interested in the future *La bohème*, Leoncavallo made no excuses that he was already negotiating with "two publishers," although his personal intervention later secured their requesting the German rights. Leoncavallo to Dürer at Peters, 23 January 1894, and Leoncavallo to Peters, 27 April 1894. Months later, Leoncavallo asked Peters if they wanted *Der Roland von Berlin* or—in three years' time—the Goldoni-inspired *Don Marzio* in the same "opéra-comique genre" as *La bohème*. When Peters refused Leoncavallo's offer, he retorted in a curt telegram that he had already signed a contract with Sonzogno for both *La bohème* and *Der Roland von Berlin*, occupying him "until 1898." Leoncavallo to Peters, 9 May 1894 and 10 May 1894 (SLSUD).

58. Edoardo Sonzogno to Leoncavallo, 25 April 1894 (BCL).

59. Leoncavallo to Fürstner, 14 June 1894 (Y).

60. Ibid.

61. Leoncavallo to Fürstner, 18 July 1894 (Y).

62. Giulio Ricordi to Giacomo Puccini, 29 September 1894 in Gara, *Carteggi Pucciniani*, 112.

63. *I Medici* also premiered in Frankfurt during this time.

64. Leoncavallo to Fürstner, 18 July 1894 (Y).

65. Since La Scala only staged Italian operas owned by Ricordi, Sonzogno soon acquired Milan's former Teatro della Canobbiana, opening it as the Teatro Lirico Internazionale that September. When the publisher later became impresario of La Scala for two years, Leoncavallo was able to have his works produced at Italy's foremost theater.

66. Berthe, who had remained in Italy, requested that he return immediately.

67. Leoncavallo to Cosima Wagner, 28 July 1894 (Y).

68. Leoncavallo to Hermann Levi, 13 August 1894 (BSM).

69. Leoncavallo remained at Via Vivaio rather than seeking a new home, implying that the money received from *Pagliacci*'s success was not yet that overwhelming.

70. Berthe, her mother (Thérèse Paut), Jeanne Puel, and Gastone and Leone Leoncavallo, who were still not financially independent.

71. Leoncavallo to Count Pierfrancesco Albicini, 17 September 1894 (CMU).

72. *Le Guide Musical*, 24 September 1894 (BNP).

73. Ibid.

74. The society probably realized that both *Pagliacci* and *Femme de Tabarin* owed a debt to Baus's *Un drama nuevo*. It is uncertain whether Leoncavallo offered Mendès money to drop the case.

75. Leoncavallo to Fürstner, 26 November 1894 (Y).

76. Leoncavallo to Fürstner, 17 November 1894 (Y).

77. Ibid.

78. Leoncavallo to Fürstner, 26 November 1894 (Y).

79. Leoncavallo to Fürstner, 17 November 1894 (Y).

80. Leoncavallo also signed a private contract with Sigismund Arkel, commissioning him to write a scenario taken from Goethe's *Reinecke Fuchs*. A ballet in three acts had been planned for the 1897 carnival season. Leoncavallo agreed to pay Arkel five thousand lire by October 1895.

• 5 •

Marriage and the Re-creation of *Chatterton*

1895–1897

$\mathcal{L}$eoncavallo was in Prague for the Czechoslovakian premiere of *I Medici* on 5 January 1895 at the Royal Theater. In addition, *Pagliacci* was performed at the city's Royal German Theater. Some two weeks later, on 20 January, Leoncavallo and Berthe registered at Milan's City Hall as having united in matrimony. The composer was described as a "maestro di musica" from Naples, aged thirty-seven,[1] and "Maria Rosa Jean," a "thirty-two-year-old proprietress" from Carpentras, France.[2] Curiously, the composer had usually acknowledged Berthe as his wife in his own correspondence, while the *Appunti* claims that he married in Paris during 1888. Like his date of birth, the marriage papers do not coincide with his own version. The Milan wedding is not mentioned anywhere, and there is a complete absence of congratulatory letters and telegrams.

Leoncavallo, five days following his "Milanese marriage," arrived in Brussels for *Pagliacci*'s Belgian premiere at the Théâtre Royal de la Monnaie. The opera received twenty-three enthusiastic curtain calls. He also briefly stopped in Paris in order to sort out his *Pagliacci* copyright problem with Catulle Mendès. There is no mention of the case thereafter—either publicly or privately. Unable to meet with Massenet, who was ill, Leoncavallo returned to Italy to be greeted by a letter from the French composer incorporating a "bravo de tout coeur" for his Belgian success.[3]

Leoncavallo was, once again, in contact with all of his publishers (past and present) during 1895, including Ricordi, Tedeschi, Peters, Bote und Bock, Fürstner, and Sonzogno. Believing that he could outwit most of them, he proceeded to play one against the other, and his correspondence—especially to Fürstner—amply demonstrates his opportunism. The letters abound with gossip, quarrels, and petty intrigue certain to provide additional sources for his lawyer, Ferruccio Foà. Leoncavallo also complained about his long-running court case with Casa Ricordi, having submitted a fifteen-page handwritten libretto on 9 January entitled *Tenebrae* in lieu of *I Medici* (and avoiding a penalty of twenty thousand lire). According to Ricordi, Ciampoli's novel, *Trecce nere*, on which an opera should have been based, remained "lost."[4] The libretto is in a prologue and two acts, taken from Francesco Bernardini's four-act drama *Il Cieco*.[5] It deals with the aristocratic Maria, daughter of Baron Gustavo de Latour and his wife, Luisa, who falls in love with Giulio di Savernay, following her marriage of many years to the blinded Vittorio de Noirbert.[6] The action is set in Paris, with the prologue taking place in 1795 and the concluding two acts some ten years later. The "libretto" that emerged was a rough sketch with dwindling dialogue as the action unfolded. It was a weak attempt to honor Ricordi's deadline, and the publisher demanded that Leoncavallo pay the twenty thousand lire regardless, since his work was, understandably, not acceptable.[7]

Leoncavallo now decided to devote most of his energy to *Chatterton*, working not only "well" but also "feverishly." He hoped the opera would resemble *Pagliacci*'s "colossal success."[8] He also tried to set up a music store for his brother Leone in Alexandria, Egypt, where he still had relatives. When this idea failed, Leoncavallo secured work for him with the French publisher Quinzard in Paris, where Leone took up residence for decades. The composer always claimed that Leone never did anything really well except to speak Italian, English, and French fluently.

Although Leoncavallo liked to imagine that he shunned publicity, he now had the "splendid idea" of dedicating *Chatterton* to Italy's Queen Margherita. Writing to the sovereign in March, he invited her to attend the premiere, scheduled as part of the Exposition for additional promotion. On 9 April, Leoncavallo was granted an audience, although he failed to mention the meeting to Fürstner, even though he wrote the publisher the same day, implying that his visit had not been successful, which would explain why *Chatterton* was later dedicated to a certain Giulia Luzzatto. The score had been completely revised, and Leoncavallo proudly wrote Fürstner that "not a scene, not a verse of the old *Chatterton* remained nor a note of music. . . . I have created a new work."[9] Like most of his colleagues, the composer believed each new work superior to the last and enthusiastically hoped to complete the orchestral score by June.

Fürstner was at a loss to understand why Sonzogno had offered the German and Austro-Hungarian rights to *Vie de bohème* to Peters instead of to him. Peters had promised to pay forty thousand lire if Leoncavallo completed the work by the end of the year, which was impossible, since he had not even finished *Chatterton*. Knowing that he would be "unable to complete *La vie de bohème*" in time and that Fürstner was interested in acquiring the rights, Leoncavallo suggested that the latter write Sonzogno a letter expressing his interest and agreeing to pay the same amount, but with a due date of July 1896.[10] Leoncavallo preferred that Fürstner be his "exclusive publisher" for the German rights to all his works including the future *Der Roland von Berlin*.[11] Poor Fürstner must have been even more bewildered when Leoncavallo then told the publisher that neither *Vie de bohème* nor *Der Roland von Berlin* were available and that he had only wanted to know how much Fürstner would have paid if they had been free, hoping that he could then force him to pay more than forty thousand lire. Fürstner was leery about *Der Roland von Berlin*. Believing that it would be of only local interest, he postponed a definite decision until after *Chatterton*'s premiere. Enraged, Leoncavallo quipped that he would have more than enough publishers interested in printing his operas by then and that he no longer wished to offer Fürstner his works for all the "treasures of Peru," certain that the publisher would "regret" his decision in the future.[12] Leoncavallo informed Fürstner one month later that Sonzogno had become "very angry" with the publicity resulting from Leoncavallo's royal audience—even threatening to boycott performances of the work since it detracted from the composer's operas written for his own firm. Foà reminded Leoncavallo that *Chatterton*'s contract was signed before a collaboration with Casa Sonzogno, thereby allowing him to do as he pleased. Leoncavallo felt tempted to break his contract with Sonzogno, who supposedly offered 150,000 lire to purchase *Chatterton*, *La bohème*, and *Der Roland von Berlin*. Leoncavallo made Fürstner feel worse—if that was possible—when he declared that the composer Alberto Franchetti had been willing to pay twenty thousand lire for one of his libretti. Within a month Leoncavallo defended Sonzogno to Fürstner as "the first who had faith in *Pagliacci*," as well as the only publisher who engaged superior artists while also inviting the entire European press—something that no one else did.[13] A few weeks later, Leoncavallo wrote Fürstner again advising him that Sonzogno was leaving for Paris to arrange performances of *Pagliacci* at the Opéra-Comique and would then proceed to Berlin in order to discuss *La bohème* with him. Realizing that Fürstner would not pay more, an agreement eventually reached that he would receive the German rights to *Vie de bohème* and *Der Roland von Berlin*.[14] Meanwhile, Leoncavallo could hardly restrain his enthusiasm that Mascagni's *Guglielmo Ratcliff* and *Silvano* had failed in Naples and that his rival was "finished," having even been "hissed at in the street."[15] The "Causa Ricordi-Leoncavallo" continued during April at the Milanese Tribunal, with a panel consisting of Enrico Panzacchi, Count Leopoldo Pullè, and Giovanni Pozza. They judged that *Tenebrae* could have been a good libretto if Leoncavallo had done a better job. However, having presented it on time, Leoncavallo received an extension to improve it.

   Although Queen Margherita had declined the *Chatterton* dedication, she was present at the Teatro Nazionale for the first Roman production of *Pagliacci* in May. Enthused by the work, she expressed interest in coming to a second performance. Leoncavallo—who was absent—prepared to leave for the countryside after requesting that Fürstner send him an advance sum of ten thousand lire toward the twenty-five thousand he would be paid for *Chatterton*, together with the twenty-five thousand Fürstner owed Tedeschi.

Before Leoncavallo left for a rest at Lake Maggiore's Cannero, he received a letter from Enrico Butti and Gustavo Macchi describing their intention of writing a synopsis of *Der Roland von Berlin* from the Alexis novel. They promised to finish in two months time so that Leoncavallo could send it to Wilhelm II for his approval. An announcement also appeared in Milan's *Corriere della Sera* erroneously stating that Leoncavallo was at work on *Der Roland von Berlin* and that *Vie de bohème* would soon reach completion! Sonzogno had probably released the news to make Puccini and Ricordi believe that Leoncavallo's version would appear at the same time as theirs. Not having seen any progress on the opera, Sonzogno warned Leoncavallo that whoever produced the opera first would have the greater advantage. Leoncavallo had misinformed Sonzogno that he had begun work on the Murger opera and that *Chatterton* was already complete. When Sonzogno traveled to Berlin during September, Leoncavallo even warned Fürstner that he should not mention the truth since "he (Sonzogno) believes that I am working on *La vie de bohème*."[16] Sonzogno also told Leoncavallo that Jahn was searching for an excuse to cancel *I Medici* in Vienna,[17] proposing a more "modern" work like *Vie de bohème* rather than Tedeschi's *Chatterton*.[18] Oblivious to Sonzogno's advice, Leoncavallo wrote Jahn that *Chatterton* would be perfect, while sending the opera's third act to Fürstner, including alterations for the Jenny/Giorgio duet of act 2 that he felt resembled Massenet's *Werther*.

Leoncavallo's publishing intrigues continued, with plans to let Sonzogno hear the completed *Chatterton*, after he realized that Tedeschi did not have sufficient money at his disposal. The composer even suggested that Fürstner support Tedeschi in order to compete against Sonzogno and Ricordi, since he was "a young and unknown publisher."[19] Although Tedeschi was facing hard times, Sonzogno, trying to juggle Casa Sonzogno and the 200,000 lire he owed for the Teatro Lirico, was nearly ruined. Producing operas essentially unpopular with the public such as Mascagni's *I Rantzau*, *Silvano*, and Giordano's *Mala vita* augmented the deficit. His newspaper *Il Secolo* became a corporation, and, at the same time, he lost a court case against Casa Ricordi costing 180,000 lire. He owed Giovanni Verga another 143,000 lire for *Cavalleria rusticana*. In addition, a great deal of his properties and a paper factory were mortgaged. According to Leoncavallo, Sonzogno had lost almost five million lire thanks to the Teatro Lirico alone. Leoncavallo now felt that the time was ripe for Tedeschi to become Sonzogno's partner, and Tedeschi thus offered Sonzogno 200,000 lire and another 100,000 within one month, if made an associate of the firm and owner of the Teatro Lirico. Leoncavallo thought that the 300,000 combined with *Chatterton*'s rights would help stifle Sonzogno's plans to offer his firm to

Casa Ricordi for one million lire. Although Sonzogno agreed to sell *Pagliacci's* rights back to Leoncavallo, he refused. Sonzogno supposedly liked *Chatterton*, when Leoncavallo introduced it to him following a dinner in Tedeschi's presence, although he did not "have need for an associate at the moment . . . because Tedeschi presented too many stipulations."[20]

When Fürstner expressed misgivings concerning *Chatterton's* libretto, Leoncavallo warned him that when it came to artistic judgments he was "a bit more competent" than either Fürstner or Signor Sonzogno"[21] and that Giulio Ricordi had originally thought *Pagliacci's* text to be "bad."[22] Leoncavallo was certain that Fürstner would "regret" any misgivings following the premiere. The publisher also inquired why *Chatterton* failed to include an overture,[23] to which the composer explained, "the opera must begin immediately."[24] It was not until 4 November 1895 that Leoncavallo finally signed a contract in Paris with Louis Ratisbonne, representing Alfred de Vigny's heirs, granting the composer authorization for *Chatterton*.[25]

CHATTERTON'S BELATED BIRTH

While Sonzogno hoped Leoncavallo would soon "complete" *La bohème*, the composer was delighted to hear that the premiere of Puccini's *La bohème* in Turin on 1 February 1896 had been a "terrible fiasco."[26] Residing at Rome's Hotel National on Piazza Montecitorio together with Berthe, Leoncavallo hoped to have *Tommaso Chatterton* premiere between the 7th and 9th of March 1896 at the Teatro Nazionale.[27] However, it would not open until the 10th, due to the tenor's indisposition, a repeat of the situation with Sylva in Berlin. The rehearsals had proceeded well with the orchestra applauding Leoncavallo following act 1, while the singers were "excellent" and "madly in love with their roles."[28]

The press promoted the opera by repeating the history of its inspiration, stating that it had only been edited slightly, rather than being a new version altogether. Leoncavallo supported such rumors—emerging as the young romantic, recalling Vigny. In an interview with the *Gazzetta di Torino*, Leoncavallo stated that *Chatterton* had been inspired by his bohemian Parisian days and that Marchese Pizzardi had lent him three thousand lire to have the opera produced. He also suggested that he would no longer have chosen *Chatterton* as the subject of an opera. It was impossible for the original version of *Chatterton* to have been inspired by his bohemian Parisian days, since they did not take place until after its composition!

On the evening of the premiere, Leoncavallo presented himself for two curtain calls following *Chatterton's* act 1, "Ricomposi l'antica favella." The act's conclusion beginning with "Ne' pieghi del sudario" was repeated, with Leoncavallo returning three more times.[29] After the *Intermezzo Sinfonico* of act 2 failed to impress, it was not until Chatterton's main aria "Tu sola a me rimani, o Poesia," that renewed interest arose. The Jenny/Giorgio duet passed "in silence,"[30] as did the prelude to act 3, due to a poor orchestral interpretation that critics hoped would improve during the next "two or three performances."[31] Fortunately, most of the music written for Chatterton himself was greeted warmly. The evening concluded amid much applause signifying approval, though some noted that Lucignani's vocal quality was not matchless, only indefatigable in the demanding role of Chatterton. The opera was only a mild success. Ironically, critics felt Leoncavallo's orchestration fell far below his more mature (!) works, such as *I Medici* and *Pagliacci*, resembling a "colt indulging in its own whims during a race, whose only impulse is the ardor of its passion and its youthful temperament."[32] The opera, written by a composer with much to express—though with an eye to greater potential—was too "exuberant." This prognosis seems typical of Leoncavallo's talent, which was frequently ill focused, thereby hindering complete success. The composer appeared some twenty times during the second performance, which was more successful. Leoncavallo, relieved the premiere had not been the scandal he had originally feared, thanks in part to *Chatterton's* complete revision, received numerous congratulatory telegrams, including one from Massenet.

Leoncavallo soon publicly announced that he had been working on his *Vie de bohème* in three acts during the past summer at Lake Maggiore and that it was scheduled for November 1896 at the Teatro Lirico. Not only was the date more than half a year off, but the work would also be in four acts. He declared further that his libretto—in contrast to Puccini's version—would remain faithful to Murger's novel, stressing that there would not even be minimal similarities.[33] Sonzogno was also impressed, according to one of the composer's letters:

> I will be in Switzerland in a few days to work on . . . my *Vie de Bohème*. . . . I have all my hopes set on this opera, which is proceeding so well! Has Sonzogno written you anything? You know that he is not easily enthusiastic, although when I read my adaptation he cried, declaring it the most beautiful libretto created up until now and that even without music, it would be a success.[34]

Leoncavallo still hoped for a premiere of *Der Roland von Berlin* in 1897, even though the novel's Italian translation was not complete. Still planning to finish *Crepusculum*, he implied that the libretti to *Savonarola* and *Cesare Borgia* had already been written.[35] He then boasted of the advantages of being able to create his own texts. He also felt that it was easier for younger composers to have a career than it had once been. His main concern now, he told the press, was to create a Society of Authors in Italy like the one in France. When asked whether verismo was still relevant, his response was tongue in cheek: "Realism yes, but only-to a certain degree. One shouldn't forget that the houses depicted on stage are made of cardboard!"[36]

When the excitement of *Chatterton* died down,[37] Leoncavallo returned to Milan and his worries with Tedeschi. Tedeschi finally published the piano and vocal score—in the composer's own reduction—while Fürstner held the copyright for Germany and Austria. Tedeschi's "complete ineptitude" and "lack of frankness" regarding a collaboration with Sonzogno began aggravating Leoncavallo's health.[38] He was unable to understand why Tedeschi continued to refuse "having anything to do with Monsieur Sonzogno who had made him two offers." Realizing Tedeschi only had "*Chatterton, Chatterton,* and *Chatterton,*" he was hardly in a position to compete with another publisher.[39] Tedeschi feared an agreement with Sonzogno would "lessen his importance as a publisher," regarding "the right to negotiate the rentals" of the opera,[40] and Leoncavallo believed Sonzogno would boycott *Chatterton* if he was not involved. The composer felt both firms had done "everything possible to cause the work's failure in Milan."[41] The run was also cut short due to Tedeschi's finances, his having invested no more than what Fürstner paid him. Leoncavallo hoped to reawaken Sonzogno's interest in the subject following the premiere of *La bohème*. When neither Dresden nor Prague produced the opera, Leoncavallo vied for London and Vienna. Fürstner tried assuring him that "Ricordi and Sonzogno's intrigues" had "not in the least diminished" his "complete confidence" in the composer's "masterpiece."[42] Leoncavallo was certain that if *Chatterton*—regardless of Sonzogno's apprehensions—received a presentation in Vienna with Van Dyck, it would be as popular as *Pagliacci* had been following its Viennese premiere.

The composer spent Christmas in Pallanza on Lake Maggiore, still embittered about his relations with the "idiot" Tedeschi, against whom he had now also begun legal proceedings. He hoped to regain *Chatterton*'s rights through a court hearing, thereby forcing the publisher to relinquish a work Leoncavallo felt he did "not deserve to possess." Lake Maggiore offered him peace to work on *La bohème*, with the projected premiere planned for the following spring at Sonzogno's Teatro Lirico. Switzerland was an escape from Milan's publishers and colleagues, a neutral oasis that Leoncavallo favored more intensely with each passing year. He now also considered embarking on a tour of Germany and Hungary, hoping to direct *Chatterton* in every town, certain that "without the Camorra" of his adversaries the work would be triumphant.[43] The year ended as Leoncavallo sent Van Dyck the published "Invocation à la Muse" from *La nuit de mai*, dedicated to the tenor he hoped would lead *Chatterton* to glory.

\
FROM MURGER TO LEONCAVALLO

During January 1897, the composer was concerned with the upcoming publication of the *Bohème* libretto, making sure that the Italian translation matched the
same rhythm as Murger's original French. The score remained incomplete, and
the composer asked his pharmacist for a supply of caffeine that would enable
him to work with less than five hours of sleep per night.[44] Retitled *La bohème*
rather than *Vie de bohème* thanks to the Puccini opus, the opera was now set to
premiere on 6 May 1897 at Venice's Teatro La Fenice. Puccini's version was performed in the lagoon city during the same time. Puccini wrote Illica that he was
also going to hear "Caonlevallo's" opera and, following the premiere, was relieved
that Leoncavallo's work posed no competition. He even expressed his delight by
ridiculing the composer in a poem sent to his sister Ramelde.[45] The premiere
cast consisted of Rosina Storchio (Mimì), Lison Frandin (Musette), Umberto
Beduschi (Marcello), and Rodolfo Angelini-Fornari (Rodolfo). Critics agreed
that the most interesting element was Leoncavallo's libretto, which sought to re-
create the entire novel rather than the selections Puccini's work offered. The *Corriere della Sera* considered the opera to be important and "dramatically beautiful
as a whole," although the music failed to uphold the libretto's potential.[46] Acts 1
and 2 were deemed superior, since the accompaniment served to accentuate the
dialogue, whereas acts 3 and 4 demanded more inspiration. Although "robust and
well-constructed," it gave the illusion of being prematurely aged.[47]

The production, however, was successful, thanks to Storchio's delightful
Mimì, with her aria "Musette svaria sulla bocca viva," which brought Leoncavallo before the public for seventeen curtain calls. Alfredo Edel's costumes
and scenery also helped distract from Frandin's voice, which was well beyond
its prime. Various newspapers used the occasion to resurrect the "who came
first" debate—with the *Gazzetta di Venezia* stating that Leoncavallo had already signed a contract for *La bohème* before Puccini's work had even been
announced. While reviews published in Sonzogno's *Il Secolo* were void of any
objectivity, the *Gazzetta di Venezia* took the opportunity to announce that
Leoncavallo had begun work on the "British play *Tribly* [sic]." This was a dramatization of George du Maurier's 1894 novel *Trilby*, similar to *Vie de bohème*
in its portrait of Parisian artistic life during the 1850s, a project frequently
mentioned in Sonzogno's letters to the composer that year.

THE MAHLER DÉBÂCLE

Neither Vienna nor Berlin was interested in producing *La bohème*. Fürstner
further echoed critical opinion by stating that only the first two acts were any
good, and he was no longer interested in acquiring either the work's German

or Austrian rights. Leoncavallo's numerous letters to Fürstner promising that *Chatterton* and *La bohème* would be successful were now irrelevant. The bewildered and frustrated publisher had expected a lighthearted version of Murger. Instead, he received a tragic creation recalling the ill-fated *Chatterton*. With the future of his new work at stake, Leoncavallo traveled to Vienna, hoping to remedy the situation personally. Sonzogno, certain that Puccini would not only try to hinder further performances but also the work's success, demanded that Leoncavallo undertake additional cuts prior to printing a definitive version of the libretto.[48]

When Leoncavallo arrived at Vienna's Hotel Bristol on the Kärntnerring, he received a desperate letter from Sonzogno authorizing him to make a "more than modest" financial proposal to the Vienna Opera in order to produce *La bohème*.[49] Although the artistic director, Wilhelm Jahn, was ill and therefore unable to see him immediately, he had requested that his new kapellmeister, Gustav Mahler, attend *La bohème*'s premiere, in order to inform him of the work's quality. Mahler was not impressed. He reported that the music was scarcely original in spite of some technical refinement. To Leoncavallo's chagrin, he also remained an extra day in Venice to hear Puccini's version, which he liked very much. Mahler then wrote a colleague that Leoncavallo's score mirrored his personality: hollow, bumptious, obtrusive, vulgar, and "disgusting." He made it more than clear that he preferred one bar of Puccini's opus to Leoncavallo's entire score.[50] However, as a personal favor to Leoncavallo, Jahn signed a contract to produce the opera during the middle of June. Although Leoncavallo had succeeded in gaining Jahn's refusal to Mahler's request to substitute Puccini's *Bohème*, it fueled the antagonism between Mahler and the composer. It also ruined Leoncavallo's chances in Austria once Mahler replaced Jahn as intendant the following October.

With his success for the moment in Vienna, Leoncavallo now left to meet with Count Hochberg in Berlin to discuss *Der Roland von Berlin*, as well as a possible *La bohème* premiere. Meanwhile, Sonzogno was in Paris trying to organize both a French production of the Murger opera and to secure the rights to Meilhac and Halévy's *Froufrou* (which came to nothing, as the authors both agreed that their creation could only suffer being set to music).

By September 1897, Leoncavallo was in Hamburg badmouthing Fürstner. The publisher, following both *Chatterton* and *La bohème*, earnestly believed that Leoncavallo was "finished" and unable to produce additional lasting works other than *Pagliacci*.[51] Leoncavallo, in turn, blamed Fürstner's attitude for his not being able to find a theater in Germany interested in producing *Chatterton*. He now "profoundly regretted" Fürstner's ownership of *Chatterton* and *La bohème*'s German rights.[52] On 18 September 1897 Leoncavallo wrote Ernest Van Dyck a furious letter from Hamburg, disgusted that the tenor had refused to sing Marcello in Vienna, which meant that *La bohème* would have to be postponed, further strengthening the composer's assumption that Ricordi, Puccini, and Mahler were out to destroy his fourteen-year-old reputation. Puccini's "reputation" was also in danger when Hanslick "demolished" his *La bohème*, performed at the Theater an der Wien on 5 October, finding the "second act to be trivial and boring while the third was sentimental and boring,"[53] and only an imitation of his beloved Mascagni. Puccini would have preferred to have his opera staged at the Court Opera, although Leoncavallo's work received that honor the following year, thanks to Jahn. Budapest also produced both *Bohèmes* to stimulate public interest, and Leoncavallo attended the Hungarian premiere that November, as Puccini cursed his colleague's supposed success with Mahler.[54] Leoncavallo later returned to Pallanza, where on New Year's Eve he received a letter from Edoardo Sonzogno, in which he declared that completing *La bohème* after Puccini had been a veritable disaster, since Giulio Ricordi had already booked seventeen theaters for Puccini's version. He eventually even blamed the failure of Leoncavallo's opera on the order of its creation.[55]

NOTES

1. Marriage certificate (USCM).
2. Ibid. In an early song dedicated to Berthe, the composer wrote "To Madame Berthe Rambaud." Since all unmarried women in France—regardless of age—are referred to as "mademoiselle," the possibility that Berthe may have been divorced or widowed at the time to a certain "Rambaud" cannot be excluded, thereby disproving Morini's assumption that Rambaud was her maiden name.
3. Massenet to Leoncavallo, 24 February 1895 (BCL).
4. N. Tabanelli, "La Causa Ricordi-Leoncavallo," *Rivista Musicale Italiana*, 1899.
5. Leoncavallo already had Bernardini's approval for an operatic adaptation in 1894.
6. The handwritten copy seems to ignore the fact that the characters' Christian names have not been given their French equivalent.
7. Leoncavallo sought additional money at Peters, offering his *Valse triste* for piano that he just "happened to find again." Leoncavallo to Peters, 28 February 1895 (PA).
8. Leoncavallo to Fürstner, 9 March 1895 (Y).
9. Leoncavallo to Fürstner, April 1895 (Y).
10. Leoncavallo to Fürstner, 22 April 1895 (Y).
11. Ibid.
12. Leoncavallo to Fürstner, 12 May 1895 (Y).
13. Leoncavallo to Fürstner, 29 May 1895 (Y).
14. Fürstner already owned *Chatterton*'s German rights.
15. Leoncavallo to Fürstner, 29 May 1895 (Y).
16. Leoncavallo to Fürstner, 14 August 1895 (Y).
17. One of the main problems with Vienna's *Medici* was the insufficiently dramatic voices of Paula Mark and Marie Renard.

18. *I Medici* was nevertheless presented in Prague from 5 January until 19 April 1895.

19. Leoncavallo to Fürstner, 24 August 1895 (Y).

20. Leoncavallo to Fürstner, 25 October 1895 (Y).

21. Leoncavallo to Fürstner, 19 October 1895 (Y).

22. Leoncavallo to Fürstner, 25 October 1895 (Y). Ricordi now referred to *Medici* as "Medico"—a work that all the "medici (doctors) will not be able to save." (Ricordi to Puccini, October 1895) in Gara, *Carteggi Pucciniani*, 130.

23. Leoncavallo to Fürstner, 16 December 1895 (Y).

24. Leoncavallo to Fürstner, 2 November 1895 (Y).

25. Leoncavallo's plans following *Chatterton* included *La bohème, Der Roland von Berlin, Don Marzio,* and *Crepusculum*'s *Savonarola* and *Cesare Borgia,* negating the notion that he had given up the idea of completing his trilogy following the critical lack of success of *I Medici.*

26. Leoncavallo to Fürstner, 28 February 1896 (Y).

27. Leoncavallo to Fürstner, 25 February 1896 (Y).

28. Benedetto Lucignani (Chatterton), Adalgisa Gabbi (Jenny), Scipione Terzi (Giorgio), Vittorio Coda (John Clark), and Aristide Anceschi (Lord Klifford), conducted by Vittorio Podesti. From the assembled cast the composer had discussed only Gabbi as an alternative to Darclée.

29. How the premiere could ever have been a success with the composer continuously on stage is debatable. One cannot help siding with Hanslick in deploring this custom.

30. "Tommaso Chatterton di Leoncavallo, La prima rappresentazione al Nazionale," *La Capitale,* 11/12 March 1896.

31. Ibid.

32. Ibid.

33. Years later, with the *Mimì Pinson* version of *Bohème,* Leoncavallo would strive to come closer to the Puccini opus and its success.

34. Leoncavallo to Max Abraham, 22 February 1896 (PML). Puccini was markedly less enthusiastic when hearing about Leoncavallo's "wonderful" libretto (Puccini to Illica, 22 August 1896) in Gara, *Carteggi Pucciniani,* 50.

35. They have failed to reappear.

36. "Leoncavallo e le sue opere" in *Gazzetta di Torino,* 16/17 March 1896.

37. On 28 March 1896 King Umberto I honored Leoncavallo with the "Commendatore nell'Ordine della Corona d'Italia."

38. Leoncavallo to Fürstner, 10 July 1896 (Y).

39. Leoncavallo to Count Pierfrancesco Albicini, undated (CMU).

40. Ibid.

41. Ibid.

42. Fürstner to Leoncavallo, 18 July 1896. (Y). Fürstner's stance toward Leoncavallo would change dramatically during the composition of *La bohème.*

43. Leoncavallo to Fürstner, 28 December 1896 (Y). He seems to have forgotten poking fun at Mascagni's tour one year earlier, referring to it as "charlatanesque." (Leoncavallo to Fürstner, 16 December 1895 [Y].)

44. Leoncavallo also received a commission from the Portuguese composer Augusto de Machado for a libretto that would evolve to be *Mario Wetter*, premiering at Lisbon's Teatro San Carlo on 17 February 1898.

45. "Il Leone fu trombato, il Cavallo fu suonato, di Bohème ce n'è una . . . tutto il resto è una laguna." Puccini to Ramelde Franceschini Puccini, 11 May 1897 in Gara, *Puccini Com'era*, 226–27. Alberto Franchetti and Massenet were the only composers wishing Leoncavallo well, while it seems that Giordano and Mascagni were merely present out of curiosity. According to Puccini's most recent biographer, Julian Budden, Leoncavallo was unaware of Puccini's hostility, and Giulio Ricordi even went so far to send Leoncavallo a copy of act 1 of *Tosca* "with all the latest revisions." Julian Budden, *Puccini* (New York: Oxford University Press, 2002), 186–87.

46. *Corriere della Sera*, 6 May 1897.

47. Ibid.

48. The cuts included shortening the role of Barbemuche in act 1 and cutting two waltzes in act 2. Incredibly, Sonzogno suggested the deletion of Marcello's act 3 romanza "Musette, O gioia della mia dimora!" which the composer fortunately refused, believing that Sonzogno's request had been influenced by Beduschi's poor rendition in Venice. Leoncavallo had the good sense to want to hear the aria sung once more—"at least in rehearsal"—before making a decision. Leoncavallo to Amintore Galli, 14 June 1897 (BCGR).

49. Leoncavallo to unidentified recipient (SUBF).

50. Mahler to Richard Heuberger in Karl Josef Müller, *Mahler, Leben, Werke, Dokumente* (Mainz: Piper-Schott, 1988), 157.

51. Leoncavallo to unidentified recipient, 27 September 1897 (BCL).

52. Ibid.

53. A. Goldbacher to Edoardo Sonzogno, 7 October 1897 (BCL).

54. Giacomo Puccini to Tito Ricordi, 23 November 1897 in Giuseppe Pintorno, *Giacomo Puccini—276 lettere inedite* (Milan: Fondo dell'Accademia d'Arte a Montecatini-Terme, 1974), 69.

55. Sonzogno's irritation increased when Lison Frandin threatened him with a lawsuit if he refused her waning powers as Musette for the Milanese production of *La bohème*.

· 6 ·

From Mahler to Queen Victoria

1898–1905

*M*ahler wrote Leoncavallo on 12 January 1898 that the Hofoper's *La bohème* would open on 19 February, although the date was eventually delayed until the 23rd. As rehearsals for the German-language version progressed, Leoncavallo was astounded that Mahler—who would conduct the work—had undertaken numerous spontaneous cuts, some of them without his consent. Chancing to see an invitation to the February 21st dress rehearsal, Leoncavallo crossed out his own name on the card as *La bohème*'s author, replacing it with Mahler's, declaring his editing to be an outrage. Mahler liked neither the opera nor its composer and was therefore loath to lavish on it the care it deserved and required. Leoncavallo's efforts all seemed futile; even his casting wishes fell on deaf ears. Frustrated and depressed, he and Berthe often dined with the Austrian critic Ludwig Karpath, who tried to cheer up the composer at a series of elegant restaurants.

Desperate for publicity, Leoncavallo took up a new tactic by announcing to the journalist Josef Oppenheimer (*Neuen Freie Presse*) that he was Jewish, since he believed that many influential Viennese critics were of the faith. Those who knew better were infuriated, and those who did not believed him—to his detriment. Leoncavallo's assertions were never forgotten and even led to questioning Mascagni, who was also aware that the "sly fox" would pretend to be Jewish whenever the situation decreed. Years later, Karpath asked the composer once more, who, embarrassed, replied that Berthe was Jewish and that Oppenheimer must have misunderstood.[1]

Thanks to the composer's prodding, Ernest van Dyck was double cast with Andreas Dippel as Marcello.[2] For a reason that has not been documented, Van Dyck threatened to cancel if his requests were not met by noon the day of the performance. When Mahler refused and asked Dippel to sing the premiere, Van Dyck was suddenly available; but Mahler was unrelenting, and, even

75

though he knew how much Leoncavallo had pinned his hopes on Van Dyck, it was Dippel who sang the Austrian premiere.[3] Sonzogno was furious, warning the composer to be less haughty when dealing with impresarios.[4]

As the premiere approached, Mahler confided in his friends that if he had become director of the Court Opera a few months earlier, *La bohème* would not be performed at all. When the opera was only mildly received, Leoncavallo blamed Van Dyck's absence for the work's relative lack of success, while Mahler felt justified in his original assumption, believing Leoncavallo's version to be a failure.[5] After the third performance, the Leoncavallos left for Abbazia and then Pallanza, where the composer wrote Karpath and Mahler, requesting that the tenor Fritz Schrödter replace Dippel, who was soon to leave for Russia. Mahler had no interest in contracting Schrödter or in ever again performing Leoncavallo's work, which closed after six performances. Leoncavallo told the press years later that he greatly admired Mahler as an intendant "in spite of personal differences"[6] and although he was "a bit crazy."[7]

The opera's bad luck continued in Genoa, where it was also disliked by the critics when performed on 20 January 1898, even though it combined first-rate singers who had been missing from Vienna's roster: Caruso, Storchio, and De Luca.[8] Prague was next to introduce *La bohème*, and although Leoncavallo opted to remain in Pallanza at the last moment, he heard that the performance—conducted by Franz Schalk—was warmly received, with thirty curtain calls; the *Prager Tagblatt* correctly stated that the opera's interest increased during its second half.

Settling in Riccione's Villa Tardini that June, Leoncavallo turned his attention to *Der Roland von Berlin*, requesting that publishers Bote und Bock send music written during the time Alexis's novel unfolds, thereby hoping to create an authentic atmosphere. He planned to present Wilhelm II with the completed work by 1899.[9] Recalling his experience with Mahler, Leoncavallo asked Berlin's Italian Embassy—ultimately to no avail—whether they could influence Count Hochberg to help back his choice of singers for the world premiere. The year 1898 was completed in Bologna at 4 Via Guido Reni. Leoncavallo, hard at work on *Der Roland von Berlin*, was distracted by a severe sore throat, forcing him to drink cold liquids for five days and keeping him from eating solid foods.[10] He managed to correspond with Massenet, thanking him for sending the *Thaïs* "meditation" for one of his brothers, and the French composer responded by gushing about the beauty of Italy ("Your country is music, music").[11]

Early in 1899, Leoncavallo conducted excerpts of *La bohème* at Bologna's Teatro Comunale, which he felt was a "colossal success." As his career progressed, he now, with greater frequency, led performances of his own works. The complete opera was then presented in February at the same theater, prior to a production at the Teatro Filarmonico in Verona.[12]

Hoping Massenet could put in a good word for him in France, Leoncavallo wrote Berthe a postcard from Milan signed "Roger," saying that Sonzogno was discussing a French version of *La bohème* with the publishers Choudens.[13] When Nice produced the opera in March,[14] Leoncavallo was invited to perform for Queen Victoria on the 29th of that month at the Hotel Regina in Cimiez. Victoria confided in her journal later that evening that "After dinner we had a great treat, the celebrated Italian composer Leon Cavallo [*sic*] came & played to us out of his new opera *La Bohème* & also 3 pieces out of his *Pagliaci* [*sic*]. He plays quite beautifully & the pieces out of his new opera are charming."[15] Leoncavallo was presented to Victoria for a second time a few days later, the Queen recalling: "We again had the pleasure of hearing Signor Leon Cavallo [*sic*] play a number of lovely things from his operas. He plays most deliciously, with such entrain, & such extraordinary feeling & expression & has such a beautiful touch. He is very pleasing & modest, & told us he wrote his own libretto as well as composed the music."[16] Leoncavallo sought to remain in touch with Victoria, realizing how important her influence might be when trying to place some of his operas at Covent Garden. She invited him to Windsor Castle to conduct a performance of *Pagliacci* in July,[17] although an eye ailment prevented his acceptance. The Queen recorded her impressions without the composer's participation:

A little after 9 went over to the Waterloo Gallery, where we had a very successful operatic performance. It began by a small *Opéra Comique, Le Chalet,* by Adam, composed about 60 years ago. . . . Then followed Leon Cavallo's [*sic*] celebrated Opera *Pagliaci* [*sic*] which he was to have conducted himself but was prevented from ill health. It is eminently dramatic & very tragic & full of passion. The music is beautiful, very descriptive, but chiefly sad, the orchestration very fine. I still prefer the *Cavalleria*, though this is perhaps a more powerful composition.[18]

Leoncavallo sent Victoria two specially bound scores of *Chatterton* and *La bohème* from Villa Cavalieri in Riccione, hoping that the former work would "interest Her Majesty," and perhaps lead to a possible production at Covent Garden. The Queen had requested that Leoncavallo send her a signed photo, which he inscribed to "L'Auguste Souveraine," expressing his "profound regret in having lost the opportunity" of presenting himself at Windsor.[19] His connection to the House of Windsor ended with a thank-you note from Windsor Castle. Curiously, Queen Victoria's critique regarding Leoncavallo's pianistic capabilities—which seem to have been superb—remain a unique testimony to his ability at the keyboard.

I Medici received its last performance during Leoncavallo's lifetime that April at Sonzogno's Teatro Lirico.[20] It was the publisher's final attempt at resurrecting the work following a four-year hiatus since its appearance at La Scala in

1895. Strongly associated with the verismo movement on account of *Pagliacci*, Leoncavallo was unable to find the success he dreamed of with his "historical drama," which harkened back to the days of Meyerbeer, Verdi, and Wagner.

"VIOLETTA ON ROLLER SKATES"

Despite the fact that *Der Roland von Berlin* still remained incomplete, Leoncavallo signed a contract in Paris on 10 July with Pierre Berton and Charles Simon, authorizing him to create an opera based on their hugely successful play *Zazà*, to be completed by the end of 1900.[21] *Zazà* is first mentioned in a letter dated 24 June from Sonzogno to the composer, proposing Emma Calvé the opportunity to create the role at the Opéra-Comique. From *Frou Frou* to *Don Marzio*, Sonzogno continued to advise Leoncavallo that a comedy was needed following the composer's run of tragic operas and that a successful "modern subject" not previously composed would be appropriate before returning to the heavy fare of *Der Roland von Berlin*. Leoncavallo most likely saw *Zazà* staged during one of his visits to France, considering it a continuation of a French subject so in vogue at the time,[22] reminiscent of Massenet's *Sapho*. It would be his most modern scenario to date, as well as an authentic representation of backstage life, one Viennese critic defining Zazà as a "Violetta on roller skates."

La bohème also seemed to be gaining in popularity since the Prague production, having received ten performances at Rome's Teatro Adriano during July, at which Leoncavallo was honored with twenty-six curtain calls in the presence of Queen Margherita. He hoped the opera would be presented in St. Petersburg during the coming winter with Mattia Battistini.

Leoncavallo returned to Paris in October for *La bohème*'s French premiere at the Théâtre de la Renaissance. *Le ménestrel* wrote that the opera was both "interesting" and "lively,"[23] a far cry from the composer's initial appearance in the Paris newspaper many years before, announcing his availability for piano lessons! Massenet was so elated that he wished to cable Sonzogno. While in Paris, Leoncavallo also sold Choudens two tarantellas for piano and recieved "500 francs" for the song "Nuit de décembre."[24]

LEONCAVALLO, PUCCINI, AND LOUŸS

Leoncavallo also tried visiting Pierre Louÿs, whose novel *Aphrodite* had interested him. Unfortunately, his many messages left at 147 Boulevard Malesherbes did not include his own Parisian address, thereby forcing Louÿs to search for the composer through Choudens. Having already granted *Aphrodite* as a ballet to Albéniz and as an opera to Massenet's student Ernest Moret, Louÿs suggested that Leoncavallo write an opera based on his *Femme et le pantin*. Since these arrangements were not "exclusive," Louÿs reluctantly agreed to let Leoncavallo use *Aphrodite*, as long as he was not requested to produce a libretto.[25] Puccini began searching for a new subject following *Tosca*; incredibly, he was considering *Aphrodite* at the same time Leoncavallo received Louÿs's letter. It once again seems likely that Illica let the news slip.[26]

While progress was underway for *Zazà*'s premiere, Sonzogno continued to experience difficulties placing the opera in various French theaters. When a date had still not been set by September, he warned Leoncavallo that it needed to be presented either the 8th or 10th of November as part of the Teatro Lirico's season. By this time, Sonzogno had buried some of his animosity toward Toscanini, agreeing that he conduct the world premiere. Work on the opera proceeded as Toscanini joined Leoncavallo in Brissago (on the northern shore of Lake Maggiore in Switzerland) in October in order to study the score. The composer maintained a frantic pace trying to complete the partitura, a task that had completely unnerved him, as he wrote Casa Sonzogno's artistic director Amintore Galli:

> I have begun act 4 and am exhausted! Spending nights like this it is amazing that I don't get sick. I beg you to explain to Signor Edoardo the superhuman effort it has taken to produce the orchestration with such rapidity. . . . I know that the piano and orchestral rehearsals have begun. Not even a dog has thought of informing me! Is Signor Edoardo content? And the artists? Is the orchestration good when performed? You can imagine how I am fuming being nailed here!! . . . I have given my blood and now my health to *Zazà*.[27]

When Leoncavallo confided to various newspapers that the premiere would not take place before mid-November, Sonzogno was furious, imploring the composer to finish the orchestration of *Zazà*'s first and fourth acts before 25 October in Milan, where he needed to agree on costumes and attend rehearsals.[28] Leoncavallo, however, chose to remain in Brissago, preferring to work on the orchestration in peace, since Sonzogno had written on 31 October that rehearsals were proceeding to Toscanini's satisfaction. Intent on success, Sonzogno left nothing to chance, including writing out eighty pages worth of production plans!

Zazà's world premiere was on 10 November 1900—as Sonzogno had planned—sung by Edoardo Garbin (Milio), Mario Sammarco (Cascart), and Clorinda Pini-Corsi (Anaide).[29] The young and attractive soprano Rosina Storchio—Leoncavallo's first Mimì—performed the title role. With *Zazà*, the composer had once again supplied a work that, with time, would rival *Pagliacci*'s popularity. Pierre Berton and Charles Simon attended, as did the expected army of critics, who wrote that act 1 was too long and fragmentary.[30] The *Corriere della Sera* believed act 2 to be slightly "monotonous," and it was not until Zazà's entrance in act 3 that the work was described as a success.[31] Congratulatory telegrams began arriving from Alberto Franchetti, the ever-faithful Massenet, and the actress Virginia Reiter, who had scored a success as the stage Zazà.[32]

MAHLER VS. LEONCAVALLO AND A WOULD-BE REQUIEM

After trying to interest a publisher in Chicago in purchasing some of his songs[33] and toying with the idea of writing a study on music criticism, Leoncavallo also planned a *Messa da requiem* in memory of Umberto I, who was assassinated that summer. He told the press that the work would be performed very soon and without any financial compensation. Emma Carelli and Alessandro Bonci were scheduled to sing, although they had little interest in performing without payment. Leoncavallo had originally hoped the Italian government would donate their fees, but his numerous efforts proved ultimately unsuccessful. Recalling the days when a singer like Julián Gayarré sang gratis for Vittorio Emanuele II's funeral, Leoncavallo finally decided that the *Requiem* would remain unperformed and unpublished. Only the first two movements ("Requiem" and "Kyrie") and sketches for the "Benedictus" were in fact completed (twelve pages). These would later be incorporated into the following scheme:

> *Requiem* (chorus with bells "come un mormorio")
> *Kyrie* (chorus with harp)
> *Dies irae* (soloists, chorus)
> *Tuba mirum* (soloists, chorus)
> *Rex tremendae* (baritone, men's chorus)
> *Recordare* (tenor)
> *Confutatis* (mezzo-soprano, chorus)
> *Lacrymosa* (soloists)
> *Domine Jesu* (soprano, chorus)
> *Hostias* (soloists)
> *Sanctus* (chorus)
> *Benedictus* (baritone)
> *Agnus Dei* (soloists, chorus)

The year 1900 ended with an additional chapter in the Leoncavallo/Puccini feud. When Puccini took an interest in Rostand's *Cyrano de Bergerac*, Leoncavallo sent Massenet a hurried letter about the "amazing news circulating in Italian newspapers."[34] He implied that he had been interested in the play two years earlier, even though Rostand mentioned that his verses contained sufficient music, having already refused Massenet.[35] Leoncavallo confided his frustration to his French colleague: "I believe that Puccini has launched this news and is endeavoring to get the play; but it is not true that he has succeeded in doing so, for it would be absurd to refuse it to you in order to give it to him!!!"[36]

Leoncavallo spent January 1901 immersed in Egyptian history, intent on creating his own version of *Aïda*, drawing inspiration from his time spent in the country. His research led him to believe he had discovered the "true origin of the sphinx,"[37] which, as a "scientific revelation," merited publication.[38] Still hoping to create a "popular national opera" to increase his income, Leoncavallo's latest project, like the *Requiem*, never came to fruition.[39]

When Leoncavallo attended Verdi's funeral in January, newspapers as far away as Canada printed articles describing his initial meeting with the composer through "Teresina Stoltz" [*sic*]:[40]

It was arranged that she (Stolz) and Verdi were to be on the Milan bastion between the Porta Venezia and the Porta Monforte. . . . Leoncavallo, as if quite by accident, was also to be at the same place. The younger man, as he passed, was to raise his hat with great deference, and, if Verdi noticed the salutation, the lady would intervene and introduce the two men. Verdi *did* notice Leoncavallo's bow, and the latter was duly presented to the object of his veneration. During the conversation the younger man was careful to make no reference, direct or indirect, to any of his own works, a piece of tactful restraint which evidently immensely pleased Verdi, who, the next day, sent Leoncavallo his signed portrait. To this civility the author of *Pagliacci* replied sending copies of his works, writing on each at the top in very large characters, "A Giuseppe Verdi," and at the bottom, very small, "R. Leoncavallo."[41]

February found Leoncavallo in Turin for another run of *Zazà*,[42] opening on the 11th with Storchio and conducted by Rodolfo Ferrari.[43] Toscanini sent a congratulatory telegram for the production's success, while Charles Simon spoke to the Ministry of Fine Arts, requesting that *Zazà* be presented at the Opéra-Comique in lieu of *Pagliacci*—proof that the playwright esteemed Leoncavallo's adaptation. The composer left for Bergamo after completing a hymn for the Red Cross, before emerging in Rome for an audience with the King of Italy at the Quirinale on 25 April.

When Leoncavallo heard that Puccini's *La bohème* would return to Vienna rather than his own version, he gathered that Mahler was responsible for the "grave insult," immediately writing of his concern on 2 May:

Mahler's hate regarding myself seems to have increased with time rather than subsided, although I have never done anything to him. He is presently preparing the worst affront that a famous artist can endure. He canceled my *Bohème* under ridiculous pretexts following the fifth performance, after the great success everyone remembers it having in Vienna. . . . Never allowing a second run of my work, he decided to produce Puccini's *Bohème*. . . . The outrage that Signor Mahler has committed is terrible and has immensely damaged my reputation, since the entire artistic world now believes that my *Bohème* was not successful at the Court Opera. . . . If there is a *Bohème* that has acquired the right to be played at the Hofoper . . . it is mine. On account of my artistic pride, I never asked nor had anyone question Signor Mahler, after my *Bohème* had been produced, why it wasn't taken up again gaining the public's approval. . . . It is Signor Mahler's right not to stage my opera, but he doesn't have the right to present a work with the same title and subject without taking up mine again. Why doesn't Mahler present *Manon*? He (Puccini) stole the subject from Massenet, just like he stole *Bohème* from me![44]

The question remains whether Mahler had indeed planned a production of Puccini's *La bohème* or if Leoncavallo's "humble prayer" had its effect.[45]

Emma Carelli—later a celebrated Zazà—premiered the role on 19 May in Genoa conducted by Alessandro Pomè, with Garbin as Milio and Clorinda Pini Corsi as Anaide. The management was "embarrassed" at not being able to find a child to perform Totò, but Leoncavallo soon suggested the same girl that had played the role in Turin.[46] The attention to minute details that were important for Leoncavallo's "realistic" conception made this *Zazà* another success, with no less than forty curtain calls.

Leoncavallo began proposing additional works that would never be composed, seeking to interest a French publisher in two one-act operas that June: *Le clown* (The Clown)—to a libretto by Massenet's former tenor Victor Capoul[47]—and the Neapolitan-inspired *Pazzariello* by Ferdinando Fontana. Considering the quality of the latter's *Le villi* and *Edgar* libretti for Puccini, it was perhaps fortunate that nothing came of the venture, although it is significant that Leoncavallo did not wish to write the libretto.[48] Mostly interested in the "commercialism" of these works, he hoped French publishers would also be persuaded by their "beauty."[49] Another short-lived project was Leoncavallo's decision to do an operatic adaptation of Chester Bailey Fernald's grand guignol *The Cat and the Cherub*, which was later successfully used by Franco Leoni for his opera *L'oracolo*.

At the end of 1901, the first sparks of a future scandal disputing the authorship of *Zazà*'s libretto began to appear. Mascagni wrote Illica that Giacomo Orefice was planning an opera entitled *Chopin*, commenting that "Ruggerone" should write one called *Zangarini and Ponchielli*, since Zangarini had in fact ghostwritten much of *Zazà*'s libretto.[50] Oblivious to the next conflict that awaited him, Leoncavallo sent Wilhelm II his good wishes for the coming year, also writing Berlin's Italian Embassy that he was working on *Der Roland von Berlin*, which the kaiser hoped to receive by the autumn of 1902.

After performances of *La bohème* in Verviers, Leoncavallo presented a French version of *Zazà* in Antwerp in February 1902, which was attended by Pierre Berton and the publisher Paul de Choudens, who would later write the libretto for *Maïa*.[51] In March Leoncavallo returned to Naples for *La bohème,* in which he reinstated Marcello's act 3 aria "Musette! O gioia della mia dimora!" which Sonzogno had refused to include. While there, he received a congratulatory telegram from Emma Carelli, mentioning that she hoped he would visit her in Rome. He later attended additional performances of *Zazà*—beginning 8 March—at the Teatro Massimo in Palermo. It was not until the beginning of April that Leoncavallo found time again to continue work on *Der Roland von Berlin*.

Leoncavallo's birthday reflected the melancholy he felt at turning forty-five. Although letters from young admirers and musicians enthusiastic about his new operas raised his spirits somewhat, he felt he was in a new century that "stifled all élan."[52] Unable to concentrate on *Der Roland von Berlin* in Milan, he left for the Riviera, where he found an idyllic spot at Menton's Château de la Roche Montée. While there, he chanced to read in a German newspaper on 17 April that he was supposedly planning an operetta entitled *Le gaulois* for the Théâtre de la Gaîté. He immediately responded that he never had the intention of writing an operetta and that he also *loathed* the art form. Considering that he would later write numerous operettas, this implies that he only found the genre compatible as a source of income.

DER ROLAND VON BERLIN

From Menton he again wrote Pierre Louÿs that May to discuss *Aphrodite*, after having already rejected composing *La femme et le pantin*. Louÿs claimed that Théophile Puget and Gabriel Bernard had already written an *Aphrodite* libretto in 1900 but that it was "not very good."[53] As the libretto possessed some "dramatic quality," Louÿs had tried revising act 1, only to lay it aside, overwhelmed by the enormity of the remaining work. Recalling that some ten or twelve phrases in *Pelléas et Mélisande*'s libretto were sufficient to evoke laughter during the world premiere of Debussy's opera one month earlier, Louÿs felt that the public and critics would ridicule the work. Although Louÿs believed he had done his "duty" by warning Leoncavallo, the final decision was his.[54] Upon receipt of the libretto from Louÿs, Leoncavallo proceeded to write Puget and Bernard to discuss terms for a contract.[55]

Leaving Menton for Paris, Leoncavallo set out immediately for Louÿs's home, where the author delighted in showing him some of the composer's own operas contained in his library, in addition to Arturo Berutti's version of *Aphrodite*, which Leoncavallo then borrowed. Berutti's adaptation had been produced in Buenos Aires without the author's consent, and he subsequently forbade performances of the opera in Europe until 1904. In correspondence with Leoncavallo he reminded him that he had already authorized a total of seven or eight operatic adaptations. However, Debussy, Ernest Moret, Henri Rabaud, André Pollonnais, and Albéniz never succeeded in composing a version. Upon hearing Camille Erlanger's adaptation of *Aphrodite*, Louÿs still believed there would be room for two, especially with a composer of Leoncavallo's stature. Since beginning *Aphrodite* precisely ten years earlier on 22 July 1892, the author had refused eighty requests for operatic and stage adaptations, writing some five hundred letters on the subject, without one of the propositions ever reaching the stage. Tired, Louÿs implored Leoncavallo to decide, hoping that a combination of the composer's "great talent" and "universal fame" would finally lead to a fruitful collaboration. When Leoncavallo eventually dropped the project, one cannot help concluding that *his* interest had only been inspired by Puccini's.[56]

While in Paris, Leoncavallo read a misleading report in the *Paris Tribune* that Wilhelm II had "already written two acts of" *Der Roland von Berlin*'s libretto "and was busily engaged on the remaining three."[57] Leoncavallo had continued doing his part of the work in the French capital, but his royal coworker's telegrams suggesting alterations and additions had become so numerous that he felt "forced to flee or ruin himself trying to keep up with the kaiser's pace."[58] Wilhelm's "collaboration" on *Der Roland von Berlin* would be rumored for years in the press, probably inserted there by Leoncavallo himself, who believed it to be an important promotional tactic.

Shortly after returning to Menton to continue work on *Der Roland von Berlin*, Leoncavallo learned that Carlo Zangarini had written a very long and detailed letter to *La Sera* in which he claimed to have written most of *Zazà*'s libretto based upon the composer's outline. Leoncavallo had supposedly invited him to Riccione during the summer of 1899 to work on *Zazà* and proposed that he write *Der Roland von Berlin*'s text as well. In his letter, Zangarini stated that Leoncavallo had even signed a contract with another librettist for the latter opera, while still insisting that he was its sole librettist. He asserted that the composer rarely completed a libretto without external help and that it was never acknowledged. Leoncavallo supposedly made it clear that Zangarini's name would not appear on the published libretto or score. He would receive money instead. After two requests for payment, Zangarini stated that he finally received it in front of the Duomo in Milan. He still hoped Leoncavallo would employ him as an official collaborator for the future *Cyrano de Bergerac* and for Zola's *La Faute de l'abbé Mouret* (*Idillio tragico*). When Leoncavallo's subsequent attempts with Rostand and Zola failed, Zangarini went public, declaring to have "sold his soul" in a "contract made of silence,"[59] and wreaked his revenge. Leoncavallo purposefully refrained from using Zangarini's name in his correspondence. He frantically wrote Gualtiero Belvederi to join him in Milan as a witness no later than 25 August, complaining of the harm everyone wished him, "a poor devil that has fought, fought . . . only doing good things for others."[60] Zangarini called Leoncavallo a "crocodile" in *La Sera*, and now the composer ironically wrote Belvederi of the envious "reptiles" prepared to throw "mud" on his "honored name!"[61] The Zangarini claim is more valid than it seems at first glance, since the style of *Zazà*'s libretto resembles both his *Conchita* for Zandonai and *La fanciulla del west* for Puccini. The fact that Puccini had already considered both the Rostand and the Zola subjects created yet another chapter in the ongoing Puccini-Leoncavallo feud.

During this period, Leoncavallo was constantly moving and being hunted by creditors. From Menton he spent one month with the Costa-Zenoglio family in Genoa, finally settling in Brissago at Lake Maggiore, where his landlord requested a thousand lire and threatened to sell the composer's furniture if he did not comply. Of a generous and gregarious nature, Leoncavallo gave freely, donating to various philanthropic organizations, while constantly traveling and at the same time supporting his brothers. Leoncavallo continued the futile search to create another financial goldmine like *Pagliacci*, but most of these projects were either never completed or hardly begun. Fleeting success developed into artistic uncertainty. Determined that his years of struggle and hard work would be rewarded by more than *Pagliacci*, he would attempt symphonic poems, grand operas, verismo, and operettas, trying to please both the public and himself, confounded by the changing times like so many of his colleagues. Leoncavallo was not the only composer to experiment, affected by his own ideals (*I Medici*), the meteoric rise of verismo (*Pagliacci*, *Maïa*, *Zingari*), and the success of operetta (*Reginetta delle rose*, *La candidata*, *Prestami tua moglie*, *A chi la giarrettiera?*). The correct path to financial freedom nevertheless eluded him.

He hoped Sonzogno would come to the rescue, signing a contract stipulating that the publisher would pay twenty-five thousand lire by December 1902 and another twenty-five thousand lire during April of the following year. Sonzogno now also took charge of paying off Leoncavallo's creditors, including the tenor Edoardo Garbin, Paolo Mariani (with whom he had signed a contract for the never composed *Le mannéquin*), Giovanni Mazzetti, and those who "presented themselves." Demanding 5 percent interest for the advance, Sonzogno clarified that the fifty thousand lire would be in anticipation of the royalties for *Pagliacci*, *I Medici*, *Chatterton*, *La bohème*, *Zazà*, and the still incomplete *Der Roland von Berlin*.

When the *Berliner Tagblatt* asked whether Leoncavallo could show the paper extracts from *Der Roland von Berlin,* the response was in the negative, since "the first person to know the opera both literally as well as musically should be Kaiser Wilhelm."[62] Shortly thereafter, Leoncavallo returned to Paris to prepare *Pagliacci* at the Opéra and, while there, sold Choudens the songs "Sérénade Française" and "Sérénade Napolitaine" for "400 francs."[63] He also met Francesco Finelli della Valletta again, who had been so influential during his Parisian days almost twenty years earlier. Leoncavallo was delighted to hear the still fresh and "seductive" voice of a "true artist."[64]

Leoncavallo journeyed to Milan once more toward the end of October before returning to Paris,[65] where a *Pagliacci* rehearsal for charity attended by President Loubet and the composer Ernest Reyer was performed prior to the premiere. *Paillasse* (the French translation of *Pagliacci*) opened on 17 December 1901 with Jean de Reszke, Aino Ackté, and Jean Delmas in Eugène Crosti's translation. The performance was a success with critics, who compared Leoncavallo's orchestration to the works of Beethoven, Wagner, and Berlioz. The Leoncavallos spent that Christmas Eve at a reception given by the society Oeuvre Française des Trente Ans de Théâtre, and, on the next day, a contract was signed allowing Loris Perterhoff and Emile Dürer to compose the *Pagliacci* parody *Re-paillasse.*

The following January 1902, Leoncavallo returned to Milan, where he wrote Belvederi that he had not only been "touched by the enthusiastic Parisian reception" but, most importantly, that the "Zangarini affair" was "finished," with the librettist required to make an official retraction.[66] He also had his portrait painted by Antonio Agnani and attended La Scala's world premiere of Smareglia's *Oceana,* together with Puccini, Franchetti, Giordano, and Cilèa.

He went to Brissago in March and then prepared *La bohème* in Warsaw during April. A short but unspecified "violent illness" forced his return to Italy,[67] where on 14 April he signed a private contract with Maurice Vaucaire for the drama *La loi coupable,* in which they agreed to split any royalties. Although the Vaucaire collaboration never bore fruit, Leoncavallo composed the orchestral "marche humoristique" *Cortège de Pulcinella* in his customary violet ink during 1903 and also issued a version for piano entitled *Petite marche humoristique.* On 6 July he also signed a contract with Vaucaire and George Mitchell to compose music for an opera to be entitled *Les roses de Noël.*

VILLA MYRIAM

With Sonzogno's money and a desire to remain in the Ticino, Leoncavallo increased his debt purchasing a hillside property in Brissago directly facing Lake Maggiore, surrounded by an oasis of palm trees and flowers. With its mild climate and peaceful atmosphere, Brissago was the ideal location for the composer to distance himself from the stress of Milan and the Italian music world. The Leoncavallos eventually took up residence in an enormous four-story castle-like villa worthy of D'Annunzio, both in its art deco and Moorish architecture. "Villa Myriam" was one of the most sumptuous residences ever built by a composer, reminiscent of a Hollywood set, easily surpassing in extravagance both Puccini's home at Torre del Lago and Verdi's Sant'Agata.[68] Leoncavallo made certain that the villa's interior was both luxurious and comfortable. Agnani was employed to paint a fresco in the villa depicting the youthful Leoncavallos dancing in tuxedo and ball gown—the composer as yet without his mustache. A sandstone statue of Berthe also graced the park. His study contained an upright piano and wooden lectern, where he composed most of his operas standing, sometimes gazing through the numerous large Venetian windows facing the lake. He took up fishing and sailing and was quite adept at cycling all over Brissago, where the inhabitants felt honored to have such a renowned artist in their midst. The home, like the man, was larger than life, but his daily routine was a simple one: a bowl of pasta shortly before retiring around 11:00 p.m. to rise at 5:00 a.m., then composing until noon. He frequently played cards (tresette) in the Osteria del Siro and at the Caffè della Posta, joined by the proprietor and Signor Pedroli, who owned the tobacco factory that supplied Leoncavallo with his omnipresent cigars.[69] Leoncavallo would often nap on a divan during the day fanned by a twelve-year-old servant. He also liked to cook for guests and entertained regularly.

In 1904, Leoncavallo was made an honorary citizen of Brissago. An arch was erected at the village entrance sporting a gold lyre on the festive day for the "glory of Italian music," while three flags accompanied a band brought from Cannobbio. In pictures taken at the event Leoncavallo appears lost in thought, hands perched on his stomach, thumbs facing upward, as the mayor remarked that Lake Maggiore's clear sky, blue water, and smiling women should inspire the composer, who, he continued, was not only a famous musician but also a good person. Upon hearing this, Leoncavallo arose from his seat and embraced the mayor, kissing him on both cheeks. He then proceeded to kiss the baker and the president of the festival committee, as well as his secretary, all to the applause of the gathered onlookers. Some noticed that the composer seemed to have difficulty breathing as he prepared to thank all the attendees. Now sporting his famous mustache, he looked like a combination of Wilhelm II and Victor Herbert. Barely whispering and almost inaudible, Leoncavallo gushed that it was a greater honor to become a citizen of Brissago than be honored by the kaiser. Following the ceremony, he mounted an elegant horse-drawn carriage that took him through the streets, waving like visiting royalty. Flowers were strewn from all sides, the band played, and schoolchildren followed on foot. The festivities concluded that evening with a torch-led procession, before the exhausted composer was allowed to retire. Wearing his customary ankle-length white nightgown, Leoncavallo spent most of the night staring at the ceiling with his arms folded on his chest, unable to sleep, with his dog Pompon at his side. Leoncavallo sometimes joked that Pompon had been the first to hear *Der Roland von Berlin.*

The period 1903–1904 marked Leoncavallo's happiest years, finding him at the apex of his fame, in stark contrast to the approaching precipitous decline of both his career and private life following *Der Roland von Berlin.* The fortune that smiled on him that year continued on 3 February with a production of *Zazà* in Novara and *Pagliacci* in Monte Carlo, which he attended, and culminated on 19 March with the arrival of a telegram from Paris announcing that he would receive the Légion d'Honneur.

Other honors followed, too. When the Gramophone and Typewriter Company (G&T) began making recordings in Milan's Grand Hotel, Leoncavallo was among the first asked to write a composition, which evolved into "Mattinata," his most famous song, beginning with the words "L'aurora di bianca vestita." When Puccini also received a commission, he asked Illica to supply him with lyrics not containing the word "aurora," since "Leone-Cavallo" and Franchetti had already "somberly" composed songs to the rising sun.[70] Puccini ironically suggested Illica write something about the moon to be sung by Caruso, since the tenor would record "Mattinata" to Leoncavallo's piano accompaniment on 8 April. Caruso immortalized the session with a caricature of himself singing Mattinata with the HMV dog listening above.[71]

Close to Brissago was the town of Locarno, where, in 1904, a theater was constructed that was planning a production of *Pagliacci* during April to honor the composer. The orchestra and soloists arrived from Milan to perform, although the chorus consisted of amateurs taken from the Club Locarnese. Leoncavallo directed the production as a favor, whereupon he was rewarded an ornate goblet as well as a gold-encrusted baton. On 5 May, he received a residency permit from the Canton of Ticino in Bellinzona. Showing his recently issued passport (1903), giving his birth year as 1858, he was described as a man of medium height with graying hair and chestnut-colored eyes. He later attributed the "graying" to the stress of completing *Der Roland von Berlin* in Brissago during June and July of 1903.

VISITING THE KAISER

Following a short period spent in Rome, Leoncavallo was finally ready—after ten years—to present Wilhelm II with the vocal score of *Der Roland von Berlin*, in a special edition graced with an ivory carved bas-relief statuette of Roland on its cover.[72] The composer, terrified that it might be stolen, preferred not to use a sleeping compartment for the twenty-eight-hour train journey to Berlin. Berthe remained in Italy, later joining the composer on his second trip for the premiere. Leoncavallo arrived in Berlin on 18 May 1904 clutching the new score, refusing to have anyone help him carry it. Interviewers gathered at the Central Hotel where he was staying and immediately related anything the composer said, printing it in various versions in the next day's newspapers. In one article, the composer was described as reclining on a sofa wearing his blue and white "negligé," eating breakfast, while a young woman measured his feet in order to replace the pair of shoes that Berthe had forgotten to pack. The premiere was somewhat delayed after Wilhelm ordered the Court Opera to be made fireproof following a recent fire in Chicago.

After declaring in Sonzogno's monthly magazine *Varietas* that *Der Roland von Berlin* was his best opera on account of its libretto, the composer seemed less enthusiastic and almost apologetic about his operatic "Sorgenkind" now that he was in Berlin. He attributed the decade's delay in completing the opera to his lengthy research into German history, rather than mentioning the time it had taken to translate first the novel and then the libretto, while simultaneously writing both *La bohème* and *Zazà*. He explained that although he knew as much about the history of Brandenburg and Berlin as a national, the subject, curiously, was only considered to be of "local interest" to most Italian and American critics. By this time, Leoncavallo's name had become almost mythical in Berlin, with *Der Roland von Berlin* discussed for ten years since the *Pagliacci* performances of 1894. Patience was further put to the test when Leoncavallo steadfastly refused all requests to see the music, since the visit only served to present the score to Wilhelm, who then placed it at the Court Opera's disposal.

Leoncavallo, dressed in top hat and tails and accompanied by Hülsen, left for the Neues Palais in Potsdam on 24 May in a horse-drawn carriage. They stopped at Wildpark at noon, where they joined a military reception and outdoor mass. Recognizing the composer as the only guest without a uniform, Wilhelm smiled, relieved that he would soon receive *Der Roland von Berlin*. Hülsen briefly showed Wilhelm the score before handing it back for the official presentation. The kaiser was suitably impressed with its ornate cover. At 1:00 p.m. Leoncavallo was delayed from entering the palace, having left his invitation in his coat pocket hanging in the cloakroom. Wilhelm, when the score was officially presented, thumbed through its pages, honored to read the dedication and content that his name would be forever associated with the work,[73] commenting in French, "This is Roland of Berlin, and you will be the lion of Berlin!"[74] When Wilhelm naively asked Leoncavallo whether he was happy with the work, the composer replied that it was the best of what his art was capable of offering, having taken six years. "Then," Wilhelm said, "it must be perfect, since you are the foremost Italian composer"—a remark that spread like wildfire through the German press.[75] Wilhelm concluded the stilted conversation, drawing away from Leoncavallo with the words: "I will come to admire you! Good bye!"[76] Relieved that everything had gone smoothly, Leoncavallo rewarded himself at a sumptuous buffet, where the empress told him that she was happy the opera was complete, since Wilhelm had spoken so much about the commission.

A few days later, when Leoncavallo conducted *Pagliacci* in Berlin, critics wrote that he was unable to control the orchestra, his style displaying Nordic calm at odds with his music—a judgment frequently echoed throughout his career. He favored stretching the *tempi*—as Mascagni did, too—as if savoring each note of the Nedda/Silvio duet, a lethargic style that hindered both the orchestra and the singers. Fortunately, the musicians' well-rehearsed playing saved him from derailing, and toward the work's conclusion he grew more animated.[77] At the end of the performance he received a gold-plated wreath.[78] Although Leoncavallo's trip had been a public success,[79] German critics, composers, and musicologists felt an aversion to the composer's fame, declaring *Pagliacci* to be nothing more than a mushroom sprung up from the blood-drenched soil of Italian verismo. There were also murmurs in the press that *Der Roland von Berlin* was not worthy of the honor bestowed it. The opera was likened to a specter haunting Berlin's music scene for the past decade, returning annually for the possibility of a premiere. Its "mystical future" seemed almost unreal, while some wondered whether the score contained any music at all![80] The press abounded with articles drenched in nationalism, outraged that an Italian composer had written an opera on a celebrated German theme, thereby precluding any future success.[81]

THE PREMIERE OF *DER ROLAND VON BERLIN*

From Berlin, Leoncavallo headed to Paris, then to Milan for more performances of *Zazà* at the Teatro Lirico,[82] before returning with Berthe to Berlin for *Der Roland von Berlin*'s premiere on 13 December 1904—two months later than scheduled—with Emmy Destinn (Alda), Geraldine Farrar (Eva), Wilhelm Grüning (Henning), Baptist Hoffmann (Rathenow), and Paul Knüpfer (Frederick), conducted by Karl Muck. Presented with sumptuous costumes and sets evoking the era, the opera was a public success. The critics finally had their chance to demoralize the composer, repeatedly asking why an Italian had been honored with the commission in the first place, claiming that he had given birth to a toad, with a style that hadn't progressed since *Pagliacci*. Few mentioned that Droescher's German translation of Leoncavallo's libretto was unsatisfactory, while others felt the story had little to do with the original novel, concentrating as it did solely on the romantic angle. Although called *Der Roland von Berlin*, critics wrote that the statue's significance was incomprehensible,[83] since the work's historical background had not been sincerely felt. The European edition of the *Herald* was just as one-sided, writing: "The chief drawback, from the point of view outside of Germany, is that the subject is too local. The struggle between the Elector Frederick and the rival town of Berlin and Köln [*sic*] is not a matter of great interest to people who are not German." Leoncavallo was personally attacked when Willy Pastor-Berlin wrote in *Die Musik* that the composer had not only failed, but that he had also wasted his best years in idleness rather than working on the score! Although it is known that Wilhelm had resented Leoncavallo's writing *La bohème* and *Zazà* in the interim, the composer was anything but lazy. The work was judged to be an unimportant intermezzo in Leoncavallo's output. Although most reviews were severe, the *Herald* wrote that the critics were "forming a more sober judgment of the piece. There is no doubt that the new opera is a success, without, however, being a triumph like *Pagliacci* or *La bohème*."

Wilhelm, however, was delighted with the work and presented Leoncavallo with the Order of the Crown, and Berthe with a necklace, on 13 December.[84] The Leoncavallos appeared in all the papers and the opera was the talk of the town.[85] Leoncavallo sent Wilhelm a letter in his faulty though fluent French following the premiere, expressing the "profound emotion" he felt upon receiving his decoration, which had left him "paralyzed," unable to fully express his true sentiments. Wilhelm's "very humble and grateful servant"[86] then sent his customary annual good wishes.

Leoncavallo's so-called opportunism in accepting the commission involved the thankless task of adapting a 350-page book containing some forty-eight chapters, which consisted of a thin plot about the political aspects of the Mark Brandenburg. Impressive extended descriptions of nature fail to add any thrust to the novel's static quality. Although many considered Leoncavallo's adaptation unworthy of the novel, it is astonishing that the composer was able to divine an operatic plot from it at all. Transforming an essentially political novel into a banal love story was certainly not the composer's fault, since Henning and Elsbeth were largely unaltered in the opera, while a detailed treatment of Alexis's politics would not have lent itself to the operatic stage. As "operatically unsuitable" as the novel was for reworking as a stage production, the composer created a reasonably solid scenario that was unfortunately unable to create the immortal personages inherent in such works as *Pagliacci* or *Zazà*. Leoncavallo, had the work not been commissioned, would never have composed a *Roland von Berlin* nor included a political element. He was not only berated by destructive criticism but also unjustly condemned by uninformed reviewers accusing him of having the audacity to include a clown named "Bajazzo" (Pagliaccio) in act 1.

They failed to comprehend that this character—incorporated by the composer in his usual quest for literary and historical accuracy—also plays a dominant role in the novel's development. The composer's original Italian version is vastly superior, making a fine welding of words and music that unfortunately fails to find its equal in Droescher's banal and unimaginative translation. Leoncavallo succeeded in refining his craft in this opus—not only overcoming numerous hurdles but also creating one of his most melodic works. When reviewed in the Italian press following its premiere during January 1905, *Der Roland von Berlin* was deemed inconsistent and void of inspiration and originality—a view obviously influenced by the German critics.[87] Leoncavallo nevertheless telegraphed Wilhelm of the work's success, proud that it had also generated interest in his own country, though not making nearly the impression Sonzogno had anticipated. Directors of other European opera houses were also unimpressed with the opera and refused to schedule it, thus dramatically contributing to the composition's short life. The following 12 February Vittorio Emanuele III honored Leoncavallo with the Cavaliere dell'Ordine dei Santi Maurizio e Lazzaro in Rome as a result of Wilhelm's decoration. A gala performance of *Der Roland von Berlin* at the San Carlo in Naples, with the kaiser in attendance, was unfortunately canceled following act 1 when the tenor Enzo Leliva fell ill.

From Naples, Leoncavallo then left for Nice, where *Chatterton*, after further editing, opened at the Théâtre Municipale in Maurice Vaucaire's French translation.[88] The opera was a great critical success according to the newspaper *Petit Niçois*, with elegant members of the audience wiping away a tear or two.

Leoncavallo returned to Berlin in May 1905 to mark *Der Roland von Berlin*'s twenty-fifth performance, in which he acknowledged a thunderous ovation following each act, clutching Emmy Destinn's hand.[89] There was no time for rest after Berlin: *La bohème* was scheduled at the Théâtre Sarah Bernhardt in Paris as part of an Italian season sponsored by Sonzogno. In August the composer's agenda included *Der Roland von Berlin* in Prague and *La bohème* at Berlin's Komische Oper, followed by Kassel for *Zazà*.[90]

In September 1905, a devastating earthquake struck Calabria, foreshadowing the San Francisco quake the following year. Attached to the town of Montalto Uffugo since *Pagliacci*, and recalling his own time spent in nearby Cosenza, Leoncavallo immediately composed a Latin *Ave Maria* in C major for tenor, harp, and harmonium, dedicated to Pope Pius X. His Holiness accepted the proposal with a handwritten letter expressing his "great satisfaction," sending the composer his "paternal affection" and "apostolic benediction."[91] Leoncavallo reprinted the letter when publishing the song at his own expense in Switzerland, with profits reserved for the victims. The composer tirelessly gathered lists of wealthy individuals to whom he could send copies requesting a donation, in order to reconstruct the church of Madonna della Serra. Much of the autumn and early winter was taken up with these activities, in addition to three fundraising concerts. Everyone who corresponded with him during the time received a printed donation request addressed to "all my friends in all countries" for an already mailed composition costing three francs.[92] One of these, Ernst von Hesse-Wartegg, was Minnie Hauk's husband, who resided in Wagner's Villa Triebschen. Leoncavallo immediately sent ten copies, knowing that "your wife will not refuse,"[93] and visited the couple, curious to see Wagner's former home. By November he had raised "30,000 francs" from "sovereigns, princes, prelates, nobles, or businessmen."[94] He also attended the premiere of his *La bohème* in Geneva. Unfortunately, Switzerland further aggravated Leoncavallo's already severely debilitated health, and, by late December, he was informing Vaucaire that he was in fact "gravely ill following a strong hemorrhage," from which he had lost two liters of blood, further weakened by alarming "heart problems."[95]

NOTES

1. Ludwig Karpath, *Begegnungen mit dem Genius* (Vienna: Fiba Verlag, 1934), 370.
2. Later joint manager of the Metropolitan Opera.
3. The omnipresent Marie Renard sang Musette.
4. Edoardo Sonzogno to Leoncavallo, 26 October 1898 (BCL).
5. Puccini was livid that "Leonasino" and "Leonbestia" had succeeded in getting his *La bohème* produced at the Court Opera, while he had to settle for the Theater an der Wien.
6. Leoncavallo, interviewed in *Neues Wiener Journal*, 7 June 1904.
7. Ibid. Leoncavallo was so saddened by the Viennese premiere of his work that he still referred to it in his correspondence six years later.
8. Caruso had already performed Canio at the Teatro Lirico in December 1897.
9. In June 1898, Leoncavallo also contacted the Leipzig publisher Bartholt Senff, offering a piano scherzo after the firm had already purchased his song "A Ninon" to a text by Alfred de Musset.
10. Leoncavallo to Francesco Finelli della Valletta, 13 December 1898 (MTS). The composer may have had his tonsils removed.
11. Jules Massenet to Leoncavallo, 11 December 1898 (BCL). In August, *Pagliacci* played at Livorno's Teatro Politeama, sung by Caruso, while the soprano Elvira Lucca sang Peppe!
12. Leoncavallo also managed to convince Sonzogno to purchase *Chatterton*.
13. *Pagliacci* was now firmly established repertoire following premieres in Parma, Lisbon, Frankfurt, Ljubiana, Zürich, Buenos Aires, London, Düsseldorf, Turin, Berlin, Palermo, Genoa, Naples, Prague, Budapest, Trieste, St. Petersburg, Graz, Vienna, Stockholm, New York, Rome, Zagreb, Malta, Warsaw, Riga, Oporto, Barcelona, Copenhagen, Capetown, Berlin, and Salerno.
14. In March, Leoncavallo also signed a contract with Adolfo Re Riccardi for the Italian rights to Simon and Berton's play *Zazà*.

15. Queen Victoria, RA/VIC/QVJ/29 March 1899 (RAW).
16. Ibid., RA/VIC/QVJ/1 April 1899 (RAW).
17. *Pagliacci* was given for the sixth time at Covent Garden in May.
18. Queen Victoria, RA/VIC/QVG/4 July 1899 (RAW).
19. Leoncavallo to Queen Victoria, RA/PP/VIC/1899/3608 (RAW).
20. Giovanni Zuccani conducted a cast that included Eugenio Giraldoni.
21. Leoncavallo also conducted a private performance of *Pagliacci* on 18 May at the Circle de l'Union Artistique de Paris.
22. Leoncavallo was probably also aware through Illica that Puccini had completed another French subject with Sardou's *Tosca*. Later works possibly inspired by the operatic *Zazà* were Cilèa's *Adriana Lecouvreur* and Puccini's *La rondine*.
23. Arthur Pougin in *Le ménestrel*, 15 October 1899.
24. Leoncavallo's contract, 20 October 1899 (EC).
25. Pierre Louÿs to Leoncavallo, 10 December 1899 (BCL). Although Debussy owned *Aphrodite*'s rights for two years, Camille Erlanger, Arturo Berutti, and Max Oberleithner composed three operas based on the Louÿs work. Mary Garden frequently asked "the Opéra-Comique to stage the Erlanger work." (Konrad Dryden, *Riccardo Zandonai, a Biography* [Frankfurt: Peter Lang, 1999], 73.)
26. During autumn 1900, Puccini also read in the Parisian press that Emile Zola had granted Leoncavallo the rights to his *La Faute de l'abbé Mouret*, although, when he asked the author personally, Zola responded that it was Massenet who had been interested. Puccini had also told Illica to read *Pelléas et Mélisande* even though Maeterlinck personally told him that Debussy was composing it.
27. Leoncavallo to Amintore Galli, undated (BCGR).
28. The libretto was published on 1 November 1900. Editions were also issued in New York for reasons of copyright.
29. Interviewed for a Swedish newspaper, Leoncavallo stated his correct age to be forty-three.
30. Gustavo Macchi wrote in *Il Tempo* on 11 November 1900 that Leoncavallo had progressed considerably from his earlier works "in more ways than one." Opposition came from the *Cronache Musicali*, stating that they found no evolution in Leoncavallo's music, recognizing all his preceding operas.
31. G. P. in *Corriere della Sera*, 11/12 November 1900.
32. Ponchielli's son also wrote an article on *Zazà*, prompting Leoncavallo to respond with a humorous letter warning "Ponchiellone" not to forget his father's operas.
33. These are works for piano and violin. Uncertain what to charge, Leoncavallo told them he had "never been paid less than 1000 lire for a song." Leoncavallo to Smith, 26 December 1900 (MTS).
34. Leoncavallo to Jules Massenet, undated, reprinted in *The Musical Quarterly* 37 no. 3 (1951): 350–51.
35. Coquelin supposedly also told Leoncavallo that Rostand was not in favor of an operatic adaptation.
36. Leoncavallo to Massenet, undated, reprinted in *The Musical Quarterly* 37 (1951): 350–51.
37. Leoncavallo to unidentified recipient, 8 January 1901 (BCL).

38. This supposedly was published with the help of Maurice Vaucaire in 1904 as *Le Masque de Sable*.

39. Leoncavallo signed a contract on 1 January 1901 with Sonzogno for *Der Roland von Berlin*, agreeing that the opera must reach completion within twenty months.

40. Unidentified press clipping, Montreal, Canada (BCL).

41. Ibid.

42. Enrico Toselli wrote Leoncavallo from New York on 3 February 1901 that his 1899 barcarole for piano, *Gondola* (dedicated to Toselli), was "much appreciated and frequently encored" (BCL).

43. Leoncavallo had been against casting Oreste Mieli as Milio, although he relented after hearing the tenor sing Mascagni's *Le maschere* at Sonzogno's bidding.

44. Leoncavallo to unidentified recipient, undated, 2 May 1901 (Y).

45. Ibid. There is no mention in Puccini's correspondence of any such scheduling.

46. Leoncavallo to unidentified recipient, 3 May 1901 (BCL).

47. Capoul created the role of Guy de Kerdrel in Massenet's first opera *La grand-tante* (1867), and later served as stage manager at the Paris Opéra.

48. *La bohème* probably marked Leoncavallo's last attempt at creating a libretto on his own.

49. Leoncavallo to unidentified recipient, 21 June 1901 (Y).

50. Mascagni to Illica, 22 November 1901 in Morini, *P. Mascagni: Epistolario*, I, 240.

51. Using the sobriquet "Paul Bérel."

52. Leoncavallo to unidentified recipient, 2 April 1902 (BCL).

53. Pierre Louÿs to Leoncavallo, 11 May 1902 (BCL).

54. Ibid.

55. The author requested 25 percent for himself and another 25 percent for the librettists, leaving 50 percent for Leoncavallo.

56. Pierre Louÿs to Leoncavallo, 22 July 1902 (BCL).

57. *The Paris Tribune*, 2 July 1902.

58. Ibid.

59. Carlo Zangarini to *La Sera*, September 1901.

60. Leoncavallo to Gualtiero Belvederi, 11 August 1902 (BCL).

61. Ibid.

62. Leoncavallo to Dr. Barth, 26 September 1902 (SIMB).

63. Contract signed 10 October 1902 (EC).

64. Leoncavallo to Francesco Finelli della Valletta, 7 November 1902 (NY).

65. It is uncertain whether he traveled to Marseilles for a highly successful production of *La bohème*.

66. Leoncavallo to Gualtiero Belvederi, 6 January 1903 (BCL).

67. Leoncavallo to unidentified recipient, 13 April 1903 (MTS).

68. The Comune of Brissago was unable to furnish any documents related to the villa's construction or its name. Construction work continued until autumn 1905.

69. The factory is still in operation.

70. Puccini to Illica, 10 February 1904 in Gara, *Carteggi Pucciniani*, 190.

71. This was Caruso's sixth recording session, in which he also performed Nadir's "Je crois entendre encore" from Bizet's *Les pêcheurs de perles*.

72. The libretto was published in Georg Droescher's German translation.

73. "Seiner Majestät dem deutschen Kaiser und König von Preußen, Wilhelm II. In tiefster Ehrfurcht und Dankbarkeit gewidmet! R. Leoncavallo." ("To his Majesty, the German Emperor and King of Prussia, Wilhelm II, dedicated with great respect and gratitude. R. Leoncavallo.")

74. "C'est le Roland de Berlin et vous seres le lion de Berlin," *Kölnische Volkszeitung*, 25 May 1905.

75. *Berliner Tageblatt*, 24 May 1905.

76. "Je viendrai pour vous admirer! Au revoir!"

77. "Ritardando" is the most frequently used word in the press when describing his style.

78. Emmy Destinn's Santuzza in *Cavalleria rusticana* followed *Pagliacci* "for those who remained." *Berliner Tageblatt*, 27 May 1905.

79. The press also reported that Leoncavallo had been invited for lunch in the Berlin Zoo, where a military band "honored" him by playing selections from *Pagliacci*, asking whether they would have to pay royalties since the composer was a member of the German Society of Composers. Nothing was considered too banal to be published if it involved Leoncavallo.

80. *Hannoverscher Courier*, 20 May 1905.

81. The debate concerning Leoncavallo's commission was so popular that a parody was written called *Die Bajazzi* by Benno and Eduard Jacobson.

82. Zazà was sung by Emma Carelli, while Titta Ruffo later recalled in his autobiography that he had obtained one of his "biggest successes" as Cascart, repeating the aria "Zazà, piccola zingara" three times. Performances would have continued if the baritone had not been called to sing in Russia. Titta Ruffo, *La mia parabola* (Milan: Fratelli Treves, 1937), 223.

Mascagni also wrote Leoncavallo during this time, asking if he was composing an opera called *Amica*, since his version would premiere the following year to a libretto by Paul de Choudens, who would later supply Leoncavallo with the libretto to *Maïa*.

83. The statue's significance is also extremely vague in the original novel.

84. Emmy Destinn received a bracelet with Wilhelm's initials in sapphires and the male singers received rings with the kaiser's monogram.

85. Berthe was dressed in black, holding a scarf, while the composer—as was customary throughout his career—never looked directly at the camera.

86. Leoncavallo to Kaiser Wilhem II, undated (GSPK).

87. The cast included Rina Giachetti, Margot Kaftal, Enzo Leliva, and Francesco Maria Bonini, conducted by Leopoldo Mugnone. Act 2 was preferred to act 3.

88. Leoncavallo had signed a contract on 14 January granting Vaucaire 15 percent of the French version's royalties. That was raised to 30 percent when the copyright of Vigny's play re-entered the public domain in 1913.

89. While in Berlin, he also presented Karl Muck and the orchestra with a photo showing him composing at his lectern in Brissago, inscribed to the conductor's genial direction. By the end of 1905, Berlin had witnessed thirty-nine performances of *Der Roland von Berlin* and an astounding 259 of *Pagliacci*.

90. Although these performances were included in Leoncavallo's agenda, there is no documentation proving that he actually attended.

91. Pope Pius X to Leoncavallo, undated (AMI).

92. Leoncavallo to unidentified recipient, 13 November 1905 (SLD).

93. Leoncavallo to Ernst von Hesse-Wartegg, 26 October 1905 (Y).

94. Leoncavallo to unidentified recipient, 13 November 1905 (SLD).

95. Leoncavallo to Maurice Vaucaire, 27 November 1905 (BCL).

· 7 ·

Sardou–Leoncavallo

1906–1911

$\mathcal{B}$erthe accompanied Leoncavallo to Rapallo's Grand Hotel Savoia for an extended stay during January and February, seeking to mend the composer's feeble health. While there, he wrote Maurice Vaucaire concerning the possibility of an operatic adaptation of Victorien Sardou's play *Les premieres armes de Figaro*, to be called *La jeunesse de Figaro*, which dealt with the story of Cherubino. Although numerous music encyclopedias list the work as having been performed in 1906, it was in fact never written. Leoncavallo initially mentioned the possibility of a collaboration with Sardou in a letter to Vaucaire dated 2 July 1903. Therein he stated that his contract required that he complete *La jeunesse de Figaro* by 1908, although he assured Vaucaire that it could be finished one year earlier. He again wrote Vaucaire on 21 July 1903 that he was enthralled with the idea of the work and had already begun planning to compose a Spanish malaguena accompanied by castanets for inclusion in the opera. In October, Leoncavallo asked Vaucaire to supply him with a copy of Sardou's play. However, near the end of 1904, Leoncavallo still remained undecided whether he should in fact begin work on *La jeunesse de Figaro* or on *Roses de Noël*. By August 1905, he was waiting for the libretto to reach completion, although he failed to hear anything from Sardou. It seems that the only publisher Leoncavallo was capable of interesting in the project was Joanin in Paris. Realizing that he would never be able to compose either *Jeunesse de Figaro* or *Roses de Noël*, Leoncavallo wrote Vaucaire that his health was so debilitated that the doctors had ordered complete rest for at least ten months. The year 1905 concluded with Leoncavallo's pinning his hopes on Berlin for a possible *Jeunesse de Figaro* premiere, even hoping that it could be written by 1906. The final chapter in the work's agonized existence appears in a letter the composer again wrote to Vaucaire from Rapallo on 3 February 1906, stating that Sardou was uninterested in signing a contract until viewing the completed work.

Irritated, Leoncavallo refused to enter into an agreement "like a blind dog," and, although little, if indeed anything, had been composed, Leoncavallo now hoped that Sardou would interest the prince of Monaco in premiering the work in Monte Carlo.[1] In fact, he was still willing to "complete" the score by the end of 1908. Finally, on 25 March 1907, Leoncavallo officially renounced the *Jeunesse de Figaro* project.

However, during 1906 Leoncavallo was still writing the Leipzig publishers Breitkopf & Härtel that Sardou was willing to furnish a libretto and that the opera would be printed by Heugel.[2] The German firm naturally wished to see the completed score before making a decision for the German, Austrian, Hungarian, and Swiss rights. Leoncavallo refused to show them anything because nothing had yet been written, claiming that they "lacked confidence" in a composer who had already produced many works and was thus "no great risk" for them,[3] further stating that they would lose out to another firm if no immediate decision was made. Applying his usual tactics, Leoncavallo implied that a second German publisher was willing to accept the work "immediately," even though Heugel was supposedly considering buying the rights for all countries. When Breitkopf & Härtel scribbled "Bravo!" in the letter's margin, it was obvious that Leoncavallo's threats were not taken seriously. He wrote again to them twelve days later from Rapallo's Grand Hotel Savoia, that Heugel had offered fifty thousand francs, including rights to all countries[4] and that Breitkopf & Härtel should take up the matter with Sardou himself, adding "confidentially" that the author had supposedly also agreed to sell the British as well as North American rights for an additional twenty-five thousand francs.[5] Leoncavallo implored the firm not to keep him in "suspense" for too long.[6] The story grew preposterous by mid-February, when Leoncavallo again wrote Breitkopf & Härtel that "in full accordance" with his collaborators Vaucaire and Sardou he had broken off negotiations with Heugel, since they had only agreed to buy the rights to all countries rather than a select few![7] Breitkopf & Härtel immediately pulled back, sensing Leoncavallo's insincerity, while Leoncavallo sought to convince them that a "Sardou–Leoncavallo" collaboration merited any price. Already slated to conduct *Pagliacci* in Madrid during March, he now told the firm that he was going there to "study the country's music" for *Jeunesse de Figaro*[8] and would return to Berlin on 7 May, when they could give him their final decision.[9]

Leoncavallo left for Madrid, sending a postcard signed "Roger" to Jeanne Puel on 14 March. The *Pagliacci* cast starred Francisco Viñas as Canio, and the composer's visit included lunches with the Italian ambassador and a reception by Infanta Isabella, who greeted him with "exquisite" kindness.[10] On 1 April he conducted a concert at the Teatro Real consisting of the overtures from *Der Roland von Berlin* and *Chatterton*, together with *Cortège de Pulcinella* and the omnipresent *Ave Maria* sung by Inés Salvador.[11] In a letter dated 3 April to ~

the conductor Luigi Mancinelli he lauded Spain's hospitality, and Mancinelli subsequently asked him to conduct *Pagliacci* in Lisbon.[12]

Always seeking to improve his finances, Leoncavallo embarked on his first tour of that year on 16 April, beginning in Graz with *Chatterton*, hoping that his involvement would generate international interest in the opera's renaissance. The critical failure of *Der Roland von Berlin* marked a drastic change in Leoncavallo's fortunes. Increased financial pressure, growing artistic uncertainty, and fatigue caused by years of struggle began taking their toll on the composer's patience and inspiration to create lengthy, intricate works. *Der Roland von Berlin* would be his last major effort, and, following its short-lived and disappointing career, the composer sought shorter and less demanding works, thereby increasing the dichotomy between pre– and post–*Der Roland von Berlin* operas. Although *Zazà, La bohème*, and *Pagliacci* were constantly performed, revenues went directly to Sonzogno to fulfill the publisher's loan, which left Leoncavallo only miserably compensated by strenuous tours, and which would result, finally, in the loss of his beloved property.

From Graz, Leoncavallo proceeded on to Vienna, Munich, Berlin, Hamburg, Amsterdam, The Hague, Rotterdam, Brussels, Strasbourg, Metz, Breslau, Nuremberg, Konstanz, and numerous other European cities, with the singers Augusto Barbaini, Giuseppe La Puma, and Amina Matini. Piero Schiavazzi was also part of the tour, appearing in *Zazà, Der Roland von Berlin*, and *Pagliacci*. The tenor described the composer as a calm and reflective individual, in contrast to Mascagni's nervousness.

Leoncavallo, with the tour finally behind him, conducted the first of three performances of the ever-popular *Zazà* with Emma Carelli at Florence's Teatro Verdi on 5 May. He continued to hope there would also be a chance to present *Der Roland von Berlin* in Nice, though none of his letters brought about the desired effect. During May, he also sought investors to support and realize his brother Leone's desire to construct a theater in Paris near the Champs-Elysées.

He was furious in July after reading in the Italian press that Maurice Vaucaire was supplying Puccini with an adaptation of Louÿs's *La femme et le pantin*. Holding the librettist responsible for his rival's interest in a Spanish subject,[13] Leoncavallo felt betrayed and unable to trust Vaucaire. This conflict now also made Leoncavallo decide to "think twice about *Figaro*."[14] He reasoned that not having a publisher like Ricordi who would concern himself with creating both success for his clients as well as fiascoes for his competition convinced him that his own works had to "defend themselves against publishers and journalists" alike.[15] The Leoncavallo-Puccini feud resumed, with the former fretting that Puccini was once again walking in his footsteps concerning his Spanish opera: "I would not have cared had it been for a French composer, but for Signor Puccini with his and Ricordi's *camorra* (that is what I fear and not the products of his talent)."[16] Although Leoncavallo spoke of *La jeunesse de Figaro* during his American tour, it was possibly in the hope of finding interest on the part of a theater, at which point he could compose the score.

"AS MASSIVE AS HUGO, AS IMPRESSIVE AS BISMARCK, AND AS HANDSOME AS BYRON"

With slim prospects for *Der Roland von Berlin* and earnings in Europe, Leoncavallo, seeking to revive his career, was persuaded to travel through the United States from October until December 1906 in a tour arranged by Rudolph Aronson and managed by John Cort and S. Kronberg. Seven singers took part, in addition to the seventy-five piece "La Scala orchestra."[17] The musicians departed on the steamship Princess Irene from Genoa. Leoncavallo left from Bremen on the Kaiser Wilhelm der Große on 24 September 1906, with his secretary and general factotum, Carlo Macchi. Leoncavallo's colleague, Karl Muck, was also on board with his wife, heading for his new post at the Boston Symphony Orchestra, as was the Metropolitan Opera's Arturo Vigna, returning from Italy following "conferences with the composers of the new Italian operas to be produced at the Metropolitan."[18] Yvette Guilbert and the Minneapolis violinist Heinrich Hovel—who tried to converse with Leoncavallo in a mixture of Italian and English—made the voyage more pleasing, even though he discourteously remarked that in the United States ladies "must listen without looking" at Leoncavallo in order "to prevent any heart-breaking disappointment" since the composer was "short and fat and round-about."[19] Aronson had succeeded in stimulating the press's anticipation prior to Leoncavallo's arrival, with every newspaper filled with Leoncavallo's biography, albeit modified to suit the occasion. One U.S. newspaper sported the headline that the composer was "as massive as Hugo, as impressive as Bismarck and as handsome as Byron."[20] Not only was his *Ave Maria* used promotionally, but he had also composed a short piano piece entitled *Viva l'America!*, a mixture of "Yankee Doodle" and "Dixie" dedicated to President Theodore Roosevelt, to whom he planned to present it personally.[21]

RODERICO LEON VAVELLO'S ARRIVAL

The first press photos show Leoncavallo on board the Kaiser Wilhelm docking in New York on 2 October, holding a bouquet of roses in his left hand and arm-in-arm with an embarrassed Karl Muck. Playing the *charmeur*, Leoncavallo soon spoke of American women: "There is a freedom about them, a freedom of action and thought that makes them different from all others. They are so well poised and yet so stirring and strong."[22] Over two hundred people from New York's Italian community waited to greet "Roderico Leon Vavello" [*sic*], while Aronson was also there "to receive Cavello" [*sic*].[23] The composer pointed to the sky and the shores of Staten Island, exclaiming "Splendide! Magnifique! Perhaps I shall find a theme over here for an opera!"[24] He was also greeted by Dante del Papa of the Verdi Memorial Committee, to whom he confided that he had been dreaming of coming to America for years, and was saddened that Berthe was not present, since the voyage was not nearly as strenuous as he had led her to believe: "She was afraid of the ocean voyage. . . . I was also somewhat dubious about it. I think we would have come to America long ago had it not been for that feeling."[25] He then turned to the star-struck reception, declaring his delight in coming to such a discerning country: "I know the Americans are extremely intelligent and that they appreciate good music. New York is almost as big as Milan from an Italian standpoint, and I shall feel at home, I know. . . . I find the entrance to New York even more beautiful than the Bay of Naples or the approach to Constantinople."[26] His speech as quoted in yet another newspaper was more to the point:

> My visit to America has more significance to me than a mere tour. It is my purpose while here to get the material for at least one opera based on American life. I want to go to the theatres, to see the people and meet and talk with them, to learn their ideas and ideals, and see if I can capture them in words and music. I have not studied as much American literature as I could wish but believe, after all, that it will be better for me to learn at first hand by meeting the people.[27] It is a new country, with new ideals and without the prejudices that are so apt to hamper one in the older countries.[28]

He also touched on verismo, promoting *Pagliacci*. "I wish to picture humanity as it is. The cry of a child, the sorrow of a woman, the great problems of life appeal to me far more than the contrived plots many think necessary for opera. It is such a life that I seek whenever I can, a real life that I hope to find in this new country, which is pulsating with it."[29] He added that he was working on *La jeunesse de Figaro*, having already completed two acts (!) and hoping for an American premiere, while negotiations were also underway with Oscar Hammerstein to have *Zazà* produced at the Manhattan Opera House that winter.

The composer was described as being "short but of powerful build," with a "neck of tremendous size, bushy hair, brushed well from his forehead, and a heavy black moustache," coupled with an engaging personality.[30]

> His tremendous head is made more tremendous by the big fat neck, at the bottom of which is the widest and lowest of turn down collars. His necktie is bound by a winding, gold scarf-holder. His shoulders are gigantic and

powerful, his chest great, but his legs are short. His hands are fat, but as he speaks expression enters into them, and they become the hands of a musician, the thumb being particularly long and eloquent. He speaks in a deep voice, deliberately and with emphasis . . . latent humor lurks in his eyes.[31]

Leoncavallo truthfully explained Wilhelm's "collaboration" on *Der Roland von Berlin*, although many newspapers insisted on the hearsay for publicity. Others wrote that he was busy with a Garibaldi opera called *The Red Shirt* (*Camicia rossa*) and just about to begin work on *I Medici!*[32] "While constantly looking up on the way at the big buildings and exclaiming at the wonders of America," Leoncavallo was brought to the Astor Hotel, where he would prepare for his first engagement on 8 October at Carnegie Hall.[33] The press reminded its readers that Leoncavallo had written more important things than *Pagliacci*, "and the chief feature of his mission here as composer-conductor is to make these works better known."[34] This was his reply when asked to comment on the future of Italian music:

> I do not believe . . . that the Italian school will be more Germanized than it is at present. I do not think our current tendency is to forsake the natural course of development, which our musical traditions, our language, and our stage marked out for us. To Wagner all composers stand in debt, of course. He has added to the sum total of musical knowledge, and we all profit by it. Moreover, I feel convinced that he carried his operatic form to the loftiest point attainable. . . . But we Italians, despite Verdi's example in *Falstaff*, have no reason to slavishly imitate him. I believe our duty lies in another direction. Our language must, after all, with our inherited notions of melody, guide us in the way we shall go. The German tongue suggests a style of musical declamation, the Italian one of broad, flowing phrases. . . . No, we have a distinctive field to work in, . . . and we will be wise to keep within it.[35]

Leoncavallo then stated in the *New York Telegraph* that, because of Wagner's influence,

> so little in the way of successful music-drama has come out of Germany of late. . . . The Germans have not dared to be themselves. They have imitated servilely a genius and style they cannot reach. In Italy it has been different . . . we of the younger school have worked out our destinies for ourselves. . . . Wagner deals in gods, heroines, Valkyries who fly through the air, argumentative dragons, and transmogrified toads. These things I feel to be beyond my sympathy. . . . I wish to get nearer to men. . . . The school of opera to which I belong. . . . I can characterize as the "verist." I use the phrase verist instead of "realist," a word which unfortunately has become associated with the gutter.[36]

After New York's *German Herald* criticized Leoncavallo's presumptuous interview, he presented his Carnegie Hall program, consisting of selections taken from *Zazà, Chatterton, I Medici, Der Roland von Berlin,* the new *Ave Maria,* the *Pagliacci* Nedda/Silvio duet, and concluding with the "Viva l'America!" march, which was lauded by the *New York Herald*:

> For the tune of the old "Yankee Doodle" was no more music than its rhyming words are poetry. All this has been changed, however, by the genius of Leoncavallo, who, inspired by the reforming spirit of President Roosevelt, has taken our musically impossible "Yankee Doodle" and out of it created a thing of beauty and a joy to the ear forever.[37]

Leoncavallo's "La Scala" orchestra also appeared to be self-conducting:

> It was a somewhat difficult task to secure La Scala's great orchestra for even a brief American tour. Probably no one but Leoncavallo could have induced the directors to make such an unexampled concession. . . . Signor Leoncavallo is to conduct at both concerts—a concession to popular curiosity, since La Scala's orchestra needs no conductor in works of the Italian repertoire.[38]

Most reviews were poor, describing the artists as

> a company of singers which could only bring back memories of the many operatic wrecks that have been stranded on our shores by winds blowing from Mexico and South America. . . . Ah, that tenor! Who will forget his tearfully vociferous "mai più," his stony stare across the footlights, and his deathly grip of his crush-hat? His name must not perish—it is Barbaini . . . .[39] The eight singers heard last evening (and applauded ecstatically by an audience largely Italian) are hopelessly below what New York demands.[40]

The composer seemed forlorn surrounded by semi-professional musicians; "dignified," "pathetic," and "sincere" were frequently used to describe his stage appearance:

> As for Signor Leoncavallo, he seemed strangely out of place in the surroundings in which his enthusiastic countrymen on the stage and in the stalls had put him. A dignified, earnest, importunate, modest, serious-minded musician. . . . Whatever may be the fate of the seemingly quixotic undertaking which has brought him to our shore. . . .[41] His orchestra, said to be that of La Scala, Milan, is of inferior quality, with strings and wind instruments often at variance as to pitch. . . . As a conductor, he makes no pretense of musical eccentricity, directing his orchestra calmly, indulging in no frantic gestures.[42]

Fortunately, some reviews heralded a triumphal debut:

> When the maestro stepped on the stage, he was not long left in ignorance of
> how the New World felt toward the composer of *Pagliacci*. Long continued
> cheers and applause forced him to bow at least a dozen times before he
> was enabled to signal the start to his orchestra. . . . The audience exhibited
> a voracious appetite for encores, and nearly every number on the program
> was repeated. Leoncavallo, of course, reaped the lion's share of applause, and,
> when a veritable shower of wreaths, bouquets, and floral baskets rained on
> him at the close of the concert, the uproar in the house was deafening.[43]

Leoncavallo's second concert took place on 9 October in New Jersey
(Krueger's Auditorium in Newark), before he returned on the 10th for his
second Carnegie Hall appearance, facing numerous empty seats due to singers
that "would not be tolerated in Leghorn or Pisa and an orchestra which cannot count two in a bar . . . the composer stood alone, a dignified figure in the
concert, pathetic because of his dignity."[44] The *New York Tribune* wrote "there is
so much that is admirable about this musician, so much sincerity of purpose,
so much simple dignity of bearing and unaffectedness, that it is almost pitiable
that his appeal to the music lovers of this American metropolis should elicit so
gelid a response."[45] Even "Viva l'America!" was labeled an "ill conceived and
ill constructed fantasy . . . and as sorry a tribute to the nation and its head as it
is to the talent of its author."[46] After appearing in Baltimore and Philadelphia,
Leoncavallo returned to New York for his third and final Carnegie Hall concert on 14 October.

The strenuous tour continued during the same month in Massachusetts
(October 20–22); Connecticut (October 23–24); Ohio (October 26–30),
where the approaching "Leoncavallo Opera" train killed two railway workers
upon entering Springfield; and Michigan (October 31). The troupe was now
advertised as "the largest Operatic Concert Company that ever toured America
. . . there are nearly 100 people, traveling on their own special, Grand Opera
Pullman Train, eight cars of which are required for scenery, costumes, musicians," and "instruments."[47]

"VIVA L'AMERICA!" AND THE "LA SCALA ORCHESTRA"

Aronson informed the White House on 29 October that he would personally
bring Leoncavallo's "Viva l'America!" to Washington on the 30th. It was etched
on heavy vellum and bound in silk with an embossed design by John Frew.
President Roosevelt replied that he was "delighted that a composer of the position of Leoncavallo should do me this great honor, and I shall forward to him

my letter of thanks."[48] The president wrote the same day, saying he hoped to congratulate Leoncavallo in person.[49]

Tito Ricordi was in New York during part of October to discuss the upcoming premiere of Puccini's *Madama Butterfly* at the Metropolitan Opera. Hearing that Leoncavallo was touring with the "La Scala orchestra," he immediately sent a letter to the *New York Sun* on 12 October stating that "the La Scala orchestra as a permanent organization never existed. [The] La Scala orchestra exists only for the purpose of opera and only when [the] La Scala Theatre is open. The players are simply engaged for the season, and when the theatre is closed no one who has played there can claim to be a member of [the] La Scala orchestra."[50] The press sided with Leoncavallo, claiming that "Mr. Ricordi nowhere in his letter states that the members of Mr. Leoncavallo's present orchestra have not played in the Scala Theatre. We here pay attention to Mr. Ricordi's letter because it was unnecessary, if not disingenuous."[51] Aronson retaliated in a letter to *Musical America* on 3 November, arguing that "Signor Leoncavallo states that all the members of his orchestra now on tour in this country have played at La Scala, and, hence, the management has a perfect right to announce that fact to the public."[52]

According to the *Boston Post*, Leoncavallo greeted John Philip Sousa a few days later in Boston, having first met the American composer in Moscow years earlier.[53] After explaining to the press that he was at work on *La jeunesse de Figaro*, hoping "to have it completed before very long," Leoncavallo presented a concert at Boston's Symphony Hall, where his physical appearance once again astounded.

> He does not speak a word of English but converses fluently in French. . . . Signor Leoncavallo is a rather stout specimen of the Italian race. He has thick black hair, cut a la pompadour, and has but few of the Latin characteristics. He more resembles a Russian were it not for his liquid tones when he speaks . . . [being] exceedingly cordial.[54]

Chaos reigned when the tour reached Waterbury, Connecticut, where they played in a rented hall.

> There were no programs, no ushers, no ticket takers. . . . The manager, when he arrived here, hastily enlisted a force of local amateurs and, with the aid of his Third Avenue assistant property man, who helped take tickets supported by a nasty looking cigar, he managed to worry through the evening and count up his money.[55]

The concert was a success although only two-thirds full:

> Three encores weren't considered too many for any of the selections . . . the audience was a peculiarly enthusiastic one. . . . A delay occasioned by

the stupid management of the affair did not tend to help matters. Finally the orchestra trooped in from one of the vacant offices on the Grand Street side of the hall, . . . and after a short delay the maestro stepped forward. He is a heavy, rotund figure, an ordinary middle-aged Italian who had not kept himself down to weight either by dietary abstinence or routine exercise. . . . As a conductor he gives one the impression of being easy and negligent and feeling that the orchestra is going to play with proper tempo and aroused spirit anyway.[56]

In Baltimore, Leoncavallo was described as

a man of great culture and strong intellect. He is a poet as well as a musician, and in both arts he reveals the grasp of a profound thinker. Mascagni belongs to a different type. In Leoncavallo there is a dash of the refined and diplomatic Frenchman; in the composer of *Cavalleria rusticana* one perceives, within as well as without, the impulsiveness, the impetuosity, the strong racial temperament of the full-blooded Italian . . . our local critics may differ as to the merits of *Pagliacci* and the other operatic selections performed at Leoncavallo's concert, but if any of them should ever write music half so good we shall have reason to feel very proud of home talent.[57]

Leoncavallo showed "visible evidence of fatigue"[58] upon reaching Chicago's Orchestra Hall, where he

encored the whole concert. . . . It is very delightful in these blasé times, to see such enthusiasm. . . . That the Italian master had to play his program twice over was not alone a tribute to the excellence of his music, but it demonstrated that there are still left to us a great many people who take their artistic pleasures with considerable intensity.[59]

Leoncavallo also granted an interview at Milwaukee's Hotel Blatz while being shaved, expressing his belief that the time was ripe for an American operatic composer to win European popularity:

Your country has not paid the attention to music that the old world has and for this reason is slower to take on the spirit of composition. But what has been done shows that in every phase of musical composition the American musician has the instincts and emotions of the true master. . . . Soon these attributes will be assembled in the one great American musician, and then the world will acknowledge that the American composer has arrived to bear his European brothers company.[60]

Leoncavallo also lauded Milwaukee for its pasta, enjoying "the first *real* macaroni he had ever eaten in an American hotel."[61] The composer's every move was documented in the press, from his attending the musical comedy *The Van-*

derbilt Cup at the Metropolitan Theatre,[62] to his difficulties with English ("So difficile this angliss"). Photographs of this "big son of Italy" appeared in all the papers, with Italians and Americans alike greeting the composer holding flags from both countries.[63]

The case of the "La Scala Orchestra" was still being discussed during November, although it now seemed obvious that the idea had originated from John Cort, being the great mistake of a

> scheming impresario, with fancied financial possibilities that brought the composer to this country. . . . It seems the impresario had no other mind than gain. . . . Leoncavallo is evidently a good composer, but he is evidently in the hands of fakirs. . . . It is good to have one paper in the city which is not afraid to tell the truth about humbugs of this kind, which, by mendacious and misleading notices and ambiguous and untruthful advertisements swindle the public. John Cort ought to blush with shame.[64]

A final article signed by Leoncavallo appeared on 19 November defending the "La Scala Orchestra":

> A wrong impression exists that my organization is the only La Scala orchestra of Milan. There is no fixed La Scala orchestra, as there is a symphony orchestra in Boston. In Italy today there are probably more than 200 professors who have at one time or another been members of the La Scala orchestra. . . . When Mr. Cort's representatives approached me with a view to making an American tour, I told them that it was impossible to bring over the orchestra in a body. The opera season at Milan opens at Christmas and ends in April, and if the tour had been arranged for May I could have then brought the members who played in the orchestra last season. Every musician who has ever formed part of the La Scala [orchestra] has a right to lay claim to the fact, and the orchestra which I now have is composed exclusively of La Scala players. Some of them may have played in the orchestra three or four or five years ago, while others were members of it last season, but they are all La Scala players. It is true that they have been criticized from certain sources, but my musicians are regarded as sufficiently capable for orchestra directors to steal six of my players from me since we landed in this country, and twenty-seven of those who are with me now have contracts which will keep them in this country after our tour.[65]

THE MONKEY-HOUSE INCIDENT

The press also asked Leoncavallo to comment on Caruso's so-called monkey-house incident. During his stay at the Savoy Hotel for his engagement at the Metropolitan, the tenor visited the Central Park Zoo, where he was arrested when a young woman named Hannah Graham accused him of trying to molest her in the monkey house, although she failed to appear when the case was taken up in court. Afraid of the impact on his American career, Caruso must have appreciated Leoncavallo's response, in which he stated that the attacks were

> malicious and absurd for any sane man to consider or to discuss with dignity with any intelligent person. So magnificent an artist, so cultured a gentleman, so fine a scholar, would never stoop to such depths of infamy and indecent action as to commit the immoralities with which he is charged. It was either blackmail or else that woman, what's her name, desired some cheap notoriety.[66]

Because the tour lasted longer than originally planned, Leoncavallo was eventually unable to meet with President Roosevelt. The White House was not informed until very late, with the press announcing on 28 November that the president had "cut his visit to Panama short in order to be present in Washington when Leoncavallo and his artists give their concert there."[67] Leoncavallo concluded the tour in Muncie, Indiana, supposedly including an excerpt from *La jeunesse de Figaro*.[68] He spent a few days in New York City after the tour's orchestra and soloists had returned to Italy, attending *Lucia di Lammermoor* with Caruso and Sembrich at the Metropolitan Opera on 12 December, followed by a farewell banquet. The composer finally returned to Italy on the 14th, after traveling twenty-seven thousand miles in eight weeks, leaving the stage free for the premiere of Puccini's *Manon Lescaut* at the Metropolitan Opera. Leoncavallo's efforts had brought questionable results, and, later, Puccini refrained from acknowledging his own opera's success following act 3, not wishing to appear "charlatanesque" like Leoncavallo.[69]

Although failing to secure a contract or commission for a new work in the United States, Leoncavallo at least had *Zazà*, *La bohème*, and *Pagliacci* firmly ensconced in the international repertory, with *Zazà* even performed in Havana during January 1907 with outstanding soloists accompanied by a "mediocre" orchestra.[70] Emma Carelli, who now specialized in the role, also performed the part at Trieste's Teatro Comunale in February.

RETURNING TO ITALY

In September 1907 Leoncavallo tried to interest Titta Ruffo in a baritone version of *Chatterton*, recalling Massenet's transposition of *Werther* for Mattia Battistini.[71] Ruffo had already sung Chatterton's aria, lowered, during a Parisian concert in 1905, and it now only remained a question of transposing the entire work, in the hope that the artist could promote an opera that had completely vanished. Taking a personal interest in Ruffo, who was due to perform Ambroise Thomas's *Hamlet* at Milan's Teatro Lirico on 16 October, Leoncavallo sought to secure the sets Sarah Bernhardt had used when portraying Shakespeare's prince in France. He eventually designed his own production from memory when he failed to receive the requested photos. Leoncavallo's numerous letters to Ruffo are filled with the admiration he felt for one of the few artists he addressed with the informal "tu." After Ruffo had been unable to perform in Leoncavallo's yearly benefit concert aiding the community of Brissago, he again turned his attention to *Camicia rossa* to a text by Arturo Colautti (1851–1914), who had written the libretti to *Fedora*, *Adriana Lecouvreur*, and *Gloria*, premiering that same year at La Scala.

In the meantime, Rudolf Aronson tried to convince Leoncavallo to embark on a tour of California, Mexico, and Cuba, even seeking to generate Porfirio Diaz's interest, while the composer wrote the senator Antonio Marinuzzi, Gino Marinuzzi's father, requesting financial aid, since there was hardly any money left following the U.S. tour, thanks to Aronson. Claiming that he should have received "150,000 francs" from the tour, he added that his operas were not being produced in Italy, not even "out of curiosity."[72] The bleakness of his financial future stood in stark contrast to the giant statues of Roland and Zazà recently erected in Villa Myriam's park.

Transposing *Chatterton* turned out to be "overwhelming work,"[73] and although it would represent the opera's third revision, the composer hoped that the baritone would earn a "phenomenal triumph in the role."[74] When act 1 was completed by the end of October, Leoncavallo asked Ruffo where he should send the score before tackling the remaining two acts (which were never completed, due to the artist's increasing disinterest).[75]

MAÏA

Carlo Sabajno had conducted the first complete recording of *Pagliacci* for the G & T Company during June 1907. Why Sabajno was chosen rather than the composer—who was only asked to supervise the sessions—with Antonio Paoli as Canio instead of Caruso, remains a mystery. Giuseppina Huguet immortalized her Nedda when the entire opera was recorded on twenty-one sides, with sound considered excellent for that time. Leoncavallo was proudly photographed with the cast, holding Sabajno's arm, wearing a panama hat and white shoes. The *Pagliacci* recording would be a great success for HMV. In fact, the company also signed a contract with the composer demonstrating interest in complete versions of *Chatterton*, *Maïa*, and *Camicia Rossa*, offering to pay a thousand francs per act. A slightly abridged recording of *Chatterton*, also for HMV, would be captured for posterity and poor sales during May 1908. The composer then sought relaxation during July on the beach at Bagni Margherita in Varazze, where a series of photographs captured him in a multitude of poses, including mid-air.

Leoncavallo's relations with Casa Sonzogno changed when Edoardo retired, leaving the company to his two nephews Lorenzo, the new artistic director, and Riccardo, the business manager.[76] The composer managed to convince Lorenzo ("Renzo") to accept the idea for *Camicia rossa* as well as an operatic version of *Prometheus* (*Prometeo*) for Titta Ruffo, to replace the now stifled *Chatterton*.[77] When Lorenzo requested that *Camicia rossa* be completed by 1909, Leoncavallo wrote Colautti asking that he not mention *Prometeo* to anyone, hoping to present the work "like a bomb" three months after *Camicia rossa*—two bombs that never detonated.[78] Leoncavallo signed a contract for *Camicia rossa* on 1 August 1908, planning to premiere the work for the opening of Mexico's Teatro Nacional in 1910.

The first mention of Leoncavallo's return to verismo with the opera *Maïa*, a bucolic tragedy set in Southern France, to a libretto by the composer's French publisher Paul de Choudens, is in a letter dated 25 March 1907.[79] The reason for Leoncavallo's return to verismo was, as the composer himself stated, "to earn money."[80] Leoncavallo asked Ruffo whether he would be free to create the role of Torias, hoping to premiere the work in Monte Carlo. He also requested that Georg Droescher provide a German translation, should the Berlin Court Opera wish to mount a production. Considering *Maïa* to be "short and uncomplicated," he hoped that Droescher, creator of the hopelessly stilted German translation of the *Der Roland von Berlin* libretto, would agree, since the opera was "destined to be reproduced following its premiere at the Berlin Opera."[81] Leoncavallo also secured an Italian version of Choudens's libretto from the poet and librettist Angelo Nessi, when there were as yet no prospects of performing the work in France. It cannot be a coincidence that Leoncavallo wrote an opera to a Choudens libretto in the hope of having a premiere in Monte Carlo, considering that Mascagni and Choudens' *Amica* had premiered there in 1905. Leoncavallo was still imploring Ruffo to sing the role of Torias by 1 November, even offering to play *Maïa* for him at the piano rather than going to Paris for a production of *La bohème* at the Gaité Theatre. Numerous letters followed on the composer's stationery, which was engraved with the heading "Generosus Atque Fortis."[82] He assured Ruffo that Macchi would meet him at the station and take him to the villa where he was bound to have a "marvelous" time.[83] He also tried to interest the publisher Schmidl in another tentative opera to an Illica libretto called *Avemaria*.[84]

Leoncavallo's friend Gualtiero Belvederi also reentered his life after three years' absence, having refused to answer his letters following the Zangarini affair and cultivating a silence "worthy of the Commendatore in *Don Giovanni.*" The composer now brushed aside any misgivings that melted "like fog in the sun,"[85] informing Belvederi not only of *Maïa,* but also of his new venture into the field of operetta with *Malbruk,* to a libretto by Angelo Nessi based on Boccaccio.[86] Although he had sworn never to write an operetta, Leoncavallo was prompted by financial problems that grew more dramatic with each passing month. He had invited the comic actor Luigi Maresca to Villa Myriam during the fall, when he spoke of *Malbruk* for the first time and played a few light-hearted songs to be included in the future work that still remained "closed in a drawer."[87] Maresca saw possibilities for performing *Malbruk* with his theatrical company and finally received the score in Turin during November. Leoncavallo played the opera buffa at the piano for the first time for selected guests at Villa Myriam on 8 November.[88]

Leoncavallo had hoped that *Maïa's* premiere would take place at the San Carlo in Naples during November, and that Turin's Teatro Regio would mount *Der Roland von Berlin,* which had already enjoyed fifty performances in Berlin. Believing that Toscanini was sabotaging the possibility of having *Der Roland von Berlin* performed, he asked Turin for a "frank response," which he must have received, considering that the opera never appeared there nor anywhere else. When Naples demonstrated no interest in *Maïa,* Mascagni had it produced at Rome's Teatro Costanzi, where he had been the theater's director since August. He conducted the world premiere on 15 January 1910, with a cast including Emma Carelli in the title role, Rinaldo Grassi (Sergio), and Domenico Viglione Borghese (Torias). Leoncavallo had supervised the rehearsals, and although Paul de Choudens had promised his presence by 5 January, a telegram arrived declaring that he was "sad" not to be able to take part.[89] No one from Choudens attended, nor were they aware of who sang.[90] Hülsen showed interest in the work's effect, since *Maïa* would receive a production in Berlin in March 1911.[91]

Although the Teatro Costanzi was not completely sold out, applause following the opera's first act was both "sincere and unanimous," prompting the composer to appear clutching Mascagni's hand, leading many to believe their joint effort to be the most interesting part of the production, proving Mascagni's "artistic fraternity." Act 1 was very successful, especially Maïa's aria "Mon amant me quitta," which Carelli sang with a great sense of style, repeating the selection twice when the public demanded to hear this "delicate page of genuine character" again.[92] Although act 2 was laden with Provençal songs and dances, critics believed it insufficient in relaying an authentic atmosphere and failing to capture a country's ambience as Bizet had done in *Carmen.* The critic Nicola D'Atri thought that although Leoncavallo had demonstrated great artistic intention, Paul de Choudens's libretto was a diluted version of *Amica,* with a negative influence on the music.[93] Although Leoncavallo should have perhaps been more cautious, the chaos reigning at Casa Sonzogno understandably made him hope that Editions Choudens could offer him better publishing possibilities in the future. Leoncavallo was interviewed by the *Giornale d'Italia* one day following the premiere, answering questions in a hoarse voice aggravated by rehearsals. He explained his love of *Maïa*'s scenario, presaging Zandonai's remarks concerning *Conchita* in 1911, in which he had tried to recapture what Bizet had achieved in *Carmen*, "a conscientious and continuous study of the Provence's native colors . . . from the precious memories of my youth" to "the colors and warmth, rhythm and songs of the musical countryside."[94] The critical and public response to the premiere made Leoncavallo realize that additional revisions would be necessary if the impact of acts 1 and 3 were not to be diminished by act 2. He gave Mascagni a ring in recognition of his help,[95] whereupon Mascagni melodramatically wrote that his involvement had done "little or nothing," although the ring would be a constant "symbol of binding friendship and an eternal remembrance" of Leoncavallo's "goodness."[96]

"FANTASIA COMICA-MEDIOEVALE" AND *PROMETEO*

Leoncavallo was unable to attend *Maïa*'s second performance, having left immediately for Rome's Teatro Nazionale, where *Malbruk* was scheduled to open on 20 January 1910. Pompeo Ricchieri conducted the "fantasia comica-medioevale" in three acts, performed by Ferruccio Corradetti (Malbruk), Elodia Maresca (Alba), Luigi Maresca (Apollodoro), and Giuseppe Pasquini (Arnolfo). Reviews of Leoncavallo's first "opera buffa" were largely positive, although critics feared the parody sometimes became too sentimental, approaching opera seria. *Malbruk* was nevertheless a financial success, earning some forty-six thousand francs following twelve performances in Rome.

Leoncavallo, completely debilitated as a result of the two premieres, fell ill during February and did not recover sufficiently until the middle of March, when he left to recuperate in Rapallo. It was there that he again decided that *Maïa* should not receive any further performances—either in Berlin or in Nice—without alterations, which he now judged to be "indispensable."[97] Lorenzo Sonzogno wrote from Palermo, where he was trapped by a tempestuous sea, that he was "not enthusiastic" about *Prometeo*, but nonetheless would allow additional time before making a definite decision, warning the composer that it was a "great defect" to compose an opera with a certain singer in mind—implying Ruffo.[98] He was also determined to annul the *Camicia rossa* contract upon his return to Milan.

Leoncavallo continued his regime of massages and walks and took Rapallo's medicinal waters all the while, completely ignoring Sonzogno's letter.

The composer now wrote Ruffo that he wished to "seriously" speak about *Prometeo*,[99] since Colautti was also in Rapallo working on the "splendid" libretto, written in hexameters recalling Carducci's *Odi Barbare*. Although he had already received Sonzogno's letter, he now also told Ruffo that as soon as the publisher returned from Palermo, a contract would be signed with the librettist. It was the composer's usual game of playing one person against another, trying to secure as many partisans as possible in another "hoped-for" project. Leoncavallo wished Ruffo would tell Lorenzo how wonderful *Prometeo* would be and the great public effect it was sure to have, meanwhile asking the baritone to "protect" his work and to prove his faith in his talent. "If you want to help me—which I have special need of since my last sickness!!!—the time to try has arrived."[100] He then concluded that if Ruffo convinced Lorenzo, he would stop thinking about *Camicia rossa* in order not to waste time on *Prometeo*. Colautti had promised to complete the libretto by August, in the hopes that Monte Carlo would produce the opera in "a splendid production" with colleagues worthy of Ruffo.[101] His intention was that Ruffo's influence would enable Monte Carlo's intendant Raoul Gunsbourg to agree to a premiere, since the baritone had sung five roles there since the beginning of February. Leoncavallo wrote Ruffo that he was no longer on good terms with Gunsbourg, after he had refused to mount *Maïa* in favor of Naples, which, in turn, had then refused him![102] Leoncavallo, considering the baritone to be "one of the rare authentic Italian artists honoring art and country,"[103] felt certain that his name combined with Ruffo's "authority" would inaugurate a successful campaign toward furthering *Prometeo*. Hoping he had now cleared the way, he waited for Ruffo's response as if he were a "prophet."[104]

By March, Leoncavallo wrote Lorenzo's wife, Elvira, that he now felt much better, with doctors cautioning him to eat "vegetables, white meat, and fish."[105] His knees were still weak—a condition that bothered him particularly when ascending stairs—and he therefore resolved to take an hourly walk every morning, followed by a shorter one after meals. He also gossiped with Elvira about Ferruccio Corradetti's much-publicized suicide attempt, aware that he would need another Malbruk if the artist's debilitated psyche failed to improve by November for the French premiere.[106]

Leoncavallo finally realized there would be no support for *Prometeo* from Lorenzo, who explained in Milan on 5 April that the subject was "too grandiose" to be a commercial success.[107] Frustrated in having to accept the firm's "poor" subjects based on economic statutes,[108] Leoncavallo decided to write the work on his own account. He now commissioned Colautti to furnish a libretto for five thousand lire. He also implored Ruffo to lend him the money, complaining of his increased debts due to two premieres and illness, both of which had left him "high and dry following numerous unexpected expenses."[109] Leoncavallo was "content to write the work without a publisher," aiming for the unrealistic completion date of March 1911.[110] Ruffo was the project's sine qua non, and Leoncavallo warned him that a possible disinterest would be the "greatest anguish" of his artistic career."[111] Colautti's collaboration now depended on Ruffo's response.[112] Leoncavallo signed a contract with Ruffo in Milan on 22 April, now more realistically stipulating a completion date of spring 1912, giving the baritone exclusive rights to the role for five years as well as 10 percent of its earnings. Although Leoncavallo esteemed Colautti's *Prometeo* sketches, he asked Ruffo to also review them with the librettist since he was now a legal partner.

APPROACHING TOSCANINI

That May, shortly after arriving at Hotel Montana in Rue de l'Echelle, Paris, Leoncavallo set about discussing *Malbruk*'s November premiere at the Théâtre Apollo. Toscanini and Giulio Gatti-Casazza were also in Paris to present eighteen performances of five operas at the Châtelet between 19 May and 25 June, including *Manon Lescaut*'s French premiere, attended by Puccini.[113] Toscanini met with Leoncavallo, who desperately pushed *Maïa*, seeking to interest him in something other than *Pagliacci*, before thanking the conductor for his "fraternal reception" and "honored friendship,"[114] and implying that Choudens would send Toscanini a score. Leoncavallo then made his point: "If in the righteousness of your soul you think that I have been treated unjustly, do something for me. You know the atrocious war that is made to rage against me. A war against glory and against earning."[115] When Toscanini failed to contact Leoncavallo, believing him to be a one-time composer, Leoncavallo sent off another letter two weeks later from Brissago, addressed to "mio grande amico," asking for a critique of *Maïa*.[116] He also sent a revised version of the opera, replacing the latter half of act 2 with the second part of act 3, explaining that it brought added life into Maïa's character and the work in general,[117] therefore hoping to make it "worthy of being performed."[118] He then confided in Toscanini that his career had been destroyed by a certain "enemy," resulting in his suffering for eighteen years because of malignant detractors having wreaked "commercial damage."[119] Claiming that he was not "a millionaire like Franchetti," nor wedded to the daughter of wealthy hotel owner like Giordano,[120] he begged Toscanini for help: "I live from my work. Please do everything you can for me, I implore you, for I feel that I deserve it!"[121] Leoncavallo had also spoken with Gatti-Casazza in Paris. The latter expressed interest in producing *Zazà* at the Metropolitan Opera if a suitable interpreter could be found, while Caruso was not opposed to the idea of singing Marcello again in his *La bohème*.[122] Why it took another ten years before *Zazà* reached the Metropolitan Opera with Geraldine Farrar is anyone's guess, considering that she had already worked with the composer during 1904 in *Der Roland von Berlin*.[123] Although Toscanini had conducted *Zazà*'s world premiere, his interest did not extend itself to putting in a good word for the ailing composer. Defeated, Leoncavallo still hoped that Toscanini would visit Choudens before leaving Paris or at least send his visiting card "with two sentences for *Maïa*."[124]

COLLABORATING WITH FORZANO

October marked the first correspondence between Leoncavallo and the lawyer, playwright, and journalist, Giovacchino Forzano, about creating an operetta following the success of *Malbruk* (spurred on by Maresca).[125] Forzano initially met the composer in Montecatini, where Leoncavallo mentioned that he had been thinking about writing an operetta, wondering if the young man would be interested in providing a libretto. Forzano was delighted, aware that a commission would mean "notoriety" and introduction to Milanese publishers.[126] He immediately drafted a libretto called *La principessa delle rose*, which he then mailed to Brissago, anxiously awaiting the composer's response:

> Finally one morning as I left the house. . . . I saw the mailman who gave me a letter from my fiancée as well as another volumnious one. I recognized the calligraphy: Leoncavallo. My heart began to pound. What would it say? Would he like the subject? I opened the envelope with a trembling hand. . . . I read the first words that appeared on the final page: "Dear Forzano, I cannot possibly tell you how wonderful it is."[127]

Forzano felt he had created a "useful and delightful" libretto, describing *La principessa delle rose* as "comic, sentimental, satirical, political, poetic, romantic, and elegant,"[128] and asking Leoncavallo from Marina di Carrara if they could meet prior to the composer's departure for *Maïa* in Berlin. Forzano was confident that an aristocratic and refined operetta, void of vulgar buffoonery, would be successful. The librettist also cautioned Leoncavallo that the plot would no longer seem confused when he read it in its entirety to the composer personally, hoping to have the project complete by 10 February 1911.

Although Leoncavallo and Colautti wished to discuss *Prometeo* with Ruffo, it is not known whether they were successful before the composer left for Paris, where he signed a contract with Maurice Vaucaire on 23 October for *Malbruk*'s French translation. Leoncavallo had also subsequently composed additional music, having revised the score after the world premiere, hoping that the opera buffa would have a better chance of succeeding if its style resembled Offenbach—a name frequently mentioned in Forzano's letters regarding the future of operetta.[129] Neither Luigi Maresca nor Angelo Nessi were present when *Malbruk's* French premiere took place on 16 November at the Théâtre Apollo.[130] Enormous publicity preceded the event, with newspapers publishing photos of Leoncavallo posing in front of his Brissago Zazà statue with both Vaucaire and Nessi. The composer also risked having the emotionally delicate Ferruccio Corradetti, the cast's only foreign singer, relearn the title role in French. The *Daily Mail* reported that

> The recurrence throughout the work of the old air of "Malbruk" and parodies on famous opera airs has a very quaint effect, and the final result is pleasing. Several of the scenes, such as the serenade, are quite beautiful, and in places the music rises to the level of high-class comic opera. While the work will not add much to Leoncavallo's reputation, it will doubtless hold the bill at the Apollo for some time to come … a large part of the success of the work is due to Mme. Marfa Dhervilly, the delicious comedienne, and M. Paul Ardot, who, as Alba's mother and Apollinaire, the Chamberlain, respectively, are intensely comical.[131]

French reviewers wrote that Leoncavallo had created an amusing work, less original than *Pagliacci*, but nevertheless seducing in its buffo character. The *Frankfurter Zeitung* felt that although the plot was rather weak, Leoncavallo's music was both "fluent" and "emotionally appealing." However, critics failed to comprehend why Corradetti had been summoned from Milan when a Frenchman could have portrayed the role with more finesse. Leoncavallo's apprehensions concerning Corradetti were unfortunately confirmed when he had to be replaced following the premiere due to exhaustion.[132]

The composer stated in an interview shortly before the premiere that *Malbruk's* "operetta-like theme" was "very gay, very amusing," to which he had adapted "the corresponding music," incorporating motifs from numerous well-known works. When asked whether he was planning to compose another lighthearted opus, Leoncavallo immediately announced that he was finishing *Prometeo* and considering a comic work (no doubt Forzano's *La regina delle rose*).[133] He then expounded on the difficulties of composing comic music versus the dramatic, comparing his efforts in both genres to Rossini's *Guglielmo Tell* and *Il barbiere di Siviglia*, and Donizetti's *La favorita* and *La fille du régiment*, while also expressing his admiration for the light-hearted works of Offenbach, Charles Lecocq, and Henri Hirschmann.[134] A *Malbruk* caricature graced the title page of the Parisian newspaper *La Vie Parisienne* on 26 November. Leoncavallo hoped the work would remain in the Apollo's repertory until Easter, since he had created "an ingenious Italian operetta brimming with serenades, arias and songs," combined with musical quotations from "Rossini, Meyerbeer, Gounod, and Ambroise Thomas."[135] American newspapers misunderstood what Leoncavallo had set out to do, believing "the imitation of other composers . . . too recognizable" and the "borrowing" too evident.[136] They had obviously not read Leoncavallo's interviews, wherein he stated that he had not only poked fun at his own music, but also that of Wagner and Strauss.

Returning to Brissago, Leoncavallo received a letter from Ruffo's secretary, Amleto Pollastri, explaining that the baritone expected *Prometeo* to be completed by 1911. Shocked, the composer angrily reminded Ruffo that the contract had stated 1912, and demanded to know how he was "to start work on the music without a libretto," since discussions with Colautti were still underway.[137] Although Leoncavallo proposed to meet Ruffo in Santa Margherita that winter, as he planned to remain in Florence for Christmas, he instead stayed in Brissago, later departing for Milan for "serious affairs."[138] These "affairs" concerned Lorenzo and Riccardo Sonzogno's split due to irreconcilable differences.[139] Leoncavallo initially joined forces with Lorenzo, considering Riccardo to be "inexperienced" and at odds with the firm's older composers. He supposedly lacked both financial knowledge and talent—a combination Leoncavallo felt would "bring ruin."[140] The situation greatly upset Leoncavallo, who was uncertain about the future of Lorenzo's new firm: "We shall see; perhaps God will not abandon me!"[141] New Year's Eve was spent writing Belvederi to explain why he failed to repay borrowed money "with interest" and asking for an extension of a month or two "at the most."[142] The composer was afflicted during the holidays with an attack of phlebitis but nevertheless planned to leave for Berlin's production of *Maïa* on 20 January, writing Belvederi again that he had now also revised the end of both acts 1 and 3. At the same time, Forzano wrote Leoncavallo. Wishing to discuss *La regina delle rose* in Florence or Brissago, he feared that the composer had become too preoccupied with Angelo Nessi in planning *La Foscarina* and additional libretti. He hoped his sketches would generate sufficient enthusiasm to capture Leoncavallo's interest for a project that had hardly yet begun.

PROMETEO

Leoncavallo signaled Forzano to proceed, then returned to the conflict-ridden and ultimately sterile *Prometeo*, excusing himself for not going to hear Colautti's reading of the libretto, since his doctor forbade him to travel, although, in fact, it was the weather that was the real culprit. He referred to *Prometeo* as a "poem," not "the usual libretto,"[143] since Colautti had produced an intellectual work that was "absolutely new" and worthy of Carducci, having reproduced the style of Sappho and Aeschylus.[144] Leoncavallo was convinced that Ruffo, his "new

Orpheus," would understand how to move the world with the new opera[145] and asked for his impression. Colautti was also suffering from ill health,[146] and, although he would be forced to go to Milan for "important affairs" (probably in connection with the Sonzogno problem), he refused to search for Ruffo in "Vesuvius's shadow."[147] He thus wrote "the Divo" from Genoa's Splendid Hotel in his elegant calligraphy, that he would send the "poem," with a copy destined for Leoncavallo.[148] *Prometeo* was ultimately hindered from succeeding due to the men's conflicting agendas, in which personal meetings were replaced with an endless series of letters expressing misunderstanding, damaged pride, and artistic incompatibility. When Ruffo remained unsatisfied with *Prometeo*, Colautti immediately began incorporating "new dramatic elements into the original poem."[149] Colautti's efforts to discuss the changes with Leoncavallo were also thwarted, since he was uncertain if the composer was still in Brissago or already in Berlin. Meanwhile, Ruffo's responses were reduced to informal and infrequent telegrams or, when writing to Leoncavallo, dictated to his secretary, Pollastri, which infuriated the composer.

Leoncavallo remained in Brissago inundated with problems. Not only would *Maïa's* premiere be postponed, but Berlin's general manager, Von Hülsen, refused to take *Der Roland von Berlin* back into the repertory, with the poor excuse that he was still searching for a soprano to replace Emmy Destinn, after which he would no doubt "remember the work." He didn't, and it was never performed again. Leoncavallo wrote his last letter from his beloved Villa Myriam on 23 January 1911, before moving to live in Florence at 1 Via dei Pecori, forced from his paradise by debts.[150] None of his remaining letters mention a move, although there is a break in his correspondence from the end of January to 25 February, when the relocation probably took place.

Unimpressed that he was already involved in two projects, Leoncavallo overtaxed himself again (his Achilles' heel) when he asked Belvederi that January to supply him with a passionate and violent one-act libretto recalling *Pagliacci*, that was "theater, theater, theater"—the complete opposite of Colautti's *Prometeo* text, according to the composer.[151] Planning to leave Florence for Berlin on 15 February for rehearsals beginning on the 25th, Leoncavallo promised to send Belvederi the revised version of *Maïa*, believing that it was now "perfect." He was also still waiting for the completed *Prometeo* libretto, not having more than a sketch and hoping to show it to Belvederi in Rome following his sojourn in Berlin.[152] Leoncavallo was still in Florence on 25 February, suffering from another attack of phlebitis, which demanded rest. Always searching for a new verismo subject, he now turned to the French novella *Les Trois Masques*, with a gruesome finale that he found irresistible.[153] He continued to prod Belvederi for a new libretto that Lorenzo Sonzogno could publish instead of Edoardo, who now became "that terrible uncle."[154]

When Colautti finally presented Ruffo with the revised version of *Prometeo*, the baritone was even less enthused, claiming that it was more of "an oratorio than a work for the theater."[155] He demanded that it be rewritten once more, perhaps hoping that Colautti would lose patience and relinquish the project altogether. Leoncavallo finally read the libretto toward the end of February, writing Ruffo that indeed his judgment had been correct. He believed that Colautti's revisions had mutilated a work that essentially was an oratorio, concentrating too much on secondary characters, thus enlarging its original conception. "Leoncavallo hoped he could guide Colautti—"blundering as only great men can"[156]—and his refined talent back to their original idea through a third revision. Colautti wrote Ruffo from Genoa, requesting the second half of the money owed him, and refusing to work without payment now that Leoncavallo was "completely satisfied" with *Prometeo*.[157] Colautti received a telegram from Ruffo on 5 March that he would not be paid because he didn't like the libretto, and that an explanation would follow. In response, Colautti wrote a very distressed letter on hotel stationery, telling Ruffo that he had relinquished all other jobs for the past ten months in order to work on *Prometeo*, having gained nothing:"If you abandon me now, I will be on the verge of suicide—and Ruggero knows it!"[158] Considering Ruffo's earnings, Colautti knew payment would not have been a great sacrifice, whereas for him it was a matter of life or death, and he believed that he should never have been forced to ask Ruffo for money in the first place. Colautti told Ruffo that he was willing to rework the "poem" once more with financial compensation, warning the baritone that it was too late to pull himself out of the affair, since the music world was already aware of the project, with Leoncavallo carrying "the greatest responsibility."[159] When Colautti changed his mind that afternoon, swearing that "no human force" could make him take up "the cross" again without money,[160] he began bombarding Leoncavallo with letters, asking *him* to approach Ruffo. The composer's letter sent to Monte Carlo warned Ruffo to treat Colautti with courtesy and respect:"I am the great maestro that is writing to a great artist whom I admire and for whom I wanted to create a great work of art for which you were enthusiastic!"[161] Leoncavallo reminded Ruffo that he was bound by his contract, unable to "leave an artist as worthy as Colautti without a response."[162] The composer was still convinced that a profitable collaboration could be achieved if Colautti was paid, even assuring the baritone that he would reimburse him if he still disliked the opera. Leoncavallo had not seen Ruffo for more than one year, and, although he himself had "ten times more to do," he still found time to write, whereas Ruffo continued to answer through his secretary. Leoncavallo left for Berlin on 10 March after convincing Colautti to begin a third revision—"out of friendship"—although Ruffo's disinterest would ultimately stifle any future plans.[163]

A FINAL VISIT TO BERLIN

Leoncavallo arrived at Berlin's Central Hotel without Berthe for the premiere of his "new" *Maïa*, convinced that the revised second act would be of "certain effect," while considering the heroine's aria "Mon amant me quitta" in act 1 the best he had ever written.[164] *Maïa* began at 7:30, lasting only one hour and forty-five minutes, when it opened to a sold-out house on 18 March at the Court Opera.[165] German critics were heard gossiping in the foyer, saying that the new opera contained all of Leoncavallo's attributes and defects, while audience applause was courteous rather than impassioned. Reviewers made their readers aware that the opera had been revised, including an alternative ending to act 3, when Maïa is stabbed while trying to separate her quarreling lovers, rather than drowning as in the original. Critics were relieved that Leoncavallo had returned to an intimate subject more in tune with his talent, although Choudens's libretto, in Droescher's German translation, succeeded in sabotaging the work as it had during the world premiere. *Musical America*'s evaluation on 9 April that "*Maïa* Has Good Music, Poor Book" was both objective and succinct:

> The music, it should be stated at the outset, is vastly superior to the libretto . . . the more shortcomings of the book are all the more regrettable because Leoncavallo has illustrated in *Maïa*—perhaps more than ever before—the merits of the modern Italian school. An intimate relationship seems to exist between the composer of *Maïa* and Puccini, and above all the music is not only singable but frequently vocally effective. The parts of the heroine, the tenor Renaud, and the baritone Torias are extraordinarily well characterized . . . nor is melodic originality lacking. . . . Wherever human life and passions venture forth unrestrainedly, the music at once assumes a significant and always interesting character. The strongest factor in the opera is the instrumentation, which is full of color and tonal effectiveness. . . . The performance was decidedly praiseworthy.[166]

After the conclusion of the opera, with a cast including Melanie Kurt and Francis Maclennan, and conducted by Leo Blech, Leoncavallo was presented with "an immense floral wreath" accompanying twelve curtain calls, in spite of some reservations regarding the libretto and the conductor, whose interpretation was described as lacking in temperament. Following Leoncavallo's departure, *Maïa* was canceled after its third performance, due to negative reviews on account of its libretto, which resulted in a drastic decline in ticket sales. When Leoncavallo wrote Wilhelm II demanding to know the truth, Von Hülsen responded that "outside influences" had *not* contributed to *Maïa*'s premature end, nor had the composer's "rivals" plotted against him. Von Hülsen promised to perform *Maïa* again after Easter, when memories of the reviews would be forgotten. Leoncavallo now turned to Hungary, hoping that Budapest would perform his "best work."[167]

A letter from Ruffo's secretary awaited Leoncavallo on his return to Florence. It was clear that Colautti had still not received payment. Furious, Leoncavallo demanded to see the baritone to clear up the misunderstandings of the past year. He now turned to the Tuscan lawyer Giovanni Rosadi for advice while relaxing in Villa Casati in Bagni di Montecatini, calling Rosadi his "only hope."[168]

Following an audience with HRH the Queen Mother on 24 May, Leoncavallo was told by Carl-Eduard, Duke of Saxe-Coburg and Gotha, that *Maïa* would be presented at the Hoftheater in Gotha during January 1912. In June he was also asked by New York's Italian political newspaper *Il Progresso Italo-Americano*, if he would compose a hymn to Pascoli's lyrics for the unveiling of Ettore Ximenes' Dante monument. When the composer agreed, Ximenes immediately wrote from Rome that he was "elated" to join his name with Leoncavallo's in order to "share the applause" of the Italian community.[169]

At the same time, Leoncavallo resumed work on *La regina delle rose*—now called *La reginetta delle rose*—after *Prometeo* seemed to be going nowhere. Hoping to create an operetta that would distance itself from the saccharine sentimentality of its contemporaries, Leoncavallo had almost finished by early August, when he again met with Forzano in Carrara.[170]

Leoncavallo also wrote Belvederi that he had commissioned a libretto from Enrico Cavacchioli,[171] hoping to replace *Camicia rossa* with what may have been *Zingari* (Gypsies). This short *dramma lirico* in two scenes would premiere one year later in London. It finally resolved Leoncavallo's quest for a concise and passionate work comparable to *Pagliacci*, which Belvederi had failed to furnish. He was still unable to repay the money he had borrowed from Belvederi, blaming Casa Sonzogno's division for his financial dilemma, which was comparable to his pre-*Pagliacci* days.

Leoncavallo now wrote Rosadi an intriguing letter before leaving for London to conduct *Pagliacci*, mentioning that he had spoken with their mutual acquaintance, the sculptor Raffaelle Romanelli in Viareggio, about Puccini's stepdaughter Fosca. She claimed to have documentary evidence "of the infamy perpetrated by the partners Ricordi-Puccini, damaging to all composers that could be competitors of the only maestro wanted by the royal house of Ricordi, as well as against any new composers that may appear."[172] Leoncavallo counseled Rosadi to "approach Signora Fosca as soon as possible . . . in order not to lose" the "unique occasion of having material proof."[173]

Delaying his departure to London, the composer also contacted the journalist and playwright Valentino Soldani, initiating a long and sterile collaboration for many years, aimed at producing cinematic work.[174] Leoncavallo hoped Soldani would visit him in Montecatini to discuss a project that would be "important for both" of them.[175] Although Leoncavallo failed to interest Lorenzo in commissioning a work from Soldani, he performed excerpts at their meeting from *Reginetta delle rose* that, according to the composer, was "proceeding triumphantly."[176]

LEONCAVALLO AT THE HIPPODROME

In the summer of 1911 Albert de Courville (1887–1960), the assistant manager of London's music hall, the Hippodrome, was goaded by his director, Sir Edward Moss, to seek another "big attraction" for their audiences. Considering *Pagliacci*'s popularity, Courville decided that "it would be interesting" to bring Leoncavallo to London so that the composer could lead the score himself.[177] Leoncavallo "laughed heartily at the thought of conducting *Pagliacci* at a circus,"[178] but "the idea tickled him," while Courville explained that "although the theater was called the Hippodrome, it was, in reality, one of the finest theaters in London." Leoncavallo finally accepted the proposal of conducting the work in a condensed format twice daily with two different casts. All choruses were cut, including the Nedda/Tonio scene and "the section leading from the discovery of the lovers to 'Vesti la giubba.'"[179] Courville also suggested that Leoncavallo "write the score for an operetta."[180] A small ensemble was formed to perform *Pagliacci,* and Leoncavallo resided at the Savoy awaiting his engagement, which began on 11 September, eventually spreading to six weeks rather than the originally scheduled two.

Meanwhile, the Italian press began "protesting against its hero appearing at a music-hall, just as Sarah Bernhardt was criticized for appearing at the Coliseum."[181] According to the *Daily Telegraph*, both Leoncavallo and Bernhardt had "satisfied themselves that the great variety palaces of the West End" had "nothing in common with the music-halls of the Continent."[182] In fact, Leoncavallo was surprised by "the magnificence of the Hippodrome" and its orchestra,[183] calming the Italians, who were relieved to hear that it was "one of the most elegant Music-Halls in the metropolis"[184] and that Leoncavallo would receive twenty-five thousand francs weekly, a sum only topped by Bernhardt, who had demanded fifty thousand francs a year earlier. Although performances sung by Rinalda Pavoni (Nedda), Egidio Cunego (Canio), and Ernesto Caronna (Tonio) were successful, there was little doubt that the opera lost "a good deal of its efficacy in its half-hour form, but its salient features found vivid expression by the company brought over by the composer."[185] The opera's forty-five-minute "potted version" resulted in "the omission of a good deal of action and music, which, from an artistic point of view, must be held to be a serious mistake."[186] Critics hoped that the performance would result in "making the work known to many who might otherwise have remained in ignorance of it," while photographs depicted a tired and frowning composer. Caricatures of "the famous Italian composer" conducting the orchestra soon made the rounds of London's newspapers, and laughter was audible when Leoncavallo tried to seat himself on the conductor's chair with some difficulty. His London stay was nevertheless such a success that the engagement was prolonged, while plans were discussed to have Réjane perform on the same evening.[187] The program had been the most costly ever produced at a variety theater, and Leoncavallo was both elated and relieved to return to Italy with reviews and articles on which he scribbled "tremendous succès."

NOTES

1. Leoncavallo to Maurice Vaucaire, 3 January 1906 (BCL).

2. Leoncavallo used Sardou's name as bait, knowing that Maurice Vaucaire would supply the libretto.

3. Leoncavallo to Breitkopf & Härtel, 15 January 1906 (BHA).

4. According to Leoncavallo's account, Sardou felt fifty thousand lire was insufficient if the price included all countries rather than only France, Monte Carlo, and Belgium.

5. By February it looked as if Breitkopf & Härtel would purchase *La Jeunesse de Figaro* not only for the German-speaking countries, but for Denmark, Sweden, and Norway as well.

6. Leoncavallo to Breitkopf & Härtel, 5 February 1906 (BHA).

7. Leoncavallo to Breitkopf & Härtel, 16 February 1906 (BHA).

8. Leoncavallo to Breitkopf & Härtel, 24 February 1906 (BHA).

9. Mascagni wrote Illica during March that Sardou was collaborating with Leoncavallo and Giordano. Leoncavallo's wish to write a Sardou opera was probably prompted by Giordano's interest. After the latter's Sardou-based *Fedora* (1898), he became interested in the playwright's *La fête du Nil*, purchased by Sonzogno on 14 September 1905, although Giordano later opted to use *Madame Sans-Gêne*.

10. Leoncavallo to Luigi Mancinelli, 3 April 1906 in Antonio Mariani, *Luigi Mancinelli Epistolario*, privately printed, 221. The elder sister of Alfonso XII and therefore the king's aunt, Isabella (1851–1931), was appreciated for her charm, elegance, and wit.

11. While in Madrid, Leoncavallo was also anxious to know if Franchetti's D'Annunzio based *Figlio di Iorio* was successful at its La Scala premiere on 29 March.

12. Leoncavallo to unidentified recipient, 24 May 1906, Christie's, London, 2000. Although one source states that Leoncavallo was scheduled to be in Portugal the 24th and 25th of April, documentation proves that he was there during the end of May, autographing postcards with quotations of "Ridi, pagliaccio."

13. Puccini had originally been interested a year earlier in a work by Daudet, although he now switched to *La femme et le pantin,* to Giulio Ricordi's chagrin, and

planned to meet Vaucaire on 18 August in Abetone.

14. Leoncavallo to Maurice Vaucaire, 29 July 1906 (BNO).

15. Ibid.

16. Ibid.

17. Rudolph Aronson (1856–1919) was the leading impresario of opera in America at the time. According to an interview in the *Kansas City Times* on 5 October 1906, it had taken Aronson "16 months" to convince Leoncavallo to undertake the tour.

18. *Musical America*, 6 October 1906.

19. *Minneapolis Tribune*, undated. In true Agatha Christie fashion, the liner also carried the body of a young woman killed in a car accident. "Melba's protégée" the soprano "Parkina" (Elizabeth Perkins), was on board, as was the Cincinnati conductor Franz Van der Stucken, while the tour's tenor, Nino Perya, successfully wooed the Baltimore heiress Harris, he speaking no English, she no Italian.

20. His Ph.D. from the University of Bologna, studying with "Corducci," was again touted. Unidentified newspaper clipping.

21. The march and its dedication probably originated as a publicity tactic from Aronson, who had himself composed an "unnamed march" that he had sent the president during October 1904. (Bruce Kirkby to the author, after consulting the Roosevelt papers and the president's desk diaries, 25 July 2000, LOC.)

22. Unidentified newspaper clipping, 7 October 1906.

23. Unidentified newspaper clipping, from Columbus, Ohio, 3 October 1906.

24. Unidentified newspaper clipping, Philadelphia, 3 October 1906. Leoncavallo frequently mentioned trying to find a theme for an opera in the United States, no doubt hoping that someone would commission a work.

25. Unidentified newspaper clipping, 7 October 1906.

26. Ibid.

27. *Detroit Journal*, 3 October 1906.

28. *Boston Transcript*, 3 October 1906.

29. Ibid.

30. Ibid.

31. *New York Evening World*, 3 October 1906.

32. *Camicia rossa* was another of Leoncavallo's "would-be" operas that was never completed.

33. Unidentified newspaper clipping, 7 October 1906.

34. Ibid. It did not take long for newspapers to realize that Leoncavallo's interest in a U.S. tour was mostly financial—the *New York World* caricatured the composer on 7 October 1906 under the heading "Europe's all right, but they all come back to New York."

35. Ibid.

36. *New York Telegraph*, 7 October 1906.

37. *New York Herald*, 7 October 1906.

38. Unidentified newspaper clipping, 7 October 1906.

39. *Herald Tribune*, 8 October 1906.

40. Unidentified newspaper clipping, 9 October 1906.

41. *Herald Tribune*, 8 October 1906.

42. Unidentified newspaper clipping, 9 October 1906.

43. Unidentified newspaper clipping, 10 October 1906. Oscar Hammerstein and Heinrich Conried were also present.

44. *New York Sun*, 11 October 1906.

45. *New York Tribune*, 11 October 1906.

46. Ibid.

47. J. K. Heslet to unidentified recipient, 1 November 1906 (BCL).

48. *New York Herald*, 30 October 1906.

49. Leoncavallo should have been presented to President and Mrs. Roosevelt by Sidney Lloyd Wrightson on 30 November at 2:30. The composer's conflicting dates had not been foreseen by the White House, considering that he only learned of the appointment on 13 November, receiving a telegram from Aronson in Butte, Montana, erroneously stating that the president would receive him on 7 December—the official end of the tour.

50. Unidentified Boston newspaper clipping, 20 October 1906.

51. Ibid.

52. *Musical America*, 3 November 1906.

53. *Boston Post*, 20 October 1906.

54. *Boston Post*, 21 October 1906.

55. Unidentified newspaper clipping, 24 October 1906.

56. Ibid.

57. *Baltimore Sun*, 28 October 1906.

58. *Musical Courier*, 3 November 1906.

59. *Musical Courier*, 4 November 1906.

60. Unidentified newspaper clipping, 5 November 1906.

61. *Wisconsin Press*, 6 November 1906.

62. *Bay City Tribune*, 6 November 1906.

63. *St. Paul Dispatch*, 9 November 1906.

64. *Butte Evening News*, 15 November 1906.

65. Unidentified newspaper clipping, 19 November 1906.

66. Unidentified newspaper clipping, Grand Rapids, Michigan, 27 November 1906. The article also stated "Leoncavallo claims the credit for making Caruso."

67. *Herald* (Muncie, Indiana), 28 November 1906.

68. Leoncavallo's November appearances included: Michigan, Indiana, Wisconsin, Iowa, Minnesota, North Dakota, Nebraska, Montana, Washington state, Vancouver, Oregon, Idaho, Utah, Wyoming, and Colorado. It is not known whether he also visited Tennessee, Georgia, and Louisiana.

69. Puccini to Tito Ricordi, 19 January 1907, in Gara, *Carteggi Pucciniani*, 339.

70. Telegram to Leoncavallo from unidentified sender, Havana, Cuba, 31 January 1907.

71. Titta Ruffo and Caruso were the singers Leoncavallo admired most.

72. Leoncavallo to Antonio Marinuzzi, 30 October 1907 (GMA).

73. Leoncavallo to Titta Ruffo, 26 October 1907 (BCL).

74. Ibid.

75. Leoncavallo was also making preparations for a libretto by J. F. Louis Merlet

entitled *Marchand de masques*. In addition, his preface to Gina Bertolini Marcionni's book *Le dolorose rime* was published in Florence during 1908.

76. Riccardo was the son of Edoardo's brother Alberto, while Lorenzo was the son of Edoardo's brother Giulio Cesare. The nephews soon quarreled, and Lorenzo founded his own firm in 1911, publishing Leoncavallo, Wolf-Ferrari, Franchetti, Strauss, and Mascagni. Edoardo spent most of his time at his Parisian domicile, later also selling his newspaper *Il Secolo*, which was unable to compete with the more modern *Corriere della Sera*.

77. Leoncavallo spent the rest of his life trying to create a suitable operatic vehicle for Ruffo.

78. Leoncavallo to Arturo Colautti, undated, (BCL). Only sketches for the prelude to act 3 of *Camicia rossa* have been located, making it uncertain how much of the proposed opera Leoncavallo actually completed.

79. Choudens used the sobriquet "Paul Bérel" when signing his libretti.

80. Leoncavallo to Maurice Vaucaire, 10 August 1907 (BCL).

81. Leoncavallo to Georg Droescher, 7 June 1908 (Y). Leoncavallo offered Droescher one thousand francs to translate *Maïa*. Leoncavallo was still trying to interest Berlin in *Maïa* during 1909, sending the score to the new intendant Georg von Hülsen-Haessler, who had requested it out of "personal interest." Hülsen to Leoncavallo, 24 July 1909 (BCL).

82. "Generous and Courageous."

83. Leoncavallo to Titta Ruffo, 1 November 1908 (BCL).

84. Leoncavallo spelled the opera "Avemaria," Illica called it "Ave Maria," and the current directors of Casa Musicale Sonzogno di Piero Ostali refer to it as "Avemmaria."

85. Leoncavallo to Gualtiero Belvederi, 10 August 1909 (BCL).

86. *Malbruk* is a mixture of opera and operetta in the tradition of opera buffa.

87. *Gazzetta Ticinese*, 8 November 1909.

88. Newspapers wrote that Leoncavallo no longer supplied his own libretti, while the *Corriere della Sera* stated that the operetta took place in the year "1100"—the amount of money Nessi had received.

89. Paul de Choudens to Leoncavallo, 16 January 1910 (BCL).

90. The same disinterest is also presently apparent in the Choudens archive, which contain none of Leoncavallo's letters other than three contracts.

91. Gastone Leoncavallo and Jeanne Puel sent their regards from Pavia.

92. *I Teatri*, 17 January 1910. The Royal Family attended the performance, speaking with Leoncavallo during the interval.

93. It seems naive that Paul de Choudens always chose to use the sobriquet "Paul Bérel," since all newspapers referred to him by his real name.

94. *Giornale d'Italia*, 16 January 1910.

95. The ring may have originally come from Choudens, who sent Leoncavallo a telegram mentioning a gift for one of their interpreters.

96. Pietro Mascagni to Leoncavallo, 22 January 1910 (BCL).

97. Leoncavallo to Maurice Vaucaire, 15 May 1910 (BCL).

98. Lorenzo Sonzogno to Leoncavallo, 15 March 1910 (BCL).

99. Leoncavallo to Titta Ruffo, 17 March 1910 (BCL).
100. Ibid.
101. Ibid.
102. There was now no more mention of having *Prometeo* produced in Rome, as the composer had originally planned as part of a commissional committee.
103. Leoncavallo to Titta Ruffo, 17 March 1910 (BCL).
104. Ibid.
105. Leoncavallo to Elvira Sonzogno, 18 March 1910 (BCL).
106. Now that Lorenzo headed his own firm, Leoncavallo concluded his letter to Elvira by kissing his "mascotte's" hand. He was also interested to know if she had attended Giulio Ricordi's opera *La secchia rapita.*
107. Leoncavallo to Titta Ruffo, 6 April 1910 (BCL).
108. Ibid.
109. Ibid. Leoncavallo reminded Ruffo that the sum could be paid in two halves: at the time of signing the contract and upon the libretto's completion.
110. Ibid.
111. Ibid.
112. Leoncavallo's letter to Ruffo was written in Busto Arsizio, where he had traveled with Berthe to hear the debut of one of her singing students who seemed "very promising."
113. Metropolitan Opera soloists included: Caruso, Destinn, Amato, Bori, Farrar, and Fremstad. The engagement was an enormous success, earning $10,500 daily.
114. Leoncavallo to Arturo Toscanini, 1 June 1910 (NY).
115. Ibid.
116. Leoncavallo to Arturo Toscanini, 14 June 1910 (NY).
117. Had Toscanini shown interest in *Maïa*, Leoncavallo's career may have received a boost, temporarily shielding him from an approaching series of operettas. Instead, his success stagnated as a result of the irregular qualities inherent in his latest works. Incessant effort, worry, and disappointments contributed to ill health that would terminate his life less than one decade later.
118. Leoncavallo to Arturo Toscanini, 14 June 1910 (NY).
119. Ibid. Although Leoncavallo failed to mention who the "enemy" was, his wrath was certainly directed toward Casa Ricordi and Puccini.
120. The composer Alberto Franchetti was independently wealthy, whereas Umberto Giordano had married Olga Spatz, whose father owned a string of important hotels, including Milan's Grand Hotel.
121. Leoncavallo to Arturo Toscanini, 14 June 1910 (NY).
122. Although Leoncavallo would introduce *Zazà* to the United States at San Francisco's Tivoli Theatre during 1913, it would not reach the Metropolitan Opera until after the composer's death in 1920, in a grotesquely altered version by Renzo Bianchi in 1947.
123. Although Farrar referred to Toscanini as a "musical Napoleon," her 1920 portrayal of Zazà would be a triumphant box-office success. Geraldine Farrar, *Such Sweet Compulsion* (New York: Greystone Press, 1938), 151.
124. Leoncavallo to Arturo Toscanini, 14 June 1910 (NY). Luigi Maresca expected

Leoncavallo to attend performances of *Malbruk* in Livorno opening on 27 July. The press also wrote that the composer had received another libretto by Nessi entitled *La Foscarina*.

125. Even though Forzano would later provide libretti for Puccini, Giordano, Franchetti, and Wolf-Ferrari, his first commission came from Leoncavallo.

126. Giovacchino Forzano, *Come li ho conosciuto* (Turin: Eri, 1957), 8–10.

127. Ibid.

128. Giovacchino Forzano to Leoncavallo, 15 October 1910 (BCL). Forzano's title was made up of four words that he believed would bring the piece luck. He also created it to be performed in contemporary dress.

129. Leoncavallo received a note from Félix Lagrange—director of the Trianon Lyrique—shortly after his arrival in Paris. Having heard from Charles Simon that the composer would be coming to speak of *Zazà*, Lagrange invited Leoncavallo to attend a performance of Charles Lecocq's *Petit duc* on 3 November at the Théâtre de la Gaîté.

130. Numerous Viennese operettas were also performed at the Théâtre Apollo, no doubt a reason why the site was chosen to premiere Leoncavallo's opera buffa.

131. *Daily Mail*, 17/18 November 1910.

132. Corradetti was replaced by a certain "Claudel" or "Clarel" depending on various sources.

133. The title metamorphized from *La principessa delle rose* and *La regina delle rose* to *La reginetta delle rose*.

134. Leoncavallo felt drawn to French music since his early Parisian days, never forgetting the impression made by hearing his own music played by an orchestra, even if it happened to be the scratchy Eldorado orchestra.

135. Puccini may have been inspired by Leoncavallo's musical quotations to do the same with Strauss's *Salomé* in *La rondine*.

136. A. C. in *Herald*, November 1910.

137. Leoncavallo to Titta Ruffo, 4 December 1910 (BCL).

138. Leoncavallo to Gualtiero Belvederi, 31 December 1910 (BCL).

139. Leoncavallo felt that Lorenzo had started his own firm out of jealousy regarding Riccardo's benevolent relationship with Edoardo. Riccardo would die in 1915 and Lorenzo in 1920, whereupon the firm was bought by the cotton industrialist Piero Ostali.

140. Leoncavallo to Gualtiero Belvederi, 31 December 1910 (BCL).

141. Ibid.

142. Ibid.

143. Leoncavallo to Titta Ruffo, 7 January 1911 (BCL).

144. Ibid.

145. Ibid.

146. Colautti was sixty at the time.

147. Arturo Colautti to Titta Ruffo, 12 January 1911 (BCL).

148. Leoncavallo also referred to Ruffo in all his letters as "the Divo."

149. Arturo Colautti to Titta Ruffo, 18 January 1911 (BCL).

150. Since the villa was not sold for some time, the composer probably tried to save the property while renting or leasing it.

151. Leoncavallo to Gualtiero Belvederi, 23 January 1911 (BCL).

152. A one-page sketch for *Prometeo* is all that remains in the composer's hand.

153. Leoncavallo was intrigued by the scenic possibilities of the last part, in which a father brings his son's corpse onstage dressed as a clown. The composer Isidore De Lara originally owned the rights, asking none other than Colautti to supply the libretto!

154. Leoncavallo to Gualtiero Belvederi, 25 February 1911 (BCL).

155. Leoncavallo to Titta Ruffo, 27 February 1911 (BCL).

156. Ibid.

157. Arturo Colautti to Titta Ruffo, 4 March 1911 (BCL).

158. Arturo Colautti to Titta Ruffo, 5 March 1911 (BCL).

159. Arturo Colautti to Titta Ruffo, 7 March 1911 (BCL).

160. Arturo Colautti to Titta Ruffo, 7 March 1911 (second letter) (BCL).

161. Leoncavallo to Titta Ruffo, 7 March 1911 (BCL). Ruffo was in Monte Carlo preparing to sing *Il barbiere di Siviglia* with Chaliapin, followed by *Linda di Chamounix* and *La gioconda*.

162. Ibid.

163. Arturo Colautti to Titta Ruffo, 10 March 1911 (BCL).

164. Leoncavallo to Gualtiero Belvederi, 9 March 1911 (BCL). The opera now took place during 1820 so that Renaud could wear the uniform of Napoléon's blue hussars during act 1.

165. Wilhelm II announced that he would only be present for the second performance, in order not to detract from the premiere's success!

166. *Musical America*, 8 April 1911.

167. Leoncavallo to the Budapest Opera, 22 April 1911 (HSOA).

168. Leoncavallo to Giovanni Rosadi, 12 June 1911 (BRF). Leoncavallo met Rosadi in Florence at 9 Via Cavour. The lawyer befriended many composers and authors, including Mascagni, Pizzetti, Forzano, Matilde Serao, and the actress Eleonora Duse.

169. Ettore Ximenes to Leoncavallo, 26 June 1911 (BCL).

170. *Le ménestrel* announced on 19 August 1911, that Leoncavallo had informed them on the fourteenth that he was completing *Reginetta delle rose* and that his new opera *La foresta mormora* would be completed the following spring, while he was also involved with "la musique d'un poème" on the subject of Prometheus!

171. Enrico Cavacchioli (1885–1954).

172. Leoncavallo to Giovanni Rosadi, 1 September 1911 (BRF).

173. Ibid. Fosca was the daughter of Puccini's wife Elvira and her first husband Narciso Gemignani.

174. Puccini had been interested in Valentino Soldani's (1874–1935) *Margherita da Cortona* only to later abandon it. Soldani would also offer Riccardo Zandonai a text entitled *Calendimaggio* in 1917 that the composer felt had "the makings of a good libretto" albeit too expensive. Zandonai also contemplated *Margherita da Cortona* "though later relinquishing it." Dryden, *Riccardo Zandonai, A Biography*, 189.

175. Leoncavallo to Valentino Soldani, 9 September 1911 (MTS).

176. Ibid.

177. Albert de Courville, *I Tell You* (London: Chapman & Hall, 1928), 81.

178. Ibid., 82.

179. George Hall, "Leoncavallo in London," *Opera* 35, no. 3 (1984), 246–53.

180. De Courville, *I Tell You*, 83.

181. *Daily Telegraph*, 13 September 1911.

182. Ibid.

183. Ibid.

184. Italian correspondent to *Daily Telegraph*, 3 September 1911.

185. *Daily Telegraph*, undated, September 1911.

186. *Pall Mall Gazette*, 12 September 1911.

187. Réjane had in fact organized a charity performance for survivors of the French battleship Liberté. Leoncavallo conducted *Zazà*'s third act for the occasion.

· 8 ·

Italian Lehár

1912–1915

$\mathscr{C}$ourville's idea had paid off, and he now hoped to entice Puccini to conduct *La bohème* at the Hippodrome. Puccini, not in Leoncavallo's incessant financial straits, curtly informed Courville at the Savoy Hotel that he would never agree to such an engagement, even if the assistant manager covered him with gold "up to here—and he indicated his throat."[1] Courville later decided to lure Leoncavallo back to the Hippodrome with a new opera that would rival *Pagliacci*, and, hopefully, also its success. This evolved to be *Zingari*, based on Pushkin's poem *The Gypsies*. Enrico Cavacchioli sent Leoncavallo a letter on *Il Secolo* stationery during January 1912, thanking him for his somewhat depressing New Year's wishes, while agreeing with the difficulties in finding a publisher for *Zingari*.[2] Although the composer had joined forces with Lorenzo Sonzogno, it was Riccardo whose name would be prominent in future correspondence. Leoncavallo now tried to interest Cavacchioli in collaborating with Illica on the *Avemaria* libretto that he had originally promised the publisher Schmidl three years earlier, another "would be" opera discussed *ad infinitum* with only the text of act 1 supposedly complete.[3]

Leoncavallo also contacted Lorenzo from Florence that April,[4] asking him to arrange a "sine qua non" production of *Reginetta delle rose* in Rome.[5] He even suggested that he "prepare the atmosphere" for a premiere by creating a good image in the papers,[6] while he still undertook revisions during rehearsals to guarantee "positive results."[7] Leoncavallo sent Lorenzo the operetta's second act on 29 February 1912, worried that Forzano was too involved with other projects to correct *Reginetta delle rose*.[8] Not only would *Reginetta delle rose* be produced in Rome, but an extended interview with Leoncavallo in Montecatini "prepared the atmosphere" just prior to the work's premiere, informing readers that Leoncavallo composed from 7 a.m. until 3 p.m. and that the card game tresette was the most important part of his life besides writing music.

Leoncavallo's elegant image was spoiled, however, when reporters noticed that the rented villa's walls were empty, except for a few signed photographs of Massenet and Wilhelm II. This was all that Leoncavallo had managed to save from Villa Myriam, where debts had forced him to leave behind most of his possessions, which would later, tragically, be dispersed.[9] His lectern, made of Russian wood and laden with pencils, erasers, and half-smoked cigars, also survived the move.

The composer told the reporter he considered *Reginetta delle rose* to be "an authentic operetta," while *Malbruk* was "the first work approaching an operetta."[10] He then seated himself at the piano, trying to demonstrate that Franz Lehár had incorporated his *Valse mignonne* (1898) into *Der Graf von Luxemburg* (1909), while observing that *Die Lustige Witwe* supposedly also included shades of Leoncavallo.[11] He correctly predicted that *Reginetta delle rose*'s "Rose Waltz" would be the work's most endearing selection. Leoncavallo had been supervising rehearsals for *Reginetta delle rose* since the end of May, preparing its premiere at Rome's Teatro Costanzi on 24 June 1912. It was performed by members of the theatrical company Città di Milano[12] and conducted by Costantino Lombardo. Costumes had been designed by the composer's friend Romeo Marchetti.[13] Reviewers suggested that the operetta's plot was inspired by a British scenario Leoncavallo had come across during his London sojourn a year earlier. They considered it both "modern" and sentimental, referring to Leoncavallo as the "Italian Lehár."[14] Matilde Serao offered a thoughtful review, finding it only natural that Leoncavallo, after writing both *Zazà* and *La bohème*, should have created an Italian operetta for Forzano's fresh and tasteful libretto, while Rome's *Corriere d'Italia* noted an improvement since *Malbruk* toward a form of Italian operetta that was both clear and elegant. The production was a success, with encores requested after almost every number, although only the "rose waltz," "telephone duet," and "chorus of ministers" were repeated.[15] Leoncavallo was also called to the stage "dozens of times" by enthusiastic audiences at the second performance, before leaving for an equally successful run in Naples.[16]

Turin followed on 2 July, with a visibly fatigued and hoarse composer directing daily rehearsals lasting some five hours, although he was not too weak to tell the press that *Reginetta delle rose* would not be a sole outing in order to provide *Malbruk* with a sister. He also followed Cavacchioli's advice by introducing *Zingari* at this opportune moment, in order to reestablish his reputation as a dramatic composer. When the subject turned to *Prometeo*, Leoncavallo declared that it would contain "vast proportions in which the heroic myth" would be "treated with legendary grandeur and passion, both dramatic and modern," with "severe classical forms."[17] Even at this late stage, Leoncavallo still hoped to complete the second and third operas of his *Crepusculum* trilogy: "This precious dream of my youth will not vanish until I have realized it."[18] He then claimed to have abandoned *Camicia rossa* due to its difficult subject matter.

A PAGLIACCI SEQUEL

Leoncavallo returned to Montecatini and its spa following Turin in order to lose some weight and repair his aggravated health.[19] He devoted the next "three and a half months" to *Zingari's* orchestration,[20] presenting an informal "dress rehearsal"on 28 August at 11:00 a.m. for Riccardo Sonzogno, Sir Edward Moss, Cavacchioli, and Cavacchioli's collaborator, Guglielmo Emanuel.[21] The press immediately reported that *Pagliacci's* style had been "rediscovered."

Leoncavallo granted London's *Daily Express* an interview, in which he provided insight into his work routine, shortly after his arrival at the Savoy accompanied by Berthe and his omnipresent secretary Carlo Macchi:

> From 6 o'clock until midday I composed, or sought to, for I feel that the morning is inspirational, as the afternoon is work-a-day. The morning is fresh and sweet, the afternoon full of languor, odorous; or so it is in Italy. Then from about 4 to 7 o'clock I worked on the orchestration. Silence is the first essential, harmonious colour surroundings the second. I believe that most musicians compose at the piano. To me that would be fatally distracting. The music simply floods my mind; if I may so say it, I hear every note, the complete melody, the rhythm, the expression, exactly as if it were being produced by a super-naturally perfect orchestra. There is no flaw and no hesitancy; it is an exquisitely smooth flow.[22]

He was also quite objective for once when summing up his own character:

> I am at the same time very industrious and extremely lazy. My industry is in concentration, in composing. My laziness is in a horror of having to score my compositions laboriously. Perhaps this is because I can only "hear" my music after long and very deep reflection, out of which it is difficult to raise oneself to a pitch of physical activity. I engaged an exceedingly sympathetic and musical amanuensis during the composition of *Zingari*, but the strain was so great, the fear of blundering and missing so upsetting, that I suffered a nervous breakdown at the end of the week. I am cruel thus, but it is uncontrollable unkindness. I am so feverishly eager that there is no thought for a human being, and, in fact, when I myself score I invariably use a pencil. The time lost in dipping into the ink is irritating beyond description! And yet the music does not always run so smoothly. In *Zingari*, for example, the principal baritone song was written five times before it was satisfactory. It was good (or so I thought) on each occasion, but it was not in keeping with the character, the true gipsy spirit of the opera. That is an exceptionally important point. In addition to the emotion expressed in the individual song, chorus, or intermezzo, permeating each and all of them is the character—national, racial, or even tribal. I lay special stress on this in

speaking of *Zingari*, for there I have carefully aimed at reproducing music of pure character. Many of my very sympathetic friends in London have expressed surprise that I do not compose at night. . . . I composed most of my *Bohème*, *Zazà*, and *Roland* . . . at night, and the result is, if now I attempt such work, in an hour the five lines become six, seven, eight, and then dance and jump and disappear. So I burn the midnight oil—at midday. . . . I really think that *Zingari* is as fine as *Pagliacci*. Moreover, I feel sure that when it has grown up, as has *Pagliacci*, it will be so admitted.[23]

Zingari finally opened on 16 September at London's Hippodrome as *Gipsies*.[24] Critics commented that the opera wasted no time on "introductions or recitatives. Emotions and situations mature without unnecessarily protracted accompaniment, and the opera as a whole is well proportioned. The orchestral work, too, is sound and interesting, without being pretentious; it resists any temptation to be precious and confines itself to being appropriate."[25] The same reviewer also mentioned that the opera had been "written especially for" the Hippodrome "as a sequel to the successful performances of *Pagliacci* there last October." A plot summary followed, although "the time limit, 70 minutes, necessitated the barest outline." The artists received poor ratings, with not a word dealing with Leoncavallo's conducting or Léon Bakst's production:

Neither the actors nor the chorus quite know how to make things swing along. Signor Cunego has a resonant tenor, and if his songs had not been a little over-acted and his listening to other singers a little under-acted [he] would have made something real out of the part of Radu. Signora [Rinalda] Pavoni (Fleana) will not be of much assistance to either of her lovers until she can modulate the rather strident middle notes of her voice. . . . Signor [Ernesto] Caronna (Tamar) sang in far better style and was twice recalled; this may have been partly due to the succinct and definite character of his aria, but a good deal, too, to the purity of his method.[26]

In spite of this, the composer then proceeded to conduct sixty-two performances, two per day.[27,28] He was also asked to conduct *Pagliacci* at Birmingham's Grand Theatre—his sole "visit to the provinces"—following the conclusion of *Zingari*'s run.[29] He exclaimed that he had "never met with greater kindness nor more intense enthusiasm," no longer considering the British to be "cold and unresponsive."[30] During his free time, he managed to visit the East End to donate to a poor house. It seems that he was also commissioned to write a march for suffragette rallies, an idea that may have later inspired him during the composition of *La candidata*.

Leoncavallo traveled to Milan's Hotel Victoria on 18 November to prepare *Zingari*'s Italian premiere (30 November) at Sonzogno's Teatro Lirico Internazionale, with Eugenia Burzio and Piero Schiavazzi, conducted by Giacomo Armani.[31] The year ended in Florence as Leoncavallo wrote his customary Christmas letters, hoping that 1913 would bring about "feverish and fruitful activity," with Illica working on *Avemaria*.[32] Leoncavallo attended further performances of *Zingari* during February 1913 at Naples' Teatro San Carlo with Burzio and conducted by Vittorio Gui. He then returned to Florence, where he remained at the Terminus Hotel Milano for many months after leaving his domicile at Via degli Strozzi.[33]

Money was still a major problem, and Leoncavallo now turned to France's Society of Authors for a pension, initiating a series of letters lasting for months. He also pestered Illica about *Avemaria*, writing from Naples and Florence to provide the librettist with information for the opera's plot. He then cautioned Illica about the authentic scenario, warning him "we must never say things that are not true"[34] and asking when they should travel to Naples to research the subject. Leoncavallo had planned to be in Palermo during April and suggested that he could meet Illica either there or on his return. He hoped Illica would also be able to entice Sonzogno to come, in order to "wake the publisher who fails to answer letters in which I would like to say insolent things!"[35]

FROM *BOHÈME* TO *MIMÌ PINSON*

Inspired by Puccini's successful Murger adaptation and desperate for success, Leoncavallo now decided to switch the registers of the characters in *La bohème* to resemble his colleague's opera. Thus, Rodolfo became a tenor and Marcello a baritone. Incredible as it may seem, rather than rewrite and transpose the roles, Leoncavallo simply opted to exchange Marcello's role with Rodolfo's, and Musette's with Mimì's, thereby having the opera concentrate on the Mimì-Rodolfo relationship as in Puccini's version.[36] Many of the musical changes that Leoncavallo made in this new version, entitled *Mimì Pinson*, were both necessary and beneficial, resulting in a leaner and tighter score void of superfluous characters. Revising the opera could have been an immense improvement if the composer had invested more attention rather than merely exchanging roles, which made his efforts suspect. Considering the fact that it was obvious that Leoncavallo wished to emulate Puccini, it is curious that he now opted to change the work's title, perhaps hoping audiences would thereby judge the opera anew and unhindered by comparisons. Gaetano Bavagnoli conducted the new version on 14 April at Palermo's Teatro Massimo with Giuseppe Armanini (Rodolfo), Ida Quaiatti (Mimì), Rita D'Oria (Musette), Giuseppe Danise (Marcello), and Ernesto Badini (Schaunard). Although Leoncavallo wrote Illica that he had planned to be present, he remained instead in Florence reading the reviews, all of which, "including *Corriere della Sera*," he claimed were good, even if in fact they were not.[37] While many reviewers welcomed some of Leoncavallo's revisions, most believed that although Mimì was now wearing "high heels," her stature still remained that of a "small bourgeois Parisienne."[38] The opera's new version was never performed again following its Sicilian production.[39]

Leoncavallo now turned to *Avemaria* and was tortured by the belief that Illica would never complete it. Even Von Hülsen failed to raise the composer's spirits when writing that *Pagliacci* had just received its three hundredth performance in Berlin. It was difficult for Leoncavallo to accept that his youthful work was constantly produced while most of the others lay languishing, a fact he mentioned at every opportunity. When Cavacchioli wrote Leoncavallo that Illica would only be able to supply a synopsis of *Avemaria*'s first act by the end of June, the composer insisted he required the entire scenario in order to be able to study the "admirable subject . . . which your great artistic spirit has created."[40] Although Illica had read parts of the libretto to Leoncavallo in Castell'Arquato, the composer now requested a complete typescript for Cavacchioli's revision.[41] He begged Illica to come to Milan so that Riccardo Sonzogno could discuss the work with him. He felt "obsessed with the subject," wishing to employ his "entire soul" on the new "opus magnum."[42]

Leoncavallo, now Illica's "collaborator and admirer," finally received the entire scenario in Riccione,[43] elated that the "vibrant work" was so "full of poetry, patriotism, and emotion!"[44] *Avemaria*'s third act overwhelmed the composer with the "same tears and emotion" he had experienced at Castell'Arquato, only "more intense and profound" this time.[45] The composer began studying "the opera in order to penetrate the blood of this great human work . . . crying: Viva Illica!"[46] The librettist later responded during July from Lugagnano (Piacenza) that Leoncavallo's enthusiasm for *Avemaria* had inspired him. That same July, after Belvederi mentioned he might visit a Leoncavallo swamped with work, the composer spoke of moving to Rome, an idea that he would consider for months, hoping that Belvederi would not only become his librettist but, through his position with the newspaper *La Tribuna*, also influence important acquaintances to guarantee a premiere.[47]

Albert de Courville reappeared in Leoncavallo's life, suggesting that the composer create a musical comedy for London. This was the genesis of *Are You There?*, a "farcical musical play" to which Courville himself supplied the text while Edgar Wallace—who had not yet begun writing thrillers—created the lyrics. It seems that Courville had already approached the operetta composer Leo Fall for the project after Franz Lehár was no longer considered. Leoncavallo's score would also include selections written by Lewis M. Muir, the American composer of the popular song "Hitchy-Koo." *Are You There?* was initially announced to premiere on 12 September. When the British press interviewed Leoncavallo in Montecatini in Tuscany, he expressed his opinion that the English public was not "gifted with any extensive powers of reproducing what they hear; but they are pre-eminently endowed with a refined musical soul more than any other people."[48] He planned to travel to London with Berthe the following spring, informing the press that he was "finishing an opera in three acts; but it had not been decided whether Rome or London" would be the first to hear it.[49] It was just as well that Leoncavallo avoided attending the premiere of *Are You There?*, since the work was hissed from the stage at its first performance[50] when it finally opened at London's Prince of Wales' Theatre on 1 November 1913 (after being postponed twice), presented by the American producer Ned Wayburn. There seems to have been great friction with the British cast: "When two heavy bolts fell from the flies and narrowly missed Mr. Wayburn's head, it was reported that they had not fallen by accident."[51] The production was a disaster, and the audience loudly expressed its disapproval. Courville somewhat unwisely defended the show from the stage, apologizing if it had offended "any blasé people in the audience" who refused to see anything new. His efforts were stifled with cries of "Shut up!", "Rotten," and "Montebank!" Courville's "leading lady and current wife (Shirley Kellogg) appealed in tears to the gallery," but they "were not to be placated."[52] "Courville later blamed the audience's reaction on a cabal organized by some girls dismissed during rehearsals," whose friends were actually seen in the auditorium holding megaphones.[53] It also failed to help when *Are You There?* underwent a quick revision.[54] The show closed three weeks later, leaving Miss Kellogg free to record the "Rose-Way" song. No doubt glad that he had not attended the unfortunate premiere, Leoncavallo, following a concert of some of his works in Montreux, visited Edoardo Sonzogno, where Cavacchioli read the *Avemaria* libretto in the composer's presence,[55] generating a favorable impression. Illica now blamed Leoncavallo for mentioning *Avemaria* to the *Corriere della Sera* in an interview, even though the composer swore not to have had contact with the newspaper.[56]

A SECOND U.S. TOUR

Although Leoncavallo would have preferred to remain in Montecatini working on *Avemaria*, finances forced him into accepting a second and less strenuous North American tour lasting some six weeks.[57] He left Montecatini on 4 October 1913 to board the *Oceanic*, without Berthe, during the middle of the month, following a brief stop in Paris. Without Rudolph Aronson's publicity machine, Leoncavallo's arrival in New York and presence at the Astor Hotel, where he had also resided during the 1906 tour, "never exceeded a *pianissimo*."[58] *Musical America* interviewed the exhausted composer two hours before his train was to depart for San Francisco. Included with the article was a photograph taken beside his hotel bed, capturing Leoncavallo's greying hair and puffy eyes rimmed with black circles. His dark, ill-fitting suit failed to flatter his five-foot, six-inch stature, drawing attention to his enormous head, neck, and hands. Leoncavallo's photos generally give the impression of his being taller than he actually was, and few, like the one in *Musical America*, captured a more truthful, ill, and forelorn appearance. After the interviewer described Leoncavallo's mustache as "black, white, and reddish," and all the while hoping that the chair would not topple under the composer's weight, he wrote an illuminating description of Leoncavallo's jovial personality:

> Genial is the term that most appositely pertains to the personality of the expansive Ruggiero. He radiates good nature and *bonhommie*. On occasion he is almost naïve, while satisfaction bubbles up within him and illumines his face with smiles when he meditates upon his achievements. . . . Whether or not one is disposed to esteem his works as highly as he himself values them it is impossible not to react in some fashion to the warmth of his good nature. . . . His conversation (in a far better French than is usually at the command of an Italian) was a monologue delivered with due Italian effervescence and characteristic stress of emphasis.[59]

Leoncavallo told *Musical America* many of the same things he had said during his original tour, finding it a shame that only *Pagliacci* was known in the United States,[60] and again taking the opportunity to express his bitterness regarding Casa Ricordi and Puccini:

> Is it not a pity that there are opera houses over which a publisher exercises so powerful an influence that the operas of one particular composer are constantly exploited and those of another barred? Mr. Puccini's works are always heard. Naturally I am not in the least objecting to this, for they are thoroughly worthy of that honor. But it is the idea of restraining others that I find unjust. My operas I am sure would be well received. Think of the successes I have enjoyed and the esteem I have been held in in so many music centers in Europe! Think of *Zingari*! Think that the emperor of Germany selected me above innumerable German composers to write a work for his Royal Opera House! Think that, despite all the harsh criticism and ill will with which it was met, *Roland of Berlin* has already been sung between sixty and seventy times. In Paris there are numberless French composers clamoring for and receiving hearings. And what does the public prefer, what receives the widest attention? Italian works, mine included. They love me and treat me like a god in Vienna. I was lionized at the Opera there one evening when I was coming down the stairs after a performance of *Lohengrin*. Does it not seem unfair in the face of all this that only one of my ten operas can be given a hearing in this part of the world?[61] Oh! I should so much like to introduce the others myself.[62]

When asked to name his favorite operas, a "bland smile" pervaded his face, as he realized that *Zingari* would be performed in San Francisco. "That I cannot tell you. . . . a father cannot say which of his children he prefers, and my works are my children. I am very fond of *Zingari*. . . . I am a hard worker; in twenty years I have composed some ten operas."[63] He again mentioned trying to complete *Crepusculum* and spoke of his latest project: "I am about to begin a new one, *Avemaria*. The libretto is Illica's; anything more beautiful I have never read. I have only had it for a month, though, and have not yet started work on it. Ah! but when it is done!" When asked about what happened to the planned *Camicia rossa*, he replied, lowering his voice, that he had never completed it: "I was advised not to by many important persons. It dealt with the Irredentists, you see, and there was danger that it might arouse political feelings at an inopportune moment."[64]

Although *Musical America* was probably unaware of the Zangarini-*Zazà* scandal, they noticed that it was a "painful" subject when asking him why he no longer wrote his own libretti, since he was unhappy with "most librettists in Italy" who were journalists . . . not the most pleasant of persons to cooperate with."[65] He then changed the subject with "celerity," claiming that "Strauss and Debussy will not last because they are not natural. . . . My *Pagliacci* has succeeded because I wrote it in a spirit of absolute sincerity."[66] Leoncavallo felt music was synonymous with melody, something he was unable to glean from a younger generation steadily overtaking him: A "composer has accomplished something great when he writes a work that insinuates itself into the public ear and refuses to be dislodged from there. And therefore I hold it a greater accomplishment to have written "La donna è mobile" than to have composed *Salome*. Verdi's air is a greater piece of art than Strauss's opera."[67] While Mascagni and Alfano would experiment with impressionism in *Parisina*, *La leggenda di Sakùntala*, and *Cyrano de Bergerac*, Puccini also altered his sound palette in *La fanciulla del West*, as had Verdi with *Otello* and *Falstaff*. Although it may be considered laudable that Leoncavallo was unique in remaining faithful to his original style, *Pagliacci*'s emotional force later became stagnant in works that were not innovative, intellectually satisfying, or memorable. Leoncavallo's opinion of Wagner also changed—at least for the press—during his last years:

> I can treat operatically only such themes as are vital, natural, and true. It would not be possible, for instance, for me to write music for fishes that sing and Valkyries that fly through the air. I have never seen such things in life, and so I should be at a loss when it came to treating them. But give me men who can laugh, men who can weep, and I can laugh and weep with them. Such has always been my aim. Art should concern itself primarily with the truth. The artist must not tie himself down with theories. Wagner, man of genius that he was, laid down many theories which he purported to follow

but in the last analysis never did. He was unwilling, he averred, to write ensembles, concerted numbers, duets, and he claimed to have written "endless
melody". . . . yet Wagner was constantly refuting himself in practice.[68]

If anyone refuted himself it was Leoncavallo, incorrectly asserting that *Der Ring
des Nibelungen* originated during Wagner's early years:

> When he gave concerts in the days of his struggles for recognition what sort
> of things did he give out of his own works—the "Ride of the Valkyries"
> . . . the "Siegfried Funeral March," the "Magic Fire" music. All of them are
> numbers with a definite beginning and a perfectly well-defined ending.
> Take the wonderful last act of *Götterdämmerung*, which makes it worth one's
> while to sit through the first two, and what have you but a string of detach-
> able pieces. . . . And even in *Parsifal*, supposedly the broadest exemplification
> of his system, we find precisely the same thing.[69]

The composer communicated in French, still unable to grasp the English
language:

> The only thing that troubles me is that people over here speak English so
> differently from the way I was taught to pronounce it. I cannot understand
> those who try to talk to me in this country, and they, in their turn, are not
> able to understand me. If I tell a taxi driver I want to go to the Hippodrome
> he doesn't seem to know what I'm talking about. Then, when I show him
> the name in writing, he says it in a curious guttural way. . . . If I say I want
> to go to the Savoy Hotel the same thing happens. I cannot grasp the funda-
> mental principles of your enunciation over here. Still, as you people are able
> to understand each other when you speak there's nothing to hinder mutual
> comprehension in singing, I should think (!).[70]

Even though Leoncavallo had aroused considerable irritation over his claim
to have brought the "La Scala Orchestra" with him during his 1906 tour,
this time he became the "musical director" of the "Western Metropolitan
Opera Company," regardless as to whether or not it had just as little affilia-
tion with New York's theater as the original orchestra had with La Scala.[71]
The company's managing directors, Ettore Patrizi and Eugene D'Avigneau,
announced a "grand opera season" in San Francisco lasting from 13 October
until 23 November 1913, presenting "a great and thoroughly equipped organization of 150 people, orchestra of 50, chorus of 60, and ballet of 12." These
performances took place at the Tivoli Opera House with a superb ensemble
of singers, consisting of Carmen Melis, Piero Schiavazzi, Luigi Montesanto,
Luca Botta, Lucia Crestani, and Fanny Anitua.[72] On 22, 23, 25, and 26 October Leoncavallo conducted a program consisting of *Maïa*'s intermezzo and
"Danse Musette," the *Roland von Berlin* overture, and a "Tarantella Napoletana,"

followed by *Pagliacci* with Maria Mosciska, Piero Schiavazzi, and Luigi Montesanto singing Silvio *and* Tonio's prologue![73] The "Marcia Reale" conducted by Maestro Bellucci preceded the performance, while Melis threw a branch of laurels that landed at Leoncavallo's feet from one of the boxes, prompting him to declare a stentatorian "Viva l'America!" The *San Francisco Chronicle* announced on 28 October that Leoncavallo would conduct *Pagliacci* in a double bill with *Cavalleria rusticana* sung by Schiavazzi, who chose not to perform Canio and Turiddu at the last moment.[74] On 30 October Leoncavallo conducted the North American premiere of *Zingari*, sung by Marie Moscisca, Umberto Chiodo, and Montesanto, alternating with Melis's free and arrogant Fleana. Further performances of the opera followed on 1, 2, 4, 9, and 18 November, sometimes accompanying *Pagliacci*. Leoncavallo also conducted *Zazà* with Melis, Botta, and Montesanto on 19 and 22 of November. Critics were touched by Melis's interpretation, especially the third act with Totò, prompting one reviewer to write that "when she and the little one are seated on the sofa, singing and crying, one forgets that one is seated before a stage."[75] Leoncavallo also received a telegram from Cleofonte Campanini after attending a reception at the Bohemian Club,[76] asking whether he could conduct the Chicago premiere of *Zingari* (coupled with *Pagliacci*) on 8 December. The date was later postponed until the fifteenth. After the composer had traveled to Los Angeles to conduct *Zingari* at the Auditorium Theatre,[77] he finally telegraphed Campanini his acceptance and willingness to conduct both operas.

Arriving in Chicago and staying at the Congress Hotel and Annex, Leoncavallo immediately began writing his Christmas letters. From Illica he sought news about *Avemaria*, as he had been advertising the opera wherever possible. He also wrote Belvederi that he had kept the prestige of Italian art *in alto* during his California trip, still feeling well following twenty-four performances. Leoncavallo hoped to return to San Francisco for another tour in 1915 to coincide with the Panama Pacific International Exposition. He had also arranged to visit Mexico for two months, although these plans ultimately fell through. The composer returned to Florence during January 1914 and, feeling the ostracism his works encountered in Italy, considered a Russian tour during March 1914 if his health permitted.

AVEMARIA, ILLNESS, AND *ÇA-IRA!*

Upon his return, Leoncavallo had Illica and Cavacchioli working on *Avemaria*, Belvederi creating a patriotic libretto entitled *Ça-Ira!* that dealt with the French Revolution, and Forzano trying to recapture *Reginetta delle rose*'s success with another operetta to be called *La candidata*.[78]

After time spent in Magonza and Milan, before going to Castell'Arquato, where he hoped to discuss *Avemaria* with Illica (who was unfortunately ill), Leoncavallo returned to Florence's Hotel Terminus Milano, where he wrote the librettist not to undertake any unecessary plot changes in act 3 that would outweigh minor details in act 1. He also wished to exclude the chorus in the "sublime scene in which Avemaria accuses her father and brothers to discover if her lover is really a traitor."[79] The composer insisted that the second act remain an "intimate" one, counseling Illica to concentrate on the psychological development of his characters.[80] He approved of acts 1 and 3, as well as the opera's ending with "Viva l'Italia libera! Morte al Borbone!,"[81] inspiring feelings of "redemption and patriotism."[82]

Leoncavallo once again toyed with the idea of moving to Rome that March. He asked Belvederi to search for a furnished apartment that was centrally located and included an antechamber, living and dining room, and master bedroom for Berthe and himself, as well as rooms for Jeanne and the maid, Mariuccia. He also requested electric light, gas, and an elevator, but nothing higher than the third floor. His finances allowed him to spend between 300 and 450 lire per month. But the kind of Roman apartments that would have interested Leoncavallo—on the Via Veneto—were financially beyond his reach, costing at least 650 lire. Thus, he instead decided to rent a small house called Villino du Puget in Viareggio, at less cost and near the sea, where he might find some peace and quiet to concentrate on *Avemaria*. A severe bout of bronchitis demanding sixteen days' bed rest halted the move. Although he was not running a fever, Mariuccia was not available, and the composer felt sad and depressed, packing his few belongings at Florence's Terminus Hotel Milano to leave for Rome.

Next, Leoncavallo developed pustules on his hands and feet because of uremia. At the same time Berthe also contracted a fever, leaving Jeanne to run from Berthe's bed to Leoncavallo's chair, the composer being incapable of much movement.[83] When Jeanne also fell ill, Leoncavallo was forced to hire a nurse. After recovering somewhat, he wrote of his depression, feeling abandoned in a region without friends, "without a dog" to comfort him.[84]

When this period of illness was behind him, Leoncavallo agreed to take part in a benefit concert on 10 May for Pisa's Dante Alighieri Society. Soon thereafter, he informed the Société des Auteurs et Compositeurs Dramatiques in Paris that he was planning a cinematic adaptation of Goethe's *Reinecke Fuchs*. He complicated matters by also telling Titta Ruffo that he and Illica were preparing a new libretto entitled *Papa Lebounard* to replace *Prometeo*. Ruffo unfortunately fell into the trap once again, cabling from Salsomaggiore that he would visit Leoncavallo during the beginning of July, while Leoncavallo immediately wrote Illica that the baritone was "jubilant. . . . I wrote that you had two subjects, and you must present him with two in order to maintain a serious proposal."[85] Leoncavallo insisted that three days would be sufficient for Illica to create a scenario, after which they could all meet in Viareggio to discuss the matter further, intent on not letting Ruffo "escape."[86] He also found time to consider a cinematic version of both *Pagliacci* and *Chatterton* after hearing that Mascagni had supposedly received fifty thousand lire for a Garibaldi film. Leoncavallo and Illica also wrote Salvatore di Giacomo, director of Naples's Biblioteca Lucchesiana, requesting a series of songs called *Grida dei Venditori di Napoli* for *Avemaria*. Illica hoped to have "an authentic Cavacchioli in di Giacomo," after the former relinquished any further interest in a collaboration.[87]

WITH TOSCANINI AND CARUSO

Leoncavallo bragged to Illica on 20 July that Caruso, whom he had spoken to in Viareggio, was interested in singing *Avemaria*'s world premiere. He also wrote to Cleofonte Campanini to ask if the opera could be unveiled in Chicago. Leoncavallo's inability to begin the project during 1914, let alone complete it, forced Campanini to write the composer from Bad Nauheim that it would be impossible for the work to be scheduled in Chicago in the foreseeable future.[88] Illica now suggested that Leoncavallo read *Avemaria*'s libretto to Caruso and Giulio Gatti-Casazza in Montecatini during July, not expecting that Toscanini would also accompany them. Leoncavallo did so and was shocked that the "idiots" remained unimpressed after the reading of "an artistic masterpiece that was capable of moving a block of stone."[89] Excuses were sought when Caruso asked who would produce the work, while Gatti-Casazza felt it dangerous to cast such a famous artist in case the venture failed.[90] The hearing ended with Leoncavallo and Berthe telling the "rotten spectators" off, claiming that Caruso was afraid of singing in Italy because he "felt old" and because his role was not the name part, additionally shocked when the tenor asked him what "the word 'crimenlese' [high treason] meant!!!!!!!!!!"[91] Leoncavallo was still upset five days later, writing Illica that it didn't matter whether Caruso was a Neapolitan or not, since he was a stupid tenor, above all, and one that was "finished in Italy."[92] According to Leoncavallo, Gatti-Casazza was "afraid of a possible disaster" because Caruso had received "ferocious reviews" singing *Rigoletto* and *La fanciulla del West* in Paris during 1912.[93] Leoncavallo was convinced that neither Gatti-Casazza nor Toscanini were really Illica's friends, whereas Illica wondered whether their lack of interest resulted from Leoncavallo's having read those parts of the libretto authored by Cavacchioli (although, in fact, such was not the case).[94] Leoncavallo was still discussing changes in the *Avemaria* libretto with Illica during August, including the possibility of a trio, although the "damned war" dampened his spirits, especially after some of Berthe's cousins joined in the fight.

Leoncavallo celebrated Berthe's birthday on 15 August before receiving a devastating letter from Riccardo Sonzogno on the 24th, in which he bluntly explained the financial problems that had "completely paralyzed" Casa Sonzogno, and which would no longer allow them to commission new works. Engulfed in debts without any profits ("not even a few lire"),[95] Riccardo now hoped for an American loan since all commerce had ceased. He was only able to offer the composer five hundred lire payable between 10 and 15 September. "But then?"[96] Although Sonzogno encouraged him to be patient, Leoncavallo could hardly believe that after working for twenty-two years for the firm he would not even be entitled to receive royalties for previously published works until the situation had improved.[97]

Leoncavallo signed a private contract with Belvederi on 26 August in Montecatini, stipulating that he would also collaborate on *Ça-Ira*'s libretto, which was now taking the form of an *episodio storico* in one act. The composer read Ruffo an outline of the work and reported that the baritone was so enthused that he hoped the opera could be produced in Chicago during January 1915. Leoncavallo prepared himself for a "superhuman effort," pledging to compose the opera before the end of the year if Belvederi could provide the libretto during the first half of September. He then signed his letter to Belvederi with his name, followed by *Ça-Ira!* repeated three times.[98] Leoncavallo later confided to Vaucaire that the work would serve as a pendant to *Pagliacci*. Campanini then informed the composer on 9 September from Salsomaggiore that the opera could not premiere in Chicago, since the coming season would have to be suspended due to the war, with only the Metropolitan Opera still performing. Belvederi continued work nonetheless, presenting Leoncavallo with the completed libretto on 13 September.

Without the possibility of performing in Chicago, Leoncavallo wrote an imaginary interview between himself and Belvederi, which he then asked his friend to publish. Speaking of Europe's political situation as well as the many theaters that remained closed, he said "I hope that in this state of things a sentiment of *italianità* will rise among us for the protection of our works as well as our artists . . . and that our theaters will not be open solely to foreign *maestri* and to a privileged few . . . but also to those *maestri* that have proven themselves to be the glory of Italian art."[99] Leoncavallo again blamed Casa Ricordi's "camorra" for his works, except for *Pagliacci* and *Zazà*, not being produced in Italy, informing readers that he was prepared to join the socialists, knowing "many of its leaders."[100]

In the meantime, Belvederi's work on *Ça-Ira!* made an "excellent" impression on Leoncavallo.[101] The opera opens in Paris in 1793, showing the home of Bernard Guitry, Marquis de Boisdauphin, whose daughter, Josette, is in love with the thirty-year-old "popular poet" Gabriel Marais, who is a combination of Chatterton and André Chenier, another Illica poet.[102] Gabriel enables Guitry to escape the revolutionaries only to be guillotined at the end. Not only is Gabriel allowed to burn his poetry in the fireplace, like Chatterton, but large portions of the text, including Gabriel's aria "Tu sola a me rimani, o poesia" (which would later reappear for a third time in *Mameli*) had originated previously in *Chatterton*. Leoncavallo revised and edited most of Belvederi's work on additional sheets of paper, pasting his alterations alongside the existing libretto.

Leoncavallo also sent Illica a letter from Montecatini's Grand Hotel, fearing that the librettist might have become jealous of Forzano's work on *La candidata*. He made it clear that the operetta had resulted out of economic necessity, thanks to Casa Sonzogno, in addition to his responsibilities of supporting a family that still included his brother in Paris. He told Illica that it would be difficult to have *Avemaria* "worthily" produced even if it were completed by the following spring.[103] The composer grew increasingly worried now that Chicago was no longer available, believing that Italian opera houses would not be interested. He suggested that these extended delays would offer Illica time to rework the libretto, while he also wished to write a final scene for the opera himself.

Leoncavallo resumed work on *La candidata* and began planning *Ça-Ira!* at Viareggio's Via Amerigo Vespucci, where he rented a small *villino*. Having heard that Giordano seemed willing to offer Sonzogno financial support, Leoncavallo jealously referred to him once again as the "Spatz heir."[104] By 26 September Leoncavallo realized that Riccardo Sonzogno was considering a merger with Casa Ricordi in order to survive. He hoped Illica would be better informed and requested that he write him something "immediately dealing with the subject, since you know how much the situation interests me for all of my works and for *Avemaria*."[105] Leoncavallo's letters during this time reveal great uncertainty, despair, and enormous frustration. The composer worked "like a thunderbolt," completing *La candidata*'s second act, while Belvederi sent another revised version of *Ça-Ira!*[106]

WAR

When World War I broke out in all its force, Italy chose to remain neutral for many months, until they were forced to make a decision, thus causing a rift between the "pro-German" and the "pro-Allied sympathizers."[107] A protest was also drawn up against the German bombardment of Rheims; German newspapers reported that both Puccini and Leoncavallo were among the signatories, and threatened to ban their operas. Puccini stated that he was unaware of the protest and had not signed, hoping to remain "between chairs," realizing that a ban would signify a serious loss of income now that numerous Italian opera houses had been closed. Many composers opted to remain neutral as long as possible, fearing that their works would not be performed, hoping that "the situation could not continue for long." Although these musicians truthfully claimed that they had "nothing to do with the war," the global conflict proved stronger, forcing them to take a stance whether they wished to or not.[108] This enforced political partisanship went against the grain of Leoncavallo's international persona as an artist, in which Germany had played a significant role. The *Neues Wiener Tagblatt* published an article that was instantly reprinted by the *Corriere della Sera* on 15 October, stating that the Cologne Opera had canceled all further performances of *Pagliacci* "because of [the composer's] ingratitude and hostile feelings toward Germany." Leoncavallo and Riccardo Sonzogno realized that something would have to be done immediately to salvage his German career. They drafted a letter to the German newspapers in response to Adolph Fürstner's request, stating that the "Associazione Artistica Romana" had been responsible for inviting him to join the protest. They stressed that, although it would have been impossible as an Italian not to comply, Leoncavallo had not attended the meeting, excusing his absence while expressing his support, thereby suggesting that he had, in fact, not signed the manifesto and, in addition, was unwilling to assume any responsibility for it. Riccardo Sonzogno now also warned Leoncavallo to avoid the subject in his correspondence and not to speak negatively about Germany, hoping to protect both their interests. Germany soon demanded that Leoncavallo make a public statement in favor of their country, in light of their long collaboration, mentioning both Wilhelm II and *Der Roland von Berlin*.[109]

Fürstner received the letter from Leoncavallo and Sonzogno on 2 November and immediately presented it to the German newspapers. He later wrote Sonzogno that its publication failed to have the necessary effect and that both the lawyer Artur Wolff and Von Hülsen claimed that Leoncavallo had indeed signed the protest on 26 September. Fürstner now requested that Leoncavallo "present an explanation to the Society (Deutscher Bühnenverein) withdrawing his protest."[110] In addition, he also deemed it necessary for Leoncavallo to announce an "unconditional official denial" to the press. Fürstner felt that if the composer followed his suggestions there would be a good chance of his works returning to the German repertory. On 9 November Leoncavallo complained to Belvederi that two German theaters had canceled his operas, claiming that both their country and the kaiser were offended.[111] The *Corriere della Sera* and *La Tribuna* ran articles entitled "Leoncavallo Placed on the Index of German Theaters" as if it signified a "national feast."[112] Leoncavallo was soon forced to realize that any efforts to appear as an "independent artist"[113] were nullified, thanks to the "polemics" surrounding his name that he felt were in "bad taste" during a cruel moment in history.[114]

The time that Leoncavallo had spent away from Switzerland living in Italy had sufficed to convince him to consider a move to North America after "completing" *Avemaria*. He wished to publish "all the nude and crude truth" concerning the "camorras" that had "boycotted" his works in Italy.[115] Leoncavallo considered his homeland to be ruled by "envy, jealousy, slander, and intrigue."[116]

On 20 November, Riccardo Sonzogno managed to send the composer one thousand lire for the past three months of royalties. He also blamed Leoncavallo for having instigated the rumor that he was being boycotted by the firm. The Rheims protest was still in effect, and Wiesbaden would therefore be unable to present *Pagliacci* if Leoncavallo could not prove his "innocence."[117] Sonzogno was well aware of the financial losses if Leoncavallo's works continued to remain unperformed throughout Germany and Austria.[118] Following Sonzogno's advice, Leoncavallo tried to convince the Germans that he had documentary evidence of not signing the protest. He first contacted Viareggio's Telegraphic Office, requesting that they trace the telegram he had originally sent the "Associazione Artistica Internazionale" on 29 September [*sic*]. A copy was sent the composer on 25 November. He then wrote the Association in Rome requesting further evidence, stating that he did not want to retract any of his statements, only wishing to clear up any misconceptions about his not having been in Rome on 26 September. Leoncavallo naively hoped to convince the Germans of his innocence, although he in fact personally did support the protest. As an "honest man," he now threatened to take the Italian authorities to court.[119] On 19 December he received a letter from the Association stating that he had not personally participated at the meeting but had sent a telegram on 25 September from Viareggio to Via Margutta 54 in Rome, stating that he could not personally attend.[120, 121]

Virulent attacks continued to appear in the German press, suggesting that Leoncavallo had turned his back on them after realizing he could no longer derive any financial gains. The composer was now referred to as "poor Bajazzo," and the press once again released all their previous anger over Leoncavallo's commission. He was scoffed at and branded an "enemy of German culture," doomed as both man and composer in Germany. Fürstner now also sent Riccardo Sonzogno a copy of a Puccini letter published in the *Berliner Tageblatt* in which he had stated that he had always refrained from any manifestations against Germany, urging Leoncavallo to do the same. Meanwhile, anti-German caricatures of Leoncavallo, Bernard Shaw, Maurice Maeterlinck, and D'Annunzio that had originally appeared in German newspapers now also found their way to the United States.

While trying to rescue his name in Germany, Leoncavallo became extremely disheartened that Casa Sonzogno failed to promote its own composers in the same manner as Casa Ricordi did. Puccini remained in Torre del Lago able to work unimpeded while Ricordi organized his career, whereas Leoncavallo was forced to undertake any and all kinds of promotion himself. He felt that Mascagni was suffering too: "Where are they producing *Ratcliff, Isabeau, Amica, Fritz, Rantzau*, etc.? Other than *Cavalleria* only some performances of *Iris* are given because it belongs to Ricordi."[122] Leoncavallo failed to understand why Turin's Teatro Regio should keep their "doors closed" to his works when *Zazà* had enjoyed such an "extraordinary triumph" there in 1901. On Christmas day, Leoncavallo was told that if he did not wish to be boycotted by 120 German and Austrian theaters it would be necessary for him to travel to Rome in order to personally declare that he had not been "correctly informed" regarding the protest.

LA CANDIDATA

Leoncavallo's year ended orchestrating *La candidata*, while also considering whether he should pay a Roman journalist five hundred lire a month to write articles inspired and "guided" by his own ideas.[123] Although Leoncavallo was probably alluding to Belvederi, the latter had suggested Nicola D'Atri, whom the composer refused. Leoncavallo hoped that 1915 would mark the premieres of *Candidata, Avemaria*, and *Ça-Ira!*, while he still planned to rework *Ça-Ira!* with Belvederi. Leoncavallo also felt that *Avemaria* was now a timely and "marvelous artistic monument" thanks to the ongoing war,[124] since it was a patriotic work expressing Italy's "redemption and liberty."[125]

During January 1915, he began making arrangements for *La candidata*'s February world premiere at Rome's Teatro Nazionale. His finances were at such a low ebb that he could only remain in Rome if the hotel room cost less than 10 lire per day. Forzano bolstered the composer's spirits, certain that the operetta would be a success. While in Rome, Leoncavallo informed his Neapolitan friend, Enrico Pessina, that he wished to meet Antonio Salandra during his stay, in the hope of clearing up any lingering inconsistencies regarding the Rheims affair. With Leoncavallo having to seek the most modest of accommodations, he was understandably frustrated reading about Giordano's successful *Madame Sans-Gêne* premiere at the Metropolitan Opera, conducted by Toscanini, while his own works languished. Leoncavallo's letters to Illica and Belvederi frequently speak of his animosity regarding the successes of his colleagues, particularly Giordano, whom he claimed had paid "hundreds of thousands of lire" to stage *Madame Sans-Gêne*.[126] He had "jealously saved" for posterity Riccardo Sonzogno's letter accompanying the last thousand lire he had received; it was all he could show after "22 years working for Casa Sonzogno, during which time I gave them continuous profitable successes such as *Pagliacci, Medici*,

Bohème, Zazà, Rolando, and, finally, *Zingari!*"[127] With "five" family members to support, Leoncavallo confided to Illica that it was miraculous that he had not gone insane on account of the financial ruin that had almost destroyed him. He planned to tell Salandra that Casa Ricordi's power and omnipresence should be curtailed to ensure that other composers would be able to survive.

In a letter to Illica he confirmed that he was working on *Avemaria*, while having to again borrow money in order to survive, and noting that the house in Viareggio failed to offer even the most basic comfort. He initially promised to complete the work by spring, declaring the political situation to be too unstable to consider producing the opera before autumn. Illica, in turn, suggested that Leoncavallo reemploy Cavacchioli, since he had also signed the contract to collaborate on *Avemaria* in order to avoid any future legal conflicts. Leoncavallo also sought Illica's opinion regarding Lorenzo Sonzogno's future, having heard rumors that he might rejoin forces with his uncle, Edoardo, or sell the firm to Casa Ricordi. Leoncavallo claimed that Riccardo Sonzogno owed him 4,600 lire, but that instead of paying him at least a portion of that sum, Sonzogno had in fact spent fifty lire on cologne and silk socks during his last trip to Viareggio.[128]

The premiere of *La candidata* at Rome's Teatro Nazionale, which Leoncavallo finally managed to attend, took place on 6 February, sung by Emma Vecla,[129] Gino Vannutelli (Franz), Annetta Peretti (Sofronia), and Francesco Gargano (Presidente Consiglio dei Ministri). Reviewers deemed the score to be "easy and gracious," while Vecla's interpretation was "admirable." She was called back to the stage repeatedly with both Leoncavallo and Forzano.[130] The octet, tango, and "Dance of the Seven Veils" were especially lauded, while some critics remarked, unbelievably, that Leoncavallo had turned his back on Viennese operetta, since that genre had become increasingly Wagnerian. The Forzano/Leoncavallo collaboration was considered an heir to Offenbach, resembling a modern satire of contemporary life, which is precisely how the librettist had originally envisioned it. Leoncavallo told Illica that *La candidata* had received good reviews "for the most part" and that both the second and third performances were already sold out.[131]

Now that Leoncavallo's operas were banned in Germany, he looked to France, where he took the complete opposite stance, drafting an article wherein he wrote that he had had "the courage to sign the protest," being unique among Italian composers for having done so. As thanks for this "noble act . . . , 120 theaters in Germany and Austria" had boycotted his operas, thereby raising his esteem in France. He was not besmirching Puccini's name, claiming that his colleague's works had been completely "expelled from the repertory of all French theaters" to be replaced by *Pagliacci* to "great enthusiasm and acclaim"![132] He then sent Illica and Riccardo a clipping from *Il Messaggero* on 8 February that quoted Puccini's letter to Wolff and his French fall from grace.

Leoncavallo rejoiced in his momentary triumph over Illica's "ex-collaborator" and now looked to Paris as a possible venue to display his works, including a production of *Zazà* at the Opéra-Comique. He also hoped to collaborate with Maurice Vaucaire on a new opera to complement *Pagliacci*.[133] Vaucaire's only reservation was whether Leoncavallo would be able to produce a publisher.[134] Vaucaire also defended the composer in the French press when they recalled that Leoncavallo had also written Wolff and, in fact, never signed the declaration.[135]

Noting that Leoncavallo had in fact not signed the Rheims protest,[136] *Le Figaro* now published an extended article on 18 February that included a letter Leoncavallo had written from Viareggio stating that he *had* signed.[137] Trying to whitewash himself once more by using "Down with Austria" slogans, Leoncavallo finally opted for the truth, stating that he had not been present but had posted a telegram with his approval, now quoted in full, instead. The article's second part was aimed against Puccini, while *L'Echo de Paris* carried an article the same day questioning some "suspect information" regarding Leoncavallo's involvement. Confusion continued its course when the newspaper *L'Intransigeant* stated on 16 February that Leoncavallo had not signed, but the paper retracted the statement three days later. The controversy continued as late as 1926, with some still claiming that Leoncavallo had returned Wilhelm's medals.[138]

The demands of jockeying between the German and French sides had begun to take their toll on Leoncavallo, and he suffered under the strain of constantly promoting his name and works. He grew increasingly irritated when younger composers (such as Zandonai) received the esteem he was denied and so desperately craved. He felt that his compatriots had done little to promote his career. This had led him to live in Switzerland during the happiest times of his life, while a large part of his youth had been spent in Egypt and France. The continuous struggle now resulted in "demoralizing" him "as an artist and as a man."[139] No longer believing in a renaissance of his art, Leoncavallo wrote, "The battles are all right when one is young and when one has all the illusions of the future."[140] Disheartened, he now toyed with the idea of either "following D'Annunzio's example" by going to France[141] or trying to earn his living as a music critic for *La Tribuna* or *Giornale d'Italia*, if Belvederi could arrange such a position, reminding his friend that both the Vatican and Salandra would support his self-nomination.

Seeking a way out of his financial difficulties, he now considered founding a "co-operative society" to purchase Casa Sonzogno. He announced this concept to Illica, the wealthy Franchetti, Giordano, Mascagni, and one or two additional investors, believing that Riccardo would be pleased in light of the predicament he was in. He felt the new firm would enable him to do "very serious" things, like work on *Avemaria*,[142] and he planned to relocate its new offices to Rome in order to avoid competition with Casa Ricordi in Milan. Inspired by Edoardo Sonzogno's Teatro Lirico Internazionale in Milan, Leoncavallo felt confident the society could also create a "Teatro d'Opera Italiana" in the capital. According to Leoncavallo, Franchetti was both "enthusiastic and convinced" about his idea of founding a society; Mascagni's support remained uncertain.[143] Illica was unable to participate due to illness.

His hope renewed, Leoncavallo then met with Cavacchioli in Milan before attending a production of *La candidata* in Florence, where he again wrote Illica (supposedly in Franchetti's presence), concerning Franchetti's meeting with Mascagni, who was not "contrary to the idea" of founding a society, but who doubted Leoncavallo's sincerity.[144] Mascagni believed that Leoncavallo was only interested in forming a society in order to augment Sonzogno's coffers, considering that Italy already had a Society of Authors. Leoncavallo countered by arguing that Mascagni knew "very well that the Society of Authors on Corso Venezia could not be called a 'society,' since its main advisors were Tito Ricordi, Riccardo Sonzogno, and Renzo Sonzogno!" Going there is the same as "making a visit to our respective publishers."[145] Leoncavallo continued pressuring Illica to convince Mascagni and Giordano to sign a contract forming "the new and real Society of Authors."[146] He then returned to Viareggio, where he again wrote Belvederi on 28 March to inquire as to whether *Il Messagero* had decided to employ him as a music correspondent.

Sonzogno now reported to the composer's assistant, Carlo Macchi, that Franchetti and Giordano had informed him of Leoncavallo's plans to form a society.[147] Sensing that there would be no further interest, Leoncavallo brushed aside any amicable sentiments toward his colleagues. He again wrote Illica to ask his advice on whether he should start legal proceedings against his enemy "Kurfürst Riccardo." He also wished to sue his publisher for the 4,600 lire he now owed his lawyer, Giovanni Abbondio, who had already initiated a legal suit against Leoncavallo for lack of payment.[148]

Although by now Leoncavallo felt his colleagues to be "false and small-minded," he continued to keep Franchetti under surveillance to "use him" for his "holy cause" to give a million toward the realization of the authors' society, and he also tried to convince Mascagni that he had "everything to gain."[149] He now also blamed Cavacchioli for gossiping to the "detested Riccardo," while Illica suggested that Leoncavallo send someone to speak with Mascagni.[150] After attending *La candidata*'s Milanese premiere with Forzano and visiting Illica at Castell'Arquato, Leoncavallo hoped to use Walter Mocchi's influence to secure some "capitalists" for his society.[151] Although Mocchi cabled that he would be willing to meet with the composer at Genoa's Hotel Bristol, Leoncavallo had to send Macchi instead when Berthe developed an "intestinal inflammation," requiring a doctor and a special diet including resin oil.[152] Macchi walked the streets of Genoa for four hours before Mocchi agreed to see him, which Leoncavallo blamed on Riccardo, whom he believed had forewarned the impresario. Franchetti visited Leoncavallo on 27 April to inquire about the progress of the "society" and mentioned to Leoncavallo "with his false smile that he was now collaborating with Forzano."[153] Franchetti agreed to take part in forming the society if his colleagues also participated, whereupon Leoncavallo "coldly" retorted that whoever wished to join could, while those that did not would be superseded.[154]

By 7 May, Leoncavallo was livid that he would not be able to meet with Mocchi prior to his departure for South America and that Giordano and Mascagni's ("Pietrino, Pieruccio") interests were also waning, while Franchetti had now become a "true son of Judah."[155] He advised Illica to continue working on Mascagni, since it would also be in "his [Illica's] interest."[156] Although discouraged and disillusioned, Leoncavallo nevertheless reminded Illica that he was "an old fighter for bread and glory."[157]

HERR PUCCINI

Leoncavallo now turned to artistic matters once again, sending Maurice Vaucaire questions pertaining to the French Revolution for *Ça-Ira!*.[158] Vaucaire was supposedly also at work on a French translation of *La candidata*. The librettist mentioned Leoncavallo's operetta *Prestami tua moglie* for the first time on 14 May 1915, in a letter advising the composer to seek permission for an adaptation of Maurice Desvallières' farce *Prête-moi ta femme*, on which the work would be based.[159] During this same period, Illica also decided to discuss *Avemaria* with Riccardo Sonzogno, in Cavacchioli's presence, in order to promote "a bit of general peace,"[160] but the publisher expressed absolutely no interest, even when Illica added that he planned to rework most of it. As a result, Illica then swore never to set foot in Casa Sonzogno again, confiding in Leoncavallo that the "matter" was "serious indeed."[161] That didn't keep the composer from thinking that *Avemaria* still had a future; he wrote Illica that he had discovered a child singing in an acting troupe who would be perfect for the role of Aniello.

Gossip and jealousy again surfaced when Leoncavallo told Illica that Franchetti had been frequently visiting Forzano, who was trying to remain relatively isolated to avoid military duty. "I am happy at heart that the Baron has abandoned us," was all Leoncavallo could still say regarding his ex-investor.[162] His fear of a Puccini–Forzano collaboration was reinforced one evening when he saw Forzano saying goodbye to "Herr Puccini" as he and Berthe drank an espresso at Viareggio's Chalet Principe.[163] The implications were obvious. Leoncavallo now wondered if Mascagni had relinquished composing an opera based on Ouida's *Two Little Wooden Shoes* in favor of Puccini, who had expressed interest in the subject.[164] He speculated on whether "Forzano's presence with Puccini might signify an attempt on the part of the librettist to enter Casa Ricordi."[165] He then wrote Illica, demanding to know if he had seen Mascagni during his recent visit to Milan.[166]

Additional correspondence only confirms the bitter feelings Leoncavallo still held toward his rival Puccini. He again wrote Illica on 23 May that "Herr Puccini always comes to Viareggio, and the other day (knowing that he is a Germanophile) one of his authentic Italian friends met him, shouting: 'Long live Italy, long live the war, and death to the kaiser.'"[167] When Leoncavallo heard that Puccini had thereupon demonstrated his patriotism by informing the *Nuova Giornale* that one of his villas would be offered for use to the wounded, he ironically commented that the villa used would be "the one that's up in the mountains that he wanted to sell and . . . that one cannot reach since there isn't a road. Oh, patriotism at a good price!!!"[168] More gossip followed on 31 May. "Puccini comes to Viareggio almost every day. He must have a lot of entertainment in Torre del Lago to run here where there is almost no one, not even cinemas—which have closed—and the seashore is dark by order of the military command!"[169] Although now also weakened by ill health, Leoncavallo's rebellious spirit and naiveté had still not forsaken him when writing of "the Germans with their *Wagner*, with their *operette,* and with their *Kultur,*" praising Rossini, Verdi, and Italian art along with Italy's soldiers and *Avemaria*, claiming it to be "the first national opera of a resurrected Italy!"[170] The same letter concluded with renewed pleas for a job as music critic for the *Corriere della Sera* in order to support an "anti-German tendency in music" after he heard reports that the composer Antonio Orefice had been considered for the post.[171]

When Italy declared war on Austria during May, Leoncavallo wrote Illica a letter in which he judged it a "holy war against our eternal livid enemies."[172] By mid-June, he informed Belvederi that, with "great effort," he was composing the patriotic *Avemaria* and *Ça-Ira!*. Simultaneously, four parts of *Ça-Ira!* had supposedly already been written, while he was now working on "the famous patriotic hymn" that would be "something beautiful."[173] Leoncavallo hoped to interest Choudens in *Ça-Ira!*, considering that it was a French subject, now that his relations with Sonzogno had come to a standstill.[174]

Because of his bad health the composer was spending increasingly more time in Montecatini to take the waters, where he was cared for by Florence's Dr. Petrocchi and Dr. Grocco, who visited him three times weekly. He asked Belvederi to meet him there to hear portions of *Ça-Ira!* and consoled his friend that "a new Italy and a new France would rise beaming with new light."[175] He couldn't help revealing to Belvederi that Illica "at the age of 57" had presented himself as a volunteer for the war effort.[176] He wrote to Illica and his wife expressing how moved he was upon reading the news, which had even been mentioned in the *Corriere della Sera*, and also how envious (!) he was of Illica's decision, since, regretfully, he needed to remain at home for Berthe and Jeanne. "Who would take care of them if I left for the field?"[177] As Leoncavallo told the queen mother, *Avemaria* would be his war offering. He reminded Illica that with little hope in the new generation it had essentially been *his* generation that had inaugurated an artistic and political change.

Leoncavallo again requested that Belvederi come to Montecatini for "ten or twelve days" because "of an important matter concerning our work,"[178] but, in the meantime, Riccardo Sonzogno arrived there to try to cure an eye ailment that threatened to blind him. Although Leoncavallo believed the publisher had pretended not to see him sitting in a café with Berthe and Jeanne, Berthe's rage, repressed for so many years, now came to the surface as she accosted the publisher later that evening as he was strolling through Montecatini's streets with the conductor Carlo Sabajno. She not only told him everything her husband thought of him with reference both to money owed and to *Avemaria*, but also asked how he had had the audacity to support Giordano and *Madame Sans-Gêne*. According to Leoncavallo's subsequent account, Sonzogno told Berthe that Giordano had used his own money to promote and stage his recent "worthless" opera.[179] Riccardo then made a point of approaching Leoncavallo to shake his hand, afraid of a "public scandal."[180] Berthe's confrontation with Riccardo calmed Leoncavallo into believing that he had succeeded in making the publisher "submissive."[181] Lorenzo Sonzogno now also sent him a check for three thousand lire "to be cashed at some future time," followed by a letter expressing his regret that he could not be paid "due to the war." The composer recalled with great bitterness that he had been forced to write *La candidata* against his will in order to survive. His relations with Forzano had been broken, and composing another operetta ran the risk of making him appear too pro-German, although he continued to move ahead with *Prestami tua moglie* out of financial necessity.

Ironically, Riccardo Sonzogno happened to die "unexpectedly" of a heart attack in Leoncavallo's Montecatini home that July.[182] The composer refused to attend the funeral, only writing of the "kisses and embraces at poor Riccardo's tomb!"[183] He now resolved to begin a new legal battle for the money the deceased had owed him, furious that "the poor dead one" had not sent him "a penny." He also felt insulted that no one had bothered to send him a thank-you note for his wreath, in light of the fact that Cleofonte Campanini had received one.

Leoncavallo now left Italy for France to conduct *Pagliacci* at the Opéra-Comique, where he had been invited by the Amis de Paris to benefit the society Fraternelle des Artistes. Marthe Chenal sang Leoncavallo's patriotic "Hymne à la France," dedicated to President Poincaré, with a text by Senator Gustave Rivet. The composition had been requested of him shortly after his arrival to prove his pro-French sympathies. Poincaré was present at the performance, as were the Italian ambassador (Tittoni) and the pianist Alfred Cortot. Upon the song's completion, Leoncavallo received an ovation interspersed with shouts of "long live the great Italian maestro and friend of France!" as Chenal repeated the hymn again to "indescribable ovations," thus generating its desired effect.[184] After being photographed in the foyer with Poincaré, Tittoni, and the cast, Leoncavallo was honored at a banquet for two hundred guests, where he received a toast dedicated to the unshakable union between Italy and France. Poincaré expressed his pride that the composer had resolved to remain on the French side, and Leoncavallo was then asked to schedule an additional performance of his opera for 28 July, to be combined with Delibes' *Lakmé* and complemented by Chenal's singing the "Marseillaise." Leoncavallo wrote Illica from Paris on 11 August 1915 that Puccini's "pro-German" sympathies were discussed everywhere, "taking on the proportions of Balzac's *Comédie Humaine*."[185] When Leoncavallo went to the Italian Embassy to speak with Tittoni, he learned that Tito Ricordi had begun pressuring the Opéra-Comique to take Puccini's works back into their repertory and promising to donate "60,000 francs worth of royalties for French wounded."[186]

Leoncavallo left Paris in August after having prodded Vaucaire for new subjects. On his way home, he also stopped in Milan for a few days in order to speak with Edoardo Sonzogno in the presence of his lawyer, Carlo Accetti. The elder Sonzogno greeted the composer "with affection," while Leoncavallo related the story of Riccardo's death.[187] Edoardo, after hearing of his Parisian success and the money Riccardo owed him, promised to produce *Avemaria*, although he was unable to supply a specific date. Leoncavallo saw little hope, since numerous theaters remained closed and it was uncertain when either La Scala or Naples's San Carlo would reopen.

Leoncavallo now turned to the life of the patriot Goffredo Mameli with the opera *Mameli, Alba Italica*, which he hoped would be another Italian "national opera" suitable for World War I, if Belvederi supplied the libretto. While a large part of its music was culled from *Chatterton*, portions were perhaps also pieced together from *Avemaria* and *Ça-Ira!*. Leoncavallo first mentioned the future work in a letter to Belvederi from Montecatini on 26 August 1915, heralding the libretto as "a wonder" worthy of Carducci.[188] The composer also told Illica that he himself would present the "small work" *Mameli* if Edoardo Sonzogno failed to begin making plans for *Avemaria* within "one month," as it was now "a question of bread." He hoped Belvederi would supply him with *Mameli*'s final version by 15 September.[189] He still wished to secure Caruso for a world premiere, now writing Belvederi that he would try and read Mameli's libretto to the tenor, which "would be luck for both of us!!"[190] Leoncavallo planned to see Belvederi in Rome, where he would supervise a production of *Zingari* at the Teatro Eliseo. On 4 September, he also sent his friend a postcard mentioning his next operetta, *A chi la giarrettiera?*.

After Leoncavallo informed *Le Figaro*'s Georges Prestat that he would be unable to take part in a French tour beginning in Vichy that Leone had originally planned, he considered it fate when he ran into Baron Antonio de Marchi, the extremely wealthy son-in-law of Argentina's president.[191] Marchi suggested that the composer write a letter stating his wish to present *Avemaria* in South America, which he would then publish in various newspapers, hoping to attract Walter Mocchi's interest in producing the opera at the Teatro Colón. Leoncavallo hoped he would no longer have to "die of hunger" if the plan worked,[192] proud that he had managed to organize everything himself "without the help of a publisher!!!!"[193]

The composer probably introduced Caruso to *Mameli* while the tenor was performing Canio at Milan's Teatro dal Verme during September, with Claudia Muzio and Toscanini, but, from the tone of his subsequent correspondence with Caruso, the plan seems not to have succeeded. He wrote Toscanini prior to his departure not to allow Luigi Montesanto to perform Tonio's prologue in tails *and* also sing the role of Silvio, a custom originating with Mattia Battistini. He specifically stated that whoever sang the prologue must also sing Tonio and *in costume*. (He accepted the insertion of a high G at the conclusion of the prologue). Leoncavallo's review of the performance nevertheless reflected his futile efforts to promote *Mameli*: "C[aruso] is finished. T[oscanini] is a dog. *Pagliacci* is a great opera!!!"[194]

When Leoncavallo read in the *Corriere della Sera* on 17 September that a play entitled *Goffredo Mameli* would be presented at Milan's Teatro Olimpia, he immediately wrote a letter to a handful of Italian newspapers stating that "Maestro Leoncavallo will shortly begin a tour of Italy with a new opera in two acts entitled *L'Alba*, in which the main protagonist is *Goffredo Mameli*."[195] He was relieved when the critics savaged the work the following day, while he continued working on Belvederi's version with "total commitment,"[196] wishing to incorporate an orchestral theme similar to the "fourth act of *Roland*" into *Mameli*'s battle scene, believing it would make a "very powerful effect."[197]

Leoncavallo sent Illica an eight-page letter in October enumerating his debts,[198] which had increased dramatically since Riccardo's 1914 letter in which he had stated that he would no longer be able to pay him any future royalties. Leoncavallo estimated that the firm owed him twenty-two thousand lire and had hoped to be paid two thousand lire for a half year on a monthly basis in order to complete *Avemaria*. He opposed Lorenzo's decision to merge the two firms and refused to accept a contract for *Avemaria* without payment or royalties. Leoncavallo threatened to take Lorenzo to court, considering his new position at Casa Sonzogno to be nothing less than an incomprehensible "disaster."[199]

The composer was fortunately consoled by his work on Mameli, which demanded "three quarters of the day."[200] Delia and Mameli's love duet had now been composed, and Leoncavallo hoped to complete the entire first episode in the near future, having signed a contract to produce the opera in Chicago during December. Belvederi had already begun sending costume designs, while the composer still hoped that either Tiber or Caesar Films would produce a cinematic version. Leoncavallo felt that a filmed version of *Mameli* would be a "splendid epos."[201] Although still unable to compensate Belvederi for his efforts, he promised him payment after his Chicago engagement.[202]

Leoncavallo soon headed for Milan searching for "a capitalist" capable of financing a planned North American *Mameli* tour.[203] He also counseled Belvederi to secure a film contract guaranteeing him fifteen thousand lire, reducing the sum to 10,000 lire at year's end. However, Leoncavallo soon cabled Belvederi from the Victoria Hotel that there was "nothing to hope for" and that the American tour would have to be postponed or completely canceled.[204]

The year 1915 came to a close with Leoncavallo urging Belvederi to complete the final version of *Mameli*'s second episode in order not to waste the time that had been gained by canceling the tour. At the same time he was working on *Avemaria*, and he also completed *Prestami tua moglie*'s orchestration on 17 January 1916. Leoncavallo only managed to send Edmondo Corradi, *Prestami tua moglie*'s librettist, 140 lire rather than the agreed-upon 360 lire for furnishing the libretto, suggesting that his collaborator immediately select a new theme, the future *A chi la giarrettiera?*.

NOTES

1. Albert de Courville, *I Tell You* (London: Chapman & Hall, 1928), 87.

2. Cavacchioli hoped Eugenia Burzio would create the role of Fleana in the first Neapolitan production of *Zingari* during 1913.

3. Leoncavallo chose not to attend the Gotha production of *Maïa* that was produced in a double bill with *Pagliacci*, opening on 25 January as a "soirée Leoncavallo." W. de Holthoff to Leoncavallo, 4 January 1912 (BCL).

4. Leoncavallo was still living at Via degli Strozzi, 4.

5. Leoncavallo to Lorenzo Sonzogno, 5 April 1912 (BCL).

6. Ibid.

7. Ibid.

8. "A new source of sorrow" was Pascoli's death, reminding Leoncavallo of his early days in Bologna. Leoncavallo to Gualtiero Belvederi, 8 April 1912 (BCL). Berthe's mother, Thérèse Paut, died in Florence on 26 April 1912.

9. Even the signed photographs, manuscripts, and books would later come close to being pawned.

10. Piero Asso in *Corriere d'Italia*, 12 June 1912.

11. Although there is a very short and slight resemblance to *Der Graf von Luxemburg*, Leoncavallo's ungallant assumption was aimed at demonstrating that his own

compositions were so popular abroad that even someone like Lehár would chose to "borrow." However, he may also have said it to belittle Lehár, who shared a friendship with Puccini based on mutual esteem.

12. It was also performed in Naples at the Politeama the same evening by the Magnani company.

13. Stefi Csillag (Lilian) was lauded more for her acting than for her singing.

14. Leoncavallo himself had aimed at being an "Italian Lehár," thereby calling the public's attention to their musical similarities in his prepremiere interview.

15. The Royal Anthem was played interspersed with shouts of "Viva l'Italia" before act 2.

16. Cavacchioli sent Leoncavallo a telegram three days following the Roman premiere that the time was ripe to begin announcing *Zingari*.

17. *Gazzetta del Popolo*, 3 July 1912.

18. Ibid. Leoncavallo's continued interest in *Crepusculum* during 1912 negates the assumption that the composer had lost interest in completing the trilogy following *I Medici's* lack of success.

19. It is uncertain whether Leoncavallo was also present at the premiere of his operetta in Potenza during July, where it was performed by the Magnani company at the Teatro Stabile with enormous success.

20. Leoncavallo interviewed in the *Daily Express*, 18 September 1912.

21. This informal "world premiere" performed by the original cast also served the composer as a form of copyright.

22. *Daily Express*, 18 September 1912.

23. Ibid.

24. The cast included Pavoni and Cunego, who had already performed in *Pagliacci* during Leoncavallo's earlier engagement at the Hippodrome.

25. *The Times*, 17 September 1912.

26. Ibid.

27. Fifty-four performances according to other sources.

28. Leoncavallo to Gualtiero Belvederi, 24 November 1912 (BCL).

29. *Birmingham Weekly Post*, 2 November 1912.

30. Ibid.

31. Leoncavallo only seemed to conduct in foreign countries, where he was certain to be distanced from Italy's critics.

32. Leoncavallo to Luigi Illica, 30 December 1912 (BCP).

33. He wrote Soldani on 17 March that he was unable to locate his libretto of *Margherita da Cortona*, which the author requested he return. It was not until the beginning of June that the composer found it in his desk underneath some "important papers," thereby ending his collaboration. Leoncavallo to Valentino Soldani, 4 June 1913 (BCL).

34. Leoncavallo to Luigi Illica, 26 March 1913 (BCP).

35. Ibid.

36. Only the roles of Schaunard and Colline remained unaltered in *Mimì Pinson*.

37. Leoncavallo to Gualtiero Belvederi, 17 April 1913 (BCL).

38. Alberto Favara in *L'Ora*, 14–15 April 1913.

39. Perhaps inspired by Puccini's interest in Ouida's *Two Little Wooden Shoes* and the fact that Forzano would make an adaptation for Mascagni as *Lodoletta*, Leoncavallo also wished to compose an opera based on a Dutch subject, even requesting the address of the Amsterdam publisher Alsbach and Doyer.

40. Leoncavallo to Luigi Illica, 12 June 1913 (BCP).

41. Ibid.

42. Ibid.

43. Ibid.

44. Leoncavallo to Luigi Illica, 20 June 1913 (BCP).

45. Ibid.

46. Ibid.

47. Leoncavallo considered Belvederi and Aurelio Nappi to be his "only true friends," signing his correspondence with a rare "Ruggiero." Leoncavallo to Gualtiero Belvederi, 7 July 1913 (BCL).

48. *The Times*, 16 September 1913.

49. Ibid. Leoncavallo was probably referring to *Avemaria*, hoping it would be finished by the following year.

50. *Le ménestrel*, 15 November 1913.

51. Hall, "Leoncavallo in London," 252.

52. Ibid., 253.

53. Ibid.

54. "Several songs were replaced, some forty-five minutes of dialogue removed, and the popular comedian Billy Merson introduced." Ibid.

55. At this point, Leoncavallo was also contemplating an Italian tour with the Maresca Company to conduct *Zazà*, *Mimì Pinson*, *Zingari*, *Pagliacci,* and "the new opera which I am writing." Leoncavallo to Gea Della Garisenda, 10 September 1913 in *Gea Della Garisenda* (Faenza, 1999) 152–53.

56. Although Leoncavallo did not reveal *Avemaria*'s title to the British press, he made up for it in the United States when no longer under Illica's watchful eye.

57. The *Times* mentioned on 16 September that the tour would last ten weeks.

58. Herbert F. Peyser in *Musical America*, 25 October 1913.

59. Ibid.

60. "It is really not fair that only one of them [operas] should be heard in so many places." Ibid.

61. This would imply that all of his stage works, including *Zingari*, total ten, with Leoncavallo himself excluding *La jeunesse de Figaro*.

62. Peyser in *Musical America*, 25 October 1913.

63. Ibid.

64. Ibid.

65. Ibid.

66. Ibid.

67. Ibid.

68. Ibid.

69. Ibid.

70. Ibid.

71. Before leaving for San Francisco, Leoncavallo told New York's Italian newspaper *La Follía* that he was honored to be in the land of "progress and light in occasion of the centennial of Giuseppe Verdi's birth." *La Follía*, 16 October 1913.

72. The Tivoli Opera House was originally located on Eddy Street near Market Street.

73. Contraltos Fanny Anitua and Luisa Cecchetti alternated as Peppe/Arlecchino.

74. Reviewers felt that "these operettas [*sic*] were made up of pleasing melody and dramatic action." *San Francisco Chronicle*, 29 October 1913.

75. Reprinted in Adonide Gadotti, *Carmen Melis, Un grande soprano del verismo* (Roma: Bardi, 1985), 227.

76. *Rigoletto*, *Thaïs*, and performances of *Otello* to mark Verdi's centennial were also presented.

77. Leoncavallo stayed at the Alexandria Hotel in Los Angeles.

78. The composer first mentioned *La candidata* in a letter to Belvederi dated 24 February 1914.

79. Leoncavallo to Luigi Illica, 17 March 1914 (BCP).

80. Avemaria, Leone Fonte, and the Schoolmaster.

81. Leoncavallo to Luigi Illica, 17 March 1914 (BCP).

82. Ibid.

83. Berthe was also suffering from a second abscess.

84. Leoncavallo to Gualtiero Belvederi, 14 April 1914 (BCL).

85. Leoncavallo to Luigi Illica, June 1914 (BCP).

86. Leoncavallo to Luigi Illica, 17 July 1914 (BCP).

87. Luigi Illica to Leoncavallo, 17 July 1914 (BCP).

88. After Leoncavallo tried organizing a possible tour covering Hamburg, Munich, Budapest, and Vienna for September, Forzano wrote the composer on 20 August that he would soon bring the completed *La candidata* libretto to Viareggio.

89. Leoncavallo to Luigi Illica, 31 July 1914 (BCP).

90. The composer hoped Eugenia Burzio could create the title role, convinced that she would "understand *Avemaria*'s value." Ibid.

91. Ibid.

92. Leoncavallo to Luigi Illica, 5 August 1914 (BCP). Apart from two further Italian engagements, the remainder of Caruso's career was spent performing in North and South America.

93. Ibid.

94. Now that Cavacchioli had relinquished any interest in a further collaboration on *Avemaria*, Riccardo Sonzogno described him as a "disreputable fellow, false, and a Judas" after supposedly speaking badly of the publisher to Illica.

95. Riccardo Sonzogno to Leoncavallo, (recopied in the composer's hand) 24 August 1914 (BCP).

96. Ibid.

97. Leoncavallo to Luigi Illica, 5 September 1914 (BCP).

98. Leoncavallo hoped Ruffo would create the North American premiere of *Ça-Ira!* in Chicago, while Battistini would sing the Italian premiere at the San Carlo in Naples.

99. Leoncavallo to Gualtiero Belvederi, 9 September 1914 (BCL).
100. Ibid.
101. Leoncavallo to Gualtiero Belvederi, 13 September 1914 (BCL).
102. The revolutionary songs "Ça-ira!" and "Carmagnole" were to be included in the opera, recalling Giordano's *Andrea Chenier*.
103. Leoncavallo to Luigi Illica, 15 September 1914 (BCP).
104. Leoncavallo to Luigi Illica, 21 September 1914 (BCP).
105. Leoncavallo to Luigi Illica, 28 September 1914 (BCP).
106. Leoncavallo to Gualtiero Belvederi, 4 October 1914 (BCL).
107. Mosco Carner, *Puccini: A Critical Biography* (Surrey: Duckworth, 1958), 207.
108. Konrad Dryden, *Riccardo Zandonai: A Biography* (Frankfurt: Peter Lang, 1999), 159.
109. In the interim, when not plying Illica for information concerning Casa Sonzogno, Leoncavallo hoped to maintain his interest in *Avemaria* by stating that a wealthy American had proposed to present the opera with Eugenia Burzio as part of another North American tour beginning in San Francisco.
110. Adolph Fürstner to Edoardo Sonzogno, 2 November 1914 (BCL).
111. Leoncavallo to Gualtiero Belvederi, 9 November 1914 (BCL).
112. Ibid.
113. Max Rikoff to Leoncavallo, 14 November 1914 (BCL).
114. Draft of a Leoncavallo letter to Max Rikoff, 19 November 1914 (BCL).
115. Leoncavallo to Gualtiero Belvederi, 9 November 1914 (BCL).
116. Ibid.
117. Performances of *Zingari* in Breslau were also canceled.
118. Riccardo Sonzogno to Leoncavallo, 20 November 1914 (BCL).
119. Leoncavallo to Cesare Bazzani, undated drafted letter (BCL).
120. A letter that Leoncavallo drafted to Bazzani (undated) stated that he sent the telegram on 24 September 1914 (BCL).
121. Cesare Bazzani to Leoncavallo, 29 December 1914 (BCL).
122. Leoncavallo to Gualtiero Belvederi, 1 December 1914 (BCL). Leoncavallo was probably unaware that Mascagni had also loaned Sonzogno money, prompting the former to write to his mistress Anna Lolli that Lorenzo was both base and vile.
123. Leoncavallo to Gualtiero Belvederi, 30 December 1914 (BCL).
124. Leoncavallo to Luigi Illica, 14 January 1915 (BCP).
125. Leoncavallo to Gualtiero Belvederi, 30 December 1914 (BCL).
126. Leoncavallo to Luigi Illica, 29 January 1915 (BCP).
127. Ibid.
128. Ibid.
129. Emma Vecla was Italy's first Hanna Glawari in *Die Lustige Witwe*.
130. Eugenia Burzio also sent Leoncavallo a congratulatory telegram, perhaps still hoping to create *Avemaria* in the near future.
131. Leoncavallo to Luigi Illica, 8 February 1915 (BCP). The operetta had also been produced simultaneously at Turin's Teatro Chiarella.
132. Draft of a letter written by Leoncavallo, undated (BCL).
133. Yet another planned project with Vaucaire that never came to fruition was *Bataille d'amour*.

134. Maurice Vaucaire to Leoncavallo, 1 February 1915 (BCL).

135. Puccini tried to defend his stance by stating that he refused to become involved in a manifestation of "germanophobia," feeling a sense of rebellion at the excesses rampant among the press and public concerning nationalism. *Giornale d'Italia*, 10–11 February 1915 (BCL).

136. Leoncavallo injured his left elbow during his return journey to Viareggio. An inflammation necessitating compresses made it impossible for him to meet with Illica to discuss *Avemaria*.

137. "I have signed, and if everything would begin again I would sign the protest once more." *Le Figaro*, 18 February 1915.

138. Maurice Vaucaire to Leoncavallo, 23 February 1915 (BCL).

139. Leoncavallo to Gualtiero Belvederi, 28 February 1915 (BCL).

140. Ibid.

141. Ibid.

142. Leoncavallo to Luigi Illica, 7 March 1915 (BCP).

143. Leoncavallo to Luigi Illica, 17 March 1915 (BCP).

144. Leoncavallo to Luigi Illica, 26 March 1915 (BCP).

145. Ibid.

146. Ibid.

147. Macchi also sporadically signed his name following the composer's on Leoncavallo's letters to Illica. Leoncavallo to Luigi Illica, 7 April 1915 (BCP).

148. Ibid.

149. Leoncavallo to Luigi Illica, 10 April 1915 (BCP).

150. Ibid. Illica wrote a letter to Mascagni's wife, Lina, instead, suggesting that she allow her husband more freedom in his affair with Anna Lolli, comparing their situation to Verdi, Strepponi, and Teresa Stolz. Needless to say, the letter incensed Lina to such a degree that it resulted in a "terrible scene" that "succeeded in poisoning the festivities celebrating *Cavalleria rusticana*'s 25th anniversary." Leoncavallo to Luigi Illica, 13 April 1915 (BCP).

151. Walter Mocchi was an impresario who successfully managed to inaugurate annual seasons of Italian opera in Buenos Aires, earning money unavailable in wartime Italy. Married at the time to soprano Emma Carelli, he would later wed Bidù Sayao.

152. Leoncavallo to Luigi Illica, 24 April 1915 (BCP).

153. Leoncavallo to Luigi Illica, 28 April 1915 (BCP).

154. Ibid.

155. Leoncavallo to Luigi Illica, 7 May 1915 (BCP).

156. Ibid.

157. Ibid.

158. Vaucaire was also in contact with Leoncavallo's brother, Leone, who still lived in Paris.

159. Maurice Vaucaire to Leoncavallo, 14 May 1915 (BCL).

160. Luigi Illica to Leoncavallo, undated (BCP).

161. Ibid.

162. Leoncavallo to Luigi Illica, 18 May 1915 (BCP).

163. Leoncavallo to Luigi Illica, 23 May 1915 (BCP).

164. Puccini had initially been interested in the subject in 1911, again taking up the idea in 1912 at Illica's insistence. Puccini had also asked Giuseppe Adami to make an adaptation after hearing that Mascagni had been interested, encouraging Ricordi to purchase the rights to Ouida's novel for Puccini at public auction on 22 March 1915.

165. Leoncavallo to Luigi Illica, 23 May 1915 (BCP).

166. Forzano had spoken of *Two Little Wooden Shoes* to Mascagni during the summer of 1914. Nevertheless he initially offered Puccini the completed libretto, to Mascagni's consternation. Mascagni to Anna Lolli, 12 March 1916, Morini, *Pietro Mascagni: Epistolario*, I, 30.

167. Leoncavallo to Luigi Illica, 23 May 1915 (BCP).

168. Ibid.

169. Leoncavallo to Luigi Illica, 31 May 1915 (BCP).

170. Ibid.

171. Ibid.

172. Leoncavallo to Luigi Illica, 23 May 1915 (BCP).

173. Leoncavallo to Gualtiero Belvederi, 2 June 1915 (BCL).

174. Leoncavallo mentioned in the same letter that Giuseppe Andriulli was writing a biography of his life, and one may assume this to be proof of the *Appunti*'s authenticity.

175. Leoncavallo to Gualtiero Belvederi, 7 June 1915 (BCL).

176. Ibid.

177. Leoncavallo to Luigi Illica, 8 June 1915 (BCP).

178. Leoncavallo to Gualtiero Belvederi, 16 June 1915 (BCL).

179. Leoncavallo to Luigi Illica, 1 July 1915 (BCP).

180. Ibid.

181. Ibid.

182. This information was confirmed in a letter written to the author on 21 June 2001 by Nandi Ostali of Casa Musicale Sonzogno di Piero Ostali, Milan. The original source was not given.

183. Leoncavallo to Luigi Illica, 15 July 1915 (BCP).

184. Ibid.

185. Leoncavallo to Luigi Illica, 11 August 1915 (BCP).

186. Ibid.

187. Ibid.

188. One of Leoncavallo's first suggestions concerning *Mameli* was that the baritone role of Terzaghi should have an aria commencing with the words "Italia, Italia!" that he felt would resemble Colautti's prose, although he may have been influenced by the same text that opens Archibaldo's scene in act 1 of Montemezzi's *L'amore dei tre re*.

189. Leoncavallo also hoped to use *Mameli* as the basis for a film. Leoncavallo to Luigi Illica, 27 August 1915 (BCP).

190. Leoncavallo to Gualtiero Belvederi, 3 September 1915 (BCL).

191. Leoncavallo to Luigi Illica, 6 September 1915 (BCP).

192. Ibid.

193. Ibid.

194. Leoncavallo to Gualtiero Belvederi, 27 September 1915 (BCL).

195. Leoncavallo to Gualtiero Belvederi, 17 September 1915 (BCL).

196. Leoncavallo to Gualtiero Belvederi, 11 October 1915 (BCL).

197. Ibid. Leoncavallo planned to dedicate *Mameli* to Antonio Salandra.

198. Leoncavallo to Luigi Illica, October 1915 (BCL).

199. Leoncavallo to Gualtiero Belvederi, 28 October 1915 (BCL).

200. Leoncavallo still referred to *Mameli* as "Alba" in his correspondence.

201. Leoncavallo to Gualtiero Belvederi, 9 November 1915 (BCL).

202. Ibid. Leoncavallo's lifelong interest in film work originated after seeing a cinematic version of *Prête-moi ta femme*, resulting in *Prestami tua moglie*.

203. Leoncavallo to Gualtiero Belvederi, 3 December 1915 (BCL).

204. Leoncavallo to Gualtiero Belvederi, 29 November 1915 (BCL).

· 9 ·

I Also Have a Right to Live!

1916–1919

$\mathcal{L}$eoncavallo's lawyer, Giovanni Abbondio, officially began court proceedings against his client on 21 January 1916, demanding payment for legal services rendered after 6 June 1908, which Leoncavallo had been promising to pay for eight years, amounting to 8,053 francs, in addition to another 2,600 francs for "material and moral damages." The composer's new lawyer, Alberto Vigizzi, was engaged to reduce the requested amount and to delay payment. Leoncavallo read the court papers, scribbling his views in the margins, believing much of it to be "greatly exaggerated."[1] The papers also stated that Leoncavallo had frequently affirmed—both personally and in writing—that he had paid all costs, although Abbondio had only received one thousand Swiss francs on 3 October 1911 and fifty lire on 29 January 1913. Following these dates, "the maestro continuously pleaded with us to have patience, but many years passed without him keeping his promise to satisfy his obligations."[2] On 5 January, Leoncavallo also received the official sequestration papers for Villa Myriam and its contents for debts amounting to 50,866 Swiss francs, while Macchi was already in Brissago trying to find a buyer.[3] On 10 March, Leoncavallo had Vigizzi draw up a "notification of postponement" asking for a delay of forty days.

The composer continued to look for other employment, writing from Viareggio to his Roman acquaintance Giovanni Rosadi, still hoping to find a position in one of Italy's conservatories. He reminded the lawyer that "there exists a maestro Leoncavallo, student of the Conservatory of Naples, who also possesses a diploma in literature earned in Bologna under Carducci, and who knew how to write the libretti for the operas *Pagliacci, Medici, Bohème, Chatterton, Zazà,* and *Rolando,* which have brought glory to his name and Italian culture in this country and abroad for 23 years."[4] The composer was beginning to wonder whether anyone even still remembered that he existed, since "Maestro Leoncavallo *is not even consulted to direct a conservatory.*"[5] The composer still felt that Casa Ricordi was waging a war against him since he had won his court case with the firm. "I also have a right to live," was but one of his numerous statements bound up with the threat of leaving Italy following the war. "But before leaving my homeland, *at my age*, I will create a scandal which certainly will not shed a positive light on the government. . . . I will speak with Salandra and to the socialists with proof in hand of all the baseness of this world. . . . If my words do not obtain justice I will leave."[6]

He asked Tito Ricordi to let him have the rights to his libretto entitled *Vendetta* that he had written in collaboration with Ettore Gentili during 1891, and he again tried arranging a *Mameli* tour after the opera was completed in February 1916. He also informed Belvederi that he had begun negotiating a contract with "the swindler and thief" Renzo Sonzogno for *Mameli*,[7] without any kind of financial compensation or payment, since the publisher failed to "have faith in a patriotic work."[8] Leoncavallo was expected to pay for half of the costs, including the score's publication, while the composer suggested that money made from the premiere should benefit the Italian Red Cross, excluding what was needed for the singers and production.[9]

MAMELI

After contemplating writing a comic opera or operetta adapted from Fred Grésac's *La Passarelle*,[10] Leoncavallo was thrilled with his "iron nerves," and aware that he was tied to a publisher that had "no faith in the subject" of *Mameli*.[11] The composer had sketches sent from Milan's Museo del Risorgimento for the opera's main characters, before leaving to attend the world premiere with Berthe at Genoa's Teatro Carlo Felice, as soon as he was able to travel after a cold that had also affected his ears. Leoncavallo arrived in Genoa armed with photos of himself for the program as well as a short biographical sketch. The city's newspapers immediately announced that *Mameli*'s proceeds would benefit the Red Cross, while Leoncavallo told the *Giornale d'Italia* that he had finished *Avemaria* and still planned to complete *Crepusculum*. He described *Mameli* as a "spontaneous" opera he had written "with great love."[12] He also read *Mameli*'s libretto at the Municipal Council for a selected audience after completing a strenuous rehearsal period.

The opera—the last for which Leoncavallo would live to see premiere— opened on 27 April 1916, sung by Eugenia Burzio (Delia Terzaghi),[13] Carmelo Alabiso (Goffredo Mameli), Emilio Bione (Terzaghi), and Vida Ferluga (Cristina Trivulzio), with Leoncavallo leading the sixty-five-member orchestra. The theater was only "discreetly filled" when the composer began the performance with the "Marcia Reale."[14] Although Leoncavallo presented himself "five or six times" onstage to acknowledge the applause during the first episode, the opera was only a modest success, while the intermezzo was described as a bore. In retrospect, it seems incredible that critics failed to notice that Leoncavallo had incorporated *Chatterton's* major arias and duets into *Mameli*, frequently only changing the text. Reviewers wrote that the opera was overtly traditional, banal, effortful, frequently vulgar, and a continuation of *Pagliacci*, failing to reveal Mameli's character "in his heroic grandeur," since the opera centered on his love for Delia, transforming the patriot into a stock operatic tenor, making the historical scenario superfluous. The second episode was considered to be notably weaker than the first, while *Mameli's* vocal writing reminded reviewers of *Das Rheingold* and *Siegfried*.[15] Although the opera had been written by a "distinguished and passionate musician," it was argued that it failed to add to his reputation as a composer.[16] Leoncavallo was furious, responding with a lengthy letter on 1 May that appeared in numerous newspapers, including the *Nuovo Giornale*, directing his rage at *Il Popolo d'Italia* and *L'Avanti*, which had (correctly) implied that he had taken advantage of the war for the opera's scenario. His counterattack in the losing battle was that he had chosen the subject as an "irresistible impetus" to his "artistic and patriotic soul."[17]

The composer conducted additional performances in Pisa in May, followed by Livorno and Rome's Teatro Morgana, asking Queen Elena for financial help, since most of the profits went to the Red Cross. He then began preparing a letter with Vigizzi from Montecatini claiming, this time officially, that Abbondio's requests were "absolutely exaggerated,"[18] listing all the facts as he saw them, hoping to postpone the proceedings. He also wished to sue the film industry for "damages" when they no longer showed interest in *Mameli* or in his second cinematic project *Anima Redenta*.[19] Leoncavallo originally hoped that a *Mameli* film would be completed to coincide with the operatic premiere.

On 8 July Leoncavallo received Abbondio's official answer to his petition, once again stating the facts and refuting all of the composer's pleas with documentary evidence. Not only had Abbondio been rendering his services for years without any kind of compensation, but Leoncavallo had also managed to borrow money from him and from his own friend Antonio Farinelli. Trying to pay his debts in Switzerland and Italy, Leoncavallo had at one point found a "speculator" in Milan who had agreed to loan him 150,000 lire to be repaid within one year with interest, totaling 180,000 lire.[20] Fortunately, Farinelli had saved him from such a "disastrous decision." It was difficult for Abbondio, who had repeatedly rescued Leoncavallo from various financial ventures, to realize that the composer now had the "audacity" to not pay his fee.[21] Leoncavallo also claimed that he had never appointed Carlo Macchi to act in his behalf concerning legal matters, but Abbondio correctly countered by stating that Macchi was Leoncavallo's "secretary, his representative, and his *factotum*,"[22] and

Leoncavallo's birth certificate proving that the composer was indeed born in 1857.

ORDINANZA
per
l' abertura di cia-
scun dibbatimento

(IN NOME DI SUA MAESTA')

VITTORIO EMANUELE II

PER GRAZIA DI DIO E PER VOLONTA' DELLA NAZIONE .

RE D' ITALIA

Noi *——————————* Presidente della
Corte di Assise sedente in *————*
Veduta l' ordinanza del Primo Presidente del dì
già pubblicata in publica udienza ed affissa alla porta di questa Corte
portante la determinata apertura delle Assisie pel dì
Atteso che il processo a carico di

D'alessandro Luigi
D'alessandro Giovanni *De Montalto*

Accusati di *anonimo*

trovansi in istato di essere spedito
Veduto l' art. 459 del codice di procedura penale;

FISSIAMO

il giorno di *Sabato — 8.* del mese di *Luglio*
per l' apertura del dibattimento cui questa ordinanza si riferisce.
Ordiniamo che questa medesima ordinanza sia notificata entro ven
tiquattro ore dalla sua data all' accusato ed alla parte civile nelleper-
sone di *Antonio Maria Nigro*
loro rispettivi difensori, a diligenza del Procurator Generale, cui se n' e
n' e data comunicazione.

Cosenza li *28 Giugno —* 1865
Il Presidente della Corte di Assise
— Galofi —
Il *————————*

Addì *detto*
Ricevutane comuni-
cazione,
Il Proc Gen del Re *sott.* L' anno mille ottocento sessanta *——* il giorno *ventotto* del mese
di *Giugno* in *Cosenza*
Io sottoscritto usciere di questa Corta ho notificato la sopra scrit-
ta ordinanza allo accusato ed alla parte civile nelle persone di *suo*
loro rispettivi difensori *D. Antonio Maria Nigro*

L' Usciere
Filippo Ferrari

A page from the original murder trial of Giovanni and Luigi D'Alessandro presided over
by Leoncavallo's father in 1865.

H. Wallis's 1856 painting of Thomas Chatterton, who greatly influenced Leoncavallo's early years. Courtesy Tate, London, 2006.

The composer's Egyptian-based uncle Giuseppe Leoncavallo in 1898.

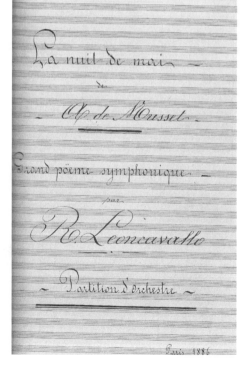

Title page from the original autograph score of *La nuit de mai,* one of the composer's earliest compositions (Paris, 1886).

An early photo of the composer, probably in France, taken in 1888.

A very young Marie Rose Jean (Berthe) photographed at the time of her meeting with the composer in 1888.

Leoncavallo playing cards in the early 1880s with the physician Guido Baccelli, the composer Alfredo Catalani, and Francesco Crispi, who was prime minister of Italy from 1887 to 1891 and from 1893 to 1896.

A postcard issued at the time of *Pagliacci*'s world premiere in 1892.

The original production of *La bohème*, 1897.

A rare photo of the composer with Marie Rose Jean (Berthe), his mother-in-law (Thérèse Paul), Jeanne Puel, and his dog "Pompon" in Brissago, 1898.

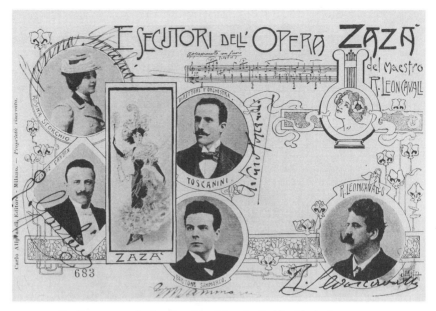

Zazà's creators: Rosina Storchio, Edoardo Garbin, Mario Sammarco,
Arturo Toscanini, and Leoncavallo.

Leoncavallo's lavish Villa Myriam in Brissago, Switzerland,
on the shores of Lake Maggiore.

Parbs　　　Mödlinger　　Berger　　Der Roland von Berlin　　Hoffmann / Destinn　　Pohl

Phot. Zander & Labisch

Act 3 of *Der Roland von Berlin* with a very youthful Emmy Destinn as Elsbeth, 1904.

Leoncavallo, with the score of *Der Roland von Berlin*, on the way to see Kaiser Wilhelm II in Berlin, 1904.

Leoncavallo with a statue of Roland, probably taken in Berlin during the time of *Der Roland von Berlin*'s premiere (1904).

Leoncavallo in Varazze, Italy, 1908.

Varazze in July 1908.

Leoncavallo, his librettist Angelo Nessi, and Ferruccio Corradetti, following the world premiere of *Malbruk* in 1910.

Leoncavallo on an Indian reservation during one of his U.S. tours, "seeking inspiration" and publicity for an American opera that was never written.

A tired and distraught Leoncavallo photographed in a New York hotel room shortly after his arrival to begin a second U.S. tour in 1913.

Leoncavallo trying to interest Enrico Caruso in *Avemaria* (1914).

The aging composer in 1914.

Leoncavallo in the midst of a heated conversation in 1916.

Leoncavallo with the famed Luisa Tetrazzini, for whom he planned *Mirandolina*.

Leoncavallo, possibly in Montecatini or Viareggio.

A weary Giacomo Puccini five years prior to his own death,
attending the Montecatini funeral, 1919.

The Montecatini funeral procession, 1919.

he regretted not having kept his correspondence with Macchi, never having anticipated the current situation. Abbondio also declared that Leoncavallo had hired Carlo Accetti's help in order to postpone payment until funds became available. Leoncavallo and Vigizzi managed to delay legal proceedings for an additional twenty days, beginning on August third. This gave Vigizzi sufficient time to prepare another counterattack of "facts" for 20 August, wherein he stated that Leoncavallo believed most of the work undertaken by Abbondio had been "personal favors," not "legal consultation" requiring payment.[23] Still finding the sum of money requested by Abbondio to be "exaggerated," Leoncavallo and his lawyer Vigizzi now demanded that there be a court ruling to determine the amount, while Vigizzi warned Abbondio not to "play with fire."[24]

Amid all the squabbling, Leoncavallo's operetta *Prestami tua moglie* received its world premiere on 2 September 1916 in Montecatini's Teatro del Casinò, sung by Dora Domar (Nanon), Pina Ciotti (Margherita), Armando Fineschi (Rissolin,) and Leopoldo Michelazzi (Rabastoul).[25] Leoncavallo and Corradi received fifteen curtain calls, with *La Nazione* heralding the work as "an authentic success." The composer himself described the operetta's reception as "enthusiastic" and "triumphant," reinforcing his opinion that the subject matter was "truly comic."[26]

Leoncavallo left Montecatini shortly after 24 September in order to sell Villa Myriam to Giuseppe Amryhn, owner of Brissago's Grand Hotel, for 150,000 lire, including furniture and art works. Amryhn agreed to pay 120,000 lire of the total sum directly to Alfonso Menotti in Cadegliano[27] to whom the composer was also indebted. Leoncavallo, Menotti, Amryhn, and two witnesses in the presence of the notary Zanolini, signed the document on 30 September in Amrhyn's office at Brissago's Grand Hotel.

Leoncavallo was hindered from attending further performances of *Prestami tua moglie* in Salsomaggiore as well as the Roman premiere, because of an incessant itch that plagued his face. Hurt by the operetta's negative criticism, Leoncavallo swore that he had made the "irrevocable decision" of never again writing another work in Italy, and began planning legal proceedings against *Il Giornale d'Italia* for a recent article that he considered damaging to his career.[28]

CONTEMPLATING *TORMENTA* AND *MIRANDOLINA*

Leoncavallo, in spite of his pledge never to write another opera in Italy, told Belvederi on 27 October about plans for a new work on a "splendid" Sardinian theme entitled *Tormenta*.[29] He hoped Belvederi would send sufficient material so that he could begin work during a trip to Paris with Berthe for a concert on 11 November, and a single performance of *Pagliacci* with Titta Ruffo at the Eldorado Theater in Nice for the Red Cross.[30] *Tormenta* remains another enigma in the chronicle of Leoncavallo's works. Although it has been supposed that the libretto was written by Belvederi, the autograph manuscript was written by the composer and signed at the beginning of each act, as if to lend credence to Leoncavallo's being its author. A French version (*Tourment*) was also typed of the complete libretto, including the composer's handwritten mise-en-scène. This copy was corrected for the composer and contains numerous suggestions regarding plot changes as well as the title itself. Curiously, nothing remains in Belvederi's hand. To confuse matters, Berthe presented her lawyer with another typed copy of *Tormenta* following Leoncavallo's death, claiming that it was the work of Cino Daspi (a pen name for the lawyer Sadoc Pini). It is doubtful that much of *Tormenta's* music had in fact been composed, although the project continued to occupy the composer until his death. This *tragedia mistica* centers on the love of three men for the same woman in Bosa (Sardinia) in 1840.[31] It includes intrigue, murder, and fratricide—a grisly yet compelling libretto that would have suited Leoncavallo's would-be return to the world of Zola-inspired verismo.

Returning to Viareggio on 1 December from Paris, Leoncavallo immediately informed Belvederi that Lorenzo Sonzogno was definitely not interested in the patriotic *Avemaria*, now asking instead for an opera in one act. Aware of the ongoing friction between Lorenzo and Illica, Leoncavallo suggested that Belvederi should temporarily postpone work on *Tormenta* to search for a scenario that would be "grand, theatrical, and new" in the manner of Oscar Wilde's *Salomé*,[32] something "alive, full of blood and action," and not based on a classical theme, which is precisely what *Salomé* was.

At the same time, Leoncavallo also had the journalist Valentino Soldani (1874–1935) working on a libretto entitled *Mirandolina*. This was a comedy in three acts inspired by Goldoni's *La locandiera* that Leoncavallo planned to compose for Luisa Tetrazzini.[33] The composer believed Soldani's libretto was "elegant," but could not begin composing until the text was complete.[34] Leoncavallo offered him three thousand lire payable in three parts: The first thousand lire following performances in London, the second after a production in the United States, and the third in Italy![35]

Leoncavallo's Christmas was an extremely melancholy one when the news reached him from Lorenzo that he would no longer receive his monthly thousand lire. He still expected a contract with Caesar Films that would help alleviate his financial difficulties, so that he could "cover" Casa Sonzogno "with mud."[36] Belvederi was somehow able to maintain the interest of Caesar Films, while also keeping an eye open for the plot of an opera in one act.[37] Leoncavallo hoped that Belvederi, a man whom he loved "more than a brother," would come to the rescue.[38] What outraged Leoncavallo most, was the "lurid ambience of the Italian theatrical world," combined with what he regarded to be the public's complete indifference.[39] He once again thought about moving to France, where his talent was "respected,"[40] believing that if D'Annunzio had not left Italy at the time he did, he would not have become the "man of great genius" that he was considered to be. "D'Annunzio returned from Paris where he had remained for five or six years having his works applauded. . . . Well then? Away! Away! There *is not one* who protests the ostracism . . . of my works . . . nor a publisher who has earned *more than 6 million* lire in 25 years ."[41]

On 11 January 1917, Leoncavallo sent Soldani a registered package containing "a first act" he had just written, which, although he did not mention its title, seems to have been *Mirandolina*.[42] Leoncavallo hoped the war would end during the coming winter, having already made plans for another North American tour to include a tryptich consisting of *Pagliacci*, *Zingari*, and a third opera yet to be written. It seems that Lorenzo's suggestion that Leoncavallo write a one-act opera was inspired by Puccini's *Il trittico* and by Soldani, with whom Puccini had conferred years earlier when debating whether he would use his *Margherita da Cortona* to follow *Il tabarro* (which instead turned out to be the similarly religious *Suor Angelica*). Leoncavallo's idea of having his triptych premiere in North America just as Puccini's would was also slightly uncanny.

Edmondo Corradi was still trying to interest Leoncavallo in a third operetta. The composer stressed that he would only accept a commission from an operetta company that also guaranteed to perform the work. He was saddened that *Prestami tua moglie* was not taken into the repertory of the Maresca operetta company, although *Reginetta delle rose* continued its immense popularity. He prepared the scenario of *Mirandolina* with Soldani, hoping the latter would soon visit him in Viareggio. He sensed that the war was about to come to an end, "*un bon mouvement*," that would offer greater possibilities of having his works produced when additional theaters reopened.[43] By 13 May, Leoncavallo informed Corradi that he was willing to collaborate on an operetta, but that it could *not* be *A chi la giarrettiera?* on account of difficulties imposed by the French Society of Authors regarding an Italian publication.[44] He also collected information dealing with Sardinia's history and customs in preparation for *Tormenta*, whereupon he discovered, to his chagrin, that they did not celebrate a festival dedicated to Hermes as implied in the libretto.

Soldani replied that there was no reason to work on *Mirandolina*, since there was no guarantee that the war would in fact end, which infuriated Leoncavallo. "It is certain that neither I nor you nor even His Highness Vittorio Emanuele III can say today that the war will *not end* by the conclusion of this year! What is certain is that *Mirandolina* must *absolutely be ready by year's end.* This is the obligation that I have undertaken toward T[etrazzini]."[45] However,

Leoncavallo personally believed that the war would soon conclude. If it did not, he warned Soldani that it would not affect *Mirandolina*'s London premiere. Leoncavallo also hoped that Tetrazzini would include the work on one of her tours, thus writing Soldani that it was "indispensable" that he receive act 3 within the next eight days, since he had already been speaking to the soprano about *Mirandolina* for over a year. "I cannot tell her that the libretto which should have been finished is not because the war will probably not end!"[46]

Leoncavallo found himself at odds with Soldani when he finally received an outline for act 3, advising the librettist that emotions were the "sine qua non" of the operatic stage, and that a scenario did not have to be "logical" in order to move an audience. He referred to some of the incongruities in Ponchielli and Boito's *La gioconda*, demonstrating his idea that opera was about the love of two protagonists, whether they were "Manon and Des Grieux" [*Manon*], "Werther and Charlotte" [*Werther*], or "Violetta and Alfredo" [*La traviata*].[47] Leoncavallo felt this maxim to be the major difference between the spoken stage and the operatic theater. He also wanted act 3 to have "a quiet sadness" in contrast to acts 1 and 2, and to center solely on the protagonists, recalling *Zazà*'s final scene. He pleaded with Soldani to respect his advice, nervous about receiving the finished product, since Tetrazzini was expected at any moment.

PIERROT AU CINÉMA, PLAGIARISM, AND THE FILM INDUSTRY

Lorenzo had heard rumors that Leoncavallo was at work on a "sketch" in one act entitled *Pierrot au cinéma* that included dance and pantomime, that the composer thought would be popular in Great Britain, France and North America's "music halls."[48] Leoncavallo reassured Lorenzo that it had nothing to do with an operetta in three acts he was planning (probably *A chi la giarrettiera?*), and that *Pierrot au cinéma* would never interest the firm. He tried enticing Lorenzo that the librettist was a banker and "one of Paris' famous personalities," who had written a text without demanding royalties, and who was supposedly arranging a production. *Pierrot au cinéma* was another of Leoncavallo's attempts at being modern and avant-garde, realizing the importance of the ever-expanding film industry.[49]

Leoncavallo finally received Soldani's scenario for *Mirandolina*'s final act toward the end of July. The librettist also asked the composer to send sufficient money to pay for his collaboration on a cinematic version of *Romeo and Juliet* that Leoncavallo was preparing, and that was to be sponsored by a Roman "capitalista."[50] Leoncavallo did not find it necessary to present this mysterious person with an outline, only informing the sponsor that Soldani was creating a "work of art" not based solely on "Schakspeare" [*sic*].[51] Leoncavallo warned

Soldani that if the "capitalista" agreed to his demands, work on *Mirandolina* would have to be postponed. Convinced that the lyric theater had gone from "bad to worse," Leoncavallo, like many of his colleagues, placed his future hope in the film world,[52] even trying to interest the actress Emma Vecla in his plan.

On 4 August 1917, Leoncavallo drew up a private contract with Soldani for *Mirandolina* that he revised repeatedly, offering the librettist three thousand lire, while securing the rights for himself.[53] He then spoke with his "capitalista," who now requested to see a completed film script before making a decision. Although nothing was definite, Leoncavallo asked Soldani to come to Viareggio to begin work without "losing a minute."[54] At the same time, Soldani was also required to undertake research for *Romeo and Juliet* in various Florentine libraries. Leoncavallo placed all his hopes in his newest project, reminding Soldani once more that "the spoken stage" offered "little guarantee of earning, whereas cinematography" presented "serious and lucrative opportunities, especially with a contract the likes of which" he hoped to secure.[55] He now also contemplated founding his own small "artistic-commercial firm" as the war continued and Tetrazzini failed to arrive due to her brother's sudden death.

Leoncavallo finally succeeded in convincing Soldani of the project's importance. However, the librettist believed it would be difficult for the "capitalista" to ascertain how expensive the entire production would be. Soldani was reluctant to give up his copyright, and demanded five hundred lire prior to beginning work. While Leoncavallo was indeed desperate for success, Soldani was not, having already received two film offers by the Tiber and Volsca companies. The "enormous success" that Soldani had garnered from his film *Demonietta* ensured that he would be able to demand a higher price and be compensated in advance, lest it be forgotten that Leoncavallo still owed him for *Mirandolina*.[56]

Realizing how difficult it was to secure money beforehand, Leoncavallo asked Soldani to "make a small sacrifice and to have patience."[57] The composer believed Soldani's estimate that the film would earn two hundred thousand lire to be "quite exaggerated,"[58] and he was ultimately unable to generate any funds. The film version of *Reginetta delle rose* had cost one hundred thousand lire for fifteen hundred meters of film and about a thousand supernumeraries. Considering that the *Romeo and Juliet* film would not be longer and could be filmed in Tuscany, the composer warned Soldani that if he did not begin drafting a film script immediately, he would be forced to look for another collaborator in order to avoid running the risk of losing the entire deal. Although Soldani realized that the cost of producing *Romeo and Juliet* would be far greater than *Reginetta delle rose*, since an entire era would have to be recreated on the screen, he agreed to complete a script between September tenth and fifteenth, on condition that he supervise the production, receive a compensation regardless of whether or not the film would be made, and, finally, own the copyright. Leoncavallo agreed, warning Soldani to create a scenario that would not "exceed 150–160,000 lire at the most," in order not to frighten his "capitalista."[59] The project was nevertheless postponed for a part of the autumn, while Leoncavallo tried to interest a new film company in the idea.[60]

In the meantime, Illica wrote a "marvelous" letter to Giulio Gatti-Casazza offering him *Avemaria*.[61] It seems that Lorenzo now told Illica that he had always liked the libretto, although Leoncavallo had kept all of Lorenzo's correspondence, which proved quite the opposite. Illica demanded to see the letters regarding Lorenzo's accusations of plagiarism on the subject, admitting that the "characters and their situations" were not very original even if the "subject's patriotism" was.[62] Illica warned Lorenzo that he had been inspired by the study of "Neapolitan history . . . the drama of a spy in apotheosis."[63] Leoncavallo reminded Illica that Lorenzo considered *Avemaria* to be a mixture of *Tosca* and *Andrea Chénier*, and that the publisher "did not have faith in patriotic subjects, particularly the Napoleonic episode of the Bourbons," which he felt would be of little or no interest.[64] Lorenzo was supposedly too embarrassed to inform Illica directly, asking for Leoncavallo's intervention, and hoping that the composer would accept another scenario entitled *Friquet*. Lorenzo made it clear that if the composer wished to continue pushing *Avemaria*, he would have to personally pay the firm in order to free himself for a contract that stipulated one opera and one operetta.[65] Lorenzo suddenly accepted *Avemaria* and Leoncavallo wondered why,[66] agreeing to take up work once more if the publisher respected the terms of Riccardo Sonzogno's contract, ensuring him twenty thousand lire and a guarantee that it would be played for three years in "ten major Italian and foreign theaters," together with some of his works other than *Pagliacci*.[67] Leoncavallo also suspected that his operas would be performed with greater frequency in the future, after hearing that Tito Ricordi planned to leave the firm.

Leoncavallo now proceeded with his idea of founding a company—without Soldani—that sought to purchase and sell films in Italy and abroad. It seems that he had convinced his Roman friend Aurelio Nappi to underwrite the project, together with Count Ernesto Cauda, while his brother Leone would be responsible for any foreign transactions from his Parisian domicile, thus leaving the position of "artistic-director" open to him.[68] The five-year contract also stipulated that the agreement could be revoked should debts amount to more than twenty thousand lire within the first year. The composer left Rome after "36 hours" on 22 October, convinced that this new venture would help secure his future.[69]

He then remained in bed "for one month" after hearing of the Italian setback by the German army. Reinforced by the Austrians, they had managed to break through the Isonzo frontier by Caporetto. The composer, residing in Montecatini's Hotel Ercolini, again insisted that he would settle in Rome as soon as he felt better. He was unable to find an apartment in Viareggio due to the influx of "rich refugees that had driven prices sky high."[70] He claimed that his impending move to Rome would take place four weeks later.[71]

While Leone felt he was making advances in securing films for his brother's new company, the composer wrote Soldani asking about his film *Demonietta*, now that he had become "director of a firm sustained by strong capitalists."[72] Soldani understandably wanted no part of Leoncavallo's new ideas after the last "capitalist" had disappeared when offered *Romeo and Juliet*, and after Tetrazzini no longer demonstrated any interest in *Mirandolina*.[73] Leoncavallo thereby succeeded in losing yet another librettist and collaborator, incapable of understanding why Soldani wrote letters in such a "harsh" vein.[74]

Lorenzo contacted Leoncavallo in January of 1918, saying that Gatti-Casazza was interested in producing *Zazà* the following season at the Metropolitan Opera. He also offered to publish *Avemaria* when the score was completed, while Leoncavallo now demanded that the work premiere in six theaters, convinced that if Lorenzo really wanted to have *Avemaria* he would accept.[75] He told Lorenzo on 12 February that he would once again take up work on *Avemaria* "in homage to Illica," after an absence of two years caused by the publisher's lack of confidence in the subject.[76] Leoncavallo also stressed Casa Sonzogno's diminished status since the loss of *Il Secolo* and the Teatro Lirico, both of which had been of utmost importance when promoting a new work. Now that most of his operas other than *Pagliacci* had all but disappeared, Leoncavallo wanted Lorenzo to guarantee that *Avemaria* would enjoy a better fate. He was livid that Lorenzo had published Puccini's *La rondine*, which, for Leoncavallo, came close to treason, considering that nothing had been done for him, and that signing a contract with Puccini was akin to dealing with the "antagonist" Casa Ricordi.[77]

FINAL ATTEMPTS

On 16 March Leoncavallo once again concentrated on his legal problems, first acquiring another lawyer, and then presenting a ten-page document against Abbondio, stating that he would only pay half of the 10,253 francs he still owed. He also offered *Malbruk*'s French rights to the Parisian publisher Max Eschig, having broken his contract with Adolph Sliwinski prior to the war. Since "two foreign publishers had demonstrated interest in *Malbruk*," Leoncavallo now wished to know whether Eschig wanted to be the first.[78] His unaltered tactics worked, since Eschig's name was soon added to all future scores.

Leoncavallo's ill-defined quest for financial success again became apparent when he invested in Milan's Fabbrica Italiana Giocattoli, a producer of "unbreakable" dolls, for which he received 10 percent of sales. It seems that he had also successfully convinced his "capitalista" to enter into the business, when the factory owner invested in Leoncavallo's film society. By August, the latter was threatening the composer with legal action due to unpaid debts, and the tension increased when Leone sent the owner a fake passport! However, Leoncavallo's charm still remained, and he managed to revive Soldani's interest in "our daughter" *Mirandolina* even after remaining bed-ridden for most of the spring with bronchial pneumonia.[79] He immediately notified Alfonso Menotti that he had no money available because Amrhyn, that "deceitful German-Swiss," had delayed paying Menotti although he had the money.[80]

After completing his last operetta, *A chi la giarrettiera?*, in July 1918, Leoncavallo planned to continue working on *Mirandolina*, while Lorenzo once again tried to free himself from *Avemaria* with an Italian translation of a French subject entitled *Il turbine*. Leoncavallo sent Soldani *Il turbine*, implying that he would be the librettist-designate, thereby bypassing Illica, whom Sonzogno disliked. Leoncavallo was unable to decide whether he should attempt *Il turbine*, still hoping that *Mameli* would be part of a tour benefiting the Red Cross in an opera company that he still planned to found!

In the meantime, Belvederi promised to send the composer "two or three kilos of spaghetti" to help him survive,[81] while the composer hoped *A chi la giarrettiera?* would receive its premiere at Montecatini's Teatro del Casinò, performed by the Lombardo Operetta Company.[82]

On 15 August 1918, Leoncavallo also signed a contract relinquishing his rights to *A chi la giarrettiera?*, *Prestami tua moglie*, *Pierrot au cinéma*, and the first act of an incomplete operetta to a text by Robert de Simone entitled *The Manicuring Girl* to Jeanne Puel.[83] He then left to spend part of the summer in Montecatini with Berthe, and to meet with Raffaele Cotugno, believing that he would be able to help. He was still passionately interested in reforming the laws governing Italy's Society of Authors, claiming that composers would continue to "live in bondage" if no improvement was made to help them.[84] He next tried uniting Puccini, Giordano, and Mascagni for his project. The latter sent someone else in his place to affirm that he agreed with Leoncavallo on necessary changes, whereas Giordano was represented by a friend.[85] Puccini failed to respond. Leoncavallo now felt "ready for a scandal."[86] In the interim he convinced Belvederi to work on the *Tormenta* libretto, while supplying the Red Cross's request for a song to be published in an anthology together with Puccini and Mascagni, sending the recently completed *C'è nel tuo sguardo*, dedicated to Cotugno's daughter Luisa. On 7 October Abbondio demanded that he receive 8,500 Swiss francs, threatening to pawn what little remained of the composer's personal belongings. Leoncavallo was able to stop him, even though Berthe would not be spared that humiliating experience shortly after her husband's death. The composer at present could only pay Abbondio 2,000 lire, during which time the trial would be "suspended."[87]

His life was almost cut short by a "fierce illness" during November necessitating the Last Sacraments, and numerous newspapers announced his imminent death if not the cause of his suffering.[88] Leoncavallo was elated by the many telegrams he received from people concerned about his health, including the Royal Family. He managed to take up work on *Tormenta* again, which Belvederi would complete by March 1919, having labored on it some four months. He felt content as his last Christmas approached, believing to have found another *Mameli* in *Tormenta*, a valuable consolation from writing numerous operettas. He was pleased with Belvederi's work, feeling that Paula's prayer had turned out very well, and wrote his friend that his eyes were "bathed in tears of emotion" after reading the conclusion of act 1, convincing him again that Belvederi was "a true poet as well as a first-rate artist."[89] He reminisced about "the once great Bologna," where he had originally made Belvederi's acquaintance, one of the few friends he was able to keep throughout his lifetime.[90] He interpreted his partial recovery as a "miracle" that would enable him to "leave some beautiful things for art," aware that his remaining days were few. Leoncavallo also planned a trip to Sardinia with Belvederi seeking inspiration for *Tormenta* during January 1919, although he warned the librettist that the text would have to be completed beforehand.[91]

Leoncavallo's last remaining letters sadly document his jealousy directed toward the Metropolitan Opera's world premiere of Puccini's *Il trittico*, which took place on 14 December 1918. A lifetime of rivalry had still not abated even at this late stage. Leoncavallo felt that both *Il tabarro* and *Suor Angelica* consisted of "empty monotony," making *Gianni Schicchi* seem like a masterpiece in comparison, believing its success was solely due to Giuseppe De Luca's interpretation of the rogue, knowing "how to give life where there wasn't any."[92] Not wishing to believe that Puccini could have an authentic triumph, he consoled himself with the illusion that the Italian newspapers had only written positively about the premiere because Gatti-Casazza had sent them a telegram, thus ensuring a "journalistic success!"[93] He hoped the opera would fail when produced in Rome on 11 January 1919, since Carlo Galeffi, a baritone he greatly disliked, would then interpret the title role. Leoncavallo's life ended with the steady conviction that his career had been hindered by not having Franchetti's or Giordano's wealth, and without the powerful support of Casa Ricordi, who, together with Puccini, he believed, had succeeded in boycotting his career.

Hoping to visit Belvederi in Rome as soon as his health allowed, he had still not given up the idea of a possible move to the capital, notwithstanding the fact that he developed a phlegmon—an acute suppurative inflammation—on the middle finger of his left hand during March, necessitating a "light operation."[94] Relatively little is known concerning the last remaining months of the composer's life, other than his work on *Tormenta* and his wish to reform the Italian Society of Authors, as well as the duration of copyright, which, he felt, should be "eighty years and not less."[95] One of his final letters states that although he was still suffering from insomnia, his health was better and he had begun to take up work.

After receiving communion from his friend Padre Alfani, the sixty-two-year-old composer passed away on 9 August 1919 at his rented home (Villino Giannini) on Via Stella at 11:30 a.m.,[96] finally succumbing to the nephritis from which he had suffered for some time.[97] Forzano and Ruffo were among the first to pay their respects as the composer lay in state surrounded by flowers and candles. Berthe placed all the condolence letters and telegrams on a table in the entrance hall, together with a book to be signed by the other mourners. Edoardo and Lorenzo Sonzogno sent a wreath that was placed alongside those of Berthe and Jeanne, Puccini, Macchi, and the lawyer Carlo Accetti, while Montecatini's town hall lowered the Italian flag to honor the deceased.

The composer's obituaries varied his year of birth from 1856 to 1858 depending on sources, documenting numerous inaccuracies about his "romantic career" that would plague his memory for many decades. British newspapers recalled that Leoncavallo had had a "horror at the German aggression"[98] of World War I, while German papers relished in reminding readers one final time of *Der Roland von Berlin*'s failure. Relatively few obituaries appeared in Italy due to a newspaper strike, while D'Annunzio's eulogy proved little more than irritating.[99] Telegrams were sent from the King of Italy (through General Cittadini), Puccini, Caruso, Cilèa, and Gatti-Casazza, followed by hundreds of others.[100]

POSTMORTEM AND A GREEK TRAGEDY

A hearse arrived at Villino Giannini's entrance on 11 August to claim Leoncavallo's body for the funeral procession at 5:00 p.m., accompanied by an additional one for the wreaths. Mascagni—who was immediately thronged by admirers despite the heat—joined the cortège, as did a visibly drawn Puccini, Berthe, Jeanne, Lorenzo Sonzogno, and Luigi Petrocchi, who served as the late composer's executor. Leoncavallo's brothers were noticeably absent, although he had supported them for most of his life. Hundreds followed, from the director of Montecatini's spa to Puccini's son Antonio.[101] The solemn procession wound its way through Via Felice Cavallotti, Ricasoli, Manzoni, and Viale Verdi, where the ceremony began following a *Stabat Mater* composed by a certain maestro Rovere. The body remained at Montecatini's Cimitero Monumentale until it was transported to Florence the following morning for burial at Porte Sante.

Berthe wrote Titta Ruffo during November, hoping he would be interested in creating Oedipus in Leoncavallo's "unfinished" opera in one act, *Edipo re*, based on Sophocles, to a libretto by Giovacchino Forzano. Berthe signed a contract with the composer Giovanni Pennacchio in Montecatini on 29 March 1920, agreeing that he would receive two thousand lire upon his "completion" of the work, that the composer had supposedly left unfinished at the time of his death, although not one page of the score remains in his own hand.[102] Berthe claimed that she was "conforming to the last wish of her deceased husband."[103] Forzano suggested in a letter to Berthe dated 26 June 1920 that they should meet with Ruffo in order to decide how the "changes" should be made. Ruffo's memoirs state that Leoncavallo had composed the opera for him, while the baritone promised Berthe "at the deathbed of her illustrious companion" that he would "bring it to the stage at the first opportunity."[104] Not one of Leoncavallo's letters remain mentioning the opera by name let alone its genesis, which is noteworthy considering that Ruffo fastidiously conserved his correspondence with the composer. Leoncavallo's brother, Gastone, also become involved, contacting France's Society of Authors in Paris, who referred to the opera's "fragments." Since almost all of *Edipo re*'s music derived from *Der Roland von Berlin*, the opera must be considered a mutual effort on the part of Leoncavallo's heirs to create a "new" work, at least until documentation in the composer's hand is found.[105]

On 15 June 1920, Berthe once again contacted Ruffo to ascertain whether or not he wished to create *Edipo re*. She now hoped that Gastone could arrange for a premiere in a French translation, at the Paris Opéra, followed by Monte Carlo, reminding Ruffo that she was only interested in producing the opera if the baritone would sing the title role, since she had no commercial interest in the project, only wishing to "vindicate the maestro's art."[106] Ruffo was sufficiently interested to have the opera "included in the program of the Auditorium Theater in Chicago and New York's Manhattan Theater."[107] Gino Marinuzzi would conduct and be in charge of the musical organization for the Chicago world premiere, replacing the recently deceased Cleofonte Campanini. He regularly informed Berthe of the work's progress toward presentation, which was made difficult since "Campanini had died before writing the stage directions."[108] Ruffo wrote Berthe from the Tyrol on 14 August that he was studying the role "with true love," looking forward to the premiere.[109] Although Berthe felt it unnecessary for Forzano to supervise the production in the United States, Ruffo tried contacting the librettist in Viareggio, hoping there still remained time for him to work with Marinuzzi. The baritone planned to leave for New York on 25 September, while Berthe described how she envisioned the opera's final scene. Ruffo finally created the title role in Chicago on 13 December 1920, in collaboration with Albert Paillard (Creonte), Teofilo Dentale (Tiresia), and Dorothy Francis (Giocasta). The baritone later wrote that the critics were "extremely generous regarding the production" if not the music, which they found "in certain moments to be lacking in orchestration."[110] Others felt that "Leoncavallo never wrote but one score that lived, and *Edipo re* was not it."[111] Pennacchio's name was printed on neither the orchestral nor the piano/vocal score.

IMPROPER FINALE

Edipo re was not the only posthumous composition Berthe "transformed." Others included the operetta *La maschera nuda* to a libretto by Luigi Bonelli and Ferdinando Paolieri, with a score "completed"—if not perhaps fully composed—by Salvatore Allegra.[112] Leoncavallo was the only composer who continued producing works for two decades following his death (!), and it is extremely doubtful whether *Edipo re*, *Maschera nuda*, or the short operetta *Il primo bacio* had anything to do with the composer at all. When *Maschera nuda* premiered at Naples' Teatro Politeama on 26 June 1925, Berthe announced in various newspapers that Leoncavallo had visited a Luxemburg museum during 1882 and was intrigued by the portrait of an unknown young woman, the "masked nude" of the work's title.[113] Berthe suggested that her husband then expressed the wish to compose an operetta on the theme of this gioconda, making sketches for a libretto, although, again, nothing remains in the composer's hand nor in his correspondence, while all that can be proven to be authentic is what has been "borrowed" from *A chi la giarrettiera?*. Berthe was nevertheless more truthful in this case, stating that Ferdinando Paolieri and Luigi Bonelli created a text to Leoncavallo's idea, while the composer Salvatore Allegra composed music to those "ideas."

Luigi Bonelli had also written the libretto to another of "Leoncavallo's" operettas, *Il primo bacio*, which premiered in Montecatini on 29 April 1923. As with so many of Leoncavallo's other posthumous compositions, it is doubtful whether the composer was ever actually involved. In the case of *Il primo bacio*, only a manuscript draft for the work's main waltz remains, although it is arguable whether this in fact stemmed from the composer or from his brother Leone, who was known to sign his famous brother's name under his own compositions. Until her death, Berthe continued to seek a way out of the financial difficulties in which Leoncavallo had left her.

After Berthe's death in Montecatini on 28 February 1926, Jeanne Puel also began producing posthumous operettas when she was made legal heir to the composer's estate.[114] On 22 October 1927, Jeanne signed a contract with the Wiener Operettenverlag—a subsidiary of Vienna's Universal Edition— claiming to have found eighteen original pieces of Leoncavallo's music that she wished to have fashioned into an operetta. A German libretto was quickly drafted by Heinrich Hermann Regel to match Leoncavallo's music, entitled *Liebesrebellion* (*Ribellione dell'Amore*), a "rococo operetta in three acts." She also made certain that the contract allowed other of the composer's compositions to be added ad libidum. On 9 May 1928, Regel signed a contract with the Wiener Operettenverlag stating that the composer Oskar Stalla had been called upon to supply music resembling Leoncavallo's style. The librettist Adolph Schütz was also asked to rewrite what Regel had written for Stalla's music, finally re-christening *Liebesrebellion* into *Rokoko*. The contract further stated that Stalla's name was not to be mentioned in the printed score or anywhere else. The project mercifully concluded on 18 January 1932, when a new round of contracts were signed voiding the work altogether.[115]

Although the composer's centennial was incorrectly celebrated in 1958, Leoncavallo's name would once again be in all the papers during 1978 when the current owners of Villa Myriam (Forster) wished to sell the house for 750,000 Swiss francs to the town of Brissago, which refused, believing the price too high. After a plan to turn the villa into a hotel failed, the house was destroyed in March 1978 to make space for an apartment building.

Leoncavallo's name once again made headlines in 1989, when it was suggested that the composer's remains be reburied in Brissago,[116] claiming that Leoncavallo had stated that he wished to be interred there. There was much talk of a letter or other document written by the composer mentioning this fact, although, in actuality, none was ever found. The only "evidence" was the speech Leoncavallo made upon becoming an honorary citizen of Brissago in 1904, wherein he mentioned that he would not mind having a final resting place in the town's Madonna di Ponte cemetery.[117] The idea of moving Leoncavallo's remains sparked great controversy as well as an endless number of newspaper articles. The approval of a Leoncavallo relative was sought and received on 22 September 1989,[118] when Piera Leoncavallo-Grand, Giuseppe Leoncavallo's descendant, began legal proceedings to have the body exhumed, stating that she was acting on behalf of the composer and his relatives, a decision she would later deeply regret.[119] Leoncavallo's remains were placed in a zinc box that were driven to Brissago the same day.[120] Most Italian officials refused to release any information at the time, prompting incomprehension on the public's part when the remains arrived on 24 September to be placed in a Swiss bank safe, until a final decision had been made for the composer's reburial. Florentines were incensed that Leoncavallo's resting place in Florence was not deemed sufficiently grand to honor his name.[121] What was left of Leoncavallo was now also filmed and photographed,[122] as many wondered when other illustrious names in Italy would be reburied. However, in recent years Brissago has fortunately been able to cultivate the composer's memory with, among other things, a museum housed in the town's center. One hopes that

Leoncavallo, a man who found little peace during his lifetime, will finally be able to treasure the serenity that now surrounds him.

NOTES

1. District Court of Locarno, 21 January 1916 (CL).
2. Ibid.
3. Leoncavallo also owed money to the Trüb Company in Aarau, the City of Brissago, and the bank Credito Ticinese in Locarno. Alone the latter two amounted to ten thousand Swiss francs.
4. Leoncavallo to Giovanni Rosadi, 29 February 1916 (BCL).
5. Ibid.
6. Ibid.
7. Leoncavallo to Gualtiero Belvederi, 29 March 1916 (BCL).
8. Leoncavallo to Gualtiero Belvederi, 16 March 1916 (BCL).
9. Leoncavallo still owed Belvederi twenty-five hundred lire for *Mameli's* libretto.
10. Victor Herbert later composed *Orange Blossoms* based on the Grésac play. Produced by Edward Royce, it opened on Broadway for ninety-five performances during 1922.
11. Ibid.
12. *Giornale d'Italia*, reprinted in *Il Secolo*, 20 April 1916.
13. Leoncavallo tried to convince Burzio—who was making her debut in Genoa—and the remainder of the cast to accept reduced fees, since profits were donated to the Red Cross.
14. *Il Secolo*, 28 April 1916.
15. Ibid.
16. Ibid. The singers—especially Burzio—were lauded, whereas Leoncavallo's production was deemed discreet.
17. *Il Nuovo Giornale*, 1 May 1916.
18. District Court of Locarno (CL).
19. Subtitled *Fiore di Malavita*, the plot evolves in Madrid dealing with the eighteen-year-old tobacco factory employee Pasquita, who spurns the love of the thirty-year-old Quirico for the poor though ten year younger Manuelo of no means. Her short-lived affair with Manuelo ends in pregnancy. Her lover and family desert her, and her child dies. Quirico appears again pledging his love. This unoriginal scenario concludes when an infant is "found" before her door. Her soul is then "redeemed"—the title's significance—and she begins a new life.
20. District Court of Locarno, 8 July 1916 (CL).
21. Ibid.
22. Ibid.
23. Ibid., 20 August 1916.
24. Ibid.

25. Luisa Tetrazzini attended the premiere.

26. Leoncavallo to Carlo D'Ormeville, 5 September 1916 (MTS).

27. Father of composer Gian Carlo Menotti.

28. Leoncavallo had also lost thousands of lire on the *Mameli* tour, although he still insisted on productions in Cremona and Malta to benefit the Italian Red Cross.

29. Leoncavallo to Gualtiero Belvederi, 27 October 1916 (BCL).

30. Cast lists state that he did not conduct, and it is therefore questionable whether he in fact even attended.

31. Two wealthy farming families, Alliuzzi and Croce, have been rival factions for a great length of time when the opera's young heroine Paula finds herself married to the handsome Marco Alliuzzi although she originally loved Bastianu Croce. (Marco's brother, Andria, is also in love with her). When Marco is murdered, all are convinced it was Bastianu until Paula eventually discovers that it was an act of fratricide, the murderer being Andria. Paula's love for Bastianu is again rekindled, and his mother, Catalina, blesses the union when the jealous Andria bursts in, intent on attacking Bastianu, only to be stabbed by Catalina, who thereby declares that "the beast is dead" ("La mala bestia è morta!"), recalling the chilling and unexpected *Pagliacci* conclusion.

32. Leoncavallo to Gualtiero Belvederi, 4 December 1916 (BCL).

33. Tetrazzini may have even commissioned the work, although there is no evidence.

34. Leoncavallo to Valentino Soldani, 9 December 1916 (MTS).

35. This seems to suggest that, as with *Zingari*, Leoncavallo hoped to present the work at the Hippodrome and then begin a tour starting in Chicago. Although the composer warned Soldani that times were difficult and that pay would not be forthcoming, he needed the libretto as soon as possible.

36. Leoncavallo to Gualtiero Belvederi, 22 December 1916 (BCL).

37. Successful films had already been made of *Pagliacci* and *Reginetta delle rose.*

38. Leoncavallo to Gualtiero Belvederi, 25 December 1916 (BCL).

38. Ibid.

40. Ibid.

41. Ibid.

42. Leoncavallo to Soldani, 11 January 1917 (MTS).

43. Leoncavallo to Valentino Soldani, 13 April 1917 (BCL).

44. Leoncavallo to Edmondo Corradi, 13 May 1917 (Y).

45. Leoncavallo to Valentino Soldani, 12 June 1917 (MTS).

46. Ibid. Leoncavallo also suggested that Soldani write a libretto for Ruffo, after the baritone completed his military duty.

47. Leoncavallo to Valentino Soldani, 19 June 1917 (BCL).

48. Leoncavallo to Lorenzo Sonzogno, undated. (BCL).

49. Originally titled *Capriccio d'amore*, it is based on an idea by Luigi Bonelli to a text by Arturo Franci.

50. The "capitalista" was probably Count Ernesto Cauda.

51. Leoncavallo to Valentino Soldani, 26 July 1917 (MTS).

52. Ibid.

53. Contract for *Mirandolina*, 4 August 1917 (BCL).

54. Leoncavallo to Valentino Soldani, 20 August 1917 (MTS).

55. Ibid.

56. Valentino Soldani to Leoncavallo, 22 August 1917 (BCL).

57. Leoncavallo to Valentino Soldani, 24 August 1917 (MTS).

58. Ibid.

59. Leoncavallo to Valentino Soldani, 29 August 1917 (MTS).

60. On 2 September 1917, Abbondio sent another list of facts refuting Leoncavallo's claims, stating clearly that the composer had "acted dishonestly," always making verbal and written promises "that he would pay his obligations," although he never kept his word (DCL).

61. Leoncavallo to Luigi Illica, 15 October 1917 (BCP).

62. Luigi Illica to Leoncavallo, 5 November 1917. The original letter has been dated 31 October by a foreign hand (BCP).

63. Ibid.

64. Leoncavallo to Luigi Illica, 12 December 1917 (BCP).

65. Lorenzo had refused all of Leoncavallo's offers to hear the *Avemaria* libretto in Viareggio, claiming that his long theatrical experience had taught him not to have confidence in subjects that composers had personally chosen.

66. Illica's outraged letters to Lorenzo accusing him of slander may have contributed to the publisher's sudden acceptance of *Avemaria*.

67. Ibid.

68. BCL.

69. Leoncavallo to Gualtiero Belvederi, 2 December 1917 (BCL).

70. Leoncavallo to Gualtiero Belvederi, 15 January 1918 (BCL).

71. On 28 December, Leoncavallo had convinced himself that he would be living in Rome by February of the following year, writing of his plans to his acquaintance Raffaele Cotugno, to whose verses he was composing a song. Leoncavallo to Raffaele Cotugno, 28 December 1917 (BNB).

72. Leoncavallo to Valentino Soldani, 29 December 1917 (MTS).

73. Valentino Soldani to Leoncavallo, 1 January 1918 (BCL).

74. Leoncavallo and Soldani's relationship was further aggravated when Berthe suddenly had the idea for a "wonderful operetta."

75. Leoncavallo to Luigi Illica, 27 January 1918 (BCP).

76. Handwritten copy by Leoncavallo of a letter to Lorenzo Sonzogno, 12 February 1918 (BCP).

77. Ibid.

78. Handwritten copy by Leoncavallo of a letter to Max Eschig, 21 January 1918 (BCL).

79. Leoncavallo to Soldani, 8 April 1918 (MTS).

80. Leoncavallo to Alfonso Menotti, 11 May 1918 (BCL).

81. Leoncavallo to Gualtiero Belvederi, 22 May 1918 (BCL).

82. The premiere was delayed when Lorenzo tried to cancel the production.

83. Berthe probably thereby wished to secure what little remained of Leoncavallo's estate for Jeanne and herself, in light of the composer's increasing ill health.

84. Leoncavallo to Raffaele Cotugno, 19 September 1918 (BNB).

85. Leoncavallo to Raffaele Cotugno, 16 October 1918 (BNB).

86. Ibid.

87. Giovanni Abbondio to Alberto Vigizzi, 27 March 1919 (BCL).

88. Leoncavallo to Raffaele Cotugno, 23 December 1918 (BNB).

89. Leoncavallo to Gualtiero Belvederi, 25 December 1918 (BCL).

90. Leoncavallo to Gualtiero Belvederi, 25 December 1918 (BCL).

91. At the same time, Leoncavallo was involved in legal proceedings against Caesar Films for not honoring their contract.

92. Leoncavallo to Gualtiero Belvederi, 7 January 1919 (BCL).

93. Leoncavallo to Gualtiero Belvederi, 19 January 1919 (BCL).

94. Leoncavallo to Raffaele Cotugno, 13 March 1919 (BNB).

95. Ibid.

96. His death certificate gives his age as being sixty-one, erroneously corresponding to his having been born in 1858, while the *Times of London* wrote that he died at age sixty.

97. Some newspaper accounts suggest that Leoncavallo had fallen into a coma at the beginning of August resulting from his lengthy battle with diabetes, while others state that he recited the Holy Litany during his last days, pleading with the Madonna for an additional three years of life in order to complete *Tormenta*.

98. *The Times*, 11 August 1919.

99. "An excellent finale for that prolific composer of melodramas and operettas who combined two noble beasts and who died suffocated by melodic adiposity."

100. The year 1919 also ended the lives of many of Leoncavallo's friends and colleagues, including Illica, Belvederi, and Cleofonte Campanini. Ironically, both Edoardo Sonzogno and Victor Maurel survived the composer by one and four years respectively.

101. Newspaper accounts fail to mention Belvederi's presence, implying that he was either unable to attend or was not recognized by the press.

102. Pennacchio had once composed the opera *Redenzione* to Leoncavallo's libretto.

103. Contract for the completion of *Edipo re* between Berthe Leoncavallo and Giovanni Pennacchio.

104. Ruffo, *My Parabola*, 310.

105. The orchestral score is written in Pennacchio's hand. Leoncavallo's transformation of *Chatterton* into *Mameli* nevertheless proved that he was capable of repackaging his works to suit potential audiences.

106. Berthe Leoncavallo to Titta Ruffo, 15 June 1920 (BCL).

107. Ruffo, *My Parabola*, 310.

108. Ibid.

109. Berthe Leoncavallo to Titta Ruffo, 14 August 1920 (BCL).

110. Ibid.

111. Edward C. Moore, *Forty Years of Opera in Chicago* (1930, Reprint, New York: Arno Press,1977), 222.

112. A ballet entitled *Danza Messicana* was also mentioned. It is worth noting that the Sicilian Salvatore Allegra also composed an opera called *Ave Maria* that premiered in 1934, albeit to a different scenario.

113. According to Berthe, Emile Collet supposedly then based his lyrics for the composer's 1893 song *Je ne sais pas ton nom* on this experience.

114. Jeanne Puel remained in contact with the great musicians of the day for decades, controlling anything and everything that had to do with Leoncavallo and possible financial gain. Ruffo was one of the first to write her regarding *Edipo re*'s copyright after she became its owner.

115. In 1929, a "fantaisie" for orchestra supposedly also composed by Leoncavallo entitled *La modèle masque* and orchestrated by F. Heurther was published in Paris by J. Yves Krier.

116. The collection was partially sold to Hildegarde Freifrau von Münchhausen and Locarno's Biblioteca Cantonale.

117. Had the composer been intent on a Brissago burial he would have certainly mentioned it before his death.

118. Although Jeanne Puel inherited the rights to the composer's estate, she had never been adopted by Leoncavallo, nor had she been granted Italian citizenship, and her companion, Ildebrando Trovatelli, inherited the rights following her death.

119. Author's interview with Piera Leoncavallo-Grand (12 April 2003).

120. Berthe's remains followed in 1993.

121. Leoncavallo's Florentine tomb had recently been renovated, and a bronze statue had also been erected on the site.

122. Leoncavallo's 1858 birth date appeared on the zinc "coffin."

2

WORKS

• *10* •

La nuit de mai

*L*eoncavallo's first symphonic poem, based on a work by Alfred de Musset, is a dialogue between a Muse (orchestra) and a Poet (tenor). The initial orchestral movement (*Poète, prends ton luth*) vividly recalls *Tannhäuser's* Venusberg, while Leoncavallo opted to use lute, mandola, two solo celli, and two harps, following ten introductory measures for violins and violas on an elevated tremolo arpeggio.[1] The second movement (*largamente, mystérieux*) introduces the Poet's first solo ("Comme il fait noir dans la vallée"), immediately creating the melancholic image of a Wertherian spirit ("C'est une étrange rêverie; elle s'efface et disparait"). The third movement for orchestra (*Poète, prends ton luth*), describes a spring night, resounding like a Chopin waltz and recalling one of Leoncavallo's Parisian piano compositions that would later be used for his 1906 song "Papillon," dealing with a rose enveloping a butterfly. Movement four ("Pourquoi mon coeur bat-il si vite?") emerges as an *assai agitato* resembling a heartbeat, with the Poet believing the pounding of his heart to be a knock at the door, foreshadowing the orchestral introduction to Canio's "Vesti la giubba" in *Pagliacci*.[2] The orchestral fifth movement again takes up the lute in reference to the Muse's unsung text (*Poète, prends ton luth*), also repeating the future *I Medici* theme as in the first movement, this time with the addition of a woodwind section, bass clarinet, and cor anglais. The impressive *largo tranquillo* of the sixth movement for tenor ("Est-ce toi dont la voix m'appelle, O ma pauvre Muse!") recalls Gounod's *Faust* in its broad sweeping melody. Frequently extracted from the symphonic poem to be performed in concert as "Invocation à la Muse," it represents the Poet's invoking the Muse as an immortal flower, a symbol of fraternal and sensuous love. The seventh orchestral movement (*Poète, prends ton luth*) is a highly theatrical, demonically driven and yet majestic *allegro con fuoco*, worthy of inclusion in any symphonic program for its shrieking and slightly macabre scherzo, recalling the spirits inhabiting the Dutchman's ship in the final act of *Der fliegende Holländer*. The Muse promises relief from earthly woes through a land of oblivion; the crimson of Italy and Greece to the green of Scotland all belong to them. The eighth movement for the Poet ("S'il ne te faut, ma soeur chérie qu'un baiser d'une lèvre amie") has a fragmentary quality, while the orchestral solo making up the ninth movement ("Crois-tu donc que je sois comme le vent d'automne") recalls Massenet.[3] This section musically recreates the first part of Musset's longest and most poetic text, wherein the Muse reminds the Poet that his pain belongs to God and that desperation and suffering can provide inspiration. Parts of the tenth movement for orchestra ("Lorsque le pélican lassé, d'un long voyage"), an *andante agitato assai*, will later return for the chorus of villagers greeting the troupe of clowns in *Pagliacci*. Here it is meant to evoke the image of a pelican feeding its young from its own flesh, a symbol of Christ's self-sacrifice for man's salvation, forcefully supported by the strings and woodwinds. The eleventh movement for orchestra ("Poète, c'est ainsi que font les grands poètes") compares the pelican to the Poet in the form of an intermezzo (*largamente*), the first part being a short recitative for the oboes followed by an *andante triste* employing horns and strings, before eventually being taken up by the entire orchestra. Closing on a note of despair, though with a rousing and driven finale (*andante mosso e solenne*), the final movement ("O Muse! Spectre insatiable ne m'en demande pas si long"), sung by the Poet, implores the Muse to spare him from immense suffering. *La nuit de mai* not only makes one aware of Leoncavallo's talent as an orchestrator but also proves his innate ability for musically expressing dramatic situations, which would find outlet in his future operas, combined with a refined sense of literature inspiring his lyrical vein.

NOTES

1. The mandola adds a curious touch of Neapolitan character, recalling the composer's origins, while the instrument was also considered a novelty in Paris at the time. The movement's main theme will be employed again for Simonetta and Giuliano's act 1 love duet in *I Medici* ("Egli è del rio").

2. Parts of the movement also recall Leonora's act 1 aria "Ma pellegrina ed orfana" from Verdi's 1862 *La forza del destino*.

3. Leoncavallo has divided the longest part of Musset's poem to include orchestral movements nine and ten.

• 11 •

Chatterton

Characters

Tommaso Chatterton, tenor	Lord Klifford, baritone
John Clark, bass	Lord Strafford, bass
Jenny Clark, soprano	Lord Lingston, tenor
Henry, soprano	Skirner, tenor
Giorgio, baritone	a servant, mute

Setting: Environs of London (1770)

Born in Bristol on 20 November 1752, Thomas Chatterton was the posthumous son of another Thomas, who had taught at Colston Hospital—the school Chatterton would later attend built "on the site of a Carmelite House."[1] Not quite fifteen, Chatterton left school to be apprenticed to a certain John Lambert for the duration of seven years "to be educated as a scrivener."[2] Precocious and eccentric, Chatterton was considered a "difficult employee," watched over like a hawk and forbidden anything that might have driven away his melancholy: "Taverns he shall not frequent, at Dice he shall not play, Fornication he shall not commit," and "matrimony he shall not contract."[3] The fact that he

---

The versions analyzed in this section pertain to those condoned by the composer during his lifetime, e.g., the second version of *Chatterton* and the first version of *Zazà*. In the first version, the opera was in four acts and the characters' names were more in keeping with their English originals: Caterina, Giovanni Bell, Lord Talbot, and Lord Beckford. The role of Skirner was originally written for a bass, while Talbot was a mezzo-soprano. Act 1 was preceded by a chorus of villagers leading directly to Chatterton's monologue and aria. Act 3 included a sextet for the soloists for which Leoncavallo made sketches without adding either text or orchestration. Most of the opera is unrecognizable when compared to its final, more compact version. As the original *Chatterton* bears no date, it is impossible to ascertain its precise year of composition.

would "often sit up all night and write by moonlight increased the friction with Lambert's staff."[4] He not only delighted in creating "fictitious pedigrees" for himself but also for his acquaintances.[5] His "heraldic dedications . . . were neither scientific, snobbish, nor would-be parvenu, but purely romantic and poetical,"[6] a trait Leoncavallo surely could identify with. His anonymous poetry was published as early as 1763 in a Bristol newspaper. His *Elinoure and Juga* (1764), which he claimed to have found, was attributed to Thomas Rowley, "a goode prieste" of the fifteenth century. The name originated in St. John's Church, where Chatterton discovered a brass plate dedicated to the merchant and sheriff Thomas Rouley.[7] Chatterton frequently used pseudonyms such as the initials "X.Y.," with which he signed his earlier *Hymn for Christmas Day*.

Chatterton remained silent regarding the original manuscript, when the Rowley pieces began attracting attention, returning "nothing but haughtiness and a refusal to give any account."[8] He then announced that he had been "employed to transcribe certain ancient manuscripts" found "in a large chest in the upper room over the chapel on the north side of Redcliff Church."[9] Chatterton's biographer, Edward Meyerstein, logically claims that the young man lied because he wanted immediate fame. Had he been honest, curiosity would have been stilled at once. For the remainder of his short life, Chatterton never wavered in declaring that he had found the manuscripts in the muniment room over the north porch at St. Mary Redcliff. The parchments on which Chatterton had written his poetry signed "Thomas Rowley" had been in his home for some time, churchwardens originally having entrusted them to Chatterton's father to cover bibles. Following Chatterton's death, his mother, "a poor woman with no antiquarian tastes whatever," stored them in a "long deal box" using the contents for thread, papers, dolls, and patterns.[10] Chatterton, having found the perfect tools to realize his creation, "was perpetually rummaging and ransacking every corner in the house for parchments and carrying away those he found by pocketsfull."[11] Hungry and in debt, Chatterton expressed his despondency to friends only three days before his suicide: "I feel the sting of a speedy dissolution. I have been at war with the grave for some time and find it is not so easy to vanquish it as I imagined; we can find an asylum to hide from every creditor but that."[12] Assuring his landlady that he was not hungry (he had in fact been without food for three days), he penned some final verses after which he "swallowed arsenick in water on the 24th of August 1770 and died, in consequence thereof, the next day."[13] Although the "Rowley poems" were published in 1777, it would take many decades of heated controversy before they were officially declared as forgeries, resulting in an eventual recognition of Chatterton's genius. Chatterton became a legendary romantic symbol, and even his handkerchief was exhibited in the British Museum; "unknown and miserable while alive," his death prompted both "curiosity and attention."[14]

The French playwright Alfred de Vigny (1797–1863) captured the image of the unhappy youth in his three-act play *Chatterton* (1835), written for his mistress Marie Dorval, with whom he had been involved over several years of jealous misery. Regarding Chatterton, he wrote that society "murders the most intelligent" in its refusal to let individuals live following the rules of their own nature.[15] A great anglophile, spending time in Britain and married to a British wife (Lydia Bunbury), Vigny not only translated *Othello* (*Le More de Venise*), but also Chatterton's own *Excelente Balade of Charitie*.

Vigny's characterization of Chatterton stands in direct relation to Goethe's *Leiden des jungen Werther* (1774) and Chateaubriand's *René* (1805), the idealistic and sensitive poet at one with nature and at odds with the world. Antiheroes, they reflect an artistic soul combined with childlike innocence, remaining passive when not in the act of writing or thinking about death and an idealized form of love. Pleasing of appearance and emotionally fragile, theirs is an aesthetic and slightly narcissistic world in keeping with the artistic egotism necessary for creation. Werther's and Chatterton's love of children—an extension of their own purity—is significant in both Goethe's novel and Vigny's play. Vigny created an idealized Chatterton beyond familial and emotional relationships, religion, and social convention, a passive victim of society. This *mal de siècle* reached its climax during the early 1900s also inspiring composers including Massenet, whose *Werther*—the most successful operatic tribute—appeared following the first version of Leoncavallo's *Chatterton* in 1892.

With "burning hands" and a "pale visage,"[16] Vigny's Chatterton is aristocratic of character, if not of birth. Solitary, he shuns worldly matters, setting him apart from the role of John Bell. As a welcome relief Chatterton frequently mentions death, even though he is only eighteen years old. A Quaker informs the reader quite early in Vigny's play that man is divided into two species: the martyrs and those that make others suffer. Chatterton is the "martyr of all," as is Kitty Bell,[17] although Kitty, like Lotte, feels largely victimized by a frustrated marriage. Both Chatterton and Werther subconsciously prefer to retain their romantic image in death rather than having it ruined by the banalities of a daily relationship. This form of "ideal love," without physical consummation, irrevocably changes both Charlotte and Kitty's lives. "Indifferent" and "continuously dreaming,"[18] Chatterton turns his room into a cloister, where he writes on his knees for lack of a table, his first love being his muse.

The Quaker adopts the role of a father figure, reminiscent of Germont in *La traviata* or even Padre Guardiano in Verdi's *La forza del destino*, while the appearance of the three lords serves as a kind of deus ex machina. The Quaker's philosophy and experience enables him to predict Chatterton's future, whereas the latter's infatuation with Kitty—his muse—would run the risk of insanity if he failed to end his own life at some point.[19] (As suicide condemned Chatterton in the eyes of society, Vigny sought to express the act as a "social homicide.")[20] Although Kitty's feelings for Chatterton are reciprocated, they are not verbalized until *after* he has swallowed poison, with no risk of rejection. Art nevertheless conquers in the end, when the striking of a clock reminds Chatterton, even in death, that he should really be writing. Chatterton informs the Quaker in act 3, scene 5, that "poetry is a mental illness" of which he believes himself cured, although without it life seems intolerable. When forced to take part in society by Lord Beckford (Lord Klifford in the opera), it signifies a loss of freedom for Chatterton comparable to having sold his soul. He therefore takes leave of a world made up of "humiliation, hate, sarcasm," and "degrading work."[21]

When transforming *Chatterton* into an opera, Leoncavallo renamed his characters in order to distance himself from Vigny:[22]

Vigny/Leoncavallo
Thomas Chatterton/Tommaso Chatterton
Catherine (Kitty) Bell/Jenny Clark
John Bell/John Clark
Quaker/Giorgio
Lord Beckford/Lord Klifford
Lord Kingston/Lord Lingston
Lord Talbot/Lord Strafford
Lord Lauderdale
Rachel
Rebecca
Skirner
Henry

Jenny's younger brother Henry replaces the children (Rachel, Rebecca) Catherine has in the play,[23] enabling her to portray a young woman not taken up with motherhood.[24] Although Leoncavallo's original version was in four acts, the second version discussed here is in three, similar to Vigny's play.[25] Act 1 commences in the "vicinity of London" during 1770, revealing John Clark's greenhouse adjoined on the one side to his home and on the other to his factory.[26] It is a cold but beautiful morning on 24 December. The curtain rises immediately to a festive, gavotte-like andante in C-major evoking a British ambience reminiscent of Handel, which will be repeated numerous times during the act in both E- and F-major, echoed by the English horn associated with John. Jenny's uncle, the elderly Quaker Giorgio, is seated at a table reading when her husband John enters, impatiently searching for his wife, telling her that Lord Klifford will be their guest during a hunting expedition with friends. Klifford's image is musically sketched with a "Tempo di gavotta" in F-major, played by the violins, which illustrates his elegant yet superficial character. John's imperious nature is immediately demonstrated when referring to his employees ("Essi lavorono, Io pago e basta") and when speaking to Jenny, reminding her that their lodger Tom (Chatterton) has failed to pay his rent, although Jenny states it is due the following day, recalling his "uncertain occupation." John exits to the opera's initial theme, having returned to C-major, as Henry enters, mimicking John to his theme.[27]

The factory bell is heard, signifying the end of a day's work. John's employees leave singing an ensemble recalling the opening bars of *I Medici*,[28] which had been written prior to *Chatterton*'s second version, not far removed in its atmosphere from one of Charles Dickens's novels, stressing the importance of Christmas generosity versus poverty. Chatterton now makes his entrance to a melancholic version of the recently heard polka in F-major, accompanied by a slowly descending chromatic scale played by the strings, thereby differentiating his character. Henry runs to greet Chatterton, who, in turn, embraces him as a sign of his love of children (i.e., innocence, similar to Werther's entrance in Massenet's opera) to a waltz-like arietta and oboe accompaniment. Henry reminds the poet that he will expect a present from him at Christmas.

Henry soon runs off to greet Lord Klifford's hunting party, as Chatterton tells Giorgio that he is saddened after having written an important letter. Giorgio chides him for being "insane," allowing Chatterton to grieve over his life ("La mia vita è un martirio"). Beginning in E-flat major, expressing the poet's pale sensitivity, supported by the orchestra, it develops into a chromatic passage in G-flat-major demonstrating his pent-up passion ("Ricomposi l'antica favella"). Chatterton's phrase "E le vecchie leggende" recalls Giuliano's "È il foco de la lucciola" from act 1 of *I Medici*, while he echoes Vigny when he sings of writing of King Harold. His sudden enthusiasm when speaking of poetry instantly lightens the music to an optimistic sounding F-major. It returns to the initial G-flat-major and is finally crowned by an optional high C. The poet's reverie is halted when Giorgio reminds him that Lord Klifford is arriving, prompting Chatterton to curse Klifford for having stolen his last refuge.[29]

A hunting theme announces Klifford's approach, before Leoncavallo proceeds to act 2, scene 3, of Vigny with the actual arrival of Lord Klifford, Strafford, and Lingston, accompanied by "six other lords in hunting attire." After greeting John and Jenny, Klifford recognizes Chatterton as his Oxford companion, introducing the poet as the author of *Harold*. It is unfortunate that Leoncavallo failed to make use of a motive for Chatterton, which could have been employed at this time, rather than the elegant one heard in keeping with Klifford's character ("Signori, vi presento). Chatterton is then forced to dine with Klifford and his companions, who make vulgar advances toward Jenny, contrasting her and Chatterton's noble character with the ironic elegance and vulgarity of the authentic aristocrat. This evolves into a septet in E-major to a spirited scherzoso accompaniment that Leoncavallo later decided to delete from the orchestral score.

Chatterton challenges Klifford to a duel when he insists on kissing Jenny's hand, unmistakably demonstrating the poet's interest in her. The dinner finally ends, leaving Chatterton and Jenny alone for the first time.[30] She now emerges as a self-secure Leoncavallo heroine with no fear of speaking her mind, furiously demanding more respect, while insisting that Chatterton seek another abode ("Ma qual donna sarà più rispettata"). Chatterton responds in a supplicating D-minor aria "Ne' pieghi del sudario" (recalling Alvaro's "Solenne in quest'ora" from Verdi's *La forza del destino*) that he is only an impoverished poet wishing to remain an additional day in John Clark's house in order to complete his work. Touched, Jenny asks forgiveness for her conduct as the poet exits, seeking comfort in Giorgio's fatherly embrace as the act ends.

Leoncavallo's talent was arguably a dramatic one, and the latter halves of his works usually find him at his most able and passionate after a weaker exposition. *Chatterton* is no exception, with its appropriately melancholic and tragic mood beginning in act 2 with an intense *intermezzo sinfonico* that essentially serves as a prelude, recalling Massenet's *La nuit de Noël* introduction preceding act 4 of *Werther*.[31] Leoncavallo's symphonic impressionism captures both the physical and emotional suffering of his protagonist, enabling the listener to experience Chatterton's anguished night following the last act. The intermezzo is introduced by slow chromatic chords in F-sharp minor (*maestoso*) leading to a lyric nocturne expressed in octaves. An impressive crescendo resulting from dynamic ascending and descending scales in syncopated octaves serves as a frenzied portrait of Chatterton's frustation and grief. Temporary release is found in a *cantabile* evoking Jenny, supported by the horns, only to be completely stifled at its violent conclusion (*tutta la forza*).

Leoncavallo contrasts this unrelenting intensity in act 2 with an a capella female chorus behind the stage singing a short religious hymn (*andante sostenuto*), reminding the listener that it is Christmas, a holiday symbolizing peace and love, in contrast to Chatterton's inner turmoil. The orchestra reprises the intermezzo's *cantabile* as the curtain rises, revealing Chatterton's sparsely furnished room and Jenny and John's bedroom directly opposite.

Chatterton is asleep at his desk after having spent the night writing.[32] Chromatic scales in sixths focus on his suffering, interspersed with motifs from the intermezzo. He laments that exhaustion has clouded his will to write, corresponding to his extended monologue "Il est certain qu'elle ne m'aime pas" in act 3, scene 1, of Vigny's play. Leoncavallo also uses the device of a clock striking, as in the original, reminding the poet to return to work. His writing is interrupted with thoughts of Jenny, whose name he invokes to the same theme with which he took leave of her in the preceding act ("Jenny! Jenny!") Contemplating suicide as a release from his unfulfilled love for Jenny and his unhappy life, he begins the opera's major aria beginning in B-flat minor, "Tu sola a me rimani, o poesia," which vaguely recalls Chopin's Prélude no. 24.

Chatterton's depressed thoughts are interrupted by Henry, intent on collecting the poet's promised Christmas gift. (His repeated theme was originally heard in act 1). Chatterton hands him a bible, explaining that Jenny will give it back to Henry when he is capable of understanding its contents, as her motif (*molto sentito*) once again resounds in the orchestra, played by the clarinets and violins. Henry immediately reads a passage devoted to Abraham ("D'acqua e di pane li provvide Abramo"), preshadowing Minnie's bible lecture in act 1 of Puccini's *La fanciulla del West*,[33] as Chatterton runs from the room in tears, passing Jenny and Giorgio, who ask Henry what is the matter, as the bible theme reappears in the strings ("E chi ti diede questo libro?"). An extended duet now begins between Jenny and Giorgio, wherein she inquires about Chatterton's poetry, remorseful for her words of the previous day. She soon rushes out when Giorgio warns her, in a "thundering voice," that it would be preferable for Chatterton to die if it saved her from an ill-fated relationship. Giorgio then leaves accompanied by a motif from the duet.

Leoncavallo brilliantly succeeds in bringing this passionate music to an abrupt halt with the sudden appearance of the evil usurer, Skirner, whose entrance is accompanied by constantly shifting, eerie-sounding tonalities played by the clarinet, bassoons, and flute. Leoncavallo grasped the dramatic viability of including Skirner into the action as a symbol of Chatterton's downfall although he never actually appears in the play.[34] A servant leads this Mephisophelean figure—reminiscent of Dr. Miracle in Offenbach's *Contes d'Hoffmann*—into Chatterton's room to await the poet, leaving sufficient time to introduce his theme, a *tempo agitato*, recalling Saint-Saëns' *Danse macabre*, that will repeatedly return throughout the scene. Chatterton offers his poetry when Skirner refuses to wait another day for repayment of his debts and extracts a document requesting that the young man make his body available to a surgical school, as the current prices on corpses are high.[35] Horrified that another human being should make such a request, Chatterton commands Skirner to be silent ("Taci! demonio."), nevertheless signing his life away. Leoncavallo's Nosferatu victoriously exits, leaving the poet to muse that although he has suffered from poverty and hunger, the latest development in his "via crucis" ranks as the most intolerable.

Giorgio soon enters, saving Chatterton from taking a large dose of opium, hoping to end his suffering indefinitely, while the Quaker admits that if Chatterton died he would also symbolically murder Jenny. Giorgio's paternal love for Jenny ("Come una figlia io l'amo") is expressed in descending chords recalling

Silvio's courtship of Nedda in *Pagliacci*. Leoncavallo remains faithful to Vigny when Chatterton finds refuge in Giorgio's embrace, just as Jenny had at the close of the preceding act, while the orchestra echoes the theme of their duet.[36]

Act 3 shows the interior of John's house that evening.[37] Jenny, John, and Giorgio are listening to Lord Klifford when the curtain rises to a descending arpeggio leading to a fugue. Chatterton has written a letter to Klifford's uncle, the Lord Mayor, requesting financial help, and Klifford now produces a response, which he hands Chatterton to menacing chords deriving from the *Intermezzo Sinfonico*.[38] All present insist that Chatterton should readily accept any position Klifford's uncle offers. Skirner's theme is again heard (*come nella scena con Skirner*), announcing that Chatterton's fate is sealed with little hope of redemption, recalling the introduction to the Dutchman's "Die Frist ist um" in Wagner's *Der fliegende Holländer*. The poet asks to be alone (to Klifford's theme) after Lord Klifford declares that he will take Chatterton with him to London that very evening. Realizing that he is no longer in control of his own destiny, Chatterton takes leave of his room and life in the short aria "Addio tranquillo asil" that bears an uncanny resemblance to Pinkerton's farewell "Addio fiorito asil" in Puccini's *Madama Butterfly*.

The poet's musings are cut short by the laughter of Klifford's friends, as he resolves to open the envelope handed him earlier, containing the note from Klifford that his "vices have been discovered." A vigorous fate-like theme from the *intermezzo sinfonico* accompanies Chatterton's trepidation, when he nervously reads an accompanying newspaper article to a succession of ascending and descending dissonant chords. All now believe that his works stem from the tenth-century monk Turgot. He feels further wounded that Klifford has offered him a position as a servant. The shame and disgrace make him realize that "all has ended" ("Tutto è finito!"), prompting him to swallow the entire contents of a vial of opium hidden in his jerkin. His words are now taken verbatim from the play: "Skirner will be paid!" ("Skirner sarai pagato!"), while the usurer's theme forcefully reappears in the orchestra, implying his evil victory. Chatterton now destroys his writings—his muse—thereby also extinguishing his immediate persona. His voice grows inspired, throwing the manuscripts into the blazing fire (musically recalling Tonio's "E voi, piuttosto" in the *Pagliacci* prologue),[39] believing the flames will purify his creation from the earth's vileness ("Addio! E voi, e voi figli de l'anima").[40] This intensely moving passage is interrupted by Jenny, who asks Chatterton why he failed to come downstairs. An extended duet commences in a frenetic vein, with themes from the originally planned *intermezzo sinfonico* once again resounding in the orchestra, as Chatterton sings Vigny's lines that all artists are egotists ("Sono tutti egoisti!"), hoping to distance Jenny's love by echoing Giorgio's warning. Although Chatterton claims that he "was" an egotist, he reminds Jenny that children are the only truth and that she must live for her family. Their voices are accompanied by the *cantabile* movement from the *intermezzo sinfonico* that Leoncavallo later deleted ("Talor ne la quiete vostra un pensier"). Jenny finally confesses her love for the poet.[41] Believing she has sinned, her thoughts turn to God, while Chatterton declares his love for her and the necessity of his death. When the poet warns her that she is speaking to a condemned person, Jenny finally realizes he has swallowed poison. Chatterton's thoughts turn once more to his destroyed opus—his family—before imagining that Skirner has come to claim his corpse. In order to provide Chatterton with additional lyrics where Vigny has failed to give him any, Leoncavallo now includes verses from act 3, scene 7, of the play, in which Chatterton curses both his country and his earthly existence. Chatterton's final moments deal with himself and not Jenny, maintaining his self-declared egocentric idealism. He then places his hand on her lips as she tries to call for help, echoing Vigny's "prie pour moi" ("pray for me"). Jenny collapses down the stairs to her death, making a last effort to raise herself upon hearing John's angry voice, then expiring in Giorgio's arms before her perplexed husband, as the Quaker invokes God's pardon.

   Chatterton is an intimate work that set the foundation for Massenet's *Werther*. Much of the opera employs a conversational tone accompanied by dance-like rhythms, while the major arias, especially Chatterton's "Ricomposi l'antica favella," seems inspired by the composer's Neapolitan origins. Like *Werther*, the opera is a study in unrelieved melancholy. However, Leoncavallo has not succeeded in creating the same flesh-and-blood characters as appear in the Massenet opus, nor has he been able to clothe these characters with much memorable music. The opera seems musically disjointed, and these problems are further hindered on account of an inferior libretto that ultimately fails to offer the composer any outstanding possibilities. Nevertheless, the opera is an early example of Leoncavallo's warm style and flowing, almost childlike music that frequently and brilliantly reflects Chatterton's inner turmoil. The personage of Chatterton was one that greatly influenced Leoncavallo and that expressed a portion of his own youthful artistic personality.

NOTES

   1. E. H. W. Meyerstein. *A Life of Thomas Chatterton* (1930 reprint, New York: Russell, 1972), 156.
   2. Ibid., 63.
   3. Ibid.
   4. Ibid., 69.
   5. Ibid., 71.
   6. Ibid., 72–73.

7. "That the name might have repeatedly occurred in deeds from the Redcliff chests is actually confirmed by a lease of 1475 where Thomas Rowley, sheriff, is witness." Ibid., 60.

8. Ibid., 110.

9. Ibid.

10. Ibid., 113.

11. Ibid., 115.

12. Ibid., 432.

13. Ibid., 435.

14. In the collection of the British Museum, London.

15. Alfred de Vigny, *Chatterton* (1835 reprint, Paris: Librarie Marcel Didier, 1967), 28.

16. Vigny, *Chatterton*, act 1, scene 5.

17. Ibid.

18. Ibid.

19. Ibid., act 2, scene 5.

20. Alfred de Vigny, 26 June 1839.

21. Vigny, *Chatterton*, act 3, scene 7.

22. Comparable to the transformation of Dumas's Marguerite Gauthier into Verdi's Violetta Valéry. Leoncavallo also paid close attention to the characters' ages, creating tension in their discrepancies—Chatterton (age eighteen), John (twenty), Jenny (twenty-five), Henry (twelve), Giorgio (sixty), and Klifford (twenty)—while also changing them from Vigny's originals—John (forty-five to fifty) and Jenny (twenty-two).

23. A "trouser role" in the opera.

24. Leoncavallo renamed the youth "Eddy" in one of his frequent revisions of the opera.

25. It is a curious fact that Vigny's name remains absent from the published score.

26. What he actually produces is mentioned neither in the opera nor in the play.

27. Henry's role provides a light-hearted foil to the ensuing tragedy, similar to Oscar in Verdi's *Un ballo in maschera* and Sophie in Massenet's *Werther*.

28. They are not present in Vigny's play.

29. The scene corresponds to act 2, scene 1 of Vigny: "Mon asil était violé."

30. They are not alone in the play.

31. Leoncavallo later included the intermezzo's first measures to be performed to a lowered curtain immediately after Chatterton's *scena*, allowing for a scene change.

32. Vigny emphasizes in his play that Chatterton writes on his knees for lack of a table.

33. This music recalls Boito (*Mefistofele*), a composer whose style greatly influenced Leoncavallo.

34. Skirner remains Leoncavallo's only portrait of a "demonic" and sadistic individual.

35. Leoncavallo later chose to replace this idea with a tamer alternative.

36. This corresponds to act 2, scene 2 of the original play.

37. Act 3 was originally preceded by a prelude in the form of a lighthearted scherzo (*con eleganza*) symbolizing Lord Klifford's frivolity—contrasting Chatterton's suffering—that the composer later wisely chose to delete.

38. The Lord Mayor actually appears in Vigny's *Chatterton*, although he is replaced by Lord Klifford in the opera.

39. The texts are also similar: *Chatterton* ("E voi, e voi, figli de l'anima"), *Pagliacci* ("E voi, piuttosto . . ."").

40. It is significant that Leoncavallo chose to portray the destruction of Chatterton's writings as if he were a father murdering his own children ("Sangue del sangue mio"), similar to the pelican (the Muse) in his *La nuit de mai*.

41. Vigny lets Chatterton initially declare his love for Jenny. Leoncavallo remains closer to Massenet's *Werther* at this point, wherein Charlotte also confesses her love to the dying poet.

• 12 •

I Medici

Characters

Lorenzo de' Medici, baritone
Giuliano de' Medici, tenor
Giambattista da Montesecco, bass
Francesco Pazzi, bass
Bernardo Bandini, tenor

Archbishop Salviati, bass
Angelo Poliziano, baritone
Simonetta Cattanei, soprano
Fioretta de' Gori, soprano
Simonetta's mother, mezzo-soprano

Note: The only character not previously mentioned historically is Fioretta de' Gori, who was the mother of Giuliano's illegitimate son, Giulio, discovered after his murder and welcomed by Lorenzo.

Setting: *Florence (1471–1478)*

The inspiration for Leoncavallo's renaissance trilogy *Crepusculum* (Twilight) derived from his interest in creating a national Italian opera influenced by Carducci's writings and Wagner's *Der Ring des Nibelungen.*[1] Admiring the same *dolce stil novo* poets as Petrarch and Dante, Lorenzo de' Medici (1450–1492) was an illustrious statesman and poet, perfectly complementing Leoncavallo's series of artistic portraits.[2] By the time Lorenzo was born, the Medicis were the most important Florentine family, with branches of their bank in every major city. Lorenzo developed into a man of extensive intellect and culture, interested in medicine, politics, poetry, music, and architecture. His handsome younger brother, Giuliano,[3] incorporated all the facets of a knightly prince, if not Lorenzo's intellectual brilliance. Giuliano's appealing appearance and early death nevertheless helped ensure his immortality. Lorenzo's intelligence enabled him to take up his father's reins in 1469, although he had not been trained in either banking or commerce. He soon married Clarice Orsini and fathered a son also named Giuliano, whose education was attended to by his Homeric protégé, Angelo Poliziano, a poor Montepulciano youth, whose translation of book 2 of the *Iliad* into Latin hexameters (1470) he found exemplary.

Although Lorenzo had once been enamored of the beautiful Simonetta Cattaneo (1453–1476),[4] it was his brother, Giuliano, who now became infatuated. Consumption claimed her at age twenty-three, thereby shattering the romantic image of Laurentian Florence.[5] Giuliano was originally interested in an ecclesiastical career as cardinal, and Lorenzo met with Pope Sixtus IV in the late summer of 1471,[6] the year in which Leoncavallo's opera begins, to congratulate him on his nomination, but not even four hundred pounds of silver could alter the pope's refusal to ordain his brother, which he had come to request. Lorenzo's relations with the Vatican deteriorated further when the pope requested a loan of forty thousand ducats, which Lorenzo was unable to pay, thus enabling the Pazzi, a rival Florentine family, to offer the sum. Conflict with the Vatican also increased when Francesco Salviati became archbishop of Pisa, rather than Lorenzo's brother-in-law Rinaldo Orsini, thus dividing Florence into pro-Medici versus pro-Salviati factions.

The Pazzi had already made plans to murder the brothers during January 1478, when Giovanni de' Pazzi's father-in-law died intestate. His wife and daughter unsuccessfully contested the inheritance, while the Medicis immediately passed a law favoring the closest male relative. The Pazzi tried convincing Jacopo Salviati, the Duke of Urbino, and the pope to forge plans for an assassination[7] to take place the morning of 26 April 1478.[8] Although Montesecco was originally asked to murder Lorenzo during Cardinal Riario's celebration of the mass at Santa Maria Del Fiore cathedral, the young priests, Antonio Maffei and Stefano da Bagnone, agreed to perform the act, while Francesco de' Pazzi and Bernardo Bandini were in charge of stabbing Giuliano. Francesco embraced Giuliano, making certain he was not wearing a mail-shirt when he entered the cathedral. After Giuliano's death from nineteen wounds, Lorenzo drew his sword, seeking refuge in the north sacristy until Sigismondo della Stufa ascertained from the organ loft that although Giuliano was dead, only pro-Medici supporters remained within the cathedral. Francesco de' Pazzi's nude corpse was hung from a window of the Palazzo della Signoria with Archbishop Salviati beside him. More than one hundred were executed on 27 April. Botticelli was given the gruesome task of creating frescoed portraits of the assassins in the Bargello and Palazzo della Signoria, as Lorenzo wrote epitaphs to be painted beneath their images.[9]

I Medici begins to the sound of hunting horns in the *preludio e fanfara da Caccia*,[10] incorporating a valkyrie-like motif in E-major that returns in a crescendo.[11] Simonetta's motif (taken from movement seven of *La nuit de mai*) now emerges following the energetic masculinity of the previous passage. This ethereal and flowing melody is repeated thrice in rapid succession. It is later taken up with intense rhythms alternating between major and minor, before the prelude's opening motif returns (*con tutta la forza e grandiosità*) in this intentionally impressive introductory sequence. The Teutonic quality expressed in the prelude—which would have been more fitting for *Der Roland von Berlin*—makes it comprehensible why Wilhelm II later presented Leoncavallo with a commission for his Hohenzollern opera. However, the opera as a whole, except for its Wagnerian model, has little if anything in common with Wagner's music.

The prelude leads directly into a conversation between the brothers. Giuliano asks Lorenzo whether he considers the pope to be an enemy, now that Lorenzo hopes to gain the pontiff's favor by traveling to Rome. Poliziano soon interrupts, wondering why Lorenzo appears so sullen, a man gifted by artistic talent amid such bucolic splendor. The triviality of the preceding dialogue is replaced by Lorenzo's caressing and elegant phrase ("E se' tu, Poliziano, tu, degno figlio di Virgilio e Dante"), considering Poliziano to be a "worthy son of Virgil and Dante." When Poliziano carries on about nature, Lorenzo speaks of the forest's peace and solitude (*largamente*) to a prominent harp accompaniment. Lorenzo now describes the forest's shade to a splendid orchestral description marking him as a peace-loving individual, seeking tranquility away from man's "vain glories."[12] When hunting horns are heard, Giuliano suggests they cease their idleness and return. Poliziano ironically remarks that only love would be able to tame the young man's fire.[13] This leads Giuliano to begin the opera's first major aria ("No, de l'antica Grecia") commencing in E-flat major, evoking visions of ancient Greece, Socrates, Plato, the olympic games, and the arena—aimed at securing his image as a muscular blonde knight—to an inspired harp, wind instrument, and violin accompaniment. After ascending to a high B-flat, Giuliano expresses his lighthearted credo that sensual passion is merely the light of a firefly, producing neither warmth nor glow, in an elegant and memorable line ("È' il foco de la lucciola") supported by harp arpeggios. Lorenzo now joins his brother and expounds on the glories of love in marked opposition, although Giuliano's music, originally introduced during his earlier aria, marks the duet's conclusion.

The stage remains empty when all return to the hunt, until a short *andantino* (played by the English horn) introduces Simonetta, who enters accompanied by Fioretta gathering flowers. The initial notes of her *rispetto* are heard in the orchestra marked by melancholy and solitude, immediately introducing her as the opera's tragic and hapless heroine. Beginning like an echo from a past age, she sings of an unfaithful knight and his pale lady who in vain awaits his return ("Come amava il suo damo!"). This haunting *rispetto* in A-flat minor forcefully evokes Simonetta's pathetic fragility, providing a metaphor of her own longing for a knight like Giuliano. Her consumption is made evident in the orchestra on account of its sudden harmonic shifts.

The initial sound of Simonetta's voice contrasts all the music previously heard in the score, supported solely by the strings, and her voice is echoed by the English horn.[14] She describes her subject's blonde hair and pallid face ("Ell'era bionda, in viso pallidetta"). An upward surge in the music dispels any doubts that the subject and protagonist are one. Fioretta tries to pull the girl from her pensive melancholy—just as Giuliano and Poliziano sought to do with Lorenzo—believing that her somber mood may be a reflection of her physical debility resulting from tubercolosis. She places one of Fioretta's freshly picked flowers in her bodice before taking up the *rispetto's* second verse, introduced by the harp. Fioretta can only utter the banal comment that she found the hauntingly beautiful song sad, preferring, upon hearing their horns, to see the men hunting. Simonetta is momentarily left alone when Fioretta seeks male company, promising to return shortly. Simonetta evokes our sympathy, assuring Fioretta that she herself is strong ("Forte son io").

Simonetta, no longer seeking to disguise her despair, feels life slowly ebbing away without her ever having loved. These feelings unite in a touching *ritornello Toscano* ("Fiorin di prato!") evoking an early renaissance manner. She concludes upon noticing that Montesecco—a standard evil bass—has listened to her singing. Resisting his embrace, Simonetta calls out for Fioretta. Montesecco, in turn, vows in a Mephistophelean manner that they will meet again.

Simonetta's motif returns when she realizes that a frightening noise she heard was a deer trying to save its life from the approaching hunting party. She is relieved that Giuliano has been unsuccessful in killing the animal—a metaphor for Montesecco and herself only a moment earlier. She introduces herself to Giuliano, whereupon flutes intone her motif. She negates Giuliano's claim that she is suffering ("È' nulla"), although Tristanesque chords in the orchestra affirm his question. He begs her to remain in a charming *andantino cantabile* recalling Wagner's *Siegfried Idyll* ("Bionda beltà che t'offri al guardo mio"), comparing her to both a nymph and Diana.[15]

Simonetta replies in the impressionistic *arioso* "Ninfa non sono" that she was born between the Ticino and the sea but left with her mother while still a child to settle in Florence.[16] When he asks whether she has ever loved, she evades the question by calling attention to noises in the forest, which, he assures her, are only branches rustling in the breeze. This metaphor of their own longing is sung to "Egli è del rio il murmure soave" taken from *La nuit de mai's* first movement, remaining one of *I Medici's* most arresting passages, musically defining Giuliano's ardor. Simonetta bridles Giuliano's passion by asking his name. He intensifies his seduction until she joins him in one of Leoncavallo's most inspired duets ("Come poterti esprimere . . ."). This leads to a *cantabile* wherein they sing the same D-major melody to varied texts ("E da prati che'l sol schiara ed inonda").

It is now Simonetta who refuses to hear Montesecco approaching, repeating Giuliano's earlier description of leaves rustling in the wind to the same original *La nuit de mai* music, signifying her approval of a physical consummation. Like the equally consumptive Violetta in Verdi's *La traviata*, Simonetta offers Giuliano a flower to return to her the following day.[17] They vocally unite once more, singing "amore" in much the same manner later employed by Puccini at the act 1 conclusion of *La bohème*, except that in *I Medici* the tenor resorts to a high B-flat while the soprano remains singing a G.

Fioretta, immediately struck by Giuliano's beauty, interrupts the tryst and is introduced by Simonetta, who then leaves to join her mother. Fioretta resolves to meet Giuliano again the following day.

Act 2 begins with the menacing "conspirators' theme" (*mosso e deciso*) consisting of descending octaves played by the trumpets, trombones, and tuba. The curtain rises, disclosing the Piazza Santa Trinità to rushing descending chromatic scales. Francesco Pazzi, Bernardo Bandini, Montesecco, and the Archbishop Salviati are secretly discussing their hatred of the Medici. Montesecco's music makes a more regal impression in this act, when he states that the Vatican must be an important link if lasting peace is to remain in Italy ("Perchè pace durevole s'abbia l'Italia intera . . ."). The conspirators then voice their assassination plans in a quartet evoking shades of Elsa's "Einsam in trüben Tagen" from act 1 of Wagner's *Lohengrin*. Francesco Pazzi concludes that both brothers must be murdered simultaneously and that he will personally kill Giuliano. Montesecco vows to extinguish Lorenzo's life. They promise to meet again later that evening, certain that the siblings will make a public appearance. All exit to the conspirators' theme.

Lorenzo now enters with Poliziano, followed by a group of musicians carrying mandolines and violas. He motions for the players to remain before Lucrezia Donati's house (although she fails to appear in the opera), where he plans to sing a serenade in the form of a charming and sophisticated gavotte in G-minor ("Ascolta el canto mio che ti falvella"), interspersed with an oriental, arabesque-sounding accompaniment. It is followed by an *andantino sostenuto* sung to the opening stanzas of the historical Lorenzo de' Medici's longer sonnet *La nencia da Barberino*:

I Medici
Ardo d'amore, e conviemmi cantare

Per una dama che mi strugge il core;
Ch'ogni otta ch'io la sento ricordare
Il cor mi brilla e par che gli esca fuore.
Ella non trova di bellezza pare;
Con gli occhi getta fiaccole d'amore;
Io sono stato in città e castella,
E mai non vidi gnuna tanto bella.

La Nencia da Barberino

Ardo d'amore, e conviemme cantare,
per una dama che strugge el cuore,
ch'ogni otta ch'i' la sento ricordare
el cuor me brilla e par che gl'esca fuore.
Ella non truova de bellezze pare,
cogli occhi gitta fiaccole d'amore;
i' sono stato in città e'n castella
e mai ne vidi ignuna tanto bella.

The stage begins to fill with townspeople who comment on Lorenzo's talent, hailing him with dramatic shouts of "Glory!" Giuliano appears with his retinue carrying torches. The conspirators also arrive, irritated by the crowd's adulation of the Medici. Salviati immediately sends Pazzi to invite Lorenzo and Giuliano to the feast where they will be murdered. Lorenzo accepts the invitation as "damsels" and "youths" dance amid glistening, descending chromatic scales.

Simonetta, her mother, and Fioretta have entered in the interim. Lorenzo asks the crowd which song they wish to hear next, and they respond by requesting one of his own. He suggests they should sing Poliziano's "Ben venga maggio" from his *Ballata xiii*. The conspirators exit as sopranos, tenors, and basses begin singing Poliziano's text to a vigorous *andante mosso*.[18] The second verse ("Venite alla frescura") is performed to a hauntingly beautiful renaissance melody in B-minor, which Leoncavallo based on "a very old Italian dance theme," without mentioning its precise origin.[19] The entire choral segment is brought to a rousing conclusion by the reappearance of the original "Ben venga maggio" theme, rounded off with a unanimous "Olà!" Simonetta wishes to join in the festivities and dance, but her mother forbids her to do so on account of her poor health. Poliziano, upon hearing their conversation, suggests that Simonetta's fervor should find release in a song. To this her mother agrees. Giuliano now passionately implores her in a most endearing manner to perform ("Canta! . . . Canta").[20]

The Simonetta of this act is both joyful and lighthearted, beginning her song ("Le coppie s'intrecciano comincia la danza") with a purposefully awkward vocal line reminding us of her shortness of breath. She is intermittently accompanied by the chorus's humming. The vocal line soars to illustrate her frenetic happiness, goading the players into performing faster and with progressive abandon.

A worried Poliziano now reminds Lorenzo that Simonetta is "tisica" (consumptive).[21] Singing that life is both oblivion and love, she joins the chorus in a finale while also taking part in a dance. Exhausted, she utters a cry and collapses in her mother's arms. Poliziano comforts Giuliano that she has only fainted. Poliziano and Lorenzo then leave while the crowd slowly disperses, supporting the ailing girl.

Giuliano notices that Fioretta is trembling, although she insists it has nothing to do with Simonetta. The chorus is heard in the distance once again taking up the antiquated "Venite alla frescura" heard earlier. Giuliano suspects, in a lengthy duet ("Ove vai tu?"), that Fioretta is enamored of someone, even if she fails to admit to whom. She finally kisses him, disclosing her secret.

Act 3 depicts the interiors of Simonetta and Fioretta's houses near the Ponte Vecchio. It is night. A sensitive and introspective prelude (*andante sostenuto*), borrowed in its entirety from movement nine of *La nuit de mai*, commences in D minor. A reserved and almost religious quality signifies a lull before the storm in a pensive yet passionate manner.

Fioretta is seen leaving Simonetta's house accompanied by the latter's mother, reassuring her that Simonetta will recover from her collapse, while the older woman blesses Fioretta for her concern. The prelude's theme resounds once more as a fragment when, inside, Fioretta trembles at the thought of being so appreciated although she, too, loves Giuliano. This leads into an extended scene beginning in a breathless and agitated manner,[22] again taken from *Nuit de mai*, depicting her conflict, before the aria's main section ("Amo, e che importa a l'animo la sua lenta agonia"), an *andante sostenuto, cantabile*. Incessant modulations between major and minor serve to express Fioretta's uncertainty.

The conspirators' theme resounds. The Archbishop Salviati, Francesco Pazzi, and Bandini appear to an eerie accompaniment briefly recalling *Chatterton's* Skirner. They hide when Giuliano enters Fioretta's house, inquiring about Simonetta, who appears on the steps of her own house admiring the beauty of the night ("O come bella è la notte!"). At the same time, Francesco Pazzi can be heard discussing the failed assassination attempt. Simonetta is so stunned by their conversation that she is unable to move ("Tremo e non so fuggir!"). Francesco now reveals that the brothers will be assassinated during Mass at Santa Maria Del Fiore the following day, although Montesecco refuses to murder anyone in church. In a septet inaugurated by Giuliano ("Me lasso!"), the protagonists' destinies are united when Fioretta tells Giuliano that she is pregnant with his child.[23] The ensemble then reaches its impressive short theme led by Simonetta ("Mio Dio! Scuoti il terror che m'ha impietrato").

Montesecco remains alone after the conspirators leave. He hears Simonetta falling on the stairs, recognizing her as "la bella di Giuliano," asking whether she has overheard their plan. She admits her knowledge and that she will try to warn Giuliano in order to save his life. Montesecco leads her to Fioretta's home, where she sees Giuliano with Fioretta, demonstrating that her beloved has in fact already forsaken her.[24] Simonetta clutches at her heart, which has now been extinguished without Montesecco's threatening dagger. Forcing her way into Fioretta's house, she fatally collapses after unsuccessfully trying to warn Giuliano "in an agonizing death rattle."

The major themes foreshadowing disaster in the strange and driven introduction (*allegro con fuoco*) to act 4 largely derive from the seventh movement of *La nuit de mai*. They will later become associated with Lorenzo's victory at the opera's conclusion. A credo is begun in F-Minor sung by eight priests (bass), while children's voices intone the word "credo" to both orchestral and organ accompaniment. Leoncavallo chose to have a portion of the credo sung before the curtain is actually raised. Most of the act takes place against the simultaneous singing of the complete credo, which takes up forty-three pages of the piano/vocal score.[25]

Santa Maria Del Fiore during Mass: Two chairs have been placed near the entrance of the sacristy for Lorenzo and Giuliano. Fioretta is seen praying. Bandini tells Montesecco that the priests Stefano da Bagnone and Antonio Maffei will murder Lorenzo. The latter now enters preceded by two servants with Poliziano at his side. The credo takes on a mysterious air when Lorenzo seats himself, while the conspirators begin negatively influencing the congregation. Fioretta then dominates the chorus in a sweeping melody in B-major also taken up in the orchestra ("Signor, prostrata in lagrime a te confesso . . ."). Giuliano's entrance coincides with the conclusion of Fioretta's plea. The credo ends to a final "amen" sung by the boys' chorus in preparation of the sanctus, while bells begin to sound the benediction.

Giuliano is fatally stabbed by Pazzi and Bandini. The crowd acknowledges its approval of the crime by shouting "Death to the tyrants." Bagnone and Maffei attack Lorenzo, who is pushed into the sacristy—and safety—by Poliziano. Fioretta tries to reanimate the dying Giuliano in a moment of "general confusion." Pazzi excites the crowd once more, announcing that Florence has now been freed, before leaving the cathedral with Bandini, Montesecco, and the other conspirators.

Lorenzo violently opens the sacristy door to face the furious crowd with folded arms. He succeeds in rousing their sympathy by speaking of the humility of the Medici family. He recalls Salvestro de' Medici, who accused his brother, Bartolomeo, of conspiring against the republic during the fourteenth century, while his descendant, Gianni de' Medici, refused honors after having put down a revolt at Ciompi in 1378.[26] Beginning in *parlando*, gathering his thoughts, Lorenzo breaks into a short though passionate passage subduing the crowd ("Pel ben de la repubblica . . .") recalling Simon Boccanegra's "Plebe! Patrizi! . . . Popolo dalla feroce storia!" from the council chamber scene of Verdi's opera. Effective choral writing expressing sympathies now in favor of Lorenzo and the Medici follows his short monologue. The entire ensemble supports Lorenzo's original melody as a sign of their solidarity. Giuliano asks Lorenzo for Fioretta to be acknowledged as his wife before he dies. While Lorenzo takes Fioretta in his arms to comfort her, the crowd, before leaving the building, again cries for revenge shouting "Palle, palle"—referring to the Medici crest. Giuliano's body is carried out, followed by Fioretta, Poliziano, and the remaining congregation. Lorenzo, after acknowledging the distant shouts for revenge, remains undefeated in his reign.

The most inspired vocal writing presents itself in acts 1 and 2. It is unfortunate that the themes Leoncavallo employed in act 1 do not reemerge as the work progresses; he is unable to add new dimensions regardless of how impressive the initial act was in its abundance of dramatic and lyric possibilities. An opera consisting of serviceable and interesting fragments ultimately fails to secure one's interest and compassion. Greater concentration and introspection should have been devoted to the psychological development of *I Medici*'s protagonists, rather than to re-creating renaissance Florence through an unsuccessful string of literary associations, which stifle the work with secondary details that ultimately only detract. *I Medici* and the *Crepusculum* in general was Leoncavallo's most ambitious project, and an almost palpable feeling of self-imposed pressure to prove the mettle that he certainly possessed hovers over this work. Collaborating with an able librettist might have rendered the drama more compact, direct, and approachable. *I Medici* remained beyond Leoncavallo's resources regardless of his effort. Sonzogno's printing of *Crepusculum*'s additional titles (*Gerolamo Savanorola* and *Cesare Borgia*) on *I Medici*'s cover also paved the way for further criticism and ridicule when the opera first appeared. Leoncavallo's talent flowered with "intimate" works such as *Zazà*, *Pagliacci*, and *La bohème*, something he had in common with most of his colleagues, notably Puccini. Although *I Medici* is "uneven" and often one-dimensional, thanks to stilted and anemic characterizations evoking little sympathy, the opera contains some sumptuous vocal writing. Its impressive arias and ensembles succeed in conveying both atmosphere and poetry, making it more interesting than just an attempt to create an Italian form of Wagner through Latin vocalism.

NOTES

1. A quote from Carducci's *Discorso sulle poesie di messer Agnolo Poliziano* also appears on the first page of the original 1893 *I Medici* piano/vocal score.

2. *Chatterton, Pagliacci, La bohème, Zazà, Mameli.*

3. Born 1453.

4. Simonetta was married to Marco di Piero Vespucci.

5. Some of Lorenzo's sonnets remain a posthumous appreciation.

6. Francesco della Rovere.

7. Captain Giovanni Battista da Montesecco also reluctantly entered into the conspiracy upon believing to have the pope's support.

8. This was due to an earlier assassination attempt having failed in 1477.

9. Montesecco, Maffei, and Bagnone were beheaded.

10. Leoncavallo had originally composed a prologue between Montesecco and the pope that he later deleted, fearing it might offend the church.

11. This opening theme fails to return throughout the course of the opera, perhaps suggesting that Leoncavallo may have also wished to use it in *Crepusculum*'s second and third parts (*Savonarola* and *Cesare Borgia*).

12. This passage was inspired by Lorenzo de' Medici's fifty-third sonnet, included in his complete *Sonetti e Canzoni*, wherein the poet-statesman discusses the little worth he places on "high honors."

13. Leoncavallo quoting from book I, xxiv of Poliziano's *Giostra*.

14. The complete lack of brass instruments also accentuates Simonetta's sensitivity, while her yearnings are expressed for her and the audience alike, similar to Leonora's "Tacea la notte placida" in act 1 of Verdi's *Il trovatore*.

15. This alludes to Poliziano's *Giostra di Giuliano* (book I, xlix) in which she is also compared to a nymph.

16. Another Poliziano quote: "Qui lieta mi dimoro Simonetta."

17. It is perhaps symbolic that she offers him Fioretta's flower, thereby implying his later love for her friend, whose name also denotes "little flower."

18. During the *Calendimaggio* (May Day) celebrations, men and women would traditionally cut branches from a tree while singing a song frequently beginning with the words "Ben venga maggio."

19. It may have been inspired by Fabrizio Caroso's ballet *Selva amorosa* originally published in 1600 in *Nobiltà di dame*.

20. This magnificent passage is not included in the original 1893 Sonzogno piano/vocal score since Leoncavallo composed it especially for Francesco Tamagno after the score's publication.

21. Leoncavallo states in the score that he opted to use the word "tisica" although aware that tuberculosis at that time was known as "mal sottile," in order that audiences comprehended.

22. This scene may have been modeled on Eboli's "O don fatale" in act 4, scene 1 of Verdi's *Don Carlo*.

23. Giulio would later become Pope Clement VII.

24. A situation strongly recalling the final act of Verdi's *Rigoletto*.

25. The credo sung against the music of the opera's main protagonists is a technique that Puccini would later employ with his te deum during act 2 of *Tosca*. Although there may be a possibility that Leoncavallo had originally written the credo during his student days at the Naples' conservatory, there is no evidence to support this hypothesis.

26. Leoncavallo drew his inspiration from Anthony's oration in Shakespeare's *Julius Caesar*, even quoting Anthony's lines ("Now let it work. Mischief, thou art afoot, take thou what course thou wilt.") from act 3, scene 2 in the score, although stating it came from scene 3.

· 13 ·

Pagliacci

Characters

Nedda/Colombina, soprano
Canio/Pagliaccio, tenor
Tonio/Taddeo, baritone
Peppe/Arlecchino, tenor
Silvio, baritone

Setting: 15 August on the Feast of the Assumption, Montalto Uffugo (Calabria) (1865–1870)

Manuel Tamayo y Baus's *Un drama nuevo* is set in England (1605) and is the story of the comic actor Yorick, his wife Alice, and the actor Walton, who are cast in "a new play" produced by the actor Shakespeare, who demands that Yorick interpret the unaccustomed dramatic role of a deceived husband (Count Octavio). Yorick soon notices that his adopted son, Edmond, is in love, warning him that his infatuation with another man's wife will create havoc. Alice originally joined the troupe two years earlier, realizing that she loved Edmond in a performance of *Romeo and Juliet*, only becoming Yorick's wife out of financial necessity. The *Pagliacci* Nedda/Silvio duet is foreshadowed when Alice tells Edmond in act 1 how she suffers trying to keep their love secret. Shakespeare hears this conversation, as Tonio will in the opera, prompting Alice to envision death as the only resolution. The jealous dramatic actor, Walton, who relishes the idea of seeing Yorick play a deceived husband, informs him of his wife and son's infidelity. Act 2 again resembles the Nedda/Silvio duet when Edmond asks Alice to flee with him, although she prefers telling Yorick the truth. Yorick now demands that Walton prove Alice's infidelity. Walton knows that "the new play" requires a "prop letter" and plans to substitute it with one of Alice's love letters to Edmond, enabling Yorick to realize the truth while onstage and in character. Yorick enters after physically threatening Alice and begging Walton to relate the name of his wife's lover. (Corresponding to Canio's "Il nome, o la tua vita! il nome!"). He also tells Walton that he is no longer an actor but a man who suffers (Canio's "No! Pagliaccio non son"). Shakespeare tries to spare bloodshed by taking the authentic love letter from Walton, only to realize that the latter has given him the blank prop letter. Infuriated, he departs, intent on murder. The play within the play now begins, showing Walton handing Yorick the real letter. Reading Alice's impassioned words to Edmond and realizing the truth, Yorick is incapable of speaking his lines. He finally kills Edmond in a duel before approaching Alice. Shakespeare tells the audience that the play cannot proceed, since Yorick has in fact mortally wounded Edmond, and that Walton's body has also just been recovered.

Although Leoncavallo borrowed heavily from the Baus work, *Pagliacci*'s conciseness was influenced by Catulle Mendès's play *La femme de Tabarin* (*Tragi-Parade en un acte*), originally published in *La semaine parisienne* during the spring of 1874. There is a short bibliographical note on the frontispiece of *La femme de Tabarin* printed by Fasquelle between 1900 and 1908, stating that Mendès originally had the idea for the play when he was twenty-five or twenty-six, which would mean 1867, precisely when *Un drama nuevo* was initially published. *La femme de Tabarin* numbers seventeen pages and, like *Pagliacci*, is divided into three parts. This Grand Guignol drama, set in the Paris of 1629, is written in an archaic style recalling D'Annunzio and Anatole France. It incorporates twice as many roles as *Pagliacci*, although the action centers on the Italian actor Tabarin (Tabarini), his wife Francesquine, and her nameless lover (Le Garde). Mendès uses a poetic and aristocratic manner for Francesquine's dialogue with Le Garde, abruptly ending as an inebriated Tabarin enters. Francesquine tells Le Garde to come to her performance, where she will try and signal him for a meeting. Suspecting his wife's infidelity, Tabarin warns Francesquine that he is neither a clown nor a drunk, only a man who ardently loves his wife ("Le bouffon, l'ivrogne n'est plus, regarde l'homme"), corresponding to another possible version of "No! Pagliaccio non son." His lengthy monologue also incorporates the "Ridi, pagliaccio" theme, when he warns his wife that his job is to make others laugh ("La parade, le fard, le chapeau qui me fut légué par Saturne, c'est pour les autres que ma bêtise fait rire"). Scene 3 commences with Tabarin eating Francesquine's soup as an elegant audience arrives to view the play. The play within the play begins when Tabarin makes his entrance amid the sound of some scratchy violins. Francesquine fails to make her entrance, and Tabarin lifts one of the stage curtains to find her sitting on Le Garde's knee, for which he calls her a slut. He then stabs his wife using a sword from one of the onlookers, prompting a spectator to suggest that, with training, he could become a great tragic actor. Tabarin returns to his senses and breaks the bloodstained weapon. Francesquine raises herself with sufficient strength to smear his lips with blood, which her husband relishes tasting ("Oui, ton sang, je veux le boire!"). No longer able to strike Tabarin, Francesquine dies after biting his thigh, screaming "Canaille!" Agreeing that the performance was "perfectly played," the spectator Artaban approaches the stage with a bouquet of flowers and is horrified to discover that the blood is real. Tabarin then calls out that he has murdered his wife and should be hanged. This small-scale shocker ends accompanied by violins playing a drinking song.

Leoncavallo was probably influenced by both plays, with Tabarin, Francesquine, and Le Garde resembling Canio, Nedda, and Silvio. Tonio may have been derived from Victor Hugo's *Notre Dame de Paris* (1831) or *Le roi s'amuse* (1832), providing a foil for Silvio and tailor-made for Victor Maurel, who had created Iago. The resemblance to *Othello* (Canio/Othello, Nedda/Desdemona, Silvio/Cassio, Tonio/Iago) was no doubt culled by Baus, if not taken directly from the Bard's play. Having lived in Montalto Uffugo, where *Pagliacci*'s action unfolds, may have reminded Leoncavallo of traveling actors, although the murder trial presided over by his father bears few similarities to the plot of his opera. *Pagliacci* is Leoncavallo's answer to *Cavalleria rusticana*, centering on a husband's vendetta (Alfio/Canio) for his wife's infidelity (Lola/Nedda) with her lover (Turridu, Silvio).[1] The opera was originally intended to be performed in one act with an intermezzo like *Cavalleria rusticana*.[2]

The first music heard in the prologue are the C-major *vivace* chords that immediately direct one's attention by their sheer vitality and force. A reply in the form of an echo somewhat recalling *La nuit de mai* immediately follows, played by the piccolos, flutes, oboes, and clarinets. This entire "dialogue" is repeated a third time in B-major, before returning once more in the original key of C. The process is again repeated until the "echo" is heard softly, preparing for Canio's "Ridi, pagliaccio" motif (*largo assai*) played by the horns. This theme immediately transforms itself to present us with Silvio's E-major motif in diminished fifths (*cantabile assai sostenuto*), the most frequently repeated theme throughout the course of the opera, which will also be associated with the sensuous charm Silvio exerts on Nedda.

This passage then returns to music of a Canio-like flavor that will once again succeed in bringing us to the original introduction in C-major with various repeats, until the echo motif again springs forth when Tonio places his head through the curtain asking if he may introduce himself, to us, his spectators. He does this at first feebly, in a broken phrase ("Si può? . . .") and then with more assurance, bowing, while excusing himself before the ladies and gentlemen making up the audience, to announce that he is in fact the prologue. He tells us that the author (Leoncavallo) wishes to set commedia dell'arte characters upon the stage, once again employing antiquated customs. This is sung to an *andantino grazioso*, musically evoking the "masks" with the difference, we are told, that the tears shed and anguish expressed will also be felt. "The author" has sought to portray an authentic "slice" of life inspired solely by reality ("L'autore ha cercato invece pingervi uno squarcio di vita"). Leoncavallo stresses the importance of "squarcio di vita" by employing a *ritornando* in addition to an up-beat on the word "squarcio." The composer now vocalizes his credo through Tonio in an exquisite *andante triste*, saying that he was inspired from deep within his soul ("Un nido di memoria in fondo a l'anima cantava un giorno"). Leoncavallo again stresses the words "authentic tears" with the use of *marcato* on "vere," while "tears" (lacrime) is to be interpreted *con dolore* (with pain/sorrow). The key now abruptly shifts to F-major when the orchestra once again takes up Silvio's motif, previously heard in the orchestral prelude. Tonio next informs us that we will be able to view the authentic human passion of love. When Tonio speaks of hate, pain, rage, and cynical laughter, the orchestra modulates to the ominous shades of Canio's vendetta motif ("Dunque, vedrete amar sì come s'amano gli esseri umani"), while on the words "e risa ciniche" Canio's "Ridi, pagliaccio" theme is forcefully echoed in the orchestra. Descending chords prepare us for Tonio's *cantabile* "E voi, piuttosto," his second major melody again sung in unison with the orchestra to a typical arpeggio accompaniment favored by Leoncavallo in both *Chatterton* and *I Medici*, reminding the audience of the actor's humanity and markedly contrasting it with his role in the opera. Now that Leoncavallo's concept has been presented, Tonio also asks that the audience pay attention to the happenings, decisively commanding the curtain to be raised, singing a D on the word "incominciate."[3] The original autograph partitura bears Leoncavallo's page markings that now resume at 1, reminding us that the prologue was in fact added later to provide Victor Maurel with an aria.

The curtain finally rises to the same solo trumpet call (*marziale deciso*) behind the scene that will return to inaugurate the second half. Tremolo chords seem to further accentuate the feeling of the blazing August sun.[4] A chorus of peasants in holiday attire greet the approaching troupe of traveling players ("Son qua! Son qua!") who announce the evening's performance—to an accompaniment taken from *La nuit de mai*—while Tonio, a hunchbacked member of the company, remains prostrate before the small temporary stage, seemingly irritated by the joyfully innocent din. While saluting Canio (the troupe's middle-aged actor) as the "prince of clowns," the crowd does not fail to notice his serious demeanor, no doubt resulting from his endless appearances, although the peasants nevertheless insist that he is capable of banishing feelings of sorrow. Leoncavallo thus immediately confronts us with a chasm between the actor's inner self and image the public wishes to see.

Canio thanks the crowd for their praise. He fails to respond as to when the spectacle will commence. His sincere wish to be heard is greeted by laughter brought on by his customary comic salutation, again reminding us of his sub-human treatment as a mere object of derision. His clown-like appeal is further accentuated in a short aria,[5] announcing that the show will begin at the very southern time of 11:00 p.m. ("Un grande spettacolo a ventitrè ore"). Canio has now completely slipped into his pseudo-farcical character that comes all too readily, holding one word for twelve beats (later expanding to fifteen). He informs the crowd that he has conceived a play that incorporates a clown's rage and vengeance toward a young suitor. The villagers promise to attend, singing the same melody that Canio had originally invited them with.

Canio helps his attractive and much younger wife, Nedda, down from the cart they had arrived in. He brusquely tells Tonio to move, thereby generating laughter from the villagers, lending additional proof of the difficulty in taking any of Canio's emotions seriously. Tonio leaves while uttering his first oath of revenge ("La pagherai! brigante!") before disappearing behind the travel-ing theater. A villager suggests that Canio join him and his friends for a drink in the tavern. This Canio agrees to do, while Peppe, a young member of the troupe, leaves his whip behind in order to accompany Canio, after changing his clothes. When Canio also asks Tonio whether he would like to come, he remarks that he'd rather remain behind in order to fix the lighting. Another peasant now warns Canio "jokingly" that Tonio only wishes to stay in order to court Nedda.[6] Laughing bitterly, Canio warns all present that such a joke better not be played on him. This develops into an extended *adagio molto* beginning in F-major ("Un tal gioco, credetemi ") revealing his persona for the first time. He not only warns the crowd still at hand, but also Tonio, that life and theater are not the same, thereby echoing what Tonio has already told us in the pro-logue. Canio makes certain to repeat the phrase to stress his point ("Il teatro e la vita non son la stessa cosa; no . . . non son la stessa cosa!!).

Realizing that he has dampened everyone's spirits, he immediately be-comes the clown again, pronouncing his words in a marionette-like man-ner—even breaking them in half. Perhaps not surprisingly, the composer has opted to have Canio sing this music ("E se lassù pagliaccio") to the same accompaniment that will blend itself with Tonio later in the play ("Lungi è lo sposo"), thus already implying that the "pagliaccio" is nothing more than a plaything in Tonio's hands. Canio sets clear differences between himself and the clown he portrays. If Pagliaccio found his wife in the company of a hand-some suitor, he would break into a comic sermon, perhaps even getting beaten. Canio warns Nedda that if she were really with a lover the story would have a tragic denouement. Canio first expresses his warning in a cordial manner ("Ma se Nedda sul serio sorprendessi . . ."). The orchestra echoes his motif, originally heard in Tonio's prologue. Canio now sings his own motif for the first time when he speaks of a "would-be" impending tragedy ("finirebbe la storia, com'è ver che vi parlo!"), his voice suddenly becoming threatening. Following a series of constantly modulating keys in keeping with his rampant emotions, Canio finally returns to the original F-major, singing the same words to the identical music as an additional warning and reminder. All attention is now turned to Nedda, who monotonously utters her first words ("Confusa io son!"), having probably heard Canio's rantings numerous times. Tired, frustrated, and annoyed, Nedda is hardly less irritable than either Canio or Tonio, all of whom have brought their problems with them from many previous engagements. The troupe's sojourn in Montalto Uffugo merely marks the setting for a final tragic outburst.

The mood suddenly relaxes, reflected in the key of C-major, as the villagers ask Canio whether he took their goadings seriously. He laughs it off with a "hardly," before excusing himself, and then, with an outburst of simple affection, lets it be known that he loves his wife. He kisses her on the forehead rather than on the mouth, realizing that his passionate feelings toward her have not been reciprocated for some time. This tender display of emotion on Canio's part slowly leads to an oboe solo from within, playing a bucolic melody in A-major, perhaps inspired by *Cavalleria rusticana*, in particular the idea of employing church bells inviting the villagers to attend vespers.[7] The preceding is now incorporated into a bell chorus, recreated verbally by the villagers in a charming *andante grazioso*. Their voices gradually fade when they leave the stage singing an echoed "Ah!"

Similar to *Cavalleria rusticana*, following this extended choral section our attention turns toward the heroine, prompting the plot to unfold. Nedda, alone, begins her lengthy *scena* by recalling the flame in Canio's eyes when he spoke of ever finding her unfaithful ("Qual fiamma avea nel guardo!"), as the orchestra once again takes up Canio's motif. Nedda then recalls that she had kept her eyes lowered fearing Canio could read her thoughts, which, the orchestra informs us, refers to Silvio, as his theme again resounds. Frightened, Nedda has again experienced the brutal side of Canio's character, prompting the orchestra to take up the latter's motif. A series of arpeggio chords form a splendid musical depiction of the sun's rays, temporarily warming Nedda's lackluster existence. When Nedda sings that she is "filled with life," a discord is simultaneously heard, reminding us of her thwarted desires. Leoncavallo not only succeeds in musically recreating the sun, he now also lets birds fly. Nedda stares into the blue sky, focusing on their mobility as a metaphor for her own desire to escape. She recalls her mother who, she believes, was capable of interpreting the meaning of these creatures' chirping. She vocally unites with the birds ("Oh! che volo d'augelli") by imitating the sound she hears prior to initiating her *ballatella* ("Stridono lassù"),[8] part of which derives from Leoncavallo's 1882 song *Tristesse*. The *ballatella* reveals Nedda's yearning for nature and sensuality in a joyful and carefree manner on this sultry afternoon, which will resurface in her duet with Silvio. The aria's center modulates to F-sharp minor, before the orchestra again takes up the sound of fluttering wings originally heard during the recitative phrases preceding the *ballatella*. Changing to F-sharp major (*con anima e passione*), Nedda's wish to follow the birds toward an unknown land that perhaps does not even exist, lends her a sense of exultation that lifts the lyric line to a rapturous crescendo, offering the illusion that she has become one with them, as her voice rises progressively by half notes.

Nedda suddenly becomes aware that Tonio, leaning against a tree, has heard her sing. The key shifts when his "Si può" motif resounds in the orchestra ("Sei la?"). Nedda immediately becomes guarded and inhibited, and Tonio's appearance ensures that the music takes on an eerie and forbidding quality (G-minor), although his text remains gentle, stating that her beautiful singing had fascinated him. When Nedda mocks his "poetry," bidding him to join Canio at the tavern, Tonio implores her not to scorn him. Ominous chords in the orchestra prepare us for the impending tragedy that will return at the duet's conclusion. Tonio soon begins a *cantabile sostenuto* that will be the only time he bares his soul. Although realizing he induces nothing but horror, he confides in Nedda that he also has a heart, and one that beats for her alone. This would-be seduction contrasts with Silvio's later *successful* conquest of Nedda, and it is worth noting that portions of Tonio's amorous fawning are presented in a similar vein ("Allor che sdegnosa mi passi d'accanto"). When Tonio grows passionate, he also resorts to an earlier melody that originally was associated with his deformity ("So ben che difforme e contorto son io") and that now gives vent to his tortured love ("Perchè, mio malgrado, subito ho l'incanto, m'ha vinto l'amor!"). Tonio again foreshadows Silvio's later ardor ("una folla non è") when implying that love has triumphed ("m'ha vinto l'amor! m'ha vinto l'amor!"). Nedda curtly interrupts Tonio's wooing, and the music takes on a Chopinesque-like passage (*scherzoso*) that supports Nedda's mocking manner. She tells him to save his passion for the evening's performance. Tonio begs Nedda to refrain from laughing, but she continues, while he once again takes up the duet's original melody. His growing anxiety and barely concealed passion is now musically underlined by Canio's theme. Nedda firmly rejects Tonio's advances to hair-raising B-minor chords, warning her that she will pay dearly for mistreating him. When Tonio practically lunges at her, Nedda strikes his face with the whip Peppe left behind, and Tonio curses her in the name of the Virgin.[9] Tonio's vendetta motif resounds again when the curse is finally verbalized: "Nedda, lo giuro . . . me la pagherai!" Nedda remains shaken at Tonio's exit, comparing his proposal to his deformed body.

The sun that was a part of her *ballatella* returns in the form of Silvio, who is now seen climbing over the wall. The orchestra shifts to F-major, inaugurating the opera's most extended duet. Silvio's theme is heard again in an *andante appassionato*. He tells Nedda that he has seen both Canio and Peppe drinking in the tavern and thereby knew it would be safe to visit. Nedda warns him that a bit sooner and he would have met with Tonio. Silvio's motif is again presented in two additional variations expressing his domination of the proceedings. Nedda relates the struggle she suffered with Tonio ("e nel bestial delirio suo, baci chiedendo"), underscored by the orchestral recreation of the hunchback's earlier threat. Silvio's theme returns when he asks Nedda how long she plans to live in such anxiety. The music suddenly shifts to D-flat major, becoming soft and intimate. Silvio begins his seduction of Nedda in earnest, imploring her to decide his fate in an elegant yet controlled manner, singing his own motif for the first time ("Decidi il mio destin").[10] Silvio implores her to remain rather than leave the following day when the festivities end. Nedda seems paralyzed and is only able to whisper "Silvio." When she half-heartedly implores him to cease, the music shifts to G-flat major accompanied by a violin tremolo and harp arpeggio, recalling the beginning of her *ballatella*. Realizing that their love must remain forbidden, she repeats her phrase "Non mi tentar!" twice, constantly ascending until she reaches a high B-flat, imploring him to have pity. Silvio then joins his voice with hers as he begs her to flee with him. Their singing in unison is interrupted by an upward sweeping chromatic scale announcing Tonio's hidden presence. The hunchback realizes that he has caught Nedda in flagrante delicto, which is underscored by the ominous chords of his vendetta motif.

His appearance marks the precise moment when Nedda assures Silvio of her love, prompting Tonio to set off in search of Canio. Silvio then begins an extended *cantabile appassionato* ("E allor perchè") that exemplifies both his sensuality and rural charm, sharply contrasting with Canio's sincerity. Nedda completely succumbs in an extended passage ("A te mi dono") that Leoncavallo culled from Mendelssohn's Trio op. 49 in D-minor (*allegro assai appassionato*).[11] This leads directly into the duet's finale, concluding with Silvio's motif. Nedda agrees to meet him that evening. They bid farewell in a final embrace ("Sí, mi guarda e mi bacia!"), capturing each other's gaze and holding it with a kiss.[12]

Tonio suddenly appears, to his own vendetta motif, accompanied by Canio. Silvio retreats over the wall to his theme twice repeated, before being broken off a third time when Canio tries to catch up with him. Syncopated chords relay a horrific accompaniment to Canio's search. Nedda listens anxiously, praying that Silvio be spared. Canio's voice is now heard to his own revenge motif, and Tonio cynically laughs to his vendetta theme. When Nedda tells the hunchback that she *had* expected such action from him, he warns her that he can still do better. He then voices his own vendetta motif for the first time upon informing her how happy the situation makes him ("Oh, non sai come lieto ne son!").

Canio reenters perspiring and short of breath, involuntarily reminding us of Silvio's physical agility and grace. His return is stressed by a rigid, almost military-sounding accompaniment (*mosso e concitato*), reminiscent of Verdi's *Otello* in its unbridled fury. When Canio demands to know the name of Nedda's lover she feigns indifference. He then produces a dagger to the vendetta motif. His lines are declaimed in a brutal manner even if Nedda still refuses to disclose her lover's name ("No, No, nol dirò giammai!"). A nervous Peppe comes to Nedda's aid, reminding Canio that the villagers are leaving the church in anticipation of the evening's performance. Ironically, Peppe asks Tonio to restrain Canio, thus symbolically placing the latter's destiny in the hunchback's hands. Aware that Silvio will return that evening, Tonio leads Canio away, advising him, in constantly modulating major/minor keys, creating an unbalanced effect, that Canio should trust him. Tonio's vendetta motif returns in an eerie B-flat minor upon telling Canio that he will watch Nedda and that Silvio will most likely turn up for the performance, thus inadvertently placing the idea of murder in Canio's mind. Calming C-major chords insinuate that Canio fully believes Tonio's compassion.

Peppe tells Canio to don his costume before sending Tonio off to beat his drum, which symbolically resounds in the orchestra.[13] Tonio's drumbeat—echoing the pounding of Canio's heart—leads to the latter's declaimed *recitativo* that "the show must go on" regardless of his emotional state ("Recitar! Mentre preso dal delirio"). He is no longer a man, merely a clown. In a lachrymose adagio in E-minor ("Vesti la giubba") "declaimed with pain" to a simple string accompaniment, (the English horn slowly supports the vocal line, after which the orchestra gradually builds in intensity), Leoncavallo has, perhaps unwittingly at the time, ensured his operatic immortality. He has also provided generations of tenors with a splendid yet relatively short *arioso* in which to demonstrate their mettle.[14] Paid by people who seek amusement, Canio sings the "Ridi, pagliacci" theme for the first time, realizing that he will be expected to make merry of the fact that Nedda is about to run off with a lover. Canio's moving soliloquy is stifled in tears as he is forced to laugh at his own "shattered love." The orchestra elegiacally elaborates this suffering, preparing us for the ensuing tragedy.[15]

A short intermezzo creates a note of despair, incorporating as it does Tonio's "Un nido di memoria" theme from the prologue. This is followed by a crescendo (*nervoso con forza*) leading to a full orchestral reprisal of Tonio's original B-flat major "E voi, piuttosto" from the prologue.

The opera's second half depicts a small traveling theater. Peppe arranges the benches, and Tonio is seen carrying a large drum before taking his place at stage left. A trumpet announces the event with the same *marziale deciso* that opened the opera. Villagers are heard approaching in the distance ("Ohe!"). The orchestra plays an archaic and bucolic melody that prepares us for the commedia dell'arte atmosphere to follow. This again corresponds to the chorus that opens the second part of *Cavalleria rusticana.*[16]

Tonio goads the people ("Avanti, avanti") to take their seats, his manner resembling the earlier trumpet call, leaving no doubt that this will be *his* show. Silvio also enters during this concertized passage—just as Tonio had foreseen—and we wonder why Nedda's lover would have chosen to be in such close proximity to Canio. In fact, Tonio even tells him where to sit. Nedda warns Silvio to remain cautious, even though Canio has not yet seen him. Silvio reminds her to meet him later that night, although she collects entrance fees without replying. Does she now have misgivings? Nedda then enters the theater, followed by Peppe. The chorus voices rise to a crescendo of anticipation.[17]

The small curtain rises "on a poorly painted scene representing a tiny room with two doors." The orchestra begins a short introductory prelude in the style of an antique air to string pizzicato. Colombina (Nedda) is seen seated by the table glancing toward the door on her right. Her vocal line is broken to accentuate an almost doll-like quality in keeping with her commedia dell'arte role, relating that her husband Pagliaccio (Canio)—a derivative of Pierrot—will not return until late that night. Colombina nervously asks herself where the "blockhead" Taddeo (Tonio) is, expecting a tryst with her lover Arlecchino (Peppe). Leoncavallo thus parallels both life and theater, except that the vendetta will in fact be carried out in this version.

Arlecchino's guitar is heard in the distance, and Colombina emits an amorous sigh upon rushing to the window. A violin pizzicato creates the illusion, and the orchestra echoes the tuning of Arlecchino's instrument. Arlecchino commences his charming serenade from offstage with a light string accompaniment, highlighted with first one and then two flute pizzicati. The *serenata* makes no great demands on the tenor and its lighthearted yet elegant melody conveys an appropriately anachronistic touch. Leoncavallo's attention to detail in the use of his text, reminding the singer not to breathe in order to maintain the legato, is further accentuated by rhyming parts of two sentences, thereby stressing the serenade's irony (". . . la tua boccuccia. Amor mi cruccia!"). The music again returns to the identical accompaniment (*tempo di Minuetto*) that was heard at the beginning of the commedia. Colombina wonders whether she should give Arlecchino the signal for their rendezvous.

Taddeo appears to interrupt the planned tryst with his own declarations of love. In a mock tragic style he sings of her beauty in an *ad libitum* coloratura flourish enjoyed by the villagers. Taddeo decides the best manner to approach Colombina is with a declaration of his love ("Se a la rubella"). His music recalls Silvio's first wooing of Nedda ("Sapea ch'io non rischiavo nulla"). When Taddeo explains that Colombina's husband is away ("Lungi è lo sposo"), leaving the scene open to his advances, the orchestra quotes from an earlier accompaniment that served to underline Canio's description of the ridicule that would be his sole reward for discovering his wife's theatrical infidelity. Drama and life have become one. Taddeo offers Colombina roast chicken, kneeling down to a charming and elegant *andante sostenuto* in A-major perfectly suiting his stage character. Without paying any heed to Taddeo's lovesickness, Colombina only asks how much he paid for the chicken. Taddeo remarks in character, though with ironic intention, that Colombina is as virtuous as a snowflake. He repeats this frequently ("Si, casta! . . . al par di neve!") until the violincelli take up one of his earlier themes recalling the only time he had ever spoken sincerely of his love ("So ben che difforme").

When Arlecchino enters, kicking Taddeo from the stage to the audience's glee, three ominous chords resound in the orchestra. Taddeo exits, vaguely recalling Tonio's search for Canio during Nedda's meeting with Silvio, signifying a sealing of fate in Tonio's/Taddeo's mind. The spectators are usually only cajoled into laughter by Taddeo, thus enlarging the irony between comedy and evil as well as widening the cleft between what the villagers actually are allowed to perceive and what the audience knows and therefore dreads. A short duet begins between Arlecchino and Colombina made up of purposefully stilted and exaggerated mannerisms. Colombina sets the table to a charming gavotte. Arlecchino hands her a vial containing a sleeping draft intended for Pagliaccio, enabling their elopement. Without warning, the music abruptly changes to rapid and menacing scales when Taddeo rushes in, announcing that Pagliaccio has discovered his wife's infidelity. Taddeo's appearance again provokes laughter from the audience, prompting Arlecchino's exit. Colombina remains, reminding Arlecchino of their planned meeting ("A stanotte"), uncannily echoing what she said to Silvio during their love duet.

Pagliaccio soon enters as his vendetta motif sounds in the orchestra, banishing any doubt concerning the situation's authenticity. A distraught Canio prays for courage to be able to perform his "comic" portrayal, subjecting himself to the part while a stuttering and deformed *andantino* generates our sympathy. Colombina steadfastly rejects his accusations of infidelity, asking whether he is drunk. "Yes," he replies with emphasis, "since one hour." When Pagliaccio wonders why the table has been set for two, Colombina lies that Taddeo had joined her but had fled upon Pagliaccio's arrival. Taddeo is called in by Colombina to testify to her innocence, which he does to the same stammering accompaniment that had been present with Canio. To this he also stakes her claim of virtuousness in an exaggerated and accentuated manner, once again not failing to draw laughter from the spectators. Repulsed by them and Nedda's playacting, Canio now demands the name of her real lover. When Nedda feigns ignorance, Canio finally sings an earlier theme ("Vo' il nome de l'amante tuo") that originally only sounded in the orchestra as he once warned the villagers of his wrath should he ever suspect her of infidelity.[18] Nedda tries to resume the play to Tonio and Canio's halting accompaniment, reminding him that he is in fact Pagliaccio. Another shift to E-flat minor unleashes a wave of rage from Canio, signifying a complete break with his role. The orchestra then unleashes itself in an irregular, agitated frenzy, supporting Canio's claim that he is no longer Pagliaccio.

Canio echoes Baus during this stinging and swift oration, reminding Nedda that he originally found her as a hungry orphan. The spectators' involvement with the impending tragedy ("Comare, mi fa piangere!") also instantly recalls Mendès. From vengeance and hate, the music now turns to one of pain and pity. Canio begins one of the score's most inspired passages and a *ritenuto molto* prepares for a superb *cantabile espressivo* in E-flat major ("Sperai, tanto il delirio accecato m'aveva"). Canio eulogizes his love, further binding the operatic and *commedia* audience in sympathy, rather than siding with the heroine as Puccini might have chosen to do.

Canio's anguish is heartily applauded by the innocent spectators, and he once again demands that Nedda answer him. Her reply is Colombina's, and she resumes the gavotte originally heard in her duet with Arlecchino. Ascending scales crowned by Canio's demands for her to cease, allow him to threaten her once more to either confide the name of her lover or face death.[19] In true Neapolitan fashion typical of one of Leoncavallo's heroines, Nedda grows furious herself and unleashes a high B while swearing upon her mother's memory that she is "not vile." Peppe hopes that Tonio will help restrain the quarreling couple. Instead, Tonio now holds Peppe back, well aware of what the outcome will be. Nedda remains defiant, passionately singing Silvio's motif once again ("Di quel . . . tuo sdegno è l'amor mio più forte!"). Silvio draws his dagger, finally realizing that Canio's threats are in earnest. The villagers restrain him, as Tonio does with Peppe, thereby allowing the tragedy to take place. Canio sinks his own dagger into Nedda, hoping that death's agonies will make her utter her lover's name. She cries out for Silvio, and Canio mortally wounds him with the same knife. The orchestra responds with Canio's vendetta theme, now fully realized. Amid a disconcerted audience and two corpses, Tonio cynically announces that the "play has ended." The opera is immediately rounded off by the dramatic "Ridi, pagliaccio" motif, before sweeping to a close in a *Cavalleria rusticana*–like manner.

Modeled on *Cavalleria rusticana*'s realism, *Pagliacci* was a radical switch from the romantic *Chatterton* and the pageantry of *I Medici*. Leoncavallo sought to theatrically present "a slice of life" just as Mascagni had done, portraying the

extremes of passion in full view of an audience. Rather than the heroine's being deceived as in *Cavalleria rusticana*, Leoncavallo's male protagonist faces his
wife's infidelity, driven on and cultivated by the Iago figure of Tonio, perhaps
the most interesting character in the work, representing a form of fate. Writing
his own libretto without having to be dependent on outside help, Leoncavallo
was able to mold the exact format he desired with an eye to success, giving
the public what it wanted, while at the same time ensuring that the process
of creation would be a short one. The opera surges in a continuous flow of
inspiration without a superfluous note. The orchestral accompaniment is as
riveting as the superb libretto, remaining Leoncavallo's only opera completely
bound by a web of motifs. The characters are not stilted or self-conscious but
authentic and passionate personages, thanks to Leoncavallo's ability to empa-
thize, without having to approach the work through an academic lens as he did
in *I Medici* and portions of *La bohème*.[20]

NOTES

1. The plot of Puccini's *Il tabarro* greatly resembles that of *Pagliacci*.
2. Leoncavallo has written "Dramma in un atto" on the cover of *Pagliacci*'s autograph orchestral score, housed at Washington's Library of Congress. The prologue
immediately leads to the introductory chorus with no mention of either the first
or second act. During the decades that passed between *Pagliacci*'s composition and
Leoncavallo's death, he perhaps authorized certain modifications of the work—or at
least tolerated them, considering his presence in the studio during 1907 for a complete
recording of the opera under Carlo Sabajno. This may account for some sixty-two
differences between the printed score and the original manuscript. Leoncavallo also
penned this opera in his customary violet ink, only this time on Casa Ricordi stationary, while the copyright was declared 1 June 1892.
3. Most of the variances between the original autograph orchestral score and today's
performing practice are additional high notes, as well as a variety of musical terms relating
to the music's interpretation. I have frequently relied on the original autograph orchestral
score housed at the Library of Congress, Washington, for my analysis of the opera.
4. Specified as being precisely 3:00 p.m. by Leoncavallo.
5. E-minor and F-sharp minor.
6. In the autograph orchestral score the word "scherzosamente" in reference to the
peasant's warning does not appear, suggesting that Leoncavallo originally wished the
heeding for its full insinuation.
7. The fact that both *Pagliacci* and *Cavalleria rusticana* (set on Easter Sunday) take
place on a religious holiday is no coincidence.
8. In the autograph score Leoncavallo has written "stridono laggiù."
9. This is a derivative of Santuzza's anguished "A te la mala Pasqua!" in *Cavalleria
rusticana*, even beginning with the same word, "Bada" (beware).

10. Although the original manuscript of Leoncavallo's song "La chanson des yeux"—based on a fragment by André Chenier—is not dated, it most probably derives from the composer's Parisian sojourn prior to writing *Pagliacci*, having thus "borrowed" his own music for this sequence, a set piece that contains no other motifs from the opera.

11. Julian Budden, "Primi rapporti fra Leoncavallo e la Casa Ricordi" in L. Guiot and J. Maehder, eds., *Ruggero Leoncavallo nel suo tempo, atti del 1° Convegno internazionale di studi su Ruggero Leoncavallo* (Milan: Casa Musicale Sonzogno, 1993), 51.

12. Similar to the final love duet in Mascagni's *I Rantzau*, which would premiere during November 1892.

13. A very similar orchestral accompaniment is to be found near the beginning of the second act quartet in Gounod's *Faust* (conclusion, 71).

14. The orchestral *tranquillo con dolore*, which appears following the aria's conclusion, seems to be inspired from the first notes of the prelude to act 3 of *Die Meistersinger*.

15. The "Ridi Pagliaccio" theme curiously evokes a portion of the requiem sequence in act 3 of Puccini's *Edgar*, composed in 1899 ("Del Signor la pupilla veglia nell'ombre eterne").

16. Leoncavallo has also taken great pains to ensure that "the first basses enter left and approach the women followed by the tenors and basses."

17. The success of the commedia dell'arte in *Pagliacci* inspired other composers to use these characters in their own works, notably Mascagni in *Le maschere* (1901).

18. Now in E-minor.

19. This musical sequence originally appeared in sketches for Leoncavallo's incomplete *Les coupe et les lèvres,* authored in the 1880s.

20. Becoming too involved in the literary genesis of his operas usually succeeded in robbing the composer of his spontaneity, incorporating superfluous details that ultimately detract from his music. Boito comes to mind as another victim of his own great culture.

• *14* •

Séraphitus-Séraphita

*H*onoré de Balzac's lengthy philosophical novel *Séraphita* deals with the mysterious and androgynous sixteen-year-old Séraphita, whose knowledge, beauty, and spirituality enchant Minna, who falls in love, envisioning a youth named Séraphitus.

Part 1 (*Sul Falberg*) of Leoncavallo's symphonic poem takes place on a Norwegian fjord during the 1800s, commencing with precisely the same Tristanesque chords (*sostenuto assai*) that Leoncavallo will again employ in *La bohème*, reprised by the violins and clarinets. The trumpets soon introduce us to the future *Der Roland von Berlin's* "victory" motif, accompanied by tremolo chords from the violins. Part 1 concludes with a *cantabile* that will later form the love duet of *La bohème*.

Part 2 (*Le Tentazioni*) deals with the process of Séraphita's/Séraphitus' purification in the face of temptation. An *allegretto ben ritmato* with prominent use of the xylophone announces a furious-sounding bacchanal. The girl/youth resists the sensuous dances that include Lucifer, who offers her all earthly wealth. *Der Roland von Berlin's* "victory" theme is heard once again (*un poco meno, grandiosamente*) as part 2 draws to a close.

Part 3 (*L'Addio e L'Assunzione*) finds both Minna and her friend, Wilfried, in search of Séraphita/Séraphitus to declare their love. When they locate her/ him she/he is ill and dying, while the introduction to part 3 seeks to express this anguish in a touching *sostenuto tristamente* performed by the celli, flutes, and violins. Leoncavallo will later reuse this in precisely the same manner for the introduction to act 4 of *La bohème*. The remembrance of the love felt for Séraphita/Séraphitus is again recalled using an earlier heard theme from part 1. Séraphita dies as a chorus welcomes her/him into heaven with a *maestoso sostenuto* sanctus sung to the *Der Roland von Berlin* victory motif, concluding the work.

Séraphitus-Séraphita differs from *La nuit de mai* in its absence of any solo vocal parts, remaining faithful to its form as a symphonic poem. Leoncavallo sought to create a religious and mysterious atmosphere, complementing Balzac's elusive action that frequently recalls Liszt. The composer was probably not very content with the work; otherwise he would not have culled parts of it for use in *La bohème*, which premiered three years later, not to mention extracting the main themes for inclusion into *Der Roland von Berlin*.

• *15* •

La bohème

Characters

Marcello, tenor	Durand, tenor
Rodolfo, baritone	Il Signore del primo piano, tenor
Schaunard, baritone	Un Becero, tenor
Barbemuche, bass	Musette, mezzo-soprano
Visconte Paolo, baritone	Mimì, soprano
Gustavo Colline, baritone	Eufemia, mezzo-soprano
Gaudenzio, tenor	

Setting: Paris (24 December 1837 to 24 December 1838)

Henri Murger's *Scènes de bohème*, a portrait of Parisian bohemian life, originally appeared in serial form between March 1845 and April 1849 in the Parisian magazine *Le Corsaire de Satan*. Jules Janin, an influential critic, suggested a stage adaptation, which resulted in a five-act dramatization by Murger and Théodore Barrière. The play, first produced on 22 November 1849 at the Théâtre des Variétés, owed a debt to Dumas fils' *La dame aux camélias* and was warmly received, securing Murger's success. He was not only made a recipient of the coveted Légion d'Honneur but, in addition, was granted a contract from the firm of Michel Lévy that enabled him to publish *Scènes de bohème* in book form under the title *Scènes de la bohème* in 1851.[1]

Murger (1822–1861)[2] created an enduring portrait of Montmartre and the Latin Quarter's bohemian lifestyle set in the 1840s that still influences the way we presently regard the era. Murger died at age thirty-nine. His novel warns against the dangers of squandering one's youth with idealism, lacking a sense of the materialism necessary for survival and, in turn, for artistic production—a book with a moral.[3] While personal experiences always flavored his writings, his famous last words "Pas de musique, pas de bruit, pas de bohème!" sheds light on a life lived with sparse nostalgia. A charming, witty, and harshly realistic book, *Scènes de la bohème* was thought to be "a triumph of socialism" by the Goncourt brothers. This may also explain why Victor Hugo admired it. The novel dealt with the working class, a practice initiated by Hugo in his *Notre-Dame de Paris* in 1831 and later taken up by Emile Zola.

Scènes de la vie de bohème is largely based on authentic personages. Considering its journalistic style, its absence of any real plot, and a constant skipping to and fro in time, it is easily apparent that the novel originally appeared in instalments before forming the whole so familiar to us now. Not only is the poet Rodolphe a self-portrait of Murger, but the book's locations are authentic as well: Rue Vaugirard, Rue de la Harpe, and Rue de la Tour d'Auvergne all served as Murger's various residences between 1841 and 1849.

The mood of *Scènes de la vie de bohème* is extremely lighthearted until chapter 18 (*Le Manchon de Francine*), when the narration suddenly grows somber. Since the real protagonist of both novel and play is essentially youth itself, the drama only begins to unfold when the characters mature. As an independent story apart from the work's main narration, *Le manchon de Francine* inspired both Puccini and Leoncavallo to have Mimì die at home, while the hopelesness of the novel's latter half was brilliantly recreated in the final two acts of Leoncavallo's opera. The book is a frequently brutal account of life as it really is, and, like Murger, Leoncavallo was less interested in the novel's characters and personal destinies than he was in portraying an entire social class.

The play by Murger and Barrière entitled *Vie de Bohème* introduced new characters, such as Rodolphe's millionaire uncle, Durandin, and the servant Baptiste. In this version, Rodolphe is a young man of excellent social standing who writes poetry in his free time, yearns for love without gloves and dinners without forks, all the while hoping to remain free of a marriage his uncle has arranged with the wealthy Madame de Rouvres. During act 3 Rodolphe tells Mimì they should separate for lack of money. Durandin then offers her three thousand francs if she agrees to leave Rodolphe, which she eventually does, recalling Dumas fils' *Dame aux Camélias*. Act 4 takes place in Madame de Rouvres' home, where she is giving a party to which Rodolphe and Durandin have been invited. When Mimì arrives looking for Rodolphe she is asked to leave by Madame de Rouvres. After hearing what has taken place, Rodolphe ends his relationship with Rouvres.

Although Puccini made greater use of the play, Leoncavallo was particularly influenced by act 4, scene 2, where Marcel and Rodolphe mourn the loss of their loves, resulting in the aria "Musette! O gioia della mia dimora!": *O petite Mimì! Joie de ma maison, c'est donc bien vrai que vous êtes partie et que je ne vous verrai plus? O petites mains blanches aux veines bleues, vous à qui j'avais fiancé mes lèvres! avez-vous donc reçu mon dernier baiser?*

Mimì returns from the hospital in act 5, scene 4 of the play. A fever overcomes her and she asks for a muff. In act 5, scene 9 Rodolphe admits that he has been an egotist, assisting in Mimì's patient martyrdom by warming himself with the fire of her love. The play ends in a most contrived manner, when Madame de Rouvres arrives at the garret with Durandin to aid the dying Mimì. She offers her money, while Durandin is convinced that her illness is a hoax, until he touches her dead hand. Schaunard leads him to the door saying: "Une comédie! . . . Eh bien, monsieur! La pièce est finie; on va éteindre," resembling *Pagliacci*'s "La commedia è finita!"

Marcel is a composite of the writer Champfleury and the painters Marcel Lazare and Tabart, from whom his name derives. Murger also painted, even though he earned a living through journalism. Tabart had originally painted "The Crossing of the Red Sea," which turns up in Puccini's opera, and Marcel is described in the novel as a young man of twenty-two wearing a white Louis XIII hat and nibbling on a bouquet of violets (chapter 1).

Schaunard, who figures quite prominently in Leoncavallo's opera, is based on the "artist" Alexandre Schanne, an acquaintance of Jules Massenet, who later sold children's toys and eventually published his memoirs in 1887. Although Murger had renamed him "Schannard," a printing error in *Le Corsaire de Satan* originally made it appear as "Schaunard," the form it retained in the book. In the novel he is described as a good musician with a pitiable character (chapter 11).

Gustave Colline is the combination of two of Murger's friends: the theologian Jean Wallon, who kept his coat pockets stuffed with books, and a certain Trapadoux, who was called the "Green Giant," due to his wearing an enormous black coat that, with age, had turned color. Colline is mentioned in the novel as having large blue eyes always in search of something, while his skin had the shade of old ivory, except for the rouge added to his cheeks. His mouth, on the other hand, had been formed by an inexperienced painter whose elbow seems to have been jostled in the process. He is a philosopher teaching mathematics, botany, and other sciences ending in "ic."

Musette is presented as an attractive twenty-year-old who became a "kept woman" shortly after arriving in Paris. Known for singing country songs with faulty intonation, she has instinctive elegance, a poetic nature, loves luxury, and is often compared to Manon Lescaut in the novel. However, unlike the Prévost heroine, she would never have become the mistress of anyone not as young and attractive as herself. Smart and witty, she loathed idiots, regardless of their titles, age, or name. She played a fair game and requested reciprocal sincerity. Her affairs were usually short-lived, and she considered herself to be the spiritual sister of Alfred de Musset's Mimi Pinson.

The twenty-four-year-old dandy, writer, and platonic philosopher, Carolus Barbemuche, was created as an attack on Murger's two enemies, Charles Baudelaire and Charles Barbara. He appears in Leoncavallo's opera, although Puccini failed to include him. Traits of Murger's first mistress, Marie-Virginie Vimal, also influence Mimi's character, including the small white hands that the author often mentions in the novel. When Vimal left Murger, he began an affair with Lucille Louvet, who died of tuberculosis in her early twenties, nevertheless finding literary immortality in the novel's Francine and in Mimi's death.[4]

There is no certainty whether Musette was originally inspired by Mariette Roux—Champfleury's mistress who had once modeled for Ingres—or whether she was the wife of Baudelaire's friend, Pierre Dupont. While it has been suggested that Murger may have developed the name "Musette" from Alfred de Musset, Musette herself later in the novel tells her current lover, Maurice, that Marcel had originally begun calling her Musette because of her songs, which would also imply that the name may have been derived from "muse," or because her singing voice left much to be desired, thus "musette" (bagpipe).

Murger immediately introduces the reader to the main characters during chapter 1 of his novel, describing how the bohemian circle of friends was originally formed. Unlike Puccini, Leoncavallo made much greater use of the novel and its characters. It is indeed easy to understand why Leoncavallo would have felt attracted to Murger's narration, reminding him of his youth and days of hunger spent in similar conditions in the French capital. Although Puccini had similar experiences during his own student days, they had not been in Paris, and he only became familiar with the city *after* his opera premiered. Leoncavallo could of course read the book in its original language. Puccini most probably worked from Felice Camerone's Italian translation, which happened to have been published by Sonzogno in 1872, replacing an earlier (1859) inadequate version. Leoncavallo, identifying with the suffering artist, envisioned another poet in Rodolphe, and Murger even mentions Chatterton in chapter 9 when Rodolphe decides to burn the manuscript of his drama *Le Vengeur*.

Murger's novel is not only Latin in lifestyle and temperament, but also in the way the action is viewed through the very masculine world of its author. Neither Rodolphe's many girlfriends nor those of the remaining "four musketeers" (Marcel, Schaunard, and Colline) ever fully comprehend the philosophic-artistic world of their lovers, a factor that bonds the men yet more strongly to one another. The author states this repeatedly, and, in chapter 15, he writes plainly that love is an improvisation, whereas friendship ripens slowly. After six years together, the bohemians feel that they have developed their own form of communication that will always remain incomprehensible to anyone else.

The novel's female characters share just as many romances as do their male counterparts, prompting Murger to write in chapter 20 that the characters are essentially egotists that love for the sake of loving. It is Musette who states in chapter 19 that her life is like a song, with each affair a verse and Marcel its refrain. Although the bohemians search for the meaning of life, theirs is essentially a superficial existence made even more formless by a lack of any enduring ties. Rodolphe narcicistically worries more that Mimì's parting will rob him of his youth than what it really means to lose her. While the men in the novel are driven to search for the meaning of life, their mistresses only seem to seek material satisfaction. Only toward the novel's conclusion do both Mimì and Musette return to Rodolphe and Marcel. However, by this time the men have exchanged their bohemian lifestyles for success and financial security.

The opera commences on the first floor of the Latin Quarter's Café Momus, where its proprietor, Gaudenzio, is seen arguing with the musician Alessandro Schaunard. The orchestra plays a short introduction in D-major (*andantino mosso*) that will serve as Gaudenzio's motif. The proprietor complains to Schaunard ("No, signor mio, così non può durare") that his intolerable friends, Rodolfo and Marcello, continue to confiscate the café's backgammon board, while Marcello insists on painting and live models (Murger, chapter 11). Gaudenzio is finally interrupted by a vagrant searching for singing lessons advertised by Schaunard. He turns the vagrant out, and Schaunard swears that Marcello will cease his painting and no music will be performed. The key then modulates to B-flat major, accompanied by trills making it difficult to believe that he will actually keep his promise. Relieved, Gaudenzio blesses the musician's words with a "Dio benedetto!" This leads to Schaunard's arietta to a gavotte-like melody in E-major ("La macchina è soppressa") in the classical style. He reminds Gaudenzio that his friends are due at any moment to dine and celebrate Christmas at the café. The proprietor asks how they will pay, believing that the money must obviously be coming from a relative since art is not profitable.[5]

Rodolfo and Marcello enter accompanied by Schaunard and his passionate muse Eufemia.[6] Marcello orders the proprietor to place everything on the spit, including chickens, dogs, and cats. Eufemia rushes into Schaunard's arms, unable to say anything other than "Alessandro" (chapter 17).[7] When Schaunard realizes their money only totals two francs forty, he hopes that their friend, Colline, who now enters, will have more. Instead, Colline rapturously informs them that he has purchased an "extremely rare Chinese dictionary," the *Iliad*, Virgil, and Plutarch.[8]

The atmosphere suddenly grows somber when Colline asks where Mimì is. Marcello says she is coming accompanied by an attractive friend who has agreed to forsake her banker lover in order to join them out of curiosity. She then enters with Musette.[9] Marcello quotes Raoul's "Ah! quel spectacle enchanteur vint s'offrir à mes yeux" from act 1 of Meyerbeer's *Les Huguenots* after setting eyes on Musette.

Schaunard begins the elegant *cantabile* "Bella dama, da questi milionari" when introducing Colline, and two elegiac chords in F-major (*dolce con poesia*) prepare us for the poet Rodolfo. Marcello is also presented in an ironically solemn manner as the artist who changed the title of his painting "The Crossing of the Red Sea," only to be six times rejected by the Institute of Art. Schaunard finally introduces himself to harp arpeggios re-evoking the beginning of his *cantabile*.[10]

Mimì takes Musette's hand and introduces her friend with the fine G-major aria "Musette svaria sulla bocca viva." This lighthearted *chanson* expands and soars ("La scorge amor") when Mimì declares that love accompanies Musette "from her last pleasure to her new hope." After Musette has been introduced as a carefree young girl who "adores one treasure only—love!" Marcello immediately asks her whether they can search for it together.

Musette immediately orders champagne (Murger, chapter 11) and Mimì settles for a "green liqueur,"[11] prompting Rodolfo's poetic response that it resembles "the smile of meadows in the sun." A nervous waiter accidentally bumps into Barbemuche, whose hat and cane fall in the process. When Musette and the other women ask who he is, Schaunard whispers that he must be an ambassador of sorts, since he possesses a watch and uses twenty-franc bills. Barbemuche sits down at a nearby table for a drink, after having greeted the adjoining women. A *Pagliacci*-inspired accompaniment seems to imply that the show—in this case the dinner—can commence, with Mimì singing "Viva la giovinezza," taken from Marcel's line in *Vie de Bohème* (act 1, scene 10).

Marcello jokes to Musette that Colline is "a platonic philosopher" even if Mimì believes the term signifies a lover not sufficiently bold to kiss.[12] Leoncavallo, interested in "cleansing" Mimì's character, has Musette define the phrase, prompting Mimì to laugh about such "stupid love," as all raise their glasses to a toast.

The men—especially Rodolfo—demand a song from Musette, who complies with one about Mimì ("Mimì Pinson la biondinetta"). This spirited C-major aria is filled with a sense of fin de siècle charm, supported by a very delicate, mostly pizzicato accompaniment.[13] Schaunard explains that he is weeping from emotion, though Rodolfo jests that it is, in fact, the onion he is eating. That leads Colline to discover that the rabbit he is devouring seems to have two heads. Schaunard describes it as being "bicephalous." Eufemia asks him to repeat the term after having unsuccessfully tried to pronounce it.[14]

Marcello voices his growing passion for Musette in the splendid *cantabile affettuoso* "O Musette, o gioconda e sorridente!" in A-major.[15] She, in turn, confides that her character is both "vain and capricious,"[16] while an inebriated Colline underpins their short but passionate duet by ranting about the origins of ice to impress Mimì (Murger, chapter 13). Musette and Marcello finally raise their voices in unison to his original "O Musette, o gioconda e sorridente!" When Mimì suggests that the evening should be continued elsewhere, all but Rodolfo—who has just received the bill totaling thirty-one francs sixty centimes—are enthused.[17] Colline continues to remain oblivious to the situation, lecturing Mimì on the origins of coffee (Murger, chapter 13).

The opera's opening theme returns to reinstate Gaudenzio into the action, as he demands payment, taking the women's cloaks from Schaunard, who snatches them back, inducing the proprietor to call for help. Three scullions appear on the stairs armed with a ladle, broom, and a spit. Schaunard confronts the one with the broom, this time quoting from act 3 of Meyerbeer's *Les Huguenots* ("Il brando mio e il mio coraggio!"). Barbemuche finally halts the fighting, asking Gaudenzio whether he would be allowed to pay the bill, thereby enabling him to meet the bohemians, whose circle he has long wished to join (Murger, chapter 11). Although Gaudenzio gladly accepts "the author and philosopher's" offer, the bohemians feign that their pride will not allow them to accept. Schaunard suggests they play a game of billiards to decide who should pick up the bill. The wager is accepted, and all but Marcello, Musette, and Gaudenzio go to the billiard room after singing a partial *a capella* ensemble ("Al giudizio, su, moviamo") in A-flat major (*marziale sostenuto*).

This gives Marcello the opportunity to court Musette in an extended scene preceded by a charming waltz-like orchestral introduction (*andantino assai sostenuto*) in D-flat major, duly recalling the café-concert Leoncavallo in its elegance and charm. Marcello's trepidation is conveyed through Leoncavallo's halting accompaniment. He begins by asking her to give him one of her flowers, as she knights him with the "Order of Spring." In a rapturous phrase he also tells her that if he were Pluto he would offer "pearls and diamonds" (Murger, chapter 6).[18] When Musette coyly reminds him that he is not Pluto, Marcello asks whether she would allow him to paint her portrait. With mounting passion, he tells Musette how wonderful he finds her in the heartwarming D-flat major phrase "Ah, voi siete adorabile!" Leoncavallo again has Marcello quote his counterpart Marcel when he tells Musette that his artistic plan will flatter: "Rubens and my lady!" (Murger, chapter 6). Musette reprimands Marcello when he demands a kiss, asking how many minutes his love usually lasts. Schaunard's voice is heard from the billiard table exclaiming "forty-five," to which Musette humorously responds "heaven replies!" Marcello implores that he will prove heaven wrong as the couple once again take up the earlier "O Musette, o gioconda e sorridente!" theme sung in unison in A-major. Musette nevertheless prefers to remain friends, realizing that she is both "flirtatious and foolish." Marcello's conquest is sealed by a kiss at the precise moment Schaunard wins the billiard game—two simultaneous victories.

Barbemuche gladly pays the bill in order to befriend the Bohemians, while bells and cries of "Natale!" remind all again that it is indeed Christmas Eve, as this long initial act consisting of numerous individual mosaics draws to an end.

Act 2 takes place on 15 April 1838, in the courtyard of Musette's apartment on the rue de la Bayère. She has been evicted after her lover, the banker Alexis, has left following her insistence that Marcello live with them.[19] A short prelude creates a splendid Parisian atmosphere that Leoncavallo would again employ when writing the orchestral introduction to act 3 of *Zazà*.

The concierge, Durand,[20] is in the process of having some of Musette's remaining kitchen furniture moved into the courtyard to be sequestered the following day (Murger, chapter 6). The tenants bid him good night ("Buona notte") using a quotation from act 2 of Verdi's *La forza del destino* (Preziosilla's "Buona notte") before the orchestra again takes up the initial prelude.

Musette enters with Marcello, who offers her "a poor little room" in the first of his two major arias, "Io non ho che una povera stanzetta," an endearing and bittersweet portrait of his sincerity. The aria once again takes up its original theme before spreading to an all-embracing climax on a high B-flat, as the voice descends again to be engulfed by caressing arpeggios.

Schaunard enters, asking Marcello if he can borrow money to pay his rent.[21] He then suggests that Musette's party be given that night in the courtyard, since she no longer has an apartment. Rodolfo enters, having heard of Musette's plight from Durand, and immediately drops a succession of six five-franc pieces, claiming them to be the earnings from his tragedy *Le Vengeur*.[22]

Marcello gives orders to prepare the courtyard for the festivities. A vivacious quartet comprising Musette, Marcello, Rodolfo, and Schaunard follows in E-major inspired by *Falstaff*'s "Tutto nel mondo è burla." Durand—who now also functions as majordomo—announces the first guests, Mimì and Eufemia, followed by Barbemuche and his pupil Viscount Paolo. Further bohemians and students arrive with grisettes and streetwalkers, who sound more like Verdi's *Macbeth* witches than a joyful gathering on a moonlit night. An intense use of brass not often heard in the opera increases until achieving Wagnerian proportions ("Fin sullo scalone si può, si può seder!") with obvious borrowings from *Der Fliegende Holländer*.

An additional quote from Wagner's opera sounds when Schaunard announces that "The Bohemian Anthem" will be sung ("Attenti a me!"). The "Inno della bohème" is a German-sounding student song beginning in D-major that loses its sparkle after a rousing and promising beginning, only to be followed by a downward discord robbing it of any joy. Leoncavallo adapted a modified version of the text almost verbatim from Murger's poem *La jeunesse n'a qu'un temps*, "Ronde de la vie de bohème," from which the writer derived the title for the final chapter of his novel, but that, curiously, does not figure as a part of it.[23]

Following the *inno* that fails to rouse, Schaunard introduces the four parts of the party's program, much in the same manner he presented the four bohemians in act 1. This includes Schaunard's "unpublished cantata," "The Influence of Blue in the Arts." (Murger, chapter 5). Durand pumps water from a well simultaneously to serve as refreshments. Viscount Paolo soon approaches Mimì, asking what hopes and joys she can expect from such surroundings, when he can offer her "wealth, fine clothes, a coach, diamonds, and a more serious love!"[24] His courting does not fall on deaf ears, although she begs him cease in what is perhaps the most riveting music of the entire act. Mimì explains how her heart would mourn thinking of Rodolfo's pain.

Musette introduces a waltz ("Da quel suon soavemente") as the evening's second offering. The lyrics for this charming piece, reminiscent of Lehár in D-major, are taken from Alfred de Musset's poem "A la mi carême."[25] It is the first time during the course of the act that Leoncavallo has managed to create an exuberant and sensuous atmosphere.

Further cries from the chorus resume heralding Musette's offering prior to a short ensemble, wherein Mimì provides the main vocal line, deciding whether she should join the viscount and desert Rodolfo.

The guests now demand the evening's third offering, which is Schaunard's "The Influence of Blue on the Arts." Approaching the piano, he begins a prelude *quasi ad libitum*, commenting that the key of D is out of tune ("Oh! questo re sempre falso!").[26] (Leoncavallo creates the impression of a discord by combining a C-sharp with a D-natural.)[27] While Schaunard's composition in Murger is in fact a symphonic poem, Leoncavallo presents us with a parody of the Rossinian style ("Alza l'occhio celeste") about a "fair maid" who looks at the "deep blue sky" in her "azure gown . . . reflected in an aquamarine colored lake."[28] The chorus responds with its own coloratura, lending the situation humor.

The gaiety is abruptly halted when tenants ask when the tumult will finally cease. An extended choral scene now unfolds that, with its nightly chaos, was certainly inspired by act 2 of *Die Meistersinger*. In the din of it all and unobserved, the viscount motions Mimì to follow him, which she now does, albeit reluctantly. The guests meanwhile suggest that Schaunard should sing a reprise of his cantata and he complies—only louder this time—with the influence of blue on the month of April, the unavoidable day of rent. The tenants respond even more violently this time,[29] throwing potatoes and buckets of water on the guests, with Leoncavallo providing appropriately chaotic music that resembles the ghoulish atmosphere in act 3 of *Der Fliegende Holländer*. A rock landing atop the piano successfully ends the party. Rodolfo leaves, realizing that Mimì has in fact left with the viscount, as the act concludes with a reprisal of the "Inno della Bohème" in B-flat major.

Act 3 takes place in October 1838 in Marcello's garret (known as the "Elysée Schaunard" in the novel). A panorama of "countless roofs" including the cupola of the Dom des Invalides sets the scene. Marcello is painting near the window in Schaunard's presence and Musette remains seated pensively at a table. A short orchestral introduction (*molto sostenuto*) modeled on the *Tristan und Isolde* prelude begins the act. (Leoncavallo originally used this to open the first part of *Séraphitus-Séraphita*, even retaining the same key of E-flat minor.)

A *tempo di minuetto* then lends a sense of *triste* joy resembling Saint-Saëns' *Danse macabre*. Not only has Mimì left Rodolfo, but Schaunard is now a "widower" as well. Rodolfo drowns his sorrow in writing the poem "Requiem for love," claiming that Mimì has broken his heart with her "little white hands."[30]

Marcello also asks Musette why she is so sullen. The rose she gave him in act 1 has died, symbolizing the end of their love. He recalls the day she came to live with him, singing a phrase from his act 2 aria "Io non ho che una povera stanzetta," inspiring the strings and woodwinds to accompany the vocal line in a descending sweep ("Qui, sotto un tetto ricco sol d'amor"). The orchestra again takes up the macabre *tempo di minuetto* before Marcello leaves, accompanied by Schaunard, with a painting to sell.[31]

Two intense chords introduce Musette's *scena*. She decides to write Marcello a farewell letter ("Marcello mio, non stare ad aspettarmi").[32] In this scene the composer was influenced by Charlotte's "letter scene" in act 3 of Massenet's *Werther*, which he had studied carefully after his French colleague provided him with a score. (A series of *declamato* phrases also appear to have been inspired by the French work.) Musette quotes a passage from Marcello's aria "Testa adorata" when she writes that she does not know whether she will in fact return ("Esco, ne so se ritornar potrò"). The aria gains momentum ("Va; se il merletto non costasse tanto!") before reprising its original theme, without, however, having really had a center. She bathes her eyes with a handkerchief in a glass of water, symbolizing her relationship with Marcello, expressed in a heartwrenching *sostenuto doloroso* in F-minor.

Mimì arrives, having come to ask Rodolfo's forgiveness. Her soaring phrases against a tense and palpitating orchestral accompaniment present us with a highly charged and more dramatic-voiced heroine than during the preceding acts. Mimì summons all her strength in the memorable D-major phrase "Vo' dirgli che nel leggere," striving to tell Rodolfo the impression his poetry has made on her. Musette, in her own misery, is not supportive, since it is she who now seeks food and warmth rather than love. Mimì proudly declares that she will defy poverty for "kisses and ardent caresses." The music takes on a positive force for the first time in the act, throwing rays of light onto the somber gloom.

Intense ascending chords announce Marcello's arrival. He enters with Musette's letter in hand as Mimì hides to the *Séraphitus-Séraphita* theme that initiated the act. We are no longer dealing with a gentle artist (as in Puccini's opera), but a Canio-inspired fury who physically threatens his mistress. Marcello, lashing out in fury with a high A that is pushed to a high B-flat (*strisciando la nota*), hurls a barrage of insults at Musette, who has now become a mere "wretch" (*sciagurata*). She responds pleadingly in an extended passage ("So che per te spremuto ho dal mio core") that her love is in fact genuine and sincere, if now threatened by "privations." She begins a *cantabile* ("So che tutt'ora)" that Leoncavallo wishes to be sung "with poetry and passion," and, at certain moments ("Con quello spento fiore/Le ore dell'amor"), even recalling *Pagliacci's* Nedda/Silvio duet.

Marcello is finally assured of Musette's sincerity in pages of rapturous music taken from Part I of *Séraphitus-Séraphita*, marking the opera's first love duet, "Tu m'ami ancora!" Musette is moved, though still resolved to leave Marcello. This unleashes a renewed attack of anguish from her spurned lover to a downward surge of the woodwinds and strings, demonstrating the unpleasant side of love that is an essential part of the novel ("Va via, fantasma del passato!"). Although the text of Marcello's *agitato* was inspired by Musset's *La nuit d'octobre*—Leoncavallo also quotes a passage from it in the score at the beginning of act 3—its music is largely culled from the twelfth movement of *La nuit de mai.*

When Marcello repulses her she "instantly rises to face him defiantly." Mimì now makes an effort to protect Musette, prompting Marcello to call Rodolfo to act as witness. Mimì implores him not to believe his friend. Descending notes relay an impression of her agitation, as she insists that she returned for his love alone.[33] Rodolfo, in an intensely elegant *andantino* in F-major ("Fra noi due 'enne inì diggià tutto finì"), tells Mimì that their love has long ceased. He even repeats Marcello's words, stating that Mimì is little more than a specter.[34] Here, Leoncavallo succeeds in portraying Rodolfo's suffering, gracefully hidden behind a mask of irony. This charming and sensuous *arietta* is continuously interspersed with Mimì's imploring him to listen, to no avail.

Marcello, finally calmed by Rodolfo's gentle manner, tells Musette to gather her things. Mimì leaves in tears, and Leoncavallo reflects the girl's anguish through the use of oboe and violin tremolo. The major theme from the Musette/Marcello duet is also reprised, implying that Musette has relived the past few moments a second time. Three somber *largo appoggiatura* chords accompany her final hushed departure. Portions of the prelude also resurface when Marcello glances out of the window as Musette had earlier.

Schaunard breaks the tense situation for a moment when he returns in good spirits before quickly departing again, offering Leoncavallo the opportunity of portraying light and dark side by side, as he will in act 4 when Musette returns for Mimì's death. Marcello, finding Musette's bonnet, which she had let fall on her way out, unleashes his despair in the opera's most famous aria ("Musette! O gioia della mia dimora!"), that begins with the sad thought that he alone has driven her away.[35] The aria's center, "Testa adorata, più non tornerai," is a deeply felt elegiac outpouring of lost love in B-flat minor. The obsession with Mimì's small white hands now also finds expression in Marcello's aria. Shifting from major to minor, from hope to despair, his voice breaks off like Canio's as the drums of *Pagliacci*'s "Vesti la giubba" return in a *maestoso* to overwhelm the painter in his misery, as the curtain slowly falls.

The pensive *sostenuto tristemente* chromatic chords that serve to open act 4 (perhaps inspired by the prelude to act 4 of *La traviata*) derive from the introduction to the third part of *Séraphitus-Séraphita* entitled "L'Addio e L'Assunzione." It is Christmas Eve of 1838, one year later. The setting is Rodolfo's garret, where he remains alone at work. The wind howling outside and recreated in the orchestra reflects his turmoil and the mood of his verses.[36] Leoncavallo presents Rodolfo—alias Murger—writing *La Ballade du désespéré*, which he also quotes in the score at the act's beginning. The composer has reduced the fourteen stanzas of Murger's poem to just over five, in which Death offers a cure for sickness and misery to his victim. Leoncavallo has thus provided not only the rugged despair of a winter storm but also a fusion of Murger and Rodolfo, lending the scene a realistic touch, while the curtain rises with a sweep of the harps depicting a gust of wind.

Rodolfo's *scena*, "Scuoti, o vento, fra i sibili" (foreshadowing Michele's aria "Nulla! . . . Silenzio!" in Puccini's *Il tabarro*) has all the anguish and pain that result of suffering and deprivation, which will mark the entire act. Rodolfo glances toward the window, commenting on the similarity between the storm outside and the verses that "hover" around his head. He reads what he has written, immediately beginning with the first line of Murger's poem ("Qui frappe à ma porte à cette heure?") that, in its Italian translation, transforms itself to similar effect as "Chi batte alla porta a quest'ora?" Death's appearance is sensitively realized by Leoncavallo through the use of taut and vigorous rhythms conjuring up dissolution. Death announces himself as "glory," ("La gloria son, vieni ad aprir!"), while two additional musical "knocks" are discerned, recalling those that threaten Verdi's Macbeth in the "Fatal mia donna! un murmure, com'io, non intendesti?" duet of act 1.

In the poem, the door is only opened after Death has introduced himself, and Leoncavallo adheres precisely to Murger at this point, making certain that the voice projects with a complete absence of strings. On the word "morte" (death) the composer has written "ppp" while drums begin to roll, followed by ominous chords from the trumpets on the word "duol" (sorrow):

Murger: « Je suis la Mort! ouvre; j'apporte pour tous les maux la guérison. »

Leoncavallo: "Apri, son io, son la Morte/E guarir posso ogni tuo duol."

The music suddenly becomes tragic, and Leoncavallo has captured the victim's desperation with grandeur. The vocal line slowly rises to E-flat major when dissolution is welcomed ("Entra! Il tugurio a te dischiudo") into a hovel of poverty and misery. This is precisely the line that Leoncavallo chose to quote in the score at the act's beginning, musically lending it the importance for which he values it, with the use of woodwinds and strings, while drums maintain a sense of apprehensive tension. The aria ends as Marcello knocks on the door: Murger/Rodolfo and Death have all become one, with Marcello as messenger.

Schaunard enters, shivering in summer clothes for want of others. Rodolfo recalls Christmas Eve as the Café Momus music resounds. Marcello admits that he has read Musette's farewell letter again and has implored her to return, but has heard nothing. The men are eating, when Mimì appears, poorly clad. Marcello immediately approaches her, but Rodolfo turns his back. She seeks shelter for the night, having nowhere to go (Murger, chapter 22). Marcello asks about the viscount, who, Mimì confides, supported by impressionistic chords that suddenly underline her sadness ("E' finita da un pezzo!"), discarded her some time ago. Coughing, she relates that she wished to go back to work, but was "badly received." Then privation set in and she fell ill, remaining at the St. Louis Hospital for one month. Leoncavallo appreciated the importance of including the touching dialogue when Mimì tells Marcello to return to his dinner. Sadly and gently he says that none of them are hungry, whereupon she herself responds "Beati voi!!!" ("Aren't you lucky!") It is now Schaunard who leads her to the table and offers her food. She clasps at a morsel of bread that she then lets fall from sheer exhaustion, bursting into tears when Rodolfo finally confronts her; she begs forgiveness in an impassioned outburst sung to her motif from act 3 ("Rodolfo mio, perdono!").

Marcello makes a fire by breaking a chair and lighting it with paper and books. The music takes on a veiled quality through C-minor chords, and Mimì again complains of the cold. Rodolfo wonders how they will be able to find medicine or even a doctor. At that moment Musette is heard approaching, singing her "Mimì Pinson" song from act 1, eventually appearing at the door elegantly dressed and in good spirits. Shocked to discover an ill Mimì in such dire circumstances, she gives Schaunard a bracelet and ring in order to get help. Mimì now realizes that she will die, although Musette tries to make her live for Rodolfo's love. Summoning her strength one final time, she sings words inspired in Leoncavallo by the "Sola, perduta, abbandonata" scene in act 4 of Puccini's *Manon Lescaut,* when Mimì sings the phrase "No!, morir non vogl'io!" twice in B-minor to string tremolos.

Leoncavallo incorporates Murger's fascination with Mimì's/Francine's small white hands when she asks Rodolfo to kiss them one last time. Almost delirious, she envisions Christmas Eve, to a tremolo accompaniment in F-sharp major ("Taci! L'altr'anno, rammentatevi . . .") A joyful scherzo from act 1 is interrupted by a "death chord" as Mimì's life rapidly ebbs away and she loses her sight, only to hear Rodolfo's cries all the more. Descending chords make the despair almost unendurable. Bells peal, ushering in Christmas, and Mimì expires following two feeble attempts to say "Natale!" She dies to the act 3 finale performed a half key higher. Thus, the final words are reserved for Mimì herself and not for Rodolfo as in the Puccini opus. Both Puccini and Leoncavallo are, of course, quite distanced from Murger's text, where Mimì returns to the hospital to die alone, since Rodolphe believes her already dead (Murger, chapter 22).

If Leoncavallo is sometimes accused of presenting Murger's novel in too harsh a light, it should be recalled that *Scènes de la vie de bohème* frequently surpasses these effects as, for example, when Mimì refuses to sleep beside Rodolphe following her final return, fearing that her body is already being coveted by the worms that wish to feed on it.[37] Leoncavallo's opera captures the novel's ambience even if it is admittedly handicapped by an overabundance of literary details. It is doubtless an important work, and it seems fair to suggest that without the competition of Puccini's masterpiece, it may have achieved a more durable success. To quote Mosco Carner from his monograph on the Tuscan composer: "Indeed, in a crudely dramatic sense, Leoncavallo's *Bohème* may be said to be superior to Puccini's."[38] What is nevertheless missing is a wealth of "memorable lyrical invention" as well as a lack of Puccini's "homogeneity of style."[39] Leoncavallo's opus is heavier and more ponderous than Puccini's, concentrating on the poverty and resulting tragedy of his characters rather than on their romantic relationships. Puccini's opera is a song of love and death whereas Leoncavallo's is a portrait of social misery and despair.

NOTES

1. The title *Scènes de la vie de bohème* was only acquired with a third edition in 1852.

2. Murger fancied that his name would sound more anglicized as "Henry," and easier to pronounce outside of France as "Mürger."

3. Murger refrained from using the word "novel" to describe his book. Instead, it is a compilation of impressions from a hitherto misjudged social class, whose only sin and sole quest it was to live a "free life" without preordained rules.

4. Murger presumably took the name "Mimi" (chaffinch) from Alfred de Musset's *Mimi Pinson*, written in 1845.

5. Leoncavallo draws added attention to this phrase in the score by marking it "*molto ritenuto con espressione.*"

6. Phémie Teinturière in the novel.

7. Eufemia is the only character that calls Schaunard by his Christian name.

8. Leoncavallo found inspiration for this part of the scene in chapter 5 of Murger's novel, in which Colline purchases books by Alexander Pope and Emanuel Swedenborg, in addition to one on Arabic grammar, a Malaysian dictionary, and a Chinese book. Deciding to retain the last one, Leoncavallo no doubt felt it appropriate to replace the rest with Italian literature that would find immediate recognition among 1897 audiences. Puccini has Colline buy a runic grammar book in act 2 of his opera. Countless similarities of such trifling details strengthen the assumption that Puccini may have known early on what was contained in Leoncavallo's libretto.

9. Musette, Durand, and Barbemuche are the opera's only characters that Leoncavallo has opted to call by their original names.

10. Leoncavallo introduces the characters to the audience as well as to each other in keeping with chapter 1 of Murger's novel.

11. Mimi orders a Beaune wine in the novel that she again mentions as being her favorite in chapter 20.

12. Phémie asks Mimi the question in Murger when Colline uses it in reference to Barbemuche.

13. Leoncavallo took the idea and part of the text from Murger's *Mimi Pinson est une blonde* (1845), reducing the author's six verses to two, thereby successfully retaining Murger's original meter.

14. It is Colline who mentions the term to Schaunard in the novel. Puccini would later incorporate a similar idea into act 2 of *Madama Butterfly*, when Sharpless tells Cio-Cio-San that he has not studied ornithology.

15. Leoncavallo was inspired by Marcello's telling Musette how wonderful she is ("O Musette! charmante fille") in chapter 6 of the novel, when he compares her singing to tinkling crystal. At this point, Leoncavallo makes it clear that his opera will center on the Musette/Marcello relationship, thereby contrasting with Puccini's version.

16. In the play, Musette tells Mimi that she herself is an egotist.

17. In the novel it amounts to twenty-five francs, seventy-five centimes.

18. Originally, in the novel, a palace more exquisite than Solomon's.

19. Puccini had initially planned this to be act 3 of his opera.

20. The role of Durand is vocally similar to Gaudenzio's, and can be performed by the same artist.

21. In chapter 10 of the novel it is Rodolphe who asks Schaunard—and many others—for the money.

22. In chapter 9 of the novel he retains the latest revision and destroys his earlier manuscripts, claiming to be inspired by Chatterton. Puccini's Rodolfo presumably

burns the same play during act 1.

23. A variation appears in act 1, scene 1 of the play ("Aux soleil de nos vingt ans!"), when Schaunard, Marcel, and Musette each sing a verse.

24. This is a character only mentioned by Rodolfo and Marcello in act 3 of Puccini's *La bohème* as "Mimì's foppish Viscontino."

25. There is also a slight resemblance to Musette's song "J'aime ce qui rayonne" in act 3 of the play.

26. The aria is sung to piano accompaniment.

27. This situation also takes place in act 2 of Puccini's opera, when Schaunard purchases an untuned trumpet while also commenting "Falso questo re!"

28. The entire idea of blue may be attributed as an ironic pendant to German romantic literature, specifically Novalis's *Heinrich von Ofterdingen*.

29. Leoncavallo again incorporates piano into the musical texture.

30. Murger's *Requiem for Love* will be quoted by Rodolfo later in the act.

31. To be played "Come un eco della prima volta."

32. Leoncavallo certainly found his literary inspiration in a similar letter that Marcel finds from Musette in chapter 9 of the novel.

33. Murger's bohemians share an intellectual bond with their own sex that is distinctly stronger than the manner in which they deal with their female counterparts. Thus, in the opera, Rodolfo immediately sides with Marcello, ironically referring to Mimì as a viscountess.

34. Here Leoncavallo quotes Murger's *Requiem d'amour*, which Rodolfo is writing in the opera, thereby combining fact with fiction.

35. This corresponds to act 4, scene 2 of the play ("O petite Mimi! joie de ma maison") while the bonnet is present in act 2, scene 12.

36. The composer emphasizes wind and death in an almost symbolical manner. Murger states that Francine has vowed that she will live until the trees shed their leaves. When a gale forces the last leaf from a tree onto her sickbed, Francine realizes that her life has come to an end and that she will die that very day. Death will enter as an unwelcome though not unexpected guest (Murger, chapter 18).

37. "Je n'ai pas voulu qu'il se couchât à côté de moi, voyez-vous, car il me semble que j'ai déjà les vers de la terre après mon corps."

38. Mosco Carner, *Puccini, A Critical Biography* (Surrey: Duckworth, 1974), 347.

39. Ibid.

· 16 ·

Zazà

Characters

Zazà, soprano
Anaide, mezzo-soprano
Floriana, soprano
Natalia, soprano
Signora Dufresne, soprano
Milio Dufresne, tenor
Cascart, baritone
Bussy, baritone

Malardot, tenor
Lartigon, bass
Duclou, baritone
Michelin, baritone
Marco, tenor
Courtois, baritone
Totò, spoken role

Additional roles: Claretta, Simona, two Spanish dancers, two singers in costume, two tailors, Augusto, waiter, a fireman, two clowns, a gentleman

Setting: Saint-Étienne and Paris (1898)

Pierre Berton and Charles Simon's play *Zazà*, inspired by the world of Flaubert and Zola, was first produced in Paris at the Théâtre du Vaudeville on 12 May 1898. It was written for the famous Gabrielle Réjane, "the actress who makes bad plays good."[1] Berton, both actor and playwright, created Count Ipanov in Sardou's *Fedora* and Scarpia in *La Tosca*.[2] Charles Simon was the son of Jules Simon, a senator of the Conservative Party.

Leoncavallo probably viewed *Zazà* as a contemporary continuation of *La bohème*. It would be his most modern scenario to date, as well as an authentic representation of the backstage café-concert life that he knew so well. Aware of Puccini's ability to capture the psychological development of his recent heroines (Manon Lescaut and Mimì), Leoncavallo now sought a female character

245

who would dominate the stage. His portrait of Zazà's personality, and his job of peering into the female psyche, would be his finest since Nedda in *Pagliacci*. Although he once again tried to include numerous allusions to time and place in his quest for an authentic atmosphere, the delineation of his heroine's character did not become lost in the process, as was often the case in his previous operas, including portions of *La bohème*.

Leoncavallo reduced the five-act play to three, remaining faithful to the original text, which is often quoted verbatim.[3] He chose to base the opera on the play's initial four acts, opting to delete dialogue rather than refashion it. Act 1 thus remains the longest in both the play and opera. The composer also cut down the play's original twenty-five roles to fifteen, while Italianizing some of the French names, as he had done in *La bohème*.[4] Characters in both the play and opera are only important as far as their relation to Zazà is concerned, since she is the sole force in both vehicles. The opera's protagonists "express themselves in the most straightforward, matter-of-fact kind of contemporary Italian; there is none of the florid poetry of the conventional opera libretto." They "are not exotic figures from the past, but ordinary, rather drab, contemporary human beings."[5]

Leoncavallo's *commedia lirica* is preceded by a rapturous introduction in C-major (*appassionato con fuoco*) immediately presenting us with Zazà's love theme, resembling a shot of adrenaline igniting a passionate heart. This motif—usually associated with desire—returns in E-flat major, before the music takes on a lilting and bittersweet quality. It then expands to an extended crescendo, culminating in a B-major *fortissimo* before the tempo subsides, exhausted in its languor.

The curtain rises on the backstage area of the Alcazar, a vaudeville theater in Saint-Étienne. The singer Floriana—Zazà's rival—is just concluding her performance with a sprightly melody in G-sharp minor ("So che son capricciosa e sventatella") accompanied solely by the dance hall orchestra, which develops into a rousing refrain ("Che s'io vi fo' l'occhietto, mio signor"), perfectly capturing both era and ambience.

The journalist Michelin, Courtois, the regisseur Duclou, and "a gentleman," join the chorus girl Claretta in ordering drinks from the waiter Augusto. Placards warn that "smoking is prohibited" even if many opt to ignore the rule, including the stage fireman.[6] Enthusiastic male spectators echo Floriana's refrain and later greet her backstage. The next vaudeville act consists of two clowns who can be heard until the stage orchestra is abruptly cut-off by a closed door.[7] Michelin asks Floriana whether the new "review" entitled *Il bacio*, by the journalist Bussy, will be rehearsed following the evening's performances. Floriana declares that it will be both performed and "a flop" for Zazà. She then sings an ironic and slightly grotesque *arietta* ("Zazà la vera stella") poking fun at Zazà, which is further accentuated when accompanied by the vaudeville orchestra during the clown scene. All partake in the merriment until Courtois warns that Zazà is approaching. Her entrance is illustrated by a descending chromatic pizzicato scale, leading up to her initial music in A-major that is both warm and friendly and as uncomplicated as her first words "Salute, ragazzi!" Zazà glances spitefully at Floriana on her way to her dressing room, realizing that neither Bussy nor Milio, "his faithful friend," have arrived.

Malardot—the Alcazar's manager—enters smoking a pipe as the clowns come offstage, making way for Claretta's oriental-sounding song. He is followed by the eccentric actor Lartigon, who seeks an audition. His entrance is musically highlighted (*tempo di minuetto funebre*) in E-major to a regal and macabre motif alluding to his seriousness. Although Malardot hopes that Lartigon will present a humorous soliloquy, the actor suggests Oreste's monologue on the death of Hermione from Racine's *Andromaque* (1667), *Hamlet*, and one of Bossuet's funeral orations written during the reign of Louis XIV.[8, 9] None of the selections interest Malardot, and Lartigon's protests concerning "art" are brutally interrupted when he reprimands a waiter to complain that the beer being served fails to contain sufficient froth.

Claretta's number soon ends to adoring kudos and Lartigon enters the vaudeville stage, deciding to recite from *Ruy Blas* after all. His initial words can still be discerned before the stage door closes, making all further acting attempts inaudible.

Cascart—Zazà's former lover, current colleague, and manager—now enters her dressing room, beginning the opera's first duet with a lighthearted and elegant greeting ("Buona sera, mia Zazà!"). It was Cascart who initiated Zazà's career as a music-hall performer, and he reminds her that whatever Zazà happened to earn, her mother would spend on alcohol. She warns him not to speak unkindly of Anaide nor to torment her ("Via! non mi torturare!"). This leads into her first aria, a splendid D-major *andante* ("Lo sai tu che vuol dire"), which is a sad account of her mother's difficult past devoid of either money or a husband. However, in Cascart's company, Zazà can be herself, without the anxiety that accompanies her mother's visits or her all-consuming passion for Milio. Leoncavallo was aware that the sheer grandeur of his music might inspire singers to "overdramatize," therefore noting in the score that it should be performed with "the utmost simplicity."[10] Cascart leaves Zazà to dress for her number while catcalls greet Lartigon's solo. Duclou then tries to save the show by pushing a performer dressed as a soldier on stage accompanied by the popular French military folk song "As-tu vu la casquette" in a *marziale allegro*.

Zazà admires the flowers gracing her dressing room brought by her numerous admirers, but there are none from Milio Dufresne, a handsome thirty-five-year-old Parisian businessman on whom she has set her heart.[11] An *allegro moderato* announces Anaide's entrance, humorously capturing Zazà's heavy set forty-five-year-old mother well past her prime. Her incessant heartburn is also musically illustrated, before she orders the waiter Augusto to bring her some punch. She speaks poorly of Cascart, envious that her daughter seeks only *his* influence and judgment. She has also come to ask Zazà to pay her debts. The entire duet is an informal dialogue in recitative style. When Anaide leaves, Zazà prepares her stage entrance by singing a pair of arpeggio vocalizes—both *legato* and *staccato*.

Zazà soon realizes that her rival Floriana is busy entertaining Bussy and Milio. Incensed, she makes a bet with Bussy that Milio will eventually succumb to her desires. Courtois, Cascart, and Michelin enter Zazà's dressing room and Bussy invites Milio to toast Zazà.[12] This infuriates Floriana, who insults Zazà, beginning a fight. A short quintet commences that concludes crowned by Zazà's high B-natural. She is then escorted to make her entrance as the vaudeville orchestra strikes up an orchestral ragtime.

Bussy, alone, and recalling Zazà's bet, asks Milio whether he has any interest in Zazà. Milio responds that he considers Zazà to be a dangerous conquest. He explains his apprehension in the delightful aria "È un riso gentile qual'alba d'april," that begins as an elegant and superficial *allegretto* in E-major, perfectly rendering his search for sexual gratification. This nimble, breathless, and charming solo incorporates all the graceful verve of the bel époque.

A bell sounds signaling Zazà and Cascart's "Il bacio" number, in which Leoncavallo has brilliantly succeeded in capturing a music hall atmosphere with this delightful D-major passage ("Non so capir perchè se m'ami tu") concerned with "lui" (him) giving "lei" (her) a kiss. Zazà returns to her dressing room following the number in order to prepare her next sketch, which Bussy suggests she should rehearse with Milio. This leads into the first major duet between the future lovers ("Signor, entrate") when a formal and reserved Milio cautiously enters the diva's dressing room. The music remains elusive and light in a conversational manner (*andante molto sostenuto e grazioso*), recalling the trepidation felt between Marcello and Musette in act 1 of Leoncavallo's *La bohème*. Zazà comes straight to the point, prodding Milio as to whether he fancies Floriana. This gives way to Zazà's initial seduction attempt incorporating the magical phrase "C'è un uomo al mondo che è tutto per me!"

Milio responds tentatively to Zazà's forthright manner, suggesting they rehearse her upcoming appearance instead. Undaunted, she commands him to unzip her corset. (This is recreated in the orchestra by a violin playing a descending chromatic scale marked "*scivolando*.") The music glows in autumnal shades of E-major when Milio sings a scintillating passage ("Scusate; non ho pratica, son così poco destro!") concerning his awkwardness, a motif that will again return to mark their love later in the opera. Zazà adopts the melody "as if in ecstasy," although this second attempt is cut short when Milio pricks himself on a pin. Zazà, donning a dressing gown, sits close to Milio, exclaiming that his hair "shines like gold," whereupon she runs her fingers through his "unwanted grey." The orchestra intensifies into a forceful *crescendo* that reprises the love motif. Zazà's efforts are then cut short when a bell reminds her that she is due on stage.[13] Milio suddenly kisses her on the neck as she sings the love motif for the first time in its original key ("Ah! . . . Perché, cattivo, non me l'avevi prima tu detto?") before being joined in song by Milio. Finally, she runs to make her entrance, bubbling with joy and chirping like a bird.

Act 2 opens in Zazà's modestly furnished living room in St. Étienne six months later.[14] A voluptuously warm lullaby-like rhythm in F-major suggests that a fulfilling *nuit d'amour* has just ended in its relaxed complacency.

The curtain rises, revealing Milio reclining on a chaise longue with Zazà standing beside him. The *berceuse* continues as Milio tells Zazà that he will not be able to take her to America for the three or four months that he will be away on business. Zazà seductively responds in the C-major *cantabile* "Quando vai a Parigi" that she only lives for Milio, and that even his Parisian sojourns seem an eternity.[15] These inspired pages highlight the work in their tender passion, and are supported by legato strings performing "like a murmur." Zazà's phrases are echoed in the orchestra before she once again sings the more nostalgic second part of her theme, "Milio, mi sembran mille giorni."

The music then modulates to E-major, employing a halting dance rhythm ("Quattro mesi a domandarmi: tornerà?") expressing Zazà's anxiety about Milio's return. It will be heard again later in the opera. She recalls their first kiss as the orchestra responds with her motif. Her aria concludes to heavy, languid chords inducing Milio to utter his beloved's name in Tristanesque rapture. Zazà finally convinces Milio to postpone the America voyage, falling into his arms and emitting a high A to an exuberant orchestral repetition (*appassionato con fuoco*) of her love motif.

Milio must leave for Paris, and Zazà calls to her maid Natalia to bring his hat and coat, promising to meet him later at the station. She watches him from the window to a bittersweet E-major *sostenuto* of her theme, that remains one of the score's most unforgettable and magical moments, commenting on his aristocratic bearing that is "kind, honest, and true." The situation strongly resembles that of Arabella's watching Mandryka cross the street from her window in act 1 of the Strauss opera that would premiere more than three decades later.[16]

Anaide makes an inopportune visit, unable to utter a word when Zazà leaves. She discusses a change in Zazà's personality with Natalia since her affair with Milio. Although Anaide is also jealous of Cascart for having separated her from her daughter, he now seems better than Milio in her estimation.[17]

Cascart arrives and awaits Zazà in Anaide's presence. She tries to break the silence by clearing her throat.[18] Leoncavallo accompanies this extended scene with a gavotte that stresses the situation's irony and unintentional humor. Zazà returns in good spirits after having seen Milio off. She laughs on staccato notes (which Leoncavallo had previously employed in *La bohème*) upon seeing the two archenemies—Anaide and Cascart—together. Anaide exits to an adjoining room, leaving Cascart and Zazà to converse in private. The Zazà/Cascart duet ("Cascart, mio camerata") begins in a conversational manner, with the diva demonstrating no interest in two theatrical engagements Cascart feels she should accept. She also refuses to renew her contract—for double the fee—at the Alcazar, wishing to remain free in order to join Milio in America. Cascart comforts her, in the aria "Buona Zazà del mio buon tempo" in B-flat major.[19] This extremely short yet highly affectionate display of genuine friendship evokes the all-embracing and selfless sincerity of Cascart's relationship with Zazà. Leoncavallo has Cascart sing the words "buona/buon" twice in one phrase, stressing the heroine's goodness, and, above all, her naiveté regarding Milio, insisting that her affair is merely "a passing fancy" that will damage her career and that she must remain as free as a bird.[20] The act 1 "Il bacio" music is heard when Cascart implores Zazà not to abandon her profession, reminding her that she once loved him and that that passion has now also passed. Bursting out on a high A echoed by three chords, Zazà brutally declares that she never loved Cascart. She liked him since he helped her, but the sensual passion that she now experiences for the first time with Milio is different, perhaps because of his elevated social status.[21] With an intense outpouring to her own love motif, she declares that she defies God to take Milio from her. Cascart, in a final effort, reveals that Milio has a mistress in Paris. Zazà is mortified. She sings a high B-flat that falls to a low F as she clutches her heart. Cascart confides that he saw Milio one evening with a woman at the theater.[22] Curiously, Leoncavallo opts for Daland's music in act 2 of *Der Fliegende Holländer* when musically sketching Madame Dufresne ("Pareva una moglietta").

Zazà's innate sadness soon expresses itself in anger and fury when Anaide returns from the adjoining room to the earlier heard gavotte. Her mother is barely able to conceal her elation upon discovering Milio's infidelity. Leoncavallo now provides Zazà with a brief moment of introspective lyricism in the heartbreaking passage "No, non dovea tradirmi!" that begins in E-minor to a somber *andantino mosso* accompaniment. The vocal line rises and blossoms when Zazà recalls that she loved Milio without demanding his faithfulness. Returning to E-minor ("Se fede avria serbato!"), there follows a strong similarity to the jailor's music in act 3 of Puccini's *Tosca*,[23] which, of course, was premiered the same year. This touching passage concludes when Zazà falls into Cascart's arms, thrice bemoaning her suffering ("quanto soffro!"), before suddenly deciding to leave for Paris. Anaide reminds her to think of her dignity, which prompts Zazà's reply that, in fact, she hasn't any. Calling for Natalia, she dresses to a short hectic trio before leaving,[24] claiming that Milio will have to make a decision.[25]

Act 3 is introduced by a tranquil Massenet-inspired *preludietto* in A-major (*andante sostenuto*) creating the atmosphere of an aristocratic Paris heightened by arpeggios evoking a sunset on the Seine. Leoncavallo opts for a very elegant apartment on the Quai Mazarin. In the play, however, the authors' stress that Bernard's (Milio's) home is arranged tastefully, though not as luxuriously as the opera's third-floor apartment at 89 rue de Châteaudun in the ninth arondisse-ment.[26]

Washerwomen from the river below can be heard singing in the background complemented by an echo effect to harp accompaniment. A sad, almost medieval sounding melody begins, expressing Milio's solitude before developing into his daughter's (Totò's) motif (*teneramente*), a simple and tender phrase coupled with an engaging sense of calm. Leoncavallo has also provided the washerwomen with a text that, while resembling a Provençal song in A-major, also reflects Milio's emotional state. It deals with the story of a certain Margot who was deserted by her lover ("Perchè soletta sei laggiù? Margot? Margot?"). The song has a peculiar veiled quality that makes it especially captivating and memorable.

The curtain rises to an equally dreamy legato in A-minor, revealing Milio seated at a small cluttered table mourning his sadness at the thought of returning to Saint-Étienne to take leave of Zazà forever,[27] a decision resulting from the realization of her increasing attachment. Milio, undecided about how he will relate the truth, sings to an accompaniment that mirrors his hesitancy and apprehension with "tortured" chromatic variations ("Il labbro mio"), musically recalling Marcello's lines prior to his aria "Musette! O gioia della mia dimora" during act 3 of *La bohème*. Leoncavallo returns to E-flat minor to commence Milio's aria "Mai più Zazà." This elegiac lament is fascinating in its passive regret. When Italianate passion dominates the lyrical French vein as Milio recalls Zazà's voice and kisses ("Oh, baci! Oh nostre tenere ebbrezze!"), Leoncavallo demonstrates his innate ability to compose sweeping phrases that, while admittedly brief, do not fail to rival those of Puccini and Mascagni in their melodic invention. Milio, aware that his love is condemned, repeats the phrase "Il nostro amore è naufragato!" twice to a rising *tessitura* in an effort to resolve his unhappiness. The aria concludes with its initial words ("Mai più!") reflecting his inability to reach a solution.

Madame Dufresne enters, offering to accompany her husband to the station. She reminds their servant, Marco,[28] that she is expecting a certain "Madame Dunoyer," that he must welcome should she return late. The Dufresnes exit, leaving Marco free to smoke Milio's cigars and to read his newspaper; he is particularly interested in the politics of the relatively unstable France of 1900.[29] Washerwomen are heard again singing their mournful song preshadowing the events to come.[30]

Intense chords announce Zazà's arrival together with Natalia. She gains entrance by claiming that *she* is the expected "Madame Dunoyer" whom Marco mentions.[31] Zazà studies the furnishings with jealousy, imagining Milio's romantic trysts enacted in the luxurious surroundings.[32] She then "discovers" a letter on the table addressed to "Madame Dufresne." Reading it—to Natalia's consternation—Zazà finally realizes that Milio is indeed married and that Cascart in fact told the truth.[33] Zazà refuses to leave the apartment even after Natalia begs her to do so. Pulsating chords present a pitiable portrait of Zazà's relentlessly clinging to a lost romance as her motif is heard.

Totò (Antonietta), Milio's seven-year-old daughter, enters, and the orchestra grows calm, resuming the *preludietto* music that opened the act. Zazà soon recognizes her as Milio's offspring. Totò is a spoken role and the composer took great care that her text be employed naturally. Her motif, an *andante sostenuto* in F-major is now heard, and Zazà immediately associates her with the apparition of a celestial being, a significant metaphor considering that she will change both Zazà's life and her opinion of love.

It seems that Zazà experiences fleeting maternal feelings, becoming a child to Totò's pressing questions of who she is and why she is lying. Zazà's vulgarity is stressed in the play, when Totò says that she is certainly *not* Madame Dunoyer, since the latter is very "proper" and does not have dyed red hair. Leoncavallo deletes this, preferring to reinforce the audience's sympathetic association with his heroine.

Totò represents the image of how Zazà herself would have liked to be as a child, with both a mother *and* father. She essentially considers herself an orphan, not believing that Anaide was an adequate mother. Totò also weighs on Zazà's conscience by telling her that she spent six months with her mother in Algeria during the time of the Zazà-Milio affair. She forces Zazà to think about how empty her life is. Zazà, admitting to the child that she is both "alone" and "abandoned," begins an aria in E-minor describing her sad childhood ("Mamma usciva di casa . . .") that exudes child-like innocence. For Zazà, the realization of not having had a father was traumatic, and she tells Totò that it is the worst misfortune that can beset a child. This is directly taken from act 3, scene 4, of the play:

> Totò: Les petits enfants qui n'ont pas de papa?
> Zazà: Oui, c'est le plus grand malheur qui puisse arriver à un petit enfant.

This heartwrenching phrase in E-major is transformed into the opera's "Questa per un fanciullo è la più gran sventura!" Zazà bursts into tears—noticed by Totò—and changes the subject by suggesting that the girl perform something on the piano. Totò plays an unspecified selection in the original. In the opera, however, Leoncavallo needed a musical basis to accompany Zazà's upcoming aria. The composer's choice of Cherubini's *Ave Maria* in F-major also reinforced Zazà's association of the child being an angel, appearing in her life warning her to change course. Totò's insistence that the *Ave Maria* is her mother's favorite, also conjures images of Madame Dufresne, the "innocent wife," in contrast to Zazà, who has a past.

When Totò begins playing, Zazà is able to continue her thoughts ("È finita! Ammogliato! . . . Ammogliato") regarding her lover's marriage.[34] Believing that it was all a dream, her voice rises just as simply and delicately as Totò's playing. She draws a comparison between women born to luxury (Madame Dufresne) and shielded from all hardship to become mothers—another allusion to the *Ave Maria*—as opposed to the suffering of those (Zazà) raised in cold and hunger, weary of so much misfortune that they seek any means of escape. Totò's playing ends parallel to the conclusion of Zazà's most famous aria, "Dir che ci sono al mondo," based on her monologue "Tout est fini! Ce n'est pas assez qu'il soit marié," in the play. Leoncavallo has supplied religious-sounding chords (*quasi religioso*) when Totò insists that, unlike in the play, Zazà should kiss her.

The world returns in the form of Madame Dufresne, and an embarrassed Zazà tells the astonished woman that she was pleasantly conversing with her daughter after having entered the wrong apartment since her name is also "Dunoyer." The theme of Zazà's arietta "Mamma usciva di casa" accompanies her words as she relates her conversation with Totò. All formality is broken when Zazà takes leave of Totò with a tender and passionate embrace. The act ends to a reprisal of Zazà's earlier "Questa per un fanciullo è la più gran sventura!" in E-major.

Act 4 commences with bleak chords forming a *sostenuto malinconico*. The scene is in Zazà's "salon" as in act 2.[35] Anaide and Malardot hope that Zazà will return soon, since her cancellations are costing him a fortune. Zazà arrives with Natalia and Cascart. She dismisses everyone, realizing that Malardot wants her to resume her career at the Alcazar. Cascart then tries to comfort Zazà in the aria "Zazà, piccola zingara," a charming and affectionate *andantino* in D-flat major. The importance of Zazà's encounter with Totò is stressed when Cascart mentions that "an angel's hand" has indeed saved her, while the solo concludes with the "questa per un fanciullo è la più gran sventura!" music in D-flat major. Cascart reminds Zazà that it is her duty to leave Milio because he is married, and that she should inform him by letter. Instead, she prefers to await his return from Lyon in order to tell him personally. Zazà promises to follow Cascart's advice. Milio is suddenly heard arriving as she sends Cascart away.

When Milio asks what is troubling her, she sings a haunting and extended *largo triste* concerning a dream she had that he no longer loved her ("Tu non m'amavi più"). This lament in E-minor, sung as if in a trance, is as captivating as it is unforgettable, and, arguably, one of the most beautiful passages written by the composer. Zazà repeats the words "mai più" twice toward the aria's center, recalling the conclusion of Milio's "Mai più, Zazà" of act 2. Now that her forebodings seem justified, the passage takes on an uncanny quality with its dance-like rhythm again presented in E-major, as it was the first time, only to an altered text.

Zazà tries to lighten the mood by asking whether Milio is hungry. His reply, "come un poeta" (like a poet), evokes tremolo chords recalling *La bohème*. Small talk continues during the dinner to a *Pagliacci*-like accompaniment. When Milio again speaks of his departure, Zazà, unable to control herself, declares that he is lying, and, on a high B, claims that he will be leaving with his wife. She explains that his inability to speak the truth has injured her most. She tells Milio in a delicate *largo* passage that he should never have entered her life.

Much of the music that follows seems uninspired, until Milio pledges his love, to Zazà's motif. When the subject turns to Totò (to a harp accompaniment), an enraged Milio demands to know if Zazà has in fact seen his daughter. Although Zazà readily admits that she said nothing to his wife regarding their relationship, Milio brutally informs her of the differences between being a mistress and being Madame Dufresne. Understandably furious, Zazà bursts into an angry and appropriately rugged *allegretto* in C-minor, claiming that, in essence, she is nothing but a dirty secret. She taunts him by claiming to have told Madame Dufresne everything about their relationship, as her love motif resounds in an altered and deformed C-minor, completely shattered and robbed of its beauty ("I nostri baci, l'ardente affetto").

Milio responds by calling her a slut as he throws her to the floor, hardly awaiting Zazà's pitiful reply "Oh, come l'ami lei!!" (Oh, how you love her!!).[36] He then begins a dramatic *largo* containing an abundance of high B's. Zazà finally speaks the truth that she has, in fact, said nothing to his wife. She asks him to leave, realizing that he seemingly loves his wife (or his sense of duty) more than he does her.[37] The orchestra resounds with a magnificent *sostenuto* in E-major when Milio leaves, just as it originally did to accompany his exit in act 2. Knowing that she has sent him away, perhaps forever, she runs to the door and then the entrance hall calling his name, and, finally, that all important window of act 2. Nervous chords underpin Zazà's frantic and desperate pleas. Her love theme is resurrected upon seeing Milio a final time from the window before losing sight of her lover to the same text as in act 2. She again echoes the words "Mai più! ... Mai più!" from Milio's act 3 aria before uttering a poignant "Tutto è finito!" prompting a forceful crescendo in E-major, bringing one of Leoncavallo's most important and successful operas to a riveting close.[38]

Zazà is the chronicle of an affair that has indelibly changed its heroine's conception of love and life. Influenced by Puccini and Massenet's probing into the feminine psyche, Leoncavallo was perhaps most guided by the latter composer's 1898 *Sapho* (based on Daudet), which treats a similar subject. *Zazà* represents Leoncavallo's last successful full-length verismo opera and presents the listener with some of the best his art has to offer. Unlike those of many of his other works, *Zazà's* character emerges as an entirely believable personage. Her actions and thoughts involve the spectator to a far greater extent than some of the numerous protagonists that would follow in the composer's canon.

Zazà is a tender, rapturous, beguiling, and intimate musical expression of the dying fin de siècle. There is an inspirational brilliance and glow to the score that reminds one of a continuous Nedda/Silvio duet. It is a cameo of a small part of Zazà's life and she is the raison d'être for a work that is more complex than an initial hearing suggests. It is a superbly constructed score with a wealth of psychological insight, tied together by a well-developed scheme of motifs. Was the real Zazà Suzanne Reichenberg of the Comédie-Française, and was Cascart modeled on Coquelin Cadet? Leoncavallo certainly felt a particular affinity for Milio, as he strolls through the backstage area seeking adventure. *Zazà* is a superb musical portrait of the composer's Parisian years, perfectly in keeping with his dramatic talent.

NOTES

1. Réjane was forty-two years old when she first performed Zazà in 1898. By the end of the year the play had already received some 103 performances.

2. Berton was also Sarah Bernhardt's leading man and lover during her engagement at the Odéon. She also appeared in his play *Léna*.

3. It is still a matter of conjecture whether Carlo Zangarini should be given credit. It seems highly probable that Zangarini was in fact Leoncavallo's collaborator, if not the sole author of *Zazà's* libretto, considering its similarity to the *Conchita* text he later authored for Casa Ricordi.

4. "Bernard Dufresne" became "Milio Dufresne" (perhaps for reasons of vocalism), "Clairette" was changed to "Claretta," while "Anaïs" emerged as "Anaide." In keeping with the play, no one but Milio had the honor of both Christian and surname, while his wife remains solely "Madame Dufresne" in order to lend her a degree of anonymity.

5. Robert Connolly in the liner notes to the MRF *Zazà* recording.

6. Leoncavallo has retained this detail from the original play.

7. Similar to Scarpia's closing the window during Tosca's singing in act 2 of Puccini's opera that premiered the same year.

8. Jacques Bossuet (1627–1704).

9. Leoncavallo substituted these works from the play's *La Grève des forgerons* (1869) by François Coppée (1842–1908) and *Les Catacombes de Rome* by the Abbé Jacques Delille (1738–1813).

10. Leoncavallo's *Zazà*, piano/vocal score (1900), 47.

11. An acquaintance Bussy met three weeks earlier, we are informed in the play.

12. This music recalls the overture to Smetana's *Bartered Bride*.

13. In the play, Zazà even sprays perfume into Milio's handkerchief.

14. The fact that a period of six months separate act 1 and act 2 is only discernible from the play.

15. This passage greatly resembles some of Magda's music in Puccini's later *La rondine*.

16. Leoncavallo was inspired by the play, where the scene takes place in act 2, scene 2, corresponding to the heroine's monologue "Il s'en va, il s'en va à Paris." Leoncavallo chooses to omit Berton and Simon's entire second and third scene of act 2, when Zazà speaks of her love for Milio to her girlfriend and ex-colleague Simone, proceeding directly to scene 4 of the play.

17. In the play Anaïs already has a future suitor lined up for Zazà in the form of Monsieur Dubuisson.

18. In the play Cascart smokes incessantly.

19. Leoncavallo was inspired for this aria by Cascart's lines in act 2, scene 7, of the play: "Voyons, Zazà, ma petite Zazà, ne nous fâchons pas. Je suis ton ami, tu sais, ton vieux camarade, je ne viens pas te faire des scènes de jalousie bête. Non, ça n'est pas à moi que je pense, c'est à toi."

20. The essence of this scene is quite similar to what Colautti and Cilèa would write for Adriana and Michonnet in act 4 of *Adriana Lecouvreur* (1902).

21. In the play Zazà tells Cascart that he speaks of her love for Milio like a blind man describing colors.

22. This takes place eight days earlier in the original play.

23. Immediately preceding 5.

24. This trio seems to have been modeled on act 2 of Puccini's *Manon Lescaut* when the Prévost heroine gathers her jewels in a thwarted attempt to escape with Des Grieux.

25. Zazà is accompanied by Simone and not Natalia in the play, while Cascart brings her to the station.

26. In the play, Bernard's wife haughtily gives orders to her servants, who later gossip about her unkindness, enabling the audience to fully sympathize with Milio's amorous conquests elsewhere. Bernard has, in fact, already left on a business trip to Lyon and does not appear in the act at all.

27. Like Massenet's "Adieu, notre petite table" in *Manon*, Milio's scene begins by his singing to his own table, employing the similar words, "O mio piccolo tavolo ingombrato."

28. The maids Mélanie and Juliette in the play.

29. Most of the original text written for the opera not found in the play was created for this scene.

30. In B-major this time.

31. It is unfortunate that Leoncavallo failed to seek a variation for this very contrived idea that robs the scene of its credibility.

32. Zazà immediately notices the piano in the play, realizing that a woman decorated the house, since Milio only plays the instrument "with one finger."

33. The chords from *Der Fliegende Holländer* reappear again as she recalls Cascart's words.

34. Leoncavallo was no doubt inspired by Giordano's onstage piano in act 2 of *Fedora*.

35. In the play, Anaïs and Dubuisson—the suitor she favors for Zazà—await the diva's return from Paris. Leoncavallo decided to replace him with the character of Malardot in the opera.

36. An ironic twist to a similar situation, when Zangarini also has Conchita respond to Mateo in the final act of Zandonai's *Conchita*: "O Mateo, come tu mi ami!" ("Oh Mateo, how you love me!") after striking her.

37. The play overflows with accusations.

38. The play includes an additional act taking place three years later, when Zazà is a successful and wealthy artist, with offers coming from New York to earn a hundred thousand francs monthly. She is now under Dubuisson's influence. He credits himself with having discovered her. There is another meeting with Bernard, and although she admits that she still loves him, she refuses his offer to begin a relationship anew for the few weeks that he will be in France, after having taken up residence with his family in the United States. (Realizing that no one knew anything of his affair, he returned to Zazà's house, although she had left Saint-Étienne without a forwarding address.) She tells him that they have both changed, sending him away for a second time and asking that he greet Totò for her.

· 17 ·

Der Roland von Berlin

Characters

Kurfürst Friedrich, bass[1]
Johannes Rathenow, baritone
Elsbeth Rathenow, soprano
Henning Mollner, tenor
Thomas Wintz, baritone
Makensprung, baritone
Bartolomäus Schum, bass[2]
Eva, soprano
Melchior, baritone
Hans Ferbirt, baritone

Mattäus, baritone
Mathias Blankenfeld, tenor[3]
Civele Baruch, tenor
Der Bajazzo, tenor
Gertrud, mezzo-soprano
Bergholz, baritone
Der Ausrufer des Rates, baritone
Conrad von Knipprode, baritone
(Konrad) Ryke, bass

Additional roles: town councilors of Cölln and Berlin, citizens, the Kurfürst's Knights

Setting: Berlin (1442)

Although Leoncavallo only labored on *Der Roland von Berlin* sporadically—composing *Zazà* in the interim—the opera profited from a decade of germination. Wilhelm II essentially wanted a German *I Medici*, and if the opera initially resembles that work with a similarly bombastic prelude, a closer look demonstrates that *Der Roland von Berlin*'s musical as well as dramaturgical structure is much more tightly knit than its earlier counterpart. However, it is unfortunate that what inevitably worked against Leoncavallo's intimate art, was a forced striving for epic grandeur that was expected of him in his Hohenzollern opera. Fortunately, and unlike *I Medici*, where such an attempt was only partially successful at best, *Der Roland von Berlin* marks a largely positive approach to Leoncavallo's form of Grand Opera.

The scenario essentially deals with the early years of Berlin's history, when the towns of Alt-Cölln (1237) and Alt-Berlin (1244) were founded.[4] These twin settlements soon became rivals with incessant feuds. In 1307, Margrave Hermann was able to unite them, and a common city hall was erected on the Lange Brücke—the bridge crossing the river Spree connecting the two towns. Although the statue of Roland is omnipresent throughout the opera, lending the work its name, present audiences largely unfamiliar with the Alexis novel—contrary to those at the time of its premiere—need to be reminded that the statue is a symbol of municipal independence. However, its presence in the novel is not particularly positive, since it symbolizes the rigid and unyielding patrician families of the Rathenows and Schums, contrasting with the innovative strength of Henning, who is initially heralded as being a new Roland in act 1. In chapter 4, Alexis describes the statue's face sporting a "large ugly mouth" with blank eyes, while in chapter 37, Roland is defined as a "symbol of a city's bloodshed." Alexis further states that Roland was supposedly a heartless Franconian prince. Thus, on Judgment Day, Saint Peter said, "You are stone—those made of stone cannot find entrance in heaven." He touched himself and found that he had indeed hardened into stone, so he returned to earth to watch over squares and city halls, where laws were made in a heathen manner. Legend has it that he is condemned to remain immobile until the patrician families no longer reign. When the mayor, Johannes Rathenow, suggests that the statue will forever remain where it is, his aunt, Gertrud, whose presence in both novel and opera resembles an Erda or Norn-like character capable of predicting the future, comments that the statue will eventually become "rubble and dust," thereby leading to Kurfürst Friedrich II's eventual successful quest to unite the city's two sections.

Statues of Roland were to be found in the main squares of many northern German towns, such as Bremen, Halle, Nordhausen, Magdeburg, Brandenburg, and Perleberg. They were supposedly later attributed to the Roland saga (*Chanson de Roland*). Leoncavallo took great pains to acquaint himself with these legends, basing a portion of his knowledge on *Die Rolande Deutschlands*, published by a Berlin historical society in 1890.

Since *Der Roland von Berlin* was tailored to be a Grand Opera in four acts, Leoncavallo began the work with a prelude—his longest and most impressive—incorporating the opera's major themes (*sinfonia*).[5] It commences "like a whisper" with a barely audible *nobile molto sostenuto* played by the harps in D-major. Trumpets then sound from the stage with a shimmering and slightly eerie modulation in a crescendo (*dolce ma sentito*) leading to an F-sharp minor *squillante* followed by a diminuendo.[6] This is the "patrician theme,"[7] which will repeatedly return, signifying the rigidity and damning pride of both the Rathenows and Schums. Drumrolls bring the music to a *fortissimo* before the theme is again taken up. The second motif (*grandioso*), which I will term "victory," remains associated with freedom throughout the opera. Its military character in B-major introduces the bombastic, hymn-like *teco sarem*[8] motif in act 1, which originally appeared in Part I of *Séraphitus-Séraphita*. The third "conflict" motif (*allegro giusto*) is then immediately taken up in E-minor, representing the rivalry between the towns of Cölln and Berlin.[9] Changing to A-minor, the theme is echoed in the treble prior to reappearing in the bass, where it is followed by *angoscioso* chords recalling the opening pages of Wagner's *Die Walküre*. It develops into Henning's sweeping theme, which will be the opera's major tune beginning in G-major, symbolizing Henning's youthful idealism and fervor combined with his strength to change old ways. *La nuit de mai* inspired the prelude's fifth motif (*sostenuto assai*), which symbolizes Henning's love for Elsbeth, a sequence that was also used with minimal variation in the Giuliano/Simonetta love duet in act 1 of *I Medici*. This motif in F-sharp major will later be vocalized during the Elsbeth/Henning duet in act 1 as well as the more extended love duet of act 2. The conflict theme is then again taken up *con vigore* in its original E-minor key. A *vivo* section marks the beginning of a Verdian finale, before introducing the prelude's final theme depicting Kurfürst Friedrich, which will also conclude the opera. This Prussian-sounding march (*marziale sostenuto e grandioso*) derived from a German song originating in 1577.

Act 1 begins with voices heard offstage singing the *Veni Creator* to organ accompaniment from the Nicholas Church.[10] It is early afternoon on the main square, which sports a huge statue of Roland (Alexis, 4). The scene shows a tavern, Mayor Johannes Rathenow's home, the Lange Brücke, which leads to the city hall, and the barber Ferbirt's house and salon. The congregation proceeds to sing an enlightened-sounding *moderato religioso*, interrupted by youths ordering drinks at the tavern. Ferbirt shaves some clients while Henning, a young weaver, watches the proceedings on what Leoncavallo describes as a "beautiful February day."[11] Henning laughs at the conclusion of one of Ferbirt's stories and then takes a seat in the tavern.[12] However, his interest is suddenly directed toward the church, where Elsbeth, the mayor's attractive daughter, is attending Mass. Ferbirt continues to shave a customer while the men at the tavern sing a German drinking song ("Sin che il vin del Reno brilla nel bicchiere come l'or") dating from 1500.

A disguised Kurfürst Friedrich enters, accompanied by Count Conrad von Knipprode, to his theme in D-flat major. He suddenly eyes the Roland statue, wondering why citizens would choose to retain it in their midst. An *andante religioso* in G-major sounds from the organ. When Count Knipprode addresses Friedrich by his formal title, the latter quickly reminds him that he must retain his anonymity in order to witness, at first hand, the rivalry between the citizens of Berlin and Cölln, in the hope of uniting them.

Angry voices are heard coming from the Lange Brücke. Hans Makensprung, a ravaged-looking merchant, arrives followed by a large crowd, explaining that he has been beaten and robbed by bandits in the forest near Spandau. He complains that he was even scoffed at when seeking help, the city councilors insinuating that he was in fact too poor to be able to demand justice. Henning retorts, in an ironic and spirited aria touching on operetta ("Essi discutono con somma gravità"), that the city council ceaselessly discusses and debates without, however, ever reaching a conclusion (Alexis, 20). Makensprung decides to take the matter into his own hands, setting off to see the Kurfürst personally (accompanied by his theme in B-major), unaware that he is in fact standing in their midst.

Henning, however, believes he can help Makensprung without the Kurfürst's intervention, rousing the crowd by singing the victory motif with "poetry and enthusiasm." He implores them to unite and search out the robbers, offering help and protection to those in need. This is sung to Henning's own motif for the first time, an enthusiastic and heroic melody in E-major ("Per quella legge che il debole oppresso").[13] The chorus responds like willing soldiers in a renewed, almost warlike reprisal of the victory motif (*guerriero e maestoso*), promising to follow Henning as their new Roland (Alexis, 18).

Although the score makes no mention of Henning's past, the novel explains that his father saved Mayor Rathenow's life, dying in the process. Rathenow saw to it that Henning was raised in his own home together with his daughter, Elsbeth. The city owes Henning the sum of "47 Böhmische Groschen" (forty-seven Bohemian pennies) in compensation for the loss of his father. However, Henning never received the amount, and is therefore anxious that Berlin/Cölln be governed by a more just system—the entire crux of the opera.

A trumpet announces the town crier, who declares that the "prostitute" Salomé will be led through the city to be flogged, temporarily subduing the crowd's fervor. We are told in the novel that Salomé had been employed in the Rathenow household, where the mayor's son seduced her.[14] She is to be punished after having had the "audacity" to greet Elsbeth on a public street (Alexis, 4). This all serves to further demonstrate the unjust way in which Berlin/Cölln is being governed.

The disguised Kurfürst now asks Ferbirt who Henning is. Their dialogue is interrupted when Elsbeth is seen leaving the church. The blonde and blue-eyed eighteen-year-old girl drops her prayer book upon seeing Henning, who then returns it to her. This initiates their love duet with a tender and gracious melody beginning in A-flat major, with Henning invoking her name ("Ave,

Alda di Rathenow").[15] Elsbeth soon tells him that her father, the mayor, will try and enable the young man's payment in the city council. This is sung to her own motif ("Il dritto tuo difendere"). She asks him to trust her father and to come to her home that evening. Henning replies that he will be leaving shortly to fight for justice, as the victory motif is heard.[16] When Elsbeth asks why Henning would wish to risk his life, he enthusiastically speaks of his mission. Shades of Chatterton's idealistic romanticism now emerge when Henning hopes that success and glory will enable him to be united with Elsbeth. The love motif (*assai amoroso*) then sounds for the first time since the prelude, when Elsbeth gives Henning her prayer book as a symbol of her love.

Elsbeth enters her house and Ferbirt asks Henning whether a simple weaver has the right to generate such conflict ("Ma un lanajuolo ha dritto a far giustizia?"). Leoncavallo underlines the word "weaver" with the "Summ' und Brumm' du gutes Rädchen" chorus from act 2 of *Der Fliegende Holländer*. When Henning again complains of the town council's uselessness, the disguised Kurfürst responds that he should present the matter to a higher level—to the Kurfürst himself. Henning nevertheless prefers to rely on himself, and Friedrich severely warns him not to become involved with the Kurfürst's rule, since he has been selected by divine right. Henning is at odds with the city council, though not with the Kurfürst. Friedrich repeats his warning to ominous chords resembling Siegfried's dragon motif.

Their conversation is interrupted by the sound of drums, hunting horns, and flutes playing a lively F-major dance, which Leoncavallo took from an English song that British touring groups made popular in Germany during the 1700s.[17] The stage soon fills with citizens greeting a cart sporting a huge puppet with four arms and legs that seemingly devours everything in its way (Alexis 8), accompanied by a man dressed as a clown.[18] The chorus asks what the meaning of the puppet is, interspersed with shouts of "carnival." The clown replies in an A-flat major *saltarello* that it represents the city councils of Berlin and Cölln,[19] before feeding its huge mouth with money bags. When the puppet motions for more, the clown symbolically feeds it petitions and protests. Henning of course immediately asks the puppet when he will finally receive his "20,000 Groschen."[20] When the puppet motions that it is still hungry, the crowd, led by Henning, calls for its death. The clown then produces a wooden sword and decapitates the puppet (Alexis, 8) as Johannes Rathenow appears, comprehending the situation. He warns "the vulgar mob" not to profane the symbol of their city. Neither the clown nor the populace is impressed, as the *saltarello* again resumes, until Rathenow suggests that the clown will be hanged unless he ceases. The clown laughs it off as a jest, asking Rathenow when Henning will be paid. Rathenow pledges to personally come up with the sum since Cölln refuses (Alexis 3, 5). The crowd is outraged, and considers tossing Rathenow into the river Spree. Henning helps Rathenow seek refuge in the church, echoing that only the Kurfürst may bring about change and not the citizens themselves. Attention is then diverted when Salomé returns from her flogging to an exotic-sounding *marcia funebre*. All follow her out as the stage darkens.

Impressed by Henning's courage, the Kurfürst asks the young man to help him leave the city unnoticed. Henning motions the Kurfürst to a boat docked behind Ferbirt's house. When the Kurfürst offers money, the young man rejects it, replying (to the *saltarello*) that he cannot devour it like the puppet. Rather than money, Henning would like to count on the Kurfürst's help, should he ever be in need (Alexis, 10). The Kurfürst is duly impressed by Henning's modesty (expressed in a rousing *quasi marziale*), and offers him a knighthood. He also suggests that Henning track down Makensprung's bandits since "the Kurfürst" would approve. He then secretly entrusts Henning with his identity as he exits to his own theme. The victory motif resumes when Henning fondly kisses Elsbeth's prayer book, wondering whether he will indeed become a knight.[21]

Act 2 takes place one month later in Rathenow's home. The statue of Roland is seen lit by the glowing reflection of the church windows. An extremely forceful C-minor *maestoso* (later also used for *Edipo re*) evoking Rathenow's inner conflict sets the scene. The somber "patrician" motif beginning in C-major and modulating into E-minor is then heard. Rathenow is in the midst of a conversation with Konrad Ryke, a Berlin city councilor, who tells him that the petition to pay Henning has ultimately been rejected, since Cölln felt Henning to be sufficiently wealthy and the Berliners were outnumbered (Alexis, 23). Ryke leaves as the orchestra plays Elsbeth's motif "as if in a dream," while a perplexed Rathenow stares out of the window, asking the statue of Roland for help as church bells mark the hour.

His old servant Mattäus enters, announcing that a man who will not reveal his name is waiting to speak with him. It is Salomé's father Civele Baruch who now enters.[22] Baruch plays an important part in the novel, since he predicts a long-awaited social change that will relieve the poor and provide tolerance (Alexis, 10). The operatic Baruch, on the other hand, is an ominous character recalling *Chatterton*'s Skirner. His theme, an *andante sostenuto*, is reinforced by constantly modulating keys. When Rathenow requests money to pay Henning, Baruch, aware that the Kurfürst appeared incognito and that his power will soon end, wonders whether Rathenow will in fact be capable of reimbursing him. Rathenow then produces a bejeweled necklace, to no avail. Leaving, Baruch furiously asks the desperate mayor how he has the audacity to ask for his help when Baruch's daughter, Salomé, has recently been flogged. He predicts Rathenow's fall, while the mayor hopes to at least save Elsbeth the approaching shame ("In essa or è tutta la mia famiglia!").

Alone, Rathenow begins his superb D-flat major aria "Dio che non vedo," a touching *affettuoso sostenuto* in the form of a prayer, asking God to forgive him if his governing has indeed been too severe. The key changes as Rathenow now becomes a Verdian father worried about his daughter, imploring God not to forsake her in phrases worthy of Rigoletto's "Cortigiani, vil razza dannata." The aria ends in soft supplication with repeated pleas for mercy in D-flat major, as the soliloquy's main theme is gently echoed in the orchestra.

Lost in thought, Rathenow is unaware that Henning has returned to see Elsbeth. (We learn from the novel that Henning realizes that Rathenow has plans to marry Elsbeth to Melchior Schum, the son of the Cölln city councilor Bartolomäus Schum, in order to unite the two parts of town). Henning's agitated and broken phrases are accompanied by drumrolls that evoke a tense and surreal atmosphere when he hears someone knocking, worried that Rathenow might discover him.[23] Still unaware of his presence, Rathenow peers through the window to see Thomas Wintz and Bartholomäus Schum on the street,[24] arriving to discuss the proposed engagement, as Henning hides.

The men conclude that Elsbeth's engagement to Melchior should be officially announced the following day at a reception in the city hall. When Rathenow brings up the subject of Henning's money, it falls on deaf ears. Elsbeth now returns from a dinner at the rectory with Gertrud. Schum kisses her on the forehead in proxy for his son and he leaves with Wintz. Elsbeth notices the bejeweled necklace and admires its brilliance in the moonlight (Alexis, 4). She insists on wearing it the next day, even if her father considers the heirloom, originally from King Karl of Bohemia (Alexis, 16), to be too precious. The necklace represents the family's honor, and Elsbeth now muses that it would bring misfortune if she lost it. When Rathenow also tells her that she is too young to wear the necklace, she informs him that she is nevertheless of patrician birth, as that motif resounds in D-major. Rathenow finally relents, kissing Elsbeth good night before retiring, as her theme is heard.

The moon now completely illuminates the room, and Elsbeth's thoughts turn to Henning, whom she has not seen for one month. The orchestra takes on the silvery quality of the moon's pale rays, perfectly capturing the medieval German spirit evoked in the novel. Unable to explain her sense of trepidation, Elsbeth begins her magical aria "Splende la luna" (F-major), which may have been inspired by Zazà's act 2 "Questa per un fanciullo è la più gran sventura!" This fascinating and meditative solo makes time stand still, enabling Elsbeth's thoughts to be revealed for the first time.

Henning appears, calling quietly in order not to frighten Elsbeth. He immediately refers to her forthcoming marriage and his experiences with the Kurfürst, in a broken yet poetic passage worthy of a Pushkin hero ("Lieto venia . . . sognando . . . altro avvenire . . ."). He then begins an appropriately passionate *andante sostenuto cantabile* in G-flat major ("Alda il Prence mi diede quest'anello") offering her a ring from the Kurfürst as a wedding present.

Elsbeth recalls their youth before Henning passionately interrupts her ("Ah! un altro sogno") to sing that he once imagined the future to be quite different. When he wishes to return her prayer book and leave forever, Elsbeth admits that her father has forced the approaching marriage and that she, in fact, does not love Melchior. Henning now responds with rapture to the love motif in G-flat major ("Alda il Prence mi diede quest'anello").[25] He takes leave of Elsbeth in pure cavalier fashion through the window, promising to return the next day. The curtain slowly descends, accompanied by the love motif that gradually grows softer and slower, resembling a cascade of moonlit tears.

Act 3 commences with a vivacious introduction (*mosso brillantissimo*) in E-major evoking the festivities celebrating Elsbeth and Melchior's engagement in a large room in the city hall. The guests praise an inebriated Wintz, who is enjoying the merriment in the company of an equally drunk Schum. A small stage orchestra strikes up when Wintz invites the guests to dance, asking Elsbeth in a slightly pompous manner to begin. He offers her his arm to harp arpeggios which introduce an elegant and anachronistic gavotte in A-major that Leoncavallo adapted from a German *Pickelhering Dance*, written in 1519.

Mathias Blankenfeld enters, commenting to Schum that he would, in fact, prefer Konrad Ryke to Rathenow as Berlin's mayor. Schum jests that he will let Rathenow know, although the latter has remained at home pleading illness. The gavotte concludes in a crude and clumsy manner befitting the host's awkwardness. Considering that Elsbeth has no interest in Melchior Schum, the bridegroom jokingly tells his father that he really only has interest in returning for the wedding night. He exits to the second dance, a *Rigaudon* in E-minor, inspired by a 1574 *Fuggerin Tanz*.

Bergholz, another Cölln city councilor, tells Schum and Blankenfeld that Kurfürst Friedrich has been asked to intervene regarding the money owed Henning. Schum in fact hopes that Rathenow will pay the sum so that Cölln will not be forced to. Both Bergholz and Blankenfeld insinuate that Rathenow's only interest in paying the debt is because Henning was seen climbing down from Elsbeth's balcony the previous night.

Henning enters costumed and masked as an elegant minstrel carrying a lute (Alexis 23). Rather than disclose his identity, he launches into the exciting ballad "Io sono il Re de la ballata," a light *allegretto moderato* in F-major crowned by a high C. His song is enthusiastically received, and, still incognito, he asks Elsbeth where her fiancé is in a short dialogue ("Fanciulla!") resembling that between Marcello and Musette in act 2 of *La bohème*. Henning declares his love once again as Elsbeth brushes the disguised man aside with an ironic laugh.

Wintz, completely inebriated, then sings the *andantino* "O vaga, eletta vergine" derived from another German song (1590), serenading Elsbeth with a bouquet of flowers that he then offers his daughter Eva by mistake. Noticing his gaffe, he snatches them back for Elsbeth, thereby embarrassing Eva. The guests grow disconcerted, and the conflict theme is sung by the Cölln guests, while the Berliners hope to subdue the mounting antagonism.

This is Blankenfeld's chance to further the mounting conflict by making the inebriated Schum aware of his daughter's tears. His approach is marked by menacing chords first heard in the prelude. Blankenfeld tells Schum that his daughter has been disrespected, while the orchestra responds with an inverted conflict motif. Although Wintz tries to excuse his actions and is supported by the Berlin faction, Schum, goaded on by the Cöllners, now sings the "conflict" motif himself, thereby signifing that any hope for a peaceful resolution has been nullified.

Elsbeth laughs when the drunken Schum loses his balance, prompting Eva to physically attack her. She tears the precious necklace from Elsbeth's throat—which Henning manages to save—while accusing her of having only financial interest in the marriage.[26] Schum now also takes up his daughter's case, telling Elsbeth—who remains dignified and silent—that she should join her lover, who was seen climbing down her balcony.

Rathenow enters at this point to save his daughter's honor although no such appearance is made in the novel (Alexis, 14).[27] Schum tells Rathenow that the engagement has been broken off because Henning is Elsbeth's lover. Rathenow symbolically protects Elsbeth's ears from hearing additional slander by covering them with his hands. An orchestral *lamentoso* similar to the "Ridi Pagliaccio" motif expresses Rathenow's suffering. Rathenow, having faith only in Elsbeth and God, refers to her as a "saintly being," declaring Schum to be a petty merchant and swearing that he doesn't need Cölln's support, since he will pay Henning's money himself. In an energetic Verdian-style *andante maestoso* in B-minor, Rathenow sings that Schum's wealth and his honor dictate that he should pay, since the wealthy are responsible for society. Rathenow's aria, which began so impressively, unfortunately now takes on shades of operetta, as his voice becomes choked with emotion, only able to utter "Mia figlia" when the act concludes.

Jealousy and hate have succeeded in finally pulling the Rathenows and Schums apart. In the novel we are told that Rathenow, accused of taking un-authorized action in trying to pay Henning (Alexis, 24), is presented with a petition citing why he should be replaced by a Cölln mayor.[28]

A nervous and agitated Wagnerian *vivace* precedes the first scene of act 4, set in the interior of Rathenow's home as in act 2. Gertrud, Elsbeth's old nurse, tells her that Rathenow was summoned to the Town Hall, and that Kurfürst

Friedrich's troops were seen approaching the city to enforce peace among the quarreling Cölln/Berlin factions. Henning then arrives bringing the necklace and asking for Elsbeth's hand in marriage. When Elsbeth asks who found it, he suggests it was a minstrel, while the orchestra reprises the *sostenuto assai* heard during their brief duet in act 3.

The frantic *vivace* chords resembling a *cavalcata* that opened the act now return, prompting Elsbeth to believe that she hears the Kurfürst's troops approaching. Henning takes the opportunity to compare the din to the amorous clamor in his heart. Elsbeth tries to resist Henning's passion, again claiming that she hears the Kurfürst. The young man is shocked when Elsbeth finally tells him that she will never be able to marry him since she is of patrician birth.[29] This example of false pride and caste thinking is accentuated by the patrician motif. Elsbeth suggests that Henning marry someone in keeping with his social station whom she will then befriend like a sister. He further negates Elsbeth's traditional way of thinking when reminding her that he need not remain a weaver, since the Kurfürst has made it possible for men to socially advance through positions in the military, culminating in a knighthood.[30] He finally accuses Elsbeth of being false when she gave him her prayer book,[31] singing the love motif, hoping that it was all a dream. She admits her love for Henning although she firmly believes that destiny has willed it otherwise. They then both sing the love motif for the first time in unison.[32]

Rathenow suddenly enters, telling Henning that the city has more impending problems than the wooing of his daughter. Still unable to accept Elsbeth's decision, Henning pleads with Rathenow to pity him (Alexis, 27–28), concluding with the same words ("Abbi pietà") that Rathenow used at the conclusion of his "Dio che non vedo" aria in act 2. This develops into a short quartet wherein Gertrud warns Rathenow to have mercy, sensing the family's imminent doom. Instead, Rathenow echoes Elsbeth's words, adding that she will not become Henning's wife unless the Roland statue topples from its base.[33] She then faints before the scene ends as Henning curses Rathenow, accusing the mayor of murdering the son whose father originally saved him.

Another *cavalcata* preceding scene 2 describes the advance of the Kurfürst's men. The stage is cloaked in complete darkness when the Kurfürst's troops demand that the city gates be opened. The inhabitants cry out in terror.[34] Rathenow now appears and the town crier announces that the gates should be opened or the Kurfürst will enter by force. The Cölln side—represented by Blankenfeld and Schum—wish to open them, even though Rathenow refuses, claiming that entrance is only possible if the men are unarmed.

A disheveled Henning then appears carrying an axe, demanding that the gates be opened. When Rathenow asks whether he wants to destroy the city, the young man proposes a counterattack, wishing to help the city to glory by freeing its oppressed. This is sung to a *maestoso marziale* ("Ghilde, patrizi, po-polo, Consiglio! . . .") modeled on Simon Boccanegra's "Plebe, patrizi, popolo!" in the council chamber scene of Verdi's opera.[35] Henning's voice grows heroic, singing a variation of the victory motif while forcing the gates open with his axe (Alexis, 30), prior to leaving for the fight. The Kurfürst then enters to his own motif that majestically bursts forth in E-major.[36]

Blankenfeld and Schum now also greet Friedrich. Rathenow rejects the new rule. The Kurfürst relates in a lengthy passage that he has come to govern like a father, simultaneously giving orders for the Roland statue to be destroyed, which Leoncavallo recreates musically.[37] The statue topples and Ra-thenow sinks to his knees handing over his mayor's necklace, thereby eradicat-ing any doubt that he represents an example of antiquated rule. Conrad von Knipprode astounds all when he reveals that the Kurfürst's men "accidentally" killed Henning believing him to have been the enemy. Henning's body is then carried into the Nicholas church to an extremely brief funeral march in E-minor,[38] accompanied by an altered and broken-sounding victory motif (*tempo di marcia funebre*). This modulates into the love motif when the Kurfürst takes leave of his "best friend," insisting that he be buried as a knight. Elsbeth gives vent to her grief in a touching liebestod ("Addio mio fedel!") in F-sharp mi-nor.[39] The chorus partakes in Elsbeth's mourning when she kisses Henning's forehead to the love motif. Extremely moving is Leoncavallo's idea to have Els-beth return to her father following the aria, once again singing its initial words before breaking off, implying a sense of unrelieved hopelessness and loss. The Kurfürst hands Elsbeth her father's necklace, and the chorus unites to praise Friedrich ("Urrà per l'Elettore, Viva Berlin!") to his own motif, concluding the opera with the victory theme.

Although *Der Roland von Berlin* is uneven as a work, it should not be considered an unsuccessful attempt at an operatic adaptation, considering the difficulties inherent in Alexis's "unoperatic" novel. It remains an energetic and interesting work worthy of revival, containing some of Leoncavallo's most in-spired music, while its major arias present the composer at his most melodic.

NOTES

1. In the Italian version of Leoncavallo's score, the characters' names become "Fed-erico," "Giovanni," and "Alda," substituting the Kurfürst, Friedrich, Johannes Rathenow, and Elsbeth respectively. Leoncavallo has eliminated some of the characters found in the novel, such as Niklas Perwenitz, Pawel Strobant, and Erich von Stettin.

2. "Bartholomeus Schumm" in the novel.

3. "Matthies Blankenfelde" in the novel.

4. Not to be confused with Cologne.

5. Leoncavallo may have been inspired by the *Die Meistersinger* prelude or the *Rienzi* overture, while the patrician theme recalls the opening sequence of Strauss's *Also Sprach Zarathustra*. A major influence was also Massenet's *Le Cid* overture.

6. The orchestral score notes that Leoncavallo has placed trumpets, trombones, and tuba onstage behind the curtain.

7. I have relied on my own titles to simplify identification of Leoncavallo's major themes for this and all other operas in part 2.

8. All quotations from the opera appear in their original Italian version, rather than the short-lived and infinitely poorer German translation.

9. This theme resembles a motif in Massenet's *Le Cid* overture.

10. The church's name is unspecified in the operatic score.

11. Not unlike the outdoor Christmas Eve in *La bohème*.

12. Ferbirt's story commences before the curtain is raised, recalling Gaudenzio and Schaunard's conversation at the beginning of *La bohème*. Alexis reminds his readers in chapter 6 that in the Middle Ages barber shops served as both the cafés and restaurants, where gossip flourished.

13. Leoncavallo added this aria by hand to the printed libretto during the time of composition.

14. Both Rathenow's sons, Christoph and Rudolf, and his wife, Brigitte, are prematurely deceased.

15. Rathenow witnesses their meeting from a window in chapter 4 of the Alexis novel.

16. There are some discrepancies between the published Italian text and what Leoncavallo originally intended at this point. For example, Henning's phrase "Oh! Potess'io conquidere tal fama e tanto onore" becomes "Oh! Potess'io conquidere tal fama e onor cotanto." The composer incessantly revised this part of the libretto, and the typed text once again sports his calligraphy at this point.

17. As in the case of most of his other historical operas, Leoncavallo chose anachronistic material usually conceived centuries after the era he wished to recall.

18. The mood and music greatly resembles the carnival festivities in act 1 of Ponchielli's *La gioconda*.

19. This is another opportunity to illustrate the citizens' dissatisfaction with the governing party. Alexis (7) describes the suffering populace left with bones while the council members have meat, failing to live by the rules they have established.

20. The amount has been changed from the novel's original forty-seven in order to correspond with the current monetary rates at the time of the opera's premiere.

21. In the novel, Henning sets out with two hundred men in search of Makensprung's bandits. He encounters Kurfürst Friedrich in the forest, believing him to be one of the bandits, not having seen him out of disguise as in the opera (Alexis 20). The Kurfürst then offers to help search for the bandits, which turn out to be two of his own men: Wedigo von Lüderitz and Busso von Anhalt. The Kurfürst then takes Henning with him to Spandau, declaring that nobles should remain united as a chain that supports the community.

22. In Alexis his name is "Joel Baruch" and the mayor seeks him out twice for money with which to pay Henning.

23. The atmosphere of this scene recalls Ghermann hiding in the Countess's bedroom in act 2 of Tchaikovsky's *Pique Dame*.

24. "Power derives from wealth." Thus lauds Alexis's description in chapter 4 of the nouveau riche merchant Schum in contrast to the patrician Rathenow.

25. Henning's ecstasy results in a high B-flat that is vocally approached in precisely the same manner as Vasco da Gama's "Oh paradis sortide l'onde" in Meyerbeer's *L'africaine*.

26. This is a further example of the "vulgar" Schums vs. the "regal" Rathenows. In chapter 14 of the novel Eva has to be physically restrained by two women.

27. Similar to Germont in act 3 of *La traviata*.

28. In the novel, Elsbeth does not realize that Eva has torn her necklace off and thus searches for it in the snow following the party. Henning breaks into the city hall later that night to retrieve it, for which he is temporarily arrested.

29. This was an important factor in European society until both world wars, after which patricians and aristocrats were no longer a class apart. The inability to accept a new social reform results in the Rathenow downfall, and is the crux of Alexis's novel. Elsbeth reminds Henning in chapter 27 that one cannot "become" a prince and that the Schums will forever remain beer brewers.

30. This relates to Wilhelm II's politics, in which it was no longer mandatory for men to be of aristocratic birth if they wished to succeed in the military. Thus, although Friedrich believes that he has been willed to reign by the grace of God, he is decidedly modern compared to Rathenow, and it was none other than Wilhelm II who wrote of his ancestor being a "modern thinker" in the chapter he devoted to Friedrich II in his memoirs, *Meine Vorfahren*.

31. Henning's rage is musically depicted in the same violent manner as was that of Canio, Marcello, and Milio.

32. This is strikingly similar to act 3 of *Werther*, when the protagonists also sing the same melody in unison for the very first time.

33. A symbolic reference to the dissolution of Rathenow's reign.

34. The Kurfürst declares in the novel (30) that he has come to create peace among the rivaling factions, as six hundred of his men enter the town. His decision follows the ceaseless strife initiated by a petition against Rathenow.

35. Henning also explains that the "old branches" (the old rule) will fall off although the tree—a further allusion to the olive branch sung in Boccanegra's aria—will sprout anew.

36. Kurfürst Friedrich is presented as a positive revolutionary who enables the citizens to embark on a new course. Audiences that attended the opera's world premiere were able to discern the obvious similarities between Friedrich and Wilhelm II although precisely four hundred years separated the novel (1840) from its historic counterpart (ca. 1440).

37. Although Wilhelm II mentions this occurrence in *Meine Vorfahren* (30), there is no evidence that it actually happened.

38. This version expresses Leoncavallo's dramatic ideals in having the hero's short life enable a political renaissance, whereas Wilhelm II would have preferred that Henning remain alive in order to marry Elsbeth.

39. Elsbeth's final scene resembles Fidelia's farewell to Edgar ("Addio, addio mio dolce amor") in Puccini's opera of the same name, where even the words are similar.

· 18 ·

Maïa

Characters

Maïa, soprano
Renaud, tenor[1]
Torias, baritone
Germain, baritone
Louison, soprano
Simette, soprano
Renaud's fiancée, soprano

Setting: Camargue (1809)

Maïa's literary genesis originally began with France's Félibrige movement in 1854, dedicated to reviving the ancient glories of the Provence and its poet Frédéric Mistral (1830–1914), who employed this theme in most of his works, writing *Mirèio*, a rural poem in twelve cantos published in provençal in 1859. Charles Gounod grew enamored of the work after spending time with Mistral, creating an operatic adaptation (*Mireille*) first performed in 1864 at the Théâtre-Lyrique. In 1897, Francesco Cilèa's opera *L'arlesiana*, a melodrama taking place in the Provence, based on Alphonse Daudet's play *L'Arlésienne* (to which Bizet had written incidental music), premiered at Milan's Teatro Lirico and was published by Sonzogno. Perhaps trying to recreate another *Mireille*, the publisher-librettist Paul de Choudens—whose own family probably originated from the south of France—created the libretto of Mascagni's opera *Amica* (1905), as well as an equally poor text for Leoncavallo's *Maïa* somewhat later. Leoncavallo decided in favor of *Maïa* in order to ingratiate himself with a publisher other than Sonzogno, while the intimate subject was welcome after the ambitious *Der Roland von Berlin*. His future works would all be relatively short

272

following the adaptation of the Alexis epic, and as his last full-length original opera *Maïa* marks a turning point in the composer's output.[2] Enormous efforts that had not brought success (*I Medici, Der Roland von Berlin*), combined with the composer's advancing age and reduced capacity for concentration, resulted in a series of shorter creations.

As Charpentier's *Louise* is a declaration of love to Paris, so *Maïa* is one to the Camargue region of France, with its burning sun, cattle, and flamingos, which the composer has successfully captured in his opera rich with original provençal songs and dances. It is also a return to verismo—French *réalisme* this time—recalling Massenet's outing in the genre with his 1894 *La navarraise*.

Act 1, scene 1 of this *Drame Lyrique* begins at the end of a beautiful summer day,[3] as a blood red sun slowly sets to the pastoral sounds of shepherds and ox men heard in the distance, accompanied by the strains of a bagpipe playing a provençal song by Saboly in A-major. Ominous discords warn that the idyllic setting will be destroyed in the opera's dramatic denouement. The bagpipe once again takes up an *allegretto vispo*—in F-major this time—and the voices resume their wordless song. The curtain rises to *sostenuto grave* chords depicting the July sunset. Children and villagers enter to cattle bells in an A-major provençal song ("A l'aubo s'es lévado") entitled "Margoutoun." It is repeated twice to a bagpipe accompaniment before returning simultaneously with an additional song entitled "La targo."

The key abruptly changes from A-major to C-major when Maïa enters. The villagers ask why she appears to be so sad, although they realize that her lover, Renaud, has been away as a soldier for one year. Maïa's melancholic motif in C-major (*assai moderato*) now accompanies her broken phrases. It contrasts with the virile and energetic sound of Torias's voice in the distance singing his ox-man song "Le fier bouvier de la Camargue" in F-major, which will later be associated with his Escamillo brand of machismo.

Maïa is both bored and irritated by Torias, and Leoncavallo expresses these emotions with her descending octave leaps ("Il m'ennuie avec ses discours cet amoureux transi!"). Her friends, Louison and Simette, poke fun at her lovesickness (C-major), before leaving with the villagers amid spirited laughter. Torias then begins the second verse of his song solely for Maïa's benefit. A duet commences at Torias's goading, while Maïa's boredom and repressed aggression sound in the orchestra. She brusquely rejects his advances, implying that she is not "free." In an impassioned *sostenuto* to a melancholic arpeggio accompaniment, Maïa tells him that she has already promised herself to be faithful to someone else. Torias replies in an equally passionate arietta, "Vas-tu rester longtemps" (beginning in D-major), recalling Cascart in *Zazà*. It is a lilting provincial theme that will return throughout the opera as his love motif, perfectly describing his slightly vulgar passion. Maïa rejects him again, singing an altered version of his theme. She expresses her passion for Renaud in an *allegro agitato* (C-minor) before Torias exclaims that "her soldier" is due to return the very next day with his fiancée! She violently accuses him of lying, but menacing chords accompany her shocked, half-spoken uncertainty as to whether Torias may in fact be telling the truth. Torias swears ("curse" motif) that Camargue ox men do not lie.[4] Maïa vows to Torias that she will be his if Renaud is in fact engaged, singing the curse motif herself ("Les filles de Camargue ne mentent pas non plus!"). An elated Torias exits. The curse motif echoes in the orchestra, leaving a bewildered Maïa to wonder if Renaud is indeed faithful.

The tension temporarily subsides when Louison and Simette reappear, telling Maïa the good news that Renaud has returned. They leave, wishing her good luck to joyous music, wherein a discord interprets the heroine's anxiety. Maïa's trepidation is accompanied by her motif, and villagers heard in the distance recall the opera's beginning. Maïa once again remains alone onstage awaiting her lover, a subtle and psychologically effective sense of dejá vu that the composer uses to full advantage. Her first aria, "Mon amant me quitta et moi," is an extremely sad *larghetto mélancolique* in C-minor, which sounds like a medieval minstrel performing an elegy, pathetic in its simplicity and haunting in its melancholy. The aria ends to broken phrases perfectly describing Maïa and the heroine of her song, who both futilely await their lovers.

Renaud finally appears, taking Maïa in his arms and promising that he has come to stay. Uncertain, Maïa (to her motif) asks him why he was released from the army, and the reason she heard nothing for one year. When she suspects that it is because Renaud's father, Germain, does not approve of their relationship, the young man changes the subject by describing her appearance, accompanied by an altered version of her motif. Renaud proceeds to dispel Maïa's doubts in his only aria, "Enfin, je la retrouve," a superb solo in D-flat major ranking with Leoncavallo's most significant tenor music and recalling *Werther's* "Pourquoi me réveiller?" The vocal line increases in passion when Renaud takes up the original theme, concluding with a high B-flat. The variations between the original libretto in the composer's hand (I) and the published aria (II) are significant when demonstrating the stages of formation between the draft and its final version:

> *I*
> *Je sais que je retrouve*
> *la femme la maîtresse*
> *que j'ai aimée,*
> *adorée,*
> *et tiens dans mes bras*
> *enfermée de toute la force*
> *de mes vingt ans!*

Je retrouve ces lèvres
et je me souviens
de ces mille baisers
donnés et reçus
dans l'ivresse
de nos heures amoureuses
et folles! Sois à moi!

II
Enfin, je la retrouve
la femme, la maîtresse,
la bien-aimée,
la bien-aimée
Que j'ai tant de fois enfermée dans mes bras!
Je les rencontre encore
ces lèvres frémissantes,
je rencontre encore
et me souviens!
De tes baisers de fièvre de ta bouche brûlante!
De toutes les promesses
de tes folles caresses!
Et dans l'ivresse heureuse
des heures amoureuses!
Viens, Maïa!
Sois à moi!
Viens! Je te retrouve encor!
Viens! Maïa!

Maïa, with forced naiveté, following an aria guaranteed to make any woman swoon, coldly lies and says that Torias is her lover. Renaud warns that he would murder her if it were indeed true. This, of course, is completely at odds with the gentle poetry of his aria that, essentially, marks the true essence of his character. However, Maïa finally embraces him and surrenders, saying that she had only been waiting for him to "prove" his love. The orchestra reprises her motif in octaves while the lovers' vocal lines express their passion, when Maïa's theme is renewed in F-major. She now sings of her love for Renaud as if "drunk with love." Following an energetic and passionate beginning, the duet's second part is a calm and sensuous *moderato cantabile* in G-flat major, "Nuit troublante! Nuit brûlante!," recalling Berlioz's *Les Troyens* in its simple grandeur. A downward cascading *largo* in D-flat major with the lovers singing the same text arriving from opposite ends of the scale is the next phase of this magnificent duo. A B-flat in unison is then heralded when Maïa again resorts to her motif. Initially only sung by Maïa and supported by the orchestra, the motif now also includes Renaud as a symbol of his consuming passion ("Contre mon coeur, brûlant de fièvre"). Their languor is echoed by voices humming in the distance. Maïa's motif gently resounds one last time. The united lovers exit voicing the word "viens!" when a nightingale's song is heard, and arpeggio chords in G-flat major bring this impressive act to a most delicate conclusion.

An intermezzo precedes act 2, beginning with an *allegro marziale* in C-minor, initially presenting the "provençal" motif. The act then commences with a joyful allegro in E-major based on the popular song "Lou boucabeu," setting the mood for the afternoon sun that shines on a square in Beaucaire, where shepherds are seen celebrating a festival.[5] Their first song, "la bello bago," supplied by the librettist, is heard before dancers perform an old and traditional *farandole* in F-major.

Renaud enters with a young girl whom his father introduces as his son's fiancée. The village girls offer the nameless fiancée some flowers. She responds with "merci!"—the only word the entire role requires. The chorus next sings a rousing greeting marking Torias's entrance atop a carriage pulled by two oxen. He is offered a goblet by the crowd, which he melodramatically accepts, drinking its contents, echoed by the orchestra in a descending chromatic scale. This prepares the way for Torias's drinking song, leaving no doubt that Leoncavallo had Escamillo in mind.[6] He announces his decision to sing in the phrase "Je veux boire, à la force, à la vie," slightly recalling *Der Roland von Berlin*'s victory motif.

The score fails to mention Maïa's entrance, and we must thus assume that it is with or shortly after Torias, since his song will be directed not only toward the passion he feels for her, but also the oath that she swore in the preceding act.[7] Renaud immediately takes notice of Torias's interest in Maïa, when the baritone finally launches into his much awaited brindisi, "Tout le monde ici doit boire." His song soon returns to its main theme, earlier heard in numerous guises during the course of the intermezzo ("Avec moi buvez tous"). The chorus joins in, leading to a rousing finale crowned with a toast to love. Shepherds and shepherdesses then perform a *musette*,[8] gently clapping their hands to its rhythm before Torias leaves.

When Renaud is asked to perform something he begins the symbolic "Corbleau Marion," a song in the form of a dialogue between a shepherd (Renaud) and his supposedly "unfaithful" shepherdess (six chorus women). The shepherd complains how his love tortures him, in an effective passage in E-minor, that is both dramatic and sincere ("Vastu mentir toute ta vie . . ."), to an accompaniment recalling the "moonlight duet" from act 1 of Massenet's *Werther*. This chilling and uncanny story concludes when the shepherd stabs his beloved, foreshadowing the opera's final denouement. A rapid *allegro* of the villagers thanking Renaud for his song breaks the haunting spell. When his fiancée offers him a wreath, Maïa furiously destroys it, accusing him of cowardice. Germain immediately asks Maïa what is wrong, and she begins an agonized and pathetic *appassionato* in E-major, recalling Renaud's promise to be hers ("Parcequ'à son amour"). Germain responds with immense irony, adding insult to injury when he flatly states that Renaud's fiancée is wealthy. He demands (in a C-sharp major *agitato*) that she cease trying to create a scandal, and, instead, return to her degradation. With a "savage cry," Maïa snatches a dagger from a nearby shepherd and lunges toward Germain in order to kill the "viper." She is stopped by Renaud. He is startled that she should in fact try to attack his own father. When Maïa now insists that both father and son are cowards, the *farandole* heard earlier returns. Germain suggests that they leave the insane girl.[9] Torias enters, and Renaud is about to attack him when held back by his father. Craving vengeance, Maïa asks whether Torias still wishes to be her husband. When he responds in the affirmative, she proudly takes his arm, triumphantly walking out before the startled crowd.

Act 3 commences with a very fine prelude initiated by mournful C-minor chords (*lugubre, sostenuto assai*) symbolizing Maïa's inner torment. A *cantabile* in F-sharp minor then introduces the theme of Maïa's aria, while palpitating chords evoke the river Rhône's flow. The prelude concludes with the menacing curse motif, reminding one of the heroine's approaching fate.

It is evening. Maïa's small house on the banks of the Rhône soon becomes visible. Maïa is dressed elegantly for her meeting with Torias, but her desperation once again sounds to chords from the prelude. She still admits her passion for Renaud regardless of what has happened, and the orchestra blatantly echoes her oath, even though she decides to remain unfaithful to it. Her aria, "Rhône, ton flot qui gronde," a *cantabile* in E-minor, is based on the Rhône motif. The *scena* concludes—similar in its construction to Lisa's aria before she ends her life in the Neva in act 3 of Tchaikovsky's *Pique Dame*—with thoughts of suicide. She is abruptly halted by Renaud, who again declares his love, to the motif of his passionate act 1 aria. He informs her that he has turned against his father because he loves her. Maïa finally submits to Renaud's ardor, wishing to begin a new life elsewhere. Torias suddenly enters, reminding Maïa of her oath, to the curse motif. A brief trio begins when the men quarrel. Renaud pulls out his dagger and Torias assaults him. He lunges at Torias but Maïa—caught between the two like Francesca da Rimini—receives the fatal wound.

Torias exits in tears to the strains of his love theme after Maïa says that he meant nothing to her. She then begins a slow and mournful passage ("Tout maintenant s'arrange"), taking leave of her life and Renaud. She begs him to return to his father and fiancée in a tender farewell ("Sur ton coeur doucement mourante"). Delirious, Maïa's last vision is of Renaud's father, as she dies to the strains of her sad *larghetto melanconique* from act 1.

Maïa's original version takes place in the *Restauration* period of 1820 rather than the Napoléonic 1809. Act 1 is identical, except that Renaud has never been a soldier. Act 2 has greater discrepancies: Torias enters *following* the *musette* sequence (performed without the chorus in the original version) and Renaud's "Corbleau Marion." (The "Corbleau" aria ends with the shepherdess being drowned rather than stabbed, alluding to Maïa's death in the original). The first version also includes a lengthy "Danse Chantée" sung by Maïa to a mostly a capella accompaniment in provençal dialect, symbolically telling the story of a young man who plans to marry, even though his father cannot provide any money. Torias's act 2 brindisi[10] was not in the original, while his aria "Ah! Maïa, tu m'appartiendras!" fails to appear in the second version, with the composer perhaps fearing that this passionate scene (at times recalling Siegmund's "Winterstürme wichen den Wonnemond" in act 1 of *Die Walküre*) would make his character appear too sympathetic. In addition, Leoncavallo deleted a short duet between Maïa and Torias for the second version that would have made the heroine's character less credible. He also failed to include the prelude's Rhône motif for Maïa's act 3 aria. Although the passage preceding the aria in both versions is largely identical, the arias themselves are completely different, with Leoncavallo substituting Maïa's theme in the second version.

Additional differences occur in the original version's final scene, in which Renaud successfully stabs Torias without harming Maïa. Villagers remove the body as Maïa pleads with Renaud to save himself. A *farandole* is heard in the background when she tells Renaud to take one of the boats and sail it down the Rhône, where he should await her. An *allegro feroce* then calls attention to angry villagers searching for Torias's murderer. Maïa, trying to save Renaud, claims that she killed Torias. Throwing the knife aside, she jumps onto a boat, where she still has time for a grand farewell based on her theme. When shepherds push her boat, Maïa loses her balance and drowns. Torias's theme sounds one last time. The opera ends with Louison murmuring a prayer to the Virgin about "poor Maïa" as the curtain falls to a gentle pianissimo.

Leoncavallo revised the opera after the world premiere reviews that focused on the inconsistencies of Maïa's character and the fact that she all too readily goes off with Torias. Critics unanimously praised act 1—especially Maïa's aria—thereby influencing the composer to use the motif again to end the second version, which, in my opinion, is a marked improvement over the first, and certainly it is the more stageworthy.

Maïa represents Leoncavallo's last successful attempt at creating a verismo opera that is both charming and compelling. Act 1 contains some of the composer's most inspired vocal writing. Although the work is handicapped by Choudens's poor libretto, the sheer beauty of Leoncavallo's music generously compensates for any of its shortcomings.

NOTES

1. "René" in the opera's original version.

2. Of the remaining operas, *Zingari* is a one-act work, whereas *Mameli* and *Edipo re* are reworkings of *Chatterton* and *Der Roland von Berlin*, respectively.

3. Judging from the autograph libretto in Leoncavallo's hand, which was perhaps copied from Choudens, it is obvious that an earlier version called for *Maïa* to stab herself and to drown in the Rhône after Torias fatally wounded Renaud. The libretto was then revised for the opera's first musical version, in which Maïa drowns "accidentally" after Renaud's murder. An analysis of the second, superior, and ultimate performing version condoned by the composer is discussed here.

4. Leoncavallo noted in the score's first version that the passage should be sung "comme en délire."

5. A major portion of this act consists of provençal songs.

6. Not only is the situation almost identical to Escamillo's scene in act 2 of *Carmen*, but Torias's text also echoes the Torero's when he refers to Maïa's eyes.

7. Maïa would have heard Germain's announcement of his son's engagement had she been present at the beginning of the scene.

8. The *farandole* is a dance that originated in the eighteenth century.

9. Maïa returns the insults, shouting "canaille" (scoundrels) in true verismo fashion, reminiscent of the same word used by Fanny in act 3 of Massenet's *Sapho*.

10. Leoncavallo hoped to entice Ruffo to sing the role and therefore may have included the drinking song inspired by the baritone's brindisi, "O vin diseppe la tristesse," in Ambroise Thomas's *Hamlet*.

· 19 ·

Malbruk

Characters

Malbruk, baritone[1]

Arnolfo, tenor

Apollodoro, bass

Vinicio, spoken role

Il Conte di Campofiorito, spoken role

Il Barone di Rocca Ventosa, spoken role

Il Marchese di Roncisvalle, spoken role

Il Visconte di Valle Serrata, spoken role

Il Barone di Selenita, spoken role

I Cinque Alì, spoken roles

Il Messo di Re Artù, spoken role

Il Capo delle Guardie, spoken role

Alba, soprano

Marchesa Basilide dell'Oca Bianca, alto

Fiammetta, spoken role

Griselda, spoken role

Adalinda, spoken role

Belcore, spoken role

Bertrada, spoken role

Setting: Malbruk's Castle, Brittany (Twelfth Century)

Angelo Nessi's adaptation of *Malbruk* is taken from the second story told during the third day of Boccaccio's *Decameron*, in which a stable boy—who remains nameless—sleeps with King Agilulf's wife, Theodelinde. When the king discovers he has been duped, he cuts half the man's hair, in order to remember who he was the next day. The stable boy then does the same to all the other servants asleep in the room, thereby ensuring his anonymity.

Malbruk commences with an extended overture (*preambolo*) in E-major introducing the song "Malbrouk s'en va-t-en guerre!,"[2] which is performed by a backstage chorus, serving as Malbruk's theme.[3] It returns as an *andantino grazioso* (C-major) before ending in a finale "alla Rossiniana" in E-major.

Act 1 begins with an introductory chorus preparing the arrival of Malbruk and his fiancée, Alba dell'Oca Bianca (Alba of White Goose). She enters "veiled like a Turk," accompanied by Arnolfo (Malbruk's nephew) and her mother Basilide.[4] Both Alba and Arnolfo express foreboding regarding her approaching marriage to Malbruk, in the elegant C-major *andantino* "Dai queti villaggi lontani." Malbruk enters to his theme as the chorus salutes him, greeting the arrival party with a *recitativo* that Leoncavallo wrote to resemble Meyerbeer ("Baroni e gentiluomini").[5] The festivities begin with a renaissance dance (*tempo di passepied*). Alba responds to Malbruk's clumsy courtship with the charming arietta "Del vostro dolce canto," promising eternal devotion.[6] Arnolfo then breaks into his charming love theme "Passa un sogno di bellezza" in G-flat major, which soon evolves into a quintet, including Basilide's lover Appollodoro (golden Apollo) and the chorus.

A "sostenuto pomposo" resounds, followed by organ and harmonium preparing for the marriage ceremony. A trumpet signals the arrival of King Arthur's messenger announcing that the Grand Turk Alì Bubù has entered the confines, urgently requesting Malbruk to lead a battle against the invaders, in spite of it being his wedding day. This takes place to an oriental-sounding melody that eventually develops into a humorous chorus led by Malbruk, declaring that he will defend his people not only from Alì Bubù, but also from Alì Bebè, Alì Babà, and Alì Bibì! He then leaves for battle as the act ends.

A short prelude precedes act 2 with a reprisal of Arnolfo's love theme in G-flat major, drawing attention to the amorous happenings during Malbruk's absence. A blindfolded Alba appears playing a game while singing a sprightly song in G-major accompanied by her ladies.[7] This is followed by a letter from Malbruk boasting of his victories ("Dolce sposa"), whereupon all retire to the charming lullaby, "Andiamo, compagne, ne attende dei sogni il velato languor!" Alone, Alba begins her main aria, "La notte effonde balsami e fragranze." Arnolfo is heard approaching, making use of the darkness to seduce Alba as if he were Malbruk, in a most convincing C-major serenade ("Scendi a me, rima fedel") that develops into a touching E-major duo ("Alba dal nome bianco") structured on the *Pagliacci* Nedda/Silvio duet.

After the lovers' tryst, Alba's mother, Basilide, and Malbruk's chamberlain, Appollodoro, express their own passion for one another in the D-flat major "Duetto Comico d'Amore," recalling a turn-of-the-century waltz, wherein Appollodoro pretends to be an enamored bird.[8] When Malbruk returns to his wife with the same intentions as Arnolfo, he finds out that he has been duped, launching into his main aria, "O Malbruk tuono e fulmin di guerra," beginning with an orchestral adagio invoking Hamlet's "To be or not to be?" The act ends with a *mattinata* in the form of lilting B-major waltz sung by a soprano chorus.

Act 3 is preceded by an intermezzo based on the previously heard *mattinata*. Prior to the act, Malbruk entered the dormitory of the sleeping guards to ascertain with whom Alba had been unfaithful. Realizing it was Arnolfo, he cut part of the young man's mustache to identify him in the morning. Arnolfo, who feigned sleep, comprehended Malbruk's intentions and cut half the mustaches from all the other guards.[9] The act commences with a "slap chorus"[10] when the guards awaken, not knowing who to blame for their embarrassment.

The chorus honors Malbruk the following morning by singing his theme upon recounting Alì Bubù's battle. He is, of course, astounded that he cannot detect Arnolfo's presence.[11] Rather than saying "che strazio" ("what torment!"), he first exclaims "che Strauss!" Alì Bubù's men approach, proving that Malbruk was not as successful in battle as believed. He is able to save himself from becoming their prisoner, however, by a stipulation that Alba marry the next man in line, which, of course, happens to be Arnolfo. All rejoice to an *allegretto marziale* as the curtain falls.

Leoncavallo succeeded in breaking new ground for the foundation of Italian operetta with *Malbruk*. Puccini would experiment with the genre with *La rondine* in 1917, followed by Mascagni's *Sì* two years later.

NOTES

1. The name "Malbruk" derives from the Duke of Marlborough.
2. The song was used by the French in ridicule of the Duke of Marlborough following the famous battle of Malplaquet in 1709.
3. The song is called "Malbruk, Duca del Cervo" in Nessi's Italian original.
4. Arnolfo is no longer a stable boy as in the *Decameron*, but captain of the Royal Guards.
5. "Parodiando l'antico recitativo Meyerberriano."
6. Leoncavallo sets a trill on the word "fedel" (faithful), leaving little doubt that Alba will be anything but that.
7. Signifying Malbruk's "blind" love.
8. Basilide and Appollodoro serve as the buffo foil to the more serious Alba/Arnolfo in customary operetta fashion.
9. In the *Decameron*, Agilulf is able to discern that the stable boy was responsible for his wife's infidelity by listening to the young man's pounding heart.
10. "Coro degli Schiaffi."
11. This is where Boccaccio's tale ends.

• 20 •

Gli zingari

Characters

Fleana, soprano
Radu, tenor
Tamar, baritone
Il Vecchio, baritone[1]
Other roles: Gypsies

Setting: banks of the Lower Danube in Rumania (1880)

What actually made Leoncavallo write an opera based on Alexander Pushkin's 1824 narrative poem *The Gypsies?*[2] Always searching for success, the composer was most likely influenced by Albert de Courville and other Londoners who had experienced Diaghilev and the Russian Ballet at Covent Garden during 1911, when the company's performance of *Le spectre de la rose*, starring Nijinsky and Tamara Karsavina, preceded *Pagliacci* on the same evening.[3] Léon Bakst, the Russian Ballet's set designer, was thus also hired to stage *Zingari*, while Leoncavallo again hoped that he had created another *Pagliacci*.

It is not certain whether the composer was aware of Sergei Rachmaninoff's *Aleko*, based on the same source and written for his final examination at the Moscow Conservatory that premiered at the Bolshoi on 9 May 1893.[4] *Aleko* was the first of Rachmaninoff's three one-act operas, and Pushkin would also inspire *The Miserly Knight*, his second lyric work. Leoncavallo perhaps felt that his own passionate Italianate style could capture the eroticism of Pushkin's gypsies with greater intensity than Rachmaninoff's version. Although both operas include an intermezzo and are in a single act divided by two scenes,[5] there are few similarities. *Aleko* makes an almost epic impression, even if it concentrates more on the protagonist's misery than on his love for Zemfira in its unrelenting melancholy.

Leoncavallo's work is all passionate verismo combined with broad melodies favoring Italian vocalism. However, *Zingari* also creates an undeniable "oriental" atmosphere that is curiously lacking in Rachmaninoff's score. On the other hand, *Aleko* is a much more complex work than the theatrical and effect-seeking *Zingari*. It nevertheless appears almost pale—with Zemfira (Fleana) and the Young Gypsy's (Tamar) deaths going largely unnoticed musically—when compared with *Zingari*'s near hysteria. Leoncavallo's librettists followed Pushkin's poem quite closely,[6] although they altered the original names.

Scene 1 (*episodio primo*) begins with a brief introduction in G-major (*brillantissimo*) capturing the atmosphere of a warm spring evening concluding with a crimson sunset, whose last rays shine on a large almond tree. The gypsies' theme, a *quasi marziale*, is then immediately introduced. The Old Gypsy (Il Vecchio)—Fleana's father—is seated before a fire while a group of men sing an anvil chorus ("Batti! Il fuoco!"). Leoncavallo's relish in recapturing the same atmosphere as act 2 of *Il trovatore* is almost palpable. The men are soon joined by the singing of their female companions.[7] All comment on the approaching evening and beauty of the star-filled sky ("Tramonta!"). The orchestra recreates the shining stars and the campfire's glowing embers through the use of flute, oboe, and piccolo, supported by the strings. The women then sing a reprisal of the gypsy theme when the fire is extinguished for the night.

Tamar, a young gypsy, approaches the Old Gypsy to the heavy chords of an *andante sostenuto*, leaving no doubt that the baritone will bring about disaster during the course of the work. Tamar relates that he has seen a stranger lurking in the shadows who has even kissed Fleana ("C'è uno straniero"). The orchestra responds with appropriately amorous and energetic rhythms—mostly influenced by Tchaikovsky—when the Old Gypsy commands Tamar to bring the couple to him bound. The Old Gypsy wonders whether Fleana might truly be in love, and Tamar's aria "Taci nol dir!" beginning in A-minor[8] expresses his longing for the girl. Leoncavallo associates Tamar with Bohemian chords that will not sound with Radu, thereby creating a psychological bond between the baritone and Fleana that will later be at odds with her new lover.

The couple is brought in, and Fleana begins a furious tirade that Radu's hands should be untied.[9] A more sensitive and tender aspect of her personality becomes apparent when she relates that Prince Radu wishes to become her husband, in a charming passage ("Ti dirà, ti dirà") supported by the oboes. Radu's initial words are sufficient to comprehend that we are again dealing with one of Leoncavallo's typically idealistic and romantic suitors, who will later be destroyed by a fatally misguided passion. His introduction ("Principe! Radu io son") is a suitable *nobile sostenuto* in E-major worthy of his station. Similar to

Chateaubriand's *René*, Radu is a Byronic hero tired of the restrictions of "civilized society," seeking excitement elsewhere as a "prince of adventure." A harp introduction leads directly to his E-major aria, "Dammi un amore selvaggio e ribelle," accompanied by arpeggios.

The Old Gypsy is immediately won over by Radu's enthusiasm, requesting that he remain in order to share "bread and blood."[10] A disgusted Tamar runs off when Fleana tells all assembled to begin the wedding preparations. The chorus then joyfully exits toward the river to the gypsy theme. A brief love duet begins ("Eccolo finalmente il sogno!") in which Radu explains that his dream of living an exotic life has now been realized. He then sings his love motif, which will frequently return throughout the opera ("In ogni nube"). This is followed by his passionate *cantabile* "Occhi azzurri!" expressing his longing for Fleana. The couple's rapture is echoed by an off-stage chorus singing of May. Radu again takes up the love theme, soon uniting with the voices of Fleana and the chorus.

Their passion is brief, however. Fleana notices Tamar lurking in the shadows with a dagger. She introduces him as a gypsy poet who has loved her since childhood. The men begin to quarrel, and Tamar physically assaults Radu, who immediately falls. Fleana—the typical Leoncavallo amazon—reminds Tamar that she is indeed the strongest. She taunts him in her aria "Addormentarmi, accarezzarmi nella pietà" with Spanish accents (flute, strings, harp) that recall Zandonai's 1911 *Conchita*—tambourine and all. Radu comforts himself, believing that Fleana loves only him, leading Tamar to make a desperate exit.

The gypsies now prepare the wedding to a rousing chorus ("Disciogli i balenanti tuoi capelli"), incorporating memorable syncopations. Fleana sings a sensual song in B-minor—to which she also dances—vocalizing without words, evoking an Eastern atmosphere."[11] She concludes with an octave leap to high B, requesting that Tamar's dagger be used to unite her blood with Radu in a ritualistic ceremony. Tamar's voice is heard in the background singing the refrains of a sad love song ("Canto notturno") that will again be heard in its entirety in scene 2. Fleana convinces Radu of her love as the first part concludes.

A pensive intermezzo begins in E-minor to Bohemian sounding *czardas* chords. A short flute solo resembles a bird chirping, before an oriental theme recalls Fleana's earlier song. This is followed by Tamar's love motif, a forceful *cantabile con passione* in E-major. Similar to Radu's, it is nevertheless more simple and carefree, before recurring in an inverted form.

Scene 2 (*episodio secondo*) takes place one year later.[12] A frantic and somewhat forbidding *agitato* in A-minor discloses the gypsy camp near an abandoned church where Fleana lives with Radu. Fleana has tired of the older Radu, and now seeks the embraces of Tamar, promising to wait for him that evening. Radu no longer trusts Fleana, although he speaks to her with great tenderness ("Fleana, io t'ho pensato nella mia strada"). Radu, seeking to fathom the break in their relationship, admits to feelings of unbridled jealousy in his C-minor aria "Qualcuno s'aggira attorno a noi," reminiscent of Canio's furious and frequently heard revenge motif in *Pagliacci*. His rage soon turns to supplication (*angoscioso animato*), and the aria takes on an intense melancholy while a distorted love motif reappears.

Fleana derides Radu's pleas, responding with Leoncavallo's rather awkward sounding and spiteful "Tagliami! Abbruciami!" in G-flat major. Her irritation intensifies into a tirade against Radu, telling him that his pleas fail to impress her. This segment is sung to a B-minor accompaniment with rapid octave leaps on the word "vento" ("Che m'importa? per me lo grido al vento!"). When Radu implores her to be silent she again takes up the "Tagliami! Abbruciami!" to harp arpeggios. Further taunting and pleading continues, until Fleana laughs hysterically, prompting a half-crazed Radu to hurl her to the ground, after which she runs off. Alone and distraught, Radu realizes that all is lost in his impressive aria "Ho perduto la pace vagabonda," an agonized lament in B-flat minor.

Radu leaves when Tamar's violin is heard serenading Fleana ("Canto notturno") to a light pizzicato string accompaniment introduced in scene 1. This succeeds in luring Fleana for her duet with the Young Gypsy wherein he, like Silvio, initiates to an amorous refrain of his own love motif ("Bella! Bella! Sei qui tutta fremente!"). Tamar then carries Fleana inside his house.

Radu appears, pallid and disheveled. Crazed with anger and jealousy, he calls for Fleana, realizing she is inside. He locks Fleana and Tamar's door and places straw around their dwelling, which he then symbolically lights from Fleana's embers when she taunted him with her song.[13] The couple's screams soon become audible, and the gypsies search for water to extinguish the flames, although Radu seeks to hinder them. Fleana's gasps are again heard from within when Radu unleashes his fury in an *andante sostenuto* in B-flat major to pulsating chords, delighting in his wife's agony. Radu, following Fleana's final bloodcurdling scream—which Leoncavallo insists should be "long and terrible"—begins a reprisal of his earlier aria to an altered text, expressing a desire for his own immolation. He is then assaulted by the gypsies. However, Fleana's father, with an agonized sigh, accuses him of insanity but enables his escape.

In Pushkin, Aleko (Radu) stabs Zemfira (Fleana) and the Young Gypsy (Tamar). Leoncavallo's alternate ending—written in order to avoid comparison to *Pagliacci*—ultimately proves to be a weak denouement undermining the opera's importance. Although *Zingari* is a moving work of riveting and memorable melodic invention, a degree of superficiality hinders it from becoming a worthy companion piece to *Pagliacci*.

NOTES

1. In Pushkin and Rachmaninoff the characters are Zemfira, the Young Gypsy, Aleko, and the Old Gypsy.

2. The *Appunti* state that Leoncavallo included Rumanian folksongs in the opera that he had become acquainted with through his association with the Rumanian soprano Novina decades earlier.

3. The ballet *Carneval* was also given. It seems that the Russian Ballet had more to offer than the operatic season, considering that *Pagliacci* was supposedly "disgracefully given" on 30 June 1911. R. Buckle, *Diaghilev* (New York: Atheneum, 1979), 206.

4. Performed together with Tchaikovsky's short opera *Iolantha*.

5. *Aleko* also includes "Bohemian" music.

6. Enrico Cavacchioli and Guglielmo Emanuel.

7. Reminiscent of the opening sequence of *Cavalleria rusticana*.

8. Inspired by Brahms', Hungarian Dance no. 11.

9. Fleana's entrance immediately suggests one of Leoncavallo's typical heroines, able to fend for herself.

10. This seems to be a faulty translation of Pushkin's "bread and roof," where the Russian word for "roof" (krov) was obviously mistaken in the Italian translation for the similar sounding Russian term for "blood."

11. There are major discrepancies between the 1912 Sonzogno piano-vocal score in Leoncavallo's reduction and the 1940 published orchestral score by Beltramo, in which the second verse of Fleana's dance is sung to a text. The two extant recordings of the opera rely on the 1940 version, which incorporates numerous text variances as well as a leaner score.

12. Pushkin specifies that it should be two years.

13. Leoncavallo has precisely marked the moment the fire should be lit in the score.

· 21 ·

Mimì Pinson

Characters

Marcello, baritone

Rodolfo, tenor

Schaunard, baritone

Barbemuche, bass

Visconte Paolo, baritone

Gustavo Colline, baritone

Gaudenzio, tenor

Durand, tenor

Il Signore del primo piano, tenor

Musette, mezzo-soprano

Mimì, soprano

Eufemia, mezzo-soprano

Setting: Paris (24 December 1837 to 24 December 1838)

Although *La bohème* triumphed over the short-lived *Mimì Pinson*, it is worth taking a closer look at the latter version to understand what Leoncavallo thought would improve his opera. The first cut that *La bohème* was subjected to is the absence of *un becero*, the loafer who takes music lessons from Schaunard in act 1. There is also a slight variation in the accompaniment to Schaunard's gavotte, "La macchina è soppressa." Marcello's role has been transformed into Rodolfo's with his initial "Salve, Gaudentius!" and the *La bohème* Rodolfo becomes Marcello with his first line, "Salve, otre da vin!" Mimì's entrance ("Siete la?") is now sung by Musette. Schaunard thus introduces the bohemians as "Poi Marcello, pittore" rather than "Poi Rodolfo, poeta," even though Leoncavallo has written *con poesia*. Rodolfo is presented as the author of *Le vengeur*. Schaunard remains the only character that the composer has left unaltered. Mimì brings on Musette with the aria "Musette svaria sulla bocca viva," as in the original. Leoncavallo then deletes Marcello's "Se insieme lo cercassimo il vostro tesoro?" The consumptive Mimì orders champagne (gone is the poetry of her "green liqueur" and the "smile of meadows in the sun")

288

as well as patties, lobster, and roast beef! Marcello addresses Musette as "O Musette!" rather than "signorina," leading to her original aria "Mimì Pinson la biondinetta."

Marcello's "O Musette, o gioconda e sorridente!" is now sung by Rodolfo as "O Mimì, vaporosa e sorridente!" The beautiful original line "Riso perenne e canto spensierato tinnulo, cristallino" has been changed to "Volto soave e blando illuminato/ Da un sorriso divino." Mimì becomes "vain and capricious" in this version, and Barbemuche's *arietta* has been entirely deleted, as has the a capella chorus "Al giudizio, su moviamo." The original courtship duet between Marcello and Musette now follows, with Rodolfo courting Mimì. Rather than asking if he can paint Musette's portrait, Rodolfo asks Mimì whether she will be his Muse ("immortal canvas" is altered to "immortal verses"), as "Rubens" becomes "Shakespeare." Off-stage dialogue has now been adjusted to a form of *recitativo*, bringing the work even closer to a feeling of realism.

Act 2 takes place in the courtyard of Mimì's house. Her furniture will now also serve to pay her debts. (Durand no longer mentions that Marcello and Musette live together.) Leoncavallo then recomposes the music for the tenants, bidding Durand goodnight.[1] Mimì enters with Rodolfo to see her furniture in the courtyard, and the latter rephrases the sentence "Non parlate così, Musette, uditemi" to "Non parlate così, ven prego, uditemi" before the aria "Io non ho che una povera stanzetta." Marcello returns with money from selling his painting "The Crossing of the Red Sea" rather than Rodolfo with *Vengeur*. Numerous pages dealing with Musette telling Durand about the planned party have been deleted, leading directly to the a capella chorus "Ed ora vengano." Leoncavallo also deleted the *Der Fliegende Holländer*–inspired chorus leading to the "Inno della bohème." Viscount Paolo then convinces Musette—rather than Mimì—to flee with him. The composer deletes another page in order to proceed directly to Mimì's touching original "E Rodolfo? Colpevole, colpevole sarebbe questo amore!" that Musette now sings to the viscount ("E Marcello?! Infrangere, infrangere potrei"). Mimì sings Musette's waltz aria ("Da quel suon soavemente"), which has been raised from D-major to E-flat major, while shortening it from "Fra i sorrisi all'avvenire!" to "Ma già l'onda armoniosa." Schaunard's "Già l'intimazion!" to the chorus's "Toh! Piove!" has been cut, as has his line "M'ha scritto l'uscier," now "Se poi dal cimurro potessi scampar." More deletions occur between the chorus's cries of "Vedrem!" following the stone that hits the piano, to their shouts of "Arrendetevi!" Editing out this portion also succeeds in eliminating Rodolfo's realization that Mimì has forsaken him for the viscount, which is of course necessary since it is in fact Musette who has left Marcello for the viscount in this version. Act 2 concludes with a reprisal of the "Inno della bohème," played with greater rapidity—*più presto ed accel. sempre*—rather than the original *un po' ritenuto.*

Act 3 takes place in Rodolfo's garret rather than Marcello's. Alfred de Musset's quote from *La nuit d'octobre* ("Va-t'en, retire toi, spectre de ma maîtresse!") has vanished, giving us a hint that the lyrics later derived from the poem will also disappear. Leoncavallo retains the *Séraphitus-Séraphita* introduction. Rodolfo is seen writing and speaking to Schaunard while Mimì is absorbed in thought. The first change in this act has to do with a quote from Murger, where Marcello suggests that he will try and sell a painting to Solomon (*Le passage de la Mer Rouge*). Leoncavallo changes the line from "Io porto a Salomone quel quadro" to "Io vo' dal brontolone mio zio!" Mimì sings Musette's letter scene, which becomes "Rodolfo mio, non stare ad aspettarmi" raised to B-flat minor.

When Musette enters calling for Marcello, Leoncavallo cuts two pages from her "Voglio Marcello!" to the altered wording of her impassioned "Vo' rivederlo e chiedere, perdon gli vo' prostrata," which was originally Mimì's touching "Vo' dirgli che nel leggere quei versi in cui narrava." Leoncavallo has now also begun to raise the *tessitura* for Mimì to sing Musette's lines. Mimì interprets Musette's original phrase "Fuggo perchè a la fin mi fa paura." Rodolfo enters taunting Mimì, until she sings Musette's original passage, "So che tutt'ora." This now leads to the opera's major duet that, in this version, is reserved for Mimì and Rodolfo, ending on a high B-flat sung in unison, rather than an F-sharp. Leoncavallo also omits Marcello's original "Va via, fantasma del passato!" Rodolfo now catches sight of Musette hiding behind a folding screen. When Marcello arrives he sings the elegant *andantino* "Fra noi due *enne inì* diggià tutto finì" to the spoken pleas of Musette in this case, although Leoncavallo unfortunately decides to omit a portion of this charming passage. Mimì gathers her belongings and leaves, while Schaunard does not return. Act 3 ends with Rodolfo uttering "Mimì!!" upon finding her bonnet as the curtain falls.

Act 4 opens to the same introduction as in the original, directly leading to the act 3 aria "Musette! O gioia della mia dimora!," which now becomes "Mimì!" O gioia della mia dimora!" Since most of *La bohème*'s act 4 centered around Mimì and Rodolfo, there is less for Leoncavallo to change. Marcello enters, with Rodolfo telling him that he "slept" rather than "wrote." Because Marcello can no longer admire Rodolfo's poetry, the scene proceeds to Schaunard's entrance. Mimì returns to die, and Rodolfo asks Schaunard and Marcello to help find a doctor—to altered notes. Musette no longer gives Schaunard her jewelry to pay for a physician but hands him her purse instead. Mimì recalls Christmas eve at the Café Momus as she did in *La bohème*, only to a slower tempo this time, as *Mimì Pinson* concludes without a musical reminiscence of its previous act.

NOTE

1. Leoncavallo has wisely omitted sections recalling *La forza del destino* and *La nuit de mai.*

· 22 ·

La reginetta delle rose

Characters

Lilian Varry, soprano
Anita de Rios Negros, mezzo-soprano
Mikalis, mezzo-soprano
Max de Los Fuegos, tenor
Don Pedro de la Valsenda, baritone
Gin, bass
Sparados, bass
Kradomos, bass

Setting: London and "Portowa" (1912)

A short introduction in D-major prepares a joyful mood before the curtain rises to an *allegro con spirito* quadrille, played onstage, recalling Leoncavallo's own past as a café-concert pianist. The setting is the exterior of the exhibition buildings of a London park, decorated for a benefit to raise money for a shelter devoted to "small melancholic dogs." A wealthy patroness arrives to ask Gin—professor of dead languages and tutor to Prince Max de Los Fuegos of Portowa and his cousin Don Pedro de la Valsenda—how much money has already been collected. She then places her dog, Bobby, in Gin's care for a few moments, before leaving to a charming G-major *arietta* ("Addio al cagnolino"), bidding the animal farewell.

Don Pedro enters, and Gin tells him that he has spoken with the flower girl Lilian, of whom Max is enamored. It seems that he has also written offering her a job tending the roses in the famous garden of Mokos. Lilian accepted without realizing that her "boss" would in fact be Max, the crown prince of Portowa. Don Pedro reminds Gin that if Lilian decides against Portowa, Max will not leave London. Gin humorously replies that he is well versed when it comes to the psychology of rulers. He reminds Don Pedro that it was he who read the *Life of Plutarch* to various presidents of the French Republic, curing them of insomnia, and that he also taught the crown prince of Germany to open a bottle of champagne and the king of Spain table manners. Max enters and asks to be left alone with Lilian, whereupon they sing a short duet ("Duettino del baciamano"). Guests begin arriving as a Scottish fanfare is heard, before Lilian sings her poignant "Rose Waltz" (Valzer delle rose) in G-flat major, which remains the operetta's main theme ("Rose argento porporine e d'or").

Lilian's beauty attracts the attention of three American tourists. Furious, Max and one American assault one another as a *marziale mosso* sounds, with snatches of "Yankee Doodle" that Leoncavallo salvaged from his 1906 *Viva l'America*. The onstage orchestra then plays a polka in F-major, before Max and Lilian are once again left alone for their charming and graceful D-major duet "Lontano, lontano Lilian," which comes across as a mixture of Leoncavallo and Lehár. Lilian and Max dream of Portowa, as Gin and the chorus rejoice and celebrate Lilian's planned departure with a round of champagne, leading to a rousing *tempo di galopp* that concludes the act.

Act 2 is preceded by a short prelude echoing the "Rose Waltz." The scene is the Kingdom of Portowa. Six ancient ministers enter carrying canes, with hands on their lower backs, complaining of rheumatism in the charming *allegro moderato* in D-major "I ministri di Portowa." Mikalis—Portowa's regent—arrives to discuss the problem of her nephew Max and Lilian, deciding that the girl should be arrested and Max made to marry the wealthy Anita de Rios Negros, although she is already engaged to Don Pedro. Gin explains what he taught the princes in a vivacious "tempo di gavotta," before being showered with abuse from the regent, who threatens that he will be banished to immediate exile if he fails to obtain Max's consent to marry Anita. All exit, leaving a miserable Gin behind, who tells Max and Don Pedro of their tragic "force of destiny."[1] Max, Don Pedro, and Anita agree to temporarily conform until a better solution is found. The others remain singing the "telephone duet," in which Anita suggests that she would rather only *hear* Don Pedro's voice at this point.

Lilian's arrest had been carried out when she entered the country. Approaching Max, she is not only astounded that he is in fact the crown prince but also furious at his actions against her. Max declares his love—allowing her to leave the country if she desires—in an extended duet ("Che dici mai") that commences with some fine touches. They then again declare their love to the "Rose Waltz."

When Don Pedro, Anita, and Gin reappear, Max suggests that he will abdicate in favor of Don Pedro, who refuses because he wishes to leave with Anita. As all decide that a revolution would be the answer, Portowa's two an-

archists—Sparados and Kradomos—are called in. They are elated that the conspiracy will be called "Nabucodonosor," enabling them to be remembered as
"Sparakramodos" in the company of Marat, Danton, and Bismarck. This is sung
to an Offenbach-inspired ensemble ("E questa notte a mezzanotte"). Mikalis
enters demanding Lilian's release as the "revolution" breaks out. The regent
refuses to accede, preferring exile, surprised that no one is willing to follow.

An intermezzo based on Max and Lilian's act 2 duet is heard before act 3
begins in an antechamber to the throne room, where Gin recounts the latest
revolutionary developments. Anita and Lilian try on some elegant robes, leading to the trio "Basta tanta confidenza!" Don Pedro enters with the news that
now, after Mikalis has entered into "voluntary exile," the populace would prefer
a constitutional government with Max as king. Lilian realizes that there will be
no place for her and that she must leave Portowa. Don Pedro seeks to console
her in the tragic-sounding E-minor duet "Piccola bimba la vita crudele!" Lilian
leaves in tears to a *triste sostenuto* with concluding chords reminiscent of *Manon
Lescaut* as Don Pedro instructs Gin to take her to the gardens of Mokos.

Max enters having decided to renounce the throne out of love. He takes
leave of his ancestors in the G-flat major aria "Innamorato son" that seems
based on Milio's "È un riso gentile" from act 1 of *Zazà*. Max refuses to sign the
decree inaugurating a new constitutional government if it means leaving Lilian.
She now enters carrying a rose that she dips into the ink, handing it back to
Max in order that he sign the document, which he does.

Max tells his people, with great dignity, that a new democratic era has
begun in which old traditions are no longer valid. And therefore, Lilian, the
flower girl, should be accepted as their new queen. Delighted with the idea, the
chorus proclaims Lilian, with an affectionate diminuitive, as their new "Reginetta delle rose."[2] All rejoice in a D-major finale (*allegro moderato marziale*) that
concludes with a reprisal of the "Rose Waltz."

Leoncavallo follows the standard operetta format of employing two
couples in love. There are few instances in the score that remind us of Leoncavallo's previous compositions. The entire opus seems to have been inspired by
a mixture of Lehár and Offenbach: brief and lighthearted melodies combined
with spoken dialogue to an orchestral accompaniment (*musica di scena*) that
frequently recalls a café-concert atmosphere. The dialogue exceeds the vocal
music with a very lengthy second act, resulting in a fairly long evening. Forzano and Leoncavallo were influenced by the almost mandatory exotic setting
dealing with royalty, similar to Lehár's *Das land des lächelns*, while the trouser
role of Regent Mikalis seems cloned from Prince Orlofsky in Johann Strauss's
Die fledermaus.

La reginetta della rose is essentially a play with vocal numbers (short selections with numerous *da capos*), that greatly depends on the manner in which

it is performed in order to be successful. The works marks a turning point for Leoncavallo as an operetta composer and Forzano as a—then unknown— librettist. *La reginetta della rose* would remain the only operetta widely associated with the composer's name.

NOTES

1. Forzano further puns on Verdi's opera when he refers to Don Pedro as "il marchese di Calatrava" and Max as "Don Alvaro," even quoting *La forza del destino*'s "Le minacce i fieri accenti."

2. "Small Queen of Roses."

· 23 ·

Are You There?

Characters (ranges unknown)

Percy Pellett	Miss Bing
Gordon Grey	Maud Waring
Antonio/Mr. Nott-Wright	Mafalda Malatesta
Bertie Carlton	Winifred Miller
Mr. Record	Miss Nora Hammersmith
Commissionaire at Exchange	Miss Gladys Kensington
Grand Vizier	Miss London Hall
Viscount Guineas	Miss Gerrard
Carlo	Miss Mayfair
Customer at the Casino	Miss Wimbledon
Gregory Lester	Miss Hopp

Setting: London, 1913

This musical comedy is a burlesque of the telephone service, involving an American millionaire who works as a telephone mechanic, thereby allowing him to listen in on conversations held by cabinet ministers, whom he then blackmails into honoring him with a title. His daughter, on the other hand, works for the telephone company in order to pursue a writer of musical comedies whose voice she has become enamored of over the phone. The "Rose Way" duet is all that presently seems to remain of a score, which, in its entirety, may have never been published.

· 24 ·

La candidata

Characters

Aurora Lefleur, soprano
Sofronia Duchy, soprano
Eleonora Banfou, alto
Clara Rivy, soprano
Evelina Delny, soprano
Marta Sabot, spoken role
Giulia Tachat, alto
Carlo, tenor
Antonio, tenor
Guido, bass

Anatolio, bass
Prince Franz de Gouvin, tenor
Prefect of the Capital, spoken role
Prefect of Noincy, spoken role
President of the Council of Ministers, bass
Foreign Minister, spoken role
the servant Pellerossa, tenor
Pevedan, spoken role
Gregorio, spoken role

Setting: "Noincy" and Paris (1990)

La candidata (The candidate) was regarded as having a social message when it was written, taking place in the "utopian" year of 1990, when women are able to vote and peace has been proclaimed between nations.

Act 1 opens in the fictitious town of Noincy, in a hall filled with women suffragettes, who eagerly await the arrival of their "candidate," Aurora Lefleur. This is preceded by a short *allegro spigliato* introduction in B-flat major consisting of the "husband" theme. A "Feminist Hymn" ("Inno femminista") is then rehearsed for the candidate's arrival ("Guerra! Guerra!"). A duet commences ("Pevedan! Pevedan!") in F-major between the suffragette Eleonora and Pevedan, her rather "sexless" male secretary. Forzano pokes fun at the entire suffragette movement, with the women (Eleonora, Sofronia, Clara, and Giulia) demonstrating dominant masculine traits, while their husbands (Carlo,

297

Antonio, Guido, and Anatolio) act like neutered slaves. The mood for the reversal of sexes is already set in the Eleonora/Pevedan duet, where Eleonora sings mostly chest voice while Pevedan replies in an extremely high falsetto. The duet continues (*sostenuto alla tirolese*) with Pevedan's "singing" resembling yodeling ("Ah! O Pevedan mio dolce").

An octet consisting of all the husbands and their wives now continues as an example of male suppression (by their wives, that is.) This is interrupted by the arrival of Aurora, who enters to the suffragette theme. Aurora is of course a model of femininity, and she does justice to her name (sunrise) with her first aria, "Egli andava predicando" in F-major, which resembles a café-concert song from the composer's early Parisian days.

The feminist hymn that had been rehearsed previously now resumes in its entirety in B-flat major. Declaring "war" against ostracism, the hymn begins dramatically, lightening to the utmost delicacy in its second verse, when the women sing of using their gowns as flags. When it is discovered that sixty centesimi are still needed to finance the upcoming elections within the next eight days, all decide that a trip to Paris in search of a sponsor will be necessary.

An interlude in B-flat major with a reprisal of the hymn ends when the curtain rises, disclosing Prince Franz de Gouvin in bed with his girlfriend, Evelina. Franz sings an aria describing a dream in which he was the president of France ("Andavo in pariglia diretto a Longchamps").

Act 2 is preceded by another "intermezzo" in the form of a waltz that is modeled on Franz's aria. A party in Paris attended by Aurora is in progress, beginning with a tango in C-major. Evelina sings her "Canzone del principe russo" (song of the Russian prince), leading to Aurora's major romanza, "Non so perchè."

Franz turns out to be the male candidate, though neither candidate realizes the other's ambition until after Aurora has performed her "Dance of the Seven Veils" in D-flat major ("Dolce brezza tepida che voli"). Franz is now completely won over by Aurora's charm, and a major duet begins ("Cadrà pel mio piacer!") that remains the crux of the operetta, reminding one again of Leoncavallo the operatic composer, as during some of Franz's music ("Ch'io ti riguardi!"). When Aurora tries to leave, Franz confesses his love. She finally tells him that she is the female candidate. Franz now also discloses that he is the male candidate. Both burst out laughing, joining in the sprightly waltz, "Con molto spirito il destin."

The prelude to act 3 (intermezzo) takes up the theme of Aurora's "Dance of the Seven Veils." This act demonstrates that even in "far away 1990" (again in Noincy) there is still intrigue and selling of votes. Franz and Aurora decide to remain together, giving up their chance of winning, while it is unanimously decided that the androgynous Prevedan should receive the position. The operetta concludes with a concise duet between Franz and Aurora ("In quella primavera" in the partitura) that, curiously, frequently resembles *Der Roland von Berlin*.

· 25 ·

Mameli

Characters

Goffredo Mameli, tenor
Carlo Terzaghi, baritone
Delia, soprano
Princess Cristina Trivulzio di Belgioioso, mezzo-soprano
Enrico Dandolo, baritone
Emilio Dandolo, tenor

Luciano Manara, bass
Il Sergente Austriaco, bass
Un vecchio servo, baritone
Primo Ufficiale, baritone

Secondo Ufficiale, tenor

Setting: Milan and Rome (1848–1849)

Mameli is based on the historical personage of the poet-soldier Goffredo Mameli (1827–1849). His early writings stem from 1846–1847, and it was not long before they contained a political message.[1] He published *La battaglia di Marengo* and *Dante e l'Italia* in 1847. A native of Genoa, Mameli soon began taking part in patriotic demonstrations. His hymn "Fratelli d'Italia" (set to music by Novaro) was sung in the streets to great enthusiasm, earning the young man immense popularity.[2] The Italian revolution had now found its poet, and, soon, "Fratelli d'Italia" simply became known as the "Inno Mameli," while its author was seen waving the still forbidden three-colored flag as a disciple of Mazzini. During March 1848 he heard that there had been uprisings in Milan, and he set out the following day leading some three hundred men, entering the city four days later. He remained a captain throughout Italy's first War of Independence. After meeting Mazzini and experiencing the failure of battle, Mameli returned to Genoa, where he then published his "Inno militare" inspired by Mazzini. When the nationalist and republican Garibaldi, after having been forced to flee,

300

returned to Italy in 1848, he led a volunteer army of three thousand followers in the fight for national independence to free Italy from domestic tyranny and foreign oppression. Mameli joined the ranks when Garibaldi reached Genoa that September. In Rome he wrote some of the last of his surviving poetry, returning there again shortly to fight against the French siege on Garibaldi's forces in Palestrina, Velletri (19 March 1859), and, finally, Gianicolo on 3 June, where he was wounded in the leg. Although it should not have cost Mameli his life, he received improper treatment at the Trinità dei Pellegrini hospital, where he died following a month of atrocious suffering.

Princess Belgioioso (1808–1871)—the other factual character to appear in Leoncavallo's opera—was born in Milan and was herself a fascinating personality. A descendant of Marshall Gian Giacomo Trivulzio, who died while she was still a child, she married the handsome and wealthy Prince Emilio Barbiano di Belgioioso d'Este. The couple soon went separate ways, with the princess moving to Lugano, Genoa, and Marseilles, after being suspected of radical Italian patriotism. From France, she supported Mazzini by selling her jewels. Hounded by the Austrian government in 1833, she settled in Paris, where she made ends meet by painting. Her beauty, combined with the name Trivulzio, assured her easy access into the Parisian salon of Madame Récamier. She soon had her own, frequented by Victor Hugo, Chopin, Liszt, Bellini, Rossini, George Sand, Alfred de Musset, Dumas père, and Mameli. Heinrich Heine had also been a guest and admirer of her charm, mentioning her in one breath with Rossini and Raphael in his *Reisebilder*. After initial writing attempts (*Essai sur la formation du dogme catholique* and *Essai sur Vico*), she realized the importance of the press. Soon she founded the newspaper *Gazzetta Italiana* in 1845—later rebaptized *Ausonio*—which she used as a mouthpiece for a liberated Italy against Austrian domination. In Naples, when the revolution of 1848 broke out, she rented a boat and enlisted a battalion to support the Milanese uprisings, entering the city carrying the tricolored flag on 6 April. She was placed in charge of Rome's military hospitals after founding two further newspapers in Milan to support the idea of fusing Lombardy with Piedmont. Following the fall of the Roman Republic, the princess left for Asia Minor, which she immortalized in the volume *Asie Mineure et Syrie*, published in Paris in 1858. Returning to Italy, she authored a history of the House of Savoy, after which she also founded two more newspapers and befriended Verdi and Giuseppina Strepponi. Following her death, rumors began that she had kept the embalmed body of her lover for one year prior to his burial, but, then again, she was also reported to have entered Milan in 1848 dressed as Joan of Arc!

Part 1 (*episodio primo*) begins with a short *preludietto* immediately introducing Terzaghi's theme (*maestoso molto sostenuto*). Drums are heard in the distance. The curtain rises disclosing a room in Terzaghi's luxurious Milanese home on

Corsia dei Servi (presently Corso Vittorio Emanuele) during the Risorgimento of November/December 1848. A large balcony appears at back from which the cathedral can be discerned. Terzaghi and his daughter, Delia, are discussing the latest executions, as well as the death of his wife (Delia's mother)—a victim of the city's fighting. Terzaghi sings his only aria, the impressive E-flat major "Italia! Italia," a forceful and patriotic homage to the liberty or death of his country, which also introduces the Risorgimento motif.[3]

A servant enters, handing Terzaghi a letter from the Dandolo brothers, informing him that a revolutionary meeting will be held in his home that very evening. He then hurriedly leaves to meet Princess Belgioioso to the Risorgimento motif. He gives Delia the letter to show to their guests later that night, one of which will be the poet and patriot Goffredo Mameli.

Alone, Delia takes out some of Mameli's poetry ("Ad un angelo") that she found in his room, wondering if it had indeed been written with her in mind, since she reciprocates his love. She begins reading the verses to the "love motif," as the orchestra accompanies her in a gentle romantic cascade of F-major chords, expressing all the tenderness and poetry so typical of Leoncavallo at his best ("Io ti trovai"). The aria's main section ("La man di dio") is a *sostenuto cantabile* followed by Delia's own motif ("Dove si soffre").

Mameli suddenly enters to find Delia in tears as she hides the verses ("Delia! piangete!"). The poet recalls his patriotic credo in suitably passionate terms ("Ben è ver ch'io sperando sognando l'ideal"), culled from *Chatterton's* act 1 aria "Ricomposi l'antica favella" in its original key of G-flat major. Delia then tells Mameli in sweeping phrases (*andantino grazioso*) that she considers him Italy's liberator. They alternate reciting the poetry in a duet based on Delia's aria.

Their languor is interrupted by Enrico and Emilio Dandolo, who enter followed by Terzaghi and Princess Belgioioso. They arrive through a hidden entrance to a *maestoso* march that Leoncavallo based on the 1848 patriotic hymn "Inno del popolo." Enrico Dandolo informs them that Luciano Manara will also come. The orchestra takes up the popular hymn "La bandiera tricolore." Princess Belgioioso greets Mameli before Terzaghi and Enrico Dandolo begin the patriotic hymn "Il popol diviso," that evolves into an oath for an independent Italy, later also joined in by Mameli, Emilio Dandolo, and the princess herself.

Manara arrives with a letter for Mameli from Rome. The love motif is heard when the poet watches Delia leave the room on her father's orders so that she will not become involved in the dangerous conspiracy. Mameli reads that Garibaldi will be entering Rome, requiring their support. A quintet (based on Mameli's own "Fratelli d'Italia") in A-major is then sung, while drums roll in the distance. Manara suggests that they leave for Rome that very evening.

The earlier heard hymn is then taken up to an altered text, concluding with a grand "A Roma! A Roma! A Roma!" All exit, as Terzaghi places the letter in a secret cabinet.

Mameli, before returning to his room, decides that leaving the letter in Terzaghi's possession may prove too risky for Delia, and he burns it. Delia returns to confess her love for Mameli in the duet "Signore . . . fratel mio!" However, Mameli is anxious to leave for Rome, and Delia realizes that their future will be marked by tears. Leoncavallo makes use of agitated *recitativo* before borrowing from himself again with part of *Chatterton's* act 3 duet ("Col dritto che prorompe").

Knocks are heard at the door. Delia utters a cry of surprise when she sees the police approaching. Terzaghi returns in time to help Mameli escape through the secret exit before a sergeant enters. Terzaghi calmly declares that he lives alone with his daughter. The police find portions of Mameli's smoldering letters in the fireplace, and it does not take long before the secret door is also discovered. Terzaghi admits to having helped Mameli escape. He is immediately escorted out in handcuffs, albeit singing a verse of "Fratelli d'Italia," thus bringing part 1 to a close.

Part 2 (*episodio secondo*) is preceded by an intermezzo that expresses the despair of a suppressed nation. It begins with a *sostenuto lamentoso* of tragically bleak chords in A-minor, recalling the opening *andante sostenuto* in act 4 of Puccini's *Manon Lescaut*. It then fades into a quiet *mormorando* section with an equally beautiful melody. This sequence constitutes the main body of the orchestral interlude—foreshadowing Delia's aria in the second episode—before concluding with an elegiac *diminuendo*.

The curtain rises to an *allegro agitato*, showing a house and vineyard outside Rome in 1849.[4] Mameli appears in uniform as cannon shots are heard in the distance. He is astounded to see Delia, who relates how her father escaped from a prison in Mantua and is heading for Rome. Princess Belgioioso enters, telling Mameli that most of Rome's citizens have taken up arms. She then proceeds to praise Garibaldi in her short but effective F-major arietta "Fra il tumulto."

An official brings Garibaldi's orders for Mameli, and the princess enters the house, preparing to transform it into a military hospital. A frightened Delia embraces Mameli to the love motif. Terzaghi arrives greeting Mameli, which leads to a short quartet, followed by distant voices singing the patriotic hymn "Fuoco contro fuoco!" in F-major. Terzaghi unsheathes his sword and leaves to fight as students shout "Viva Mameli!" but Mameli cautions them not to rejoice until the battle has been won. Pleased that his song will accompany the fighting, Mameli speaks of poetry and war in the aria "Tu sempre a me rimani, o poesia," taken almost verbatim from *Chatterton's* act 2 "Tu sola a me rimani, o poesia."[5] He leaves to fight, and Delia confides to the princess that she hopes he will not be wounded. Music from the intermezzo returns again to accompany Delia's A-minor aria "Per ogni colpo." Fearing that Mameli may die in battle, Delia prays to the Virgin to spare the man she loves. She sinks to her knees at the aria's conclusion, as chords in the orchestra simulate her tears.

Mameli soon returns, wounded and knowing that he will die, imploring Delia not to cry as the love motif sounds. He is followed by Terzaghi, who enters smeared with blood, his sword broken, accompanied by *maestoso* chords that opened act 2 of *Der Roland von Berlin* and that will later return for *Edipo re*. Three operas with an identical motif! Mameli sings of the "new Italy" as his life ebbs away. The score informs us that St. Peter's cupola is now also illuminated in the distance, thanks to Leoncavallo's effort to reach a rousing patriotic conclusion. Delia sings a final phrase from the original love duet, and Mameli dies uttering a spoken "Italia! Italia!" Terzaghi drapes Mameli's body with the tricolored flag as offstage voices sing "Fratelli d'Italia."[6] The curtain falls to the same chords in F-major originally heard in the prelude.

NOTES

1. One of these was "L'alba"—the reason Leoncavallo originally wished to call the opera by that name.

2. The family was of course not unknown, since Mameli's father, Giorgio, had been a celebrated sea captain.

3. This may have originally been composed for *Avemaria*.

4. In the original typescript libretto, the second episode commences immediately following the intermezzo with Mameli's "Tu sempre a me rimane o poesia." Leoncavallo no doubt preferred to try and stretch the opera with additional dialogue in the final version.

5. Leoncavallo had originally reworked the *Chatterton* aria to be included in *Ça-Ira!*

6. The "Fratelli d'Italia" was not originally planned to be included at this point.

· 26 ·

Prestami tua moglie

Characters

Rabastoul, bass
Gontrano, tenor
Rissolin, tenor
Beaut Iran, spoken role
Angela, soprano
Margherita, soprano

Nanon, soprano
Magay, spoken role
La Servetta, spoken role
La Fanciulla, spoken role
Il Portinaio, spoken role
Giulietta, spoken role

Setting: Paris ("The Present," circa 1916)

Prestami tua moglie (Lend me your wife) derives from a vaudeville play in two acts written by Maurice Desvallières and dedicated to his teacher Eugène Labiche (1815–1888). Labiche was famous in France for creating more than one hundred such plays in four decades at the Palais Royal. Desvallières' farce also premiered there on 10 September 1883 and was later available to readers when published in Paris (Ollendorf Editeurs) one year later.[1] Although Leoncavallo lived from 1882 onward in Paris, where he may have seen a performance, it seems more likely that he became aware of the subject through a cinematic version that appeared decades later. Leoncavallo and his librettist, Edmondo Corradi, enlarged the work to encompass three acts due to the additional vocal and orchestral material they had created. Desvallières' original title was retained, and very little, in fact, was changed. Curiously, although Corradi worked with Leoncavallo on the text, his name was not mentioned on either the published libretto (which appeared without dialogue) or the original score.

Prestami tua moglie begins with a spirited prelude in E-major reminiscent of Rossini in its vivacity. It is based on three movements, one of which, an *alle-*

305

gro moderato in A-major, presents the operetta's main theme, the "lending" motif. Act 1 is set in the salon of the newly married couple Angela and Rissolin.
A portrait of Angela hangs on the wall, reminding the spectator of her looming
presence as the future "borrowed wife." Magay, the British nanny, is knitting,
while Rissolin accepts flowers from an introductory chorus in F-major in the
form of a lullaby ("Candidi gigli offriam per il bambino"). Preparations are
underway for the baptism of Rissolin and Angela's son, Edmondo.

Angela and Rissolin sing of their domestic bliss in the duet "Mio Rissolin!
l'alba spuntò che gia sognò l'anima amante!" Their friend Gontrano then enters
in a hurry, informing them that his uncle, the elderly Captain Rabastoul, plans
to visit him in Paris. Hoping to advance his career, Gontrano has sought to remain on cordial terms with Rabastoul, since he is also in love with his daughter,
Margherita. Rabastoul wishes to hear nothing of this liaison, since he has the
sixty-year-old Beaut Iran in mind for his daughter. Thus, Gontrano has sent
Rabastoul Angela's photo, claiming that she is his wife. Panicked, Gontrano now
pleads with Rissolin to "lend him his wife" for the duration of Rabastoul's visit.
This is sung to an *allegro moderato* trio that commences with the "lending" motif
("Prestami tua moglie, non per brutte voglie"). Although Rissolin is shocked,
Angela finds the idea enticing, reminding her husband that they can then write
one another secret letters just as they had prior to their own marriage.

Rabastoul arrives with his daughter, Margherita, soon after the couple
agrees to help their friend for two days. Rissolin sings a rapturous duet with
Margherita in E-major ("Ah per te; per te batte il mio cuore"). This leads to
Rabastoul's charming aria "La femmina in istato interessante" that begins as
a gavotte in G-major. Not only is Rabastoul charmed by Angela, he is also
delighted that Gontrano is already married to her, and, even better, that they
already have a child. When the uncle insists that the child be given his Christian name at the baptism, Gontrano tells him to join them at the church for
the ceremony. However, he purposely gives him the name of a different church
in order to hinder his presence. The act concludes to a jubilant quartet in A-
flat major ("Certo che sia il battesimo lontan!") sung by Angela, Margherita,
Gontrano, and Rissolin.

A short prelude (*andante amoroso*) based on the act 1 Margherita-
Gontrano duet precedes act 2. The scene is the same as act 1. The baptism has
taken place in the interim without Rabastoul, who spent the time searching for
the wrong church. Act 2 consists largely of music already heard in the previous
act. The baptism is however celebrated with a noteworthy melancholic waltz
in F-major sung by Nanon and Gontrano ("Lenta lenta la danza ancor mi fa
vibrare d'amor!").

Act 3 begins with an extended scene for Rabastoul commencing in C-
major recalling the previous party ("Vedi? In prima! Cominciar, se lo vuoi

bene ammazzar"). This leads to Angela's main aria in E-flat major "Nella storia vecchia e novella!" after which both couples once again sing of their love to music inspired by a tarantella ("Su presto, presto amici").

In the meantime, Rabastoul has intercepted one of Rissolin's "love letters" to Angela. Believing him to be Angela's lover, Rabastoul demands that Gontrano fight a duel with Rissolin. The farce concludes at this point in the play before the dealings become mortally dangerous, whereas, in the operetta, Corradi and Leoncavallo opt to present the duel onstage in a trio with Rabastoul beginning in E-major ("Ecco a te!"). All ends well, however, when Rabastoul is informed of the truth, concluding the operetta with a short finale based on the lending theme ("Tutto ben finisce ordinato e saggio").

Prestami tua moglie is a charming and extremely lighthearted work that contains some memorable passages, such as the fresh and inspired Gontrano-Margherita duet of act 1 and the romantic Gontrano-Nanon duet of act 2. Although inferior to *Reginetta delle rose*, it is both witty and delightful, proving another success, as its numerous newspaper reviews attest.

NOTE

1. The characters' names in the original play are Gontran (Gontrano), Beautiran (Beaut Iran), Angèle (Angela), Edith (Margherita), and Juliette (Giulietta).

· 27 ·

A chi la giarrettiera?

Characters

Tilde, soprano
Adriano, tenor
Raimondetta, soprano
Leopoldo, bass
Celestino, tenor
Eulalia, soprano
Viscount Faucon, baritone

Setting: Paris ("The Present," 1918)

This charming operetta commences with an extended overture (*allegro giusto*) in E-major incorporating the work's major themes.[1] A highlight of act 1 is a waltz—the "Canzone della giarrettiera" ("Striscia di raso morbidetta e fina")— sung by Adriano, recalling the gaiety of *Reginetta delle rose*. Following a *da capo* joined by the chorus, the operetta moves on to the fox-trot duet in F-major, the "Duettino dei piccioni," with the *comprimario* couple, Raimondetta and Celestino, interpreting two cooing pigeons, complete with refrains of "glu, glu, glu."

Spanish dance music played in the orchestra (a *zapateado* in D-minor) leads to a café-concert duet in F-major ("Chiedi mia cara tutto quello che vorrai") sung by Raimondetta and Adriano. The operetta's heroine, Tilde, Adriano's wife, now enters for an extended and slightly melancholic duet in F-minor between herself and Raimondetta ("Penso che sempre noi povere illuse"). Tilde goes off in search of her husband only to discover him in Raimondetta's embrace. She swears revenge as the chorus once again takes up the "pigeon theme" originally sung by Raimondetta and Celestino, bringing act 1 to a close.

Act 2 is set at a party, preceded by a march-like quadrille in E-major, followed by Leopoldo's sprightly aria "L'uom che di donne ha pratica," wherein he sings of the difficulty men have trying to comprehend women. Tilde appears masked, still suffering from Adriano's supposed infidelity with Raimondetta, singing the work's major aria in D-major, the *sostenuto cantabile* "Ah! qual tristezza e qual melanconia invade tutto il disilluso cuor." It recalls Salomé's "Il est doux, il est bon" in act 1 of Massenet's *Hérodiade*, showing that Leoncavallo, at the end of his career, is still under the spell of the French composer. Adriano fails to detect Tilde's identity and immediately begins courting her. This develops into an extended quartet when Raimondetta and Celestino join in. Tilde begins a spirited Brindisi in E-flat major, later accompanied by a rousing chorus. Her joy is replaced by her disillusionment with love, sung to a grand ensemble. Refusing to leave with Adriano, Tilde opts to take the arm of Viscount Faucon, as Raimondetta tells Adriano to leave. Raimondetta and Celestino take up the Brindisi once more accompanied by the chorus as the act ends.

Act 3 opens at a casino with a "Mexican chorus" in D-major ("O Paris! O Paris!"). Raimondetta and Celestino once again sing of their love. The stage empties, leaving Adriano seeking Tilde's pardon in vain. The operetta nevertheless concludes joyfully—as to be expected—with Adriano receiving her forgiveness after all misconceptions have been clarified.

A chi la giarrettiera? was another attempt by Leoncavallo and his librettist, Corradi, to recapture *Prestami tua moglie*'s ambience, with its simple vaudeville scenario. The work is a charming, light pastiche that also incorporates some impressive vocal writing recalling the operatic Leoncavallo. It remains another successful attempt in a genre that the composer did much to further in Italy.

NOTE

1. Although the autograph piano-vocal score of Leoncavallo's last complete work, *A chi la giarrettiera?* (Whose Garter Is This?), could be located, an extended search for a libretto containing spoken dialogue remained futile. Since most of the action progresses by way of the spoken text as in most operettas, it is unfortunate that a more detailed synopsis could not be derived from the music's lyrics alone.

· 28 ·

Edipo re

Characters

Edipo, baritone
Giocasta, mezzo-soprano
Creonte, tenor
Tiresia, bass
a Corinthian, baritone
a shepherd, tenor
Antigone, mute
Ismene, mute
Greek chorus

Setting: Thebes (Antiquity)

The opera begins with the same impressive *allegro moderato* chords that opened act 2 of *Der Roland von Berlin*.[1] In *Edipo re* they signify the "fate" motif. Thebes' citizens are heard from within pleading with Oedipus to liberate them from the plague. The fate motif sounds once more (D-minor) when the curtain rises revealing the chorus before the Royal Palace in Thebes. An *allegro moderato* depicts their anxiety, and they repeatedly implore Oedipus (Edipo) for guidance in one of the opera's few original pages, gaining momentum in a rousing supplication theme in B-minor ("Sire, o Sire!").

Oedipus appears, seeking to comfort the populace by informing them that he is aware of their plight and that his brother-in-law, Creon (Creonte), has asked the Oracle at Delphi to consult Apollo for a solution. He then tells them that Creon has returned, in an elegant B-major phrase ("Di rose incoronato") to horn and string accompaniment. Creon soon enters, explaining that the Oracle has promised to rid Thebes of the plague if the man that killed

Laius—Oedipus's predecessor—is found and tried. The fate motif immediately sounds again in E-minor, marking the importance of these words. The theme modulates when Creon informs Oedipus that the murderer is in Thebes, although the Oracle failed to mention his name. Creon goes in search of the blind prophet Tiresias, as Oedipus again addresses the crowd in D-major ("E amore, famiglia") with music taken from *Der Roland von Berlin*.

The chorus is unable to inform Oedipus who the murderer might be. Tiresias (Tiresia) then enters to Baruch's theme from *Der Roland von Berlin*. Accompanied by violent chords, the blind man refuses to disclose the murderer, and Oedipus pleads with him to reconsider ("Ah! Tu non vedi").[2] The passage concludes when Oedipus again implores Tiresias to the supplication theme first heard from the chorus.[3] Finally, Tiresias says that it is Oedipus. However, the latter immediately suspects that Creon has planned the answer to usurp his throne. The guards hurl themselves at Creon and Tiresias, as Oedipus's consort, Jocasta (Giocasta), enters to harp arpeggios, while the chorus hums, creating a placid atmosphere. Elsbeth's motif from *Der Roland von Berlin* now becomes Jocasta's in an *andantino mosso*.

Shocked to see her brother in chains—contrary to the Sophocles version—Jocasta asks for an explanation, beginning with the lyrical phrase "Rispetta me nel fratel mio!" When she asks Oedipus how he heard the news, he replies that it was Tiresias who informed him. Curiously, this is sung to a passage bearing a distinct resemblance to the roll call in act 3 of Puccini's *Manon Lescaut*, which, of course, Leoncavallo originally collaborated on. Jocasta tells Oedipus that she has no use for prophecies ("Le profezie son come foglie"), comparing them to leaves that scatter in the wind. She relates (in *recitativo*) how an oracle once prophesied that her first husband, Laius, would be killed by his own son but, instead, was slain by assassins at the crossroads of Delphi and Daulia, where the crime was reported to her by a servant who had escaped unscathed.

Oedipus frees Creon and Tiresias, who leave. The chorus also exits, hoping that a witness can be found. Alone, Oedipus asks Jocasta whether she had had a son with Laius. She confirms this but also admits that the child was killed after three days because of the Oracle's prophesy. Oedipus now tells her that the Delphic Oracle also told him that he would murder his father and marry his mother. He thus fled from Corinth to avoid his destiny. Upon reaching Phocis he was involved in a fight following much provocation, eventually slaying all the men except one. Horrified that he may have in fact killed Laius, he sings the opera's only major aria ("Ramingo andar") taken in its entirety from Rathenow's act 2 *scena* "Dio che non vedo" from *Der Roland von Berlin*.

Jocasta's theme (alias Elsbeth's) is heard in E-major as she seeks to comfort Oedipus. She then begins one of the opera's very few original melodies

("Svaniranno dall'alma le negre nubi alfine") in E-major that is appropriately maternal in its tenderness. Moved, Oedipus joins her in a short but emotional duet ("E fra le mie carezze"), signifying a moment of repose before the approaching drama.

Heralds' trumpets announce the arrival of a Corinthian (Sophocles, scene 3) to an orchestral accompaniment (*agitato e vigoroso*), culled from the opening of act 4 of *Der Roland von Berlin*. He informs Oedipus that their king, Polybus, has died and that the people of Corinth want Oedipus to return to govern them.[4] He refuses, reminding the Corinthian of his curse, as sonorous chords in E-minor accentuate his words, recalling the orchestral finale to Canio's "Ridi Pagliaccio." The Corinthian now advises Oedipus that he not need worry about having murdered his father, since his parents were not in fact Polybus and Merope as had been supposed. When Oedipus asks for proof—as Jocasta's theme is briefly heard in C-major—the Corinthian informs him that a shepherd from the house of Laius had placed the infant Oedipus in his care and he, in turn, gave the child to Polybus. Shuddering, Jocasta and Oedipus exchange glances as the chorus demands that the shepherd be brought in, to a dramatic drum roll (Sophocles, scene 4).

The shepherd leaves little doubt that Oedipus is indeed Laius and Jocasta's son. The prophesy has therefore been fulfilled. When Oedipus finally asks the shepherd if he recognizes the murderer, the latter mutely nods, prompting both Oedipus and Jocasta to flee from the stage. Tiresias gravely announces to the stricken crowd that Oedipus is both the son and husband of their queen, as well as his father's murderer. The chorus scatters in horror, commenting in a forceful outcry—Forzano borrowing from Shakespeare's *Macbeth* rather than Sophocles—that not even the sea would be able to cleanse the crimes committed.

An orchestral intermezzo now begins, symbolizing Jocasta's offstage suicide and Oedipus's self-inflicted blindness.[5] The chorus cries "orror!" (horror!) in the background and the orchestra evokes the protagonist's turmoil, before Jocasta's theme is again taken up in the form of an *andante doloroso* in E-major.

Oedipus enters to a lachrymose *lento* in D-minor ("Oh, notte orrenda!") that once again recalls "Ridi, pagliaccio." He sings of Jocasta's suicide, pleading for atonement in the hope that serenity will one day return to Thebes. Creon brings in Oedipus's daughters, Antigone and Ismene, whose sighs resound in a D-minor chord in the orchestra. Placing his hands on their heads, he says goodbye to them ("Miei poveri fior") to Elsbeth's touching farewell ("Addio, mio fedel!)" from act 4 of *Der Roland von Berlin*. This theme modulates to F-sharp minor when Oedipus recoils at the thought of caressing his own daughters, entrusting them to Creon's care. The scene concludes as it began, with

Oedipus commenting on the horrendous and eternal night. He then walks off into the distance, stumbling at intervals and raising himself with effort, as the opera's initial opening chords are again heard, concluding what might have been a significant work—had it been original.

NOTES

1. In B-minor rather than the original C-minor.
2. Recalling Rathenow's act 2 "Dio che non vedo."
3. Sophocles's lengthy interrogation scene has been reduced to a few lines in the opera.
4. In Sophocles, this information is first told to Jocasta.
5. This corresponds to the dialogue between the Elder and a servant in scene 5 of Sophocles.

• 29 •

Pierrot au cinéma (Capriccio d'amore)

Characters

Pierrot, tenor
Pierrette, soprano
Zaleffi, spoken role
Il Capitano Matamore, mute
L'Operatore del Cinematografo, spoken role
Gregorio, spoken role

Setting: Paris ("The Present," 1916–1917)

Scene 1 commences following a short overture, showing Pierrot and Pierrette's poorly furnished Montmartre apartment.[1] Pierrot is seated pensively on the sofa, deaf to Pierrette's calls from the bedroom. She enters and tries to console him in the duet "Ne cherche pas," offering to resume her dancing career to alleviate their lack of money. Jealous of the admirers he imagines she may have, Pierrot prefers Pierrette to remain at home, expressing this desire in the *couplet* "Ah, non! revoir des gens si betes." Although Pierrot has also forsaken *his* theatrical career, he now tells Pierrette that he has been offered an "office position" in a theater by their mutual acquaintance, the impresario and "ladies' man" Zaleffi.

Zaleffi, of course, visits as soon as Pierrot leaves, feigning to know nothing concerning Pierrot's supposed engagement, leading Pierrette to believe that Pierrot is being unfaithful. She therefore decides to accept Zaleffi's offer to earn eighty francs as a film actress, although saddened that she will be unable to keep her promise of no longer performing ("Oh! Mon Pierrot"). She then writes the "unfaithful" Pierrot a letter before leaving for the cinema.

Scene 2 opens in the film studio where a pantomime is about to be shot on a luxurious rococo set.[2] Pierrot arrives to put on his makeup, singing his

314

waltz aria, "Je cherche depuis huit longs jours"—reminiscent of "Ridi, pagliac-cio"—and hoping that Pierrette will forgive him. He leaves when Pierrette enters, also hoping that Pierrot will in turn forgive her "Ah! je sens mon coeur qui palpite."

The main body of *Pierrot au cinéma* is a danced pantomime—staged as though it were being filmed—interpreted by two dancers in the roles of Pier-rot and Pierrette.[3] Pierrette enters onstage masked and costumed in a blonde wig to the sound of a minuet. She approaches her stage husband Matamore (Crazylove), and, with gestures, asks which dance she should prepare for a soirée held by Monsieur Pantalon that evening. She then performs a gavotte, wondering if that should be the proper dance, later followed by a *rigaudon*. When Matamore motions that neither is appropriate, and that it should be something more "modern," the masked Pierrot is summoned, who plays the part of her enamored dance instructor. The men decide that the tango is the dance most in vogue and that Pierrette will be instructed for "at least one hour." The lovers passionately embrace when Matamore leaves, dancing the tango. When he returns unexpectedly, Pierrette hides and Pierrot assaults him, as the pantomime concludes with the latter posing victoriously over his prostrate victim.

The lights come up after the scene has been filmed and Pierrot—now enamored of his masked Pierrette—offers her a bouquet. She recognizes his voice and is astounded to hear his declarations of love. They soon recognize each other and immediately begin explaining that they were only trying to earn money. Pierrette forgives her seemingly unfaithful Pierrot, and the couple sings a final duet ("Dans les ci-ci"), which concludes the work.

There can be little doubt that Leoncavallo's main interest in the subject of *Pierrot au cinéma* centered on the work's novelty. It contains many modern elements, especially the growing importance of the film industry, which he correctly judged as an important future influence. The work is a mixture of ballet, dialogue, and vocal numbers approaching vaudeville.

NOTES

1. The libretto was originally in Italian before the French-language orchestral score—discussed previously—was written.

2. Leoncavallo chose to omit a choral number sung by actors and actresses ("Noi la vita"), leading directly to Pierrot's entrance instead.

3. Leoncavallo originally had a completely different version of the pantomime in mind, for which ten fully orchestrated selections exist: The Man in the Moon is sad because his daughter Opale—a masked princess—is depressed and refuses to smile. Jesters and buffoons are unsuccessful. An oriental dance follows ("Le ancelle") in addi-

tion to a comic one ("Le maschere ubriache"). Pierrot is called upon to release Opale from her misery. When he sings, she is bored; when he plays an instrument, she cries. He then claps his hands, and Opale's room is transformed into a seventeenth-century garden where they both dance a minuet, waltz, tango, and, finally, a "shimmy" that succeeds in making Opale smile.

• 30 •

La maschera nuda

Characters

Princess Mita, soprano

Pompon, soprano

La Signora Berroquet, soprano

Duca Mauro di Rosal, tenor

Cirillo, tenor

Il Cinese, spoken role

D'Estrophe, spoken role

Malachia, spoken role

Chevronnet, spoken role

Maitre d'Hôtel, spoken role

Fattore, spoken role

Giovane Andaluso, spoken role

L'Alcade, spoken role

Maggiordomo, spoken role

Vecchia, spoken role

Setting: Paris and "Rosal" (circa 1925)

The operetta is preceded by a short orchestral largo in G-major introducing the "maschera nuda" theme. Act 1 opens in the eccentrically furnished Parisian salon of the Russian princess Mita. A costume party is underway as musicians in seventeenth-century attire play a gavotte. Mita begins an elegant drinking song in F-major ("Versiam nei calici l'onda giuliva") to honor her friend, Cirillo, the reception's guest of honor, whose painting "La maschera nuda" (The Masked Nude) is currently being displayed in a Luxemburg museum. Cirillo insists that the painting's beautiful model was inspired solely by his imagination.

Mita sings a romanzetta in B-flat major ("Amor vano error") that has largely been borrowed—unaltered and in the same key—from *A chi la giarrettiera?*. Duke Mauro di Rosal enters, asking Cirillo to paint him a copy of the "maschera nuda," infatuated with its subject. Cirillo refuses. A duet between Mauro and Mita ("V'è un fiore assai strano vago") then begins, whereupon he invites her to his ancestral home. Realizing his growing interest in Mita, Mauro

317

expresses his thoughts in the aria "Vision fedel," before she leaves to pick out a costume for him. However, Mauro has already left when Mita returns, and the guests depart for the Moulin Rouge.

Act 2 takes place in the courtyard of Mauro's castle in Spain, where Mita and Cirillo are guests. Mauro is still intent on knowing who posed for the painting, singing of his longing (*canzone nostalgica*) in the B-flat major aria "O vision ideal." Cirillo is soon shocked to read that his painting has been stolen from the Luxemburg museum. He hurriedly leaves as Mita and Mauro sing of their growing affection in the duet "C'è nell'aria un palpitar." He then leads Mita to an alcove displaying Cirillo's "maschera nuda" painting, which he has stolen. When rose petals are strewn onto the canvas, Mita realizes that Mauro is in love with the painted image rather than with her. She then destroys the portrait with a knife.

Act 3 opens with a slow orchestral prelude in B-flat major based on Mauro's act 2 "canzone nostalgico." Cirillo is being "detained" by Mauro until he has finished creating a copy of the "maschera nuda" painting. Cirillo opens a door to reveal the nude Mita wearing a mask, posing in the painting's frame to Mauro's amazement. He now realizes that she was the original model and thus the object of his desire.

• 31 •

Il primo bacio

Characters

La Marchesa, spoken role
Il Marchese, spoken role
La Fanciulla del sogno, soprano
Il Giovane del sogno, tenor
La Nipotina, spoken role
Giovanni, mute

Setting: The Riviera ("The Present," 1920)

This musical sketch lasts approximately thirty minutes, the same time it takes for the action to unfold. In scene 1, *Il ricordo* (The Remembrance), the Marquess (il Marchese) and Marchioness (la Marchesa), at eighty-five and eighty, respectively, are seen relaxing in the garden of their Riviera villa on a warm September evening. The sunset reflects on the Mediterranean through the marble balustrade surrounding their park. A gentle nocturne can be heard as the couple drinks chamomile tea. They are interrupted when a clock strikes 9:00. Rather than retire, the Marchioness feels enchanted by the sunset and prefers to remain seated another few minutes. Guitars and mandolins sound in the distance with a waltz, accompanying the approaching night. The Marchioness remembers that it was the first waltz they had danced at their initial meeting decades earlier, during an April costume party. The Marquess recreates the dance with some jerky movements as his wife tries to join him. She collapses onto a chair for want of breath, and both fall asleep to the dying strains of the waltz tapering off in the evening breeze.

Scene 2, *Il sogno* (The Dream), begins with a reprisal of the nocturne. Our attention is then directed to a pink light infusing the villa's garden—now in full

319

bloom—as if enchanted. A youthful Marchioness enters in a ball gown, plucking the petals of a daisy, wondering whether or not she is loved. The nocturne ceases when the last remaining petal affirms her hope. A very youthful and slender Marquess then embraces her for the work's sole duet, "Dolce fior, sfinge bianca dell'amor," as they leave the stage to dance a waltz.

Two dancers perform a minuet dressed in 1870s attire. The Marquess and Marchioness reappear to dance the impassioned waltz heard in scene 1, expressing their rapture in song ("La danza è un vol leggero, arcan, che sfiora il suol e va lontan"). The waltz—the crux of the entire piece—is a haunting, bittersweet reverie (D-major), evoking all the nostalgia inherent in this short work. The duet is sealed with a kiss, as the couple exit and the stage darkens.

Scene 3, *Il risveglio* (The Awakening), reveals the elderly couple still asleep enjoying the dream, until their ten-year-old granddaughter wakes them to say goodnight. Both now relate how the previously heard waltz provided them with the same dream of that far-away dance. When the clock strikes 9:30, the Marchioness realizes that their dream has lasted a half hour. Too long for their age, believes the Marquess, but he is reminded by his wife that "love lasts an eternity." Their servant Giovanni enters, carrying two lighted candles. He leaves with a bow as the Marquess kisses his wife's hand, at which point both sneeze simultaneously, extinguishing the flames.

The Leoncavallo Opus

Note: All works are listed in alphabetical order. Works marked with an asterisk refer to posthumous compositions attributed to Leoncavallo. This does not necessarily imply that they were in fact authored by the composer or solely by him.

OPERAS

A chi la giarrettiera?

> Libretto by Edmondo Corradi
> First perfomance at Teatro del Casinò, Montecatini, 1919
> Unidentified conductor and cast

Are You There?

> Spoken text by Albert de Courville, lyrics by Edgar Wallace
> First performance at Prince of Wales Theatre, London, 1 November 1913
> Shirley Kellog and unidentified conductor and cast

La bohème

> Libretto by Ruggiero Leoncavallo, based on Henri Murger's novel *Scènes de la Bohème* and play *La Vie de Bohème* (in collaboration with Théodore Barrière)
> First performance at Teatro La Fenice, Venice, 6 May 1897
> Alessandro Pomè, conductor

Mimì: Rosina Storchio
Musette: Lison Frandin
Marcello: Umberto Beduschi
Rodolfo: Rodolfo Angelini-Fornari

La candidata

Original libretto by Giovacchino Forzano
First performance at Teatro Nazionale, Rome, 6 February 1915
Sassuoli, conductor
Aurora Lefleur: Emma Vecla
Franz: Gino Vannutelli
Sofronia: Annetta Peretti

Chatterton

Libretto by Ruggiero Leoncavallo, based on the play *Chatterton* by Alfred
de Vigny
First performance at Teatro Nazionale, Rome, 10 March 1896
Vittorio Podesti, conductor
Jenny: Adalgisa Gabbi
Chatterton: Benedetto Lucignani
Giorgio: Scipione Terzi
John Clark: Vittorio Coda
Lord Klifford: Aristide Anceschi

Edipo re*

First performance at the Auditorium Theater, Chicago, 13 December
1920.
Gino Marinuzzi, conductor
Giocasta: Dorothy Francis
Edipo: Titta Ruffo
Creonte: Albert Paillard

Maïa

Original libretto by Paul de Choudens
First performance at Teatro Costanzi, Rome, 15 January 1910
Pietro Mascagni, conductor
Maïa: Emma Carelli
Renaud: Rinaldo Grassi
Torias: Domenico Viglione Borghese

Malbruk

Libretto by Angelo Nessi, taken from Boccaccio's *Decameron*
First Performance at Teatro Nazionale, Rome, 20 January 1910
Pompeo Ricchieri, conductor
Alba: Elodia Maresca
Malbruk: Ferruccio Corradetti
Arnolfo: Giuseppe Pasquini

Mameli

Original libretto by Ruggiero Leoncavallo and Gualtiero Belvederi
First performance at Teatro Carlo Felice, Genoa, 27 April 1916
Ruggiero Leoncavallo, conductor
Delia Terzaghi: Eugenia Burzio
Cristina Trivulzio: Vida Ferluga
Goffredo Mameli: Carmelo Alabiso
Carlo Terzaghi: Emilio Bione

The Manicuring Girl*

The score of *The Manicuring Girl* comprises various undated Leoncavallo compositions placed together by his wife Berthe following the composer's death.
Libretto by Robert di Simone
Never performed

La maschera nuda*

Libretto by Ferdinando Paolieri and Luigi Bonelli
First performance at Teatro Politeama, Naples, 30 June 1925 (or possibly Teatro Excelsior, Naples, 2 May 1925)
Luigi Rizzola, conductor
Mita: Jole Pacifici
Pompon: Luisa Abrate
Duca Mauro: M. Manfredi
Cirillo: Gino Bianchi

I Medici

Original libretto by Ruggiero Leoncavallo
First performance at Teatro dal Verme, Milan, 9 November 1893

Rodolfo Ferrari, conductor
Simonetta Cattaeni: Adelina Stehle
Fioretta De' Gori: A. Gini Pizzorni
Giuliano De' Medici: Francesco Tamagno
Lorenzo De' Medici: Ottorino Beltrami
Giambattista da Montesecco: Giovanni Scarneo
Francesco Pazzi: Ludovico Contini

Mimì Pinson (Revision of *La bohème*)

Libretto by Ruggiero Leoncavallo, based on Henri Murger's novel *Scènes de la Bohème* and play *Vie de Bohème*
First performance at Teatro Massimo, Palermo, 14 April 1913
Gaetano Bavagnoli, conductor
Mimì: Ida Quaiatti
Musette: Rita D'Oria
Rodolfo: Giuseppe Armanini
Marcello: Giuseppe Danise

Pagliacci

Libretto by Ruggiero Leoncavallo, based on the play *Un drama nuevo* by Don Manuel Tamayo y Baus and the play *La femme de Tabarin* by Catulle Mendès and Paul Ferrier
First performance at Teatro dal Verme, Milan, 21 May 1892
Arturo Toscanini, conductor
Nedda: Adelina Stehle
Canio: Fiorello Giraud
Silvio: Mario Roussel
Tonio: Victor Maurel

Pierrot au cinéma

Libretto by C. Trulet
First performance at Teatro Manzoni, Pistoia, 23 October 1993
Graziano Mandozzi, conductor
Pierrette: Chiara Taigi
Pierrot: Lorenzo Cecchele

Prestami tua moglie

Libretto by Edmondo Corradi, based on the play *Prête-moi ta femme* by Maurice Desvallières

First performance at Teatro del Casinò, Montecatini, 2 September 1916
Cuffia, conductor
Nanon: Dora Domar
Margherita: Pina Ciotti
Rissolin: Armando Fineschi
Rabastoul: Leopoldo Michelazzi

*Il primo bacio**

Libretto by Luigi Bonelli
First performance at Teatro del Casinò, Montecatini, 29 April 1923
Unidentified conductor and cast

La reginetta delle rose

Original libretto by Giovacchino Forzano
First performance at Teatro Costanzi, Rome, 24 June 1912
Costantino Lombardo, conductor
Lilian: Stefi Csillag
Max: Guglielmo Zanasi
Mikalis: Nanetta Braconi
Don Pedro: Gaetano Prudenza

Der Roland von Berlin

Libretto by Ruggiero Leoncavallo, based on the novel *Der Roland von Berlin* by Willibald Alexis
First performance at Royal Court Opera, Berlin, 13 December 1904
Karl Muck, conductor
Alda: Emmy Destinn
Eva: Geraldine Farrar
Henning: Wilhelm Grüning
Rathenow: Baptist Hoffmann
Kurfürst Friedrich: Paul Knüpfer

Zazà

Libretto by Ruggiero Leoncavallo (possibly in collaboration with Carlo Zangarini), based on the play *Zazà* by Pierre Berton and Charles Simon
First performance at Teatro Lirico, Milan, 10 November 1900
Arturo Toscanini, conductor

Zazà: Rosina Storchio
Milio: Edoardo Garbin
Cascart: Mario Sammarco
Anaide: Clorinda Pini-Corsi

Gli zingari

Libretto by Enrico Cavacchioli and Guglielmo Emanuel, based on Alexander Pushkin's narrative poem "The Gypsies"
First performance at the Hippodrome, London, 16 September 1912
Ruggiero Leoncavallo, conductor
Fleana: Rinalda Pavoni
Radu: Egidio Cunego
Tamar: Ernesto Caronna
Il Vecchio: Armando Santolini

SONGS

Note: It was not possible, although every effort has been made, to ascertain the date of composition of all of Leoncavallo's songs. Names in parentheses refer to the lyricists. Again, not all could be identified.

L'addio/Schwerer Abschied (Leoncavallo), 1893
L'andalouse (De Musset), 1908
A ninon (De Musset), 1896
A Summer Idyll (C.L.H.)
Adieu, Suzon/Suzon (De Musset), 1893
Amore! (De Vaux), ca. 1884
Amour et parapluie
Anelito d'amore/Die Allmacht der Liebe (Leoncavallo)
Aprile!/Der Lenz! (Vivanti), 1907
At Peace (Roberts)
Ave Maria, 1905
Le baiser, 1896
Barcarola
Canzone d'amore/Serenata medioevale (Nessi), 1912
Canzone appassionata/Wenn der Tag entflieht (Nicotra)
Canzone d'autunno (Leoncavallo)
La canzone della nonna/Das Lied der Grossmutter (Nigra), 1894
Canzonetta di stile antico (Malherbe)
Chanson

La chanson de Don Juan (Leoncavallo), 1904

La chanson des yeux (Chénier), ca. 1880s

C'è nel tuo sguardo (Cotugno)

C'est bien toi/Mein guter Engel (De Musset), 1898

C'est le renouveau, ma Suzon/Ma Suzon (Collet)

C'est l'heure mystérieuse/The Dreamy Twilight Is Falling (Leoncavallo)

C'était un rêve/Es war ein Traum (Collet), 1893

Chitarretta (Leoncavallo), 1893

Cloches du soir

Déclaration/Geständnis (Silvestre), 1893

De l'ombre où mon destin (Silvestre)

Derniers voeux

Dietro le nubi

Donna, vorrei morir/Möcht gern dem Leben bald entfliehen (Stecchetti), 1893

Era d'inverno (Stecchetti)

Et nunc et semper/Aujourd'hui et à jamais!/Heute und immerdar!/Oggi e sempre!/Sempre! To-day and To-day and for Ever! (Coppée), 1906

Fantasia (Carducci)

Fantasia/To-night and to-morrow/Heute und Morgen (Weatherly), 1893

Foglie d'autunno (Leoncavallo), 1913

For I Do Love You So (De Courville)

Gare au loup! (Collet)

Hue! Dia! Mon grison (Collet), ca. 1880s

Hymne à la lyre (Silvestre), 1898

Imploration éperdue

Invocation à la muse (From *La nuit de mai*), 1886

Je n'ai rien su/Ich ahnt es nicht (Silvestre), 1893

Je ne sais pas ton nom/Will nicht wissen, wer Du bist (Collet), ca. 1884

Jeunesse et printemps (Capet), ca. 1884

Lasciati amar/Come, Love, Be Mine!/Yearning for You!/Mädchen, sei mein! (Leoncavallo)

Lost Love (Roberts)

Madame avisez-y/Oh, Phillis, Have a Care! (Malherbe), ca. 1884

Mai fleuri (Dorémi), 1905

Mandolinata (Leoncavallo), 1907

Mattinata (Carducci)

Mattinata (Leoncavallo), 1904

Melodia elegiaca, 1878

Meriggiata (Leoncavallo), 1908

La morta (Pascoli)

Napuletanata (Leoncavallo)
Ne m'oubliez pas (De Vaux), 1884
Ninna Nanna (Leoncavallo), 1904
Non dirmi chi sei
Nostalgia d'amore
Notte ha stesso il gran vel (Leoncavallo), 1905
Nuit de décembre (De Musset), 1899
Nulla so
O bellezza sconosciuta
Ottobre (Stecchetti), 1893
Pensiero/Un organetto suona per la via/Gedanken (Stecchetti), 1893
Prenez garde à mon oiseau (Collet)
Qu'à jamais le soleil se voile/Bleib' O Sonne (Dumas fils), 1893
Quando la donna mia
La renouveau, ca. 1884
Rapsodia primaverile/A Spring Rhapsody (Leoncavallo)
Ruit hora (Carducci), 1893
Se!/Wenn! (Leoncavallo), 1907
Sérénade française (Collet), 1902
Sérénade napolitaine (Collet) 1902
Serenata (Carducci), 1899
Serenatella (Leoncavallo), 1897
Si c'est aimer!/Wenn das die Liebe ist (Collet), ca. 1880s
Sussurrano le mille aure del bosco (Pascoli), 1877
La symphonie des hannetons
Tristesse (De Musset), 1882
Tutto tace, ca. 1884
Un sogno
Veux-tu ?/Vuoi tu? (Vaucaire), 1908
Vieni, amor mio!/Komm, Geliebte! (Vivanti), 1907

ORCHESTRAL WORKS

Note: Names in parentheses refer to authors of short vocal texts included in some of Leoncavallo's works.

Cortège de Pulcinella, 1899
Écho (Cantata for voice and chamber orchestra), 1884
Gagliarda, 1898
Gavotta

Grand trio en sol
Karaban (Fox-Trot)
La nuit de mai (De Musset), 1886
Le modèle masqué
Pantins vivants
Romanesca
Serenade (violin, cello, piano)
Trio in re maggiore (incomplete)
Requiem (incomplete)

BALLETS

La vita di una marionetta
Séraphitus-Séraphita (Balzac), 1894

PIANO COMPOSITIONS

Au bord du lac/Träumerei
Barcarola veneziana*
Bohémienne
Brise de mer (cello), 1906
Chanson d'amour
Dolce notte*
Due pezzi di stile arabo
Flirt-Waltzer
Gagliarda
Gavotte, 1897
Gitana tango
Gondola, 1899
Granadinas
Intermezzo
La joyeuse
Marcia nuziale
Menuet d'arlequin
Nights of Italy, 1914
Notturno
Pantins vivants, 1897
Papillon 1906

Pensée d'automne, 1906
Piccola canzone
Playeras ancienne
Reverie, 1919
Romanesca, 1898
Sarabande, 1906
Sérénade (cello), 1898
Sérénade Valse/Sérénade Napolitaine
Serenata d'Arlecchino (*Pagliacci*)
Sevillana
Sous les palmiers
Tarantella, 1899
Tema di Marcia Trionfale
Träumerei, 1904
Valse à la lune/Sérénade Française
Valse coquette, 1897
Valse mélancolique, 1901
Valse mignonne, 1898
Valse passionnée, 1912

LIBRETTI

Mario Wetter (Machado)
Redenzione (Pennacchio)

HYMNS AND MARCHES

Délivrance! Hymne à la France (Rivet), 1915
Hymne (C. Trulet), soprano, tenor, and piano, 1916
Inno della Croce Rossa (Allievo), 1901
Inno della Lega Nazionale (Pitteri), 1913
Inno Franco-Italiano
Invocazione all'Italia (Leoncavallo), soprano, tenor and piano, 1916
Marcia
Marcia nuziale, 1912
Marcia Yankee (reworking of Viva L'America!), 1912
Tema di marcia trionfale per l'eroica armata Italiana di Tripoli (Leoncavallo), 1911

La victoire est à nous (Choudens), 1915
Viva L'America!, 1906

TRANSLATION

La basoche (Messager)

ARTICLES AND PREFACES

Le dolorose rime (Gina Bertolini Marcionni)
Wagner e Mazzini, 1917

Bibliography

Adami, Giuseppe. *Giacomo Puccini*. Lindau-Bodensee: Frisch & Perneder, 1948.

———. *Giulio Ricordi e i suoi musicisti*, Milan: Treves, 1933.

Ashbrook, William. "Alcuni aspetti di Ruggero Leoncavallo librettista." In Guiot and Maehder, *Atti del Iº convegno internazionale di studi su Ruggero Leoncavallo*, 139–48.

Baker, Evan. "Leoncavallo in the United States and Canada in Fall 1906." In Guiot and Maehder, *Atti del 3º convegno internazionale di studi su Ruggero Leoncavallo*, 37–164.

Barblan, Guglielmo. "Toscanini e La Scala," Milano: La Scala, 1972. Program notes.

Benoît-Jeannin, Maxime. *Georgette Leblanc*. Brussels: Le Cri, 1998.

Béringuier, Richard. "Die Rolande Deutschlands." *Verein für die Geschichte Berlins*, 1890.

Buckle, Richard. *Diaghilev*. New York: Atheneum, 1979.

Budden, Julian. "Leoncavallo and *Zazà*," Wexford: Wexford Festival Opera, 1990. Program notes.

Budden, Julian. *Puccini*. Oxford: Oxford University Press, 2000.

———. "Primi rapporti fra Leoncavallo e la casa Ricordi: dieci missive finora sconosciute." In Guiot and Maehder, *Atti del Iº convegno internazionale di studi su Ruggero Leoncavallo*, 49–60.

Carelli, Augusto. *Emma Carelli: Trent'anni di vita del teatro lirico*. Rome: Edizioni Maglione, 1932.

Carner, Mosco. *Puccini, a Critical Biography*. Surrey: Duckworth, 1958.

Cella, Franca. "Scena, messinscena e retroscena: cronaca di una società," Palermo: Teatro Massimo, 1995. Program notes.

Cellamare, Daniele. *Pietro Mascagni*. Rome: Fratelli Palombi, 1965.

Colombani, Alfredo. "L'Opera Italiana nel Secolo XIX." Milan: *Corriere della Sera*, 1900.

Conati, Marcello. "Leoncavallo operettista." Guiot and Maehder, *Atti del 2º convegno internazionale di Studi su Ruggero Leoncavallo*, 199–214.

Crivelli, Filippo. "La ricerca di un teatro perduto." Palermo: Teatro Massimo, 1995. Program notes for *Zazà*.

D'Amico, Alessandro. "*Zazà* di Pierre Berton e Charles Simon," Palermo: Teatro Massimo, 1995. Program notes for *Zazà*.

332

De Angelis, Alberto. "Il capolavoro inespresso di R. Leoncavallo *Tormenta*, opera di soggetto sardo," in *Rivista Musicale Italiana* 30 (1923): 563–76.

De Courville, Albert. *I Tell You*. London: Chapman & Hall, 1928.

Defraia, Antonio. *Piero Schiavazzi, tra mito e verità*. Bologna: Bongiovanni, 1995.

De Rensis, Raffaelle. "Per Umberto Giordano e Ruggiero Leoncavallo." Siena, 1949.

Di Tizio, Franco. *Francesco Paolo Tosti*. Francavilla al Mare: privately published, 1984.

Dizikes, John. *Opera in America, a Cultural History*. New Haven: Yale University Press, 1993.

Dryden, Konrad. *Riccardo Zandonai, a Biography*. Frankfurt: Peter Lang, 1999.

———. "In *Pagliacci*'s Shadow: Recapturing Leoncavallo." London: Royal Opera, Covent Garden, 7 July 2003. Program notes for *Pagliacci*.

———. "Gross wie Hugo, Beeindruckend wie Bismarck und Gutaussehend wie Byron." Cologne: Cologne Opera, 22 October 2002. Program notes for *Pagliacci*.

———. "O Jeunesse, Printemps de la vie: Leoncavallova *Bohèma*." Prague: State Opera, 13 March 2003. Program notes for *La bohème*.

———. "Mosaik eines Meisterportraitisten." Berlin: Deutsche Oper, 23 April 2005. Program notes for *Pagliacci*.

Farrar, Geraldine. *Such Sweet Compulsion*. New York: Greystone Press, 1938.

Fauré, Gabriel. "Leoncavallo" in *Opinions musicales*, Paris, 1930: 64–67.

Forbes, Elizabeth. "Leoncavallo's *La bohème*." Wexford: Festival Opera, 1994. Program notes.

Förster, Michael-Andree. *Das Medium Musik in der dynastischen "Reklame" Kaiser Wilhelms II*. Mainz: Johannes Guttenberg University, 2005.

Forzano, Giovacchino. *Come li ho conosciuti*. Turin: Eri, 1957.

Frandin, Lison. "Il primo passo del maestro Leoncavallo." Trieste: Piccolo della Sera, 1905.

Gadotti, Adonide. *Carmen Melis: Un grande soprano del verismo*. Roma: Bardi, 1985.

Gara, Eugenio. *Carteggi Pucciniani*. Milan: Casa Ricordi, 1958.

Gatti-Casazza, Giulio. *Memories of the Opera*. New York: Vienna House, 1973.

Gavazzeni, Gianandrea. "*Zazà*, le retrovie del melodramma." Palermo: Teatro Massimo, 1995. Program notes.

Giani, R., and A. Engelfried. "*I Medici*." *Rivista Musicale Italiana*, 1 (1894): 86–116.

Giazotto, Remo. "Uno sconosciuto progetto teatrale di Ruggero Leoncavallo." Milan: Nuova Rivista Musicale Italiana, 1968.

Girardi, Michele. "Il verismo musicale alla ricerca dei suoi tutori. Alcuni modelli di *Pagliacci* nel teatro musicale *Fin de siècle*." In Guiot and Maehder, *Atti del I° convegno internazionale di studi su Ruggero Leoncavallo*, 61–70.

Goldin, Daniela. *La Vera Fenice*. Turin: Einaudi, 1985.

Greenfield, Howard. *Puccini, Sein Leben und Seine Welt*. Königstein: Athenäum Verlag, 1982.

Groos, Arthur. "From 'Addio del passato' to 'Le patate son fredde,' Representations of Consumption in Leoncavallo's *I Medici* and *La bohème*." In Guiot and Maehder, *Atti del 2° convegno internazionale di Studi su Ruggero Leoncavallo*, 57–74.

Groos, Arthur, and Roger Parker. "Giacomo Puccini: *La bohème*" in *Cambridge Opera Handbook*. Cambridge: Cambridge University Press, 1986.

Gualerzi, Giorgio. "Rosina & Emma per sempre," Palermo: Teatro Massimo, 1995, Program notes.

————. "*Zazà* in Italia," Palermo: Teatro Massimo, 1995. Program notes for *Zazà.*

————. "Ruggero Leoncavallo: i suoi interpreti" in Milan: La Scala, 1959. Program notes.

Guarnieri-Corazzol, Adriana. "Scrittori-Librettisti e Librettisti-Scrittori tra Scapigliatura e Décadence." In Guiot and Maehder, *Atti del 2° convegno internazionale di Studi su Ruggero Leoncavallo*, 11–40.

Guiot, Lorenza, and Kurt Deggeller. "Ruggero Leoncavallo e l'inizio della produzione fonografica." In Guiot and Maehder, *Atti del 2° convegno internazionale di Studi su Ruggero Leoncavallo*, 269–85.

Guiot, Lorenza, and Jürgen Maehder, eds. *Nazionalismo e cosmopolitismo nell'opera fra '800 e '900, atti del 3° convegno internazionale di studi su Ruggero Leoncavallo*. Milan: Casa Musicale Sonzogno, 1998.

————. *Letteratura, musica e teatro al tempo di Ruggero Leoncavallo, atti del 2° convegno internazionale di studi su Ruggero Leoncavallo*. Milan: Casa Musicale Sonzogno, 1995.

————. *Ruggero Leoncavallo nel suo tempo, atti del I° convegno internazionale di studi su Ruggero Leoncavallo*. Milan: Casa Musicale Sonzogno, 1993.

Hall, George. "Leoncavallo in America." *Opera* 36, no. 2 (1985): 153–61.

————. "Leoncavallo in London." 2 *Opera* 35, no. 3 (1984): 246–53.

Hanslick, Eduard. "*Der Bajazzo* von Leoncavallo." *Der modernen Oper, vol. vii; Fünf Jahre Musik* (1891–1895): Kritiken (Berlin, 3/1911), 96–104, 1895/6.

————. "*Die Bohème.*" *Der modernen Oper, vol viii: Am ende des Jahrhunderts* (1895–1899): *Musikalische Kritiken und Schilderungen* (Berlin, 3/1911), 123–32, 1899.

Holde, A. "A Little Known Letter by Berlioz and Unpublished letters by Cherubini, Leoncavallo, and Hugo Wolf." *Musical Quarterly* 37, no. 3 (1951): 340–53.

————. "Unpublished letter of Leoncavallo to Massenet." *Musical Quarterly* 37, no. 3 (1951): 350–51.

Irvine, Demar. *Massenet, a Chronicle of His Life and Times.* Portland, Ore.: Amadeus Press, 1994.

Karpath, Ludwig. "Das Dioskurenpaar Mascagni-Leoncavallo." In *Begegnung mit dem Genius.* Vienna: Fiba Verlag, 1934, 365.

Kelkel, Manfred. "D'Une *Bohème* à l'autre." In Guiot and Maehder, *Atti del 2° convegno internazionale di Studi su Ruggero Leoncavallo*, 49–56.

Klein, J. W. "Ruggero Leoncavallo (1858–1919)." *Opera* 9 (1958): 158–62, 232–36.

Kolodin, Irving. *The Metropolitan Opera 1883–1966.* New York: Alfred A. Knopf, 1967.

Korngold, J. "Ruggiero Leoncavallo: *Zazà*, 1909." In *Die romanische Oper der Gegenwart.* Vienna: Rikola, 1922, 103–6.

Lauer, Lucinde. "Leoncavallos *Zingari*-Anmerkungen zum libretto einer italienischen Pushkin Oper." In Guiot and Maehder, *Atti del 2° convegno internazionale di Studi su Ruggero Leoncavallo*, 174–86.

Lederer, Josef-Horst. "'Er scheiterte an einem Beginnen, das sein Ehrgeiz ihn nicht hatte ausschlagen lassen' Zur Zeitkritik an R. Leoncavallos Historischem Drama *Der Roland von Berlin.*" In Guiot and Maehder, *Atti del 3° convegno internazionale di studi su Ruggero Leoncavallo*, 181–92.

Leoncavallo, Ruggero. *Manuele Dantesco ad uso della gioventù*. Livorno: Becheroni, 1859.

Leoncavallo, Ruggiero. "M. Leoncavallo par lui-même." *Le Figaro*, Paris: 9 June 1899.

———. *Appunti Vari delle Autobiografici di R. Leoncavallo*. Unpublished. Milan: Casa Musicale Sonzogno Archives, 1915.

Lerario, Teresa. "Ruggero Leoncavallo e il soggetto dei *Pagliacci*." *Chigiana* XXVI–XXVII (1971): 115–22.

Loubinoux, Gerard. "Leoncavallo e l'operetta francese." In Guiot and Maehder, *Atti del 2° convegno internazionale di Studi su Ruggero Leoncavallo*, 187–98.

Maeder, C., M. Costantino, and Bruno Moretti. "Fenomeni pragmatico-testuali e strutture metriche nei libretti di Ruggero Leoncavallo." In Guiot and Maehder, *Atti del 2° convegno internazionale di Studi su Ruggero Leoncavallo*, 74–82.

Maehder, Jürgen. "Quest'è Mimì, gaia fioraia, Zur Transformation der Gestalt Mimìs in Puccinis und Leoncavallos *Bohème*-Opern." In *Opern und Opernfiguren: Festschrift für Joachim Herz*. Anif: Müller-Speiser, 1989, 301–19.

———. "'Der Dichter spricht' Livelli di discorso musicale nella *Bohème* di Ruggero Leoncavallo." In Guiot and Maehder, *Atti del I° convegno internazionale di studi su Ruggero Leoncavallo*, 83–116.

———. "Timbri e tecniche d'orchestrazione: Influssi formativi sull'orchestrazione del primo Leoncavallo." In Guiot and Maehder, *Atti del 2° convegno internazionale di Studi su Ruggero Leoncavallo*, 141–66.

———. "*I Medici* e l'immagine del Rinascimento italiano nella letteratura del decadentismo europeo." In Guoit and Maehder, *Atti del 3° convegno internazionale di studi su Ruggero Leoncavallo*, 239–60.

———. "Paris-Bilder: Zur Transformation von Henry Murgers Roman in den *Bohème*-Opern Puccinis und Leoncavallos." *Jahrbuch für Opernforschung* 2 (1987), 109–76.

———. "Musik über Musik: Meyerbeer, Rossini e Wagner nella *Bohème* di Ruggero Leoncavallo in Dentro e fuori il melodramma," Venice, 1989. Program notes.

Maione, Rino, ed. *Franco Alfano*. Milan: Rugginenti Editore, 1999.

Mandozzi, Graziano. "*Séraphitus-Séraphita*." Pistoia: Teatro Comunale Manzoni, 1994. Program notes.

———. *I Medici von Ruggero Leoncavallo*. Master's thesis, Vienna: Universität für Musik und darstellende Kunst, 2003.

Marchetti, Arnaldo. *Puccini, Com'Era*. Milan: Curci, 1973.

———. "Lo smisurato sogno dell'autore dei *Pagliacci*." *Rassegna Musicale Curci* (1972).

Martinotti, Sergio. "Leoncavallo e la lirica da camera italiana." In Guiot and Maehder, *Atti del I° convegno internazionale di studi su Ruggero Leoncavallo*, 181–200.

Menichini, Maria. *Alfredo Catalani*. Lucca: Maria Pacini Fazzi, 1993.

Meyerstein, E. H. W. *A Life of Thomas Chatterton*, 1930 reprint, New York: Russell, 1974.

Moore, Edward C. *Forty Years of Opera in Chicago*, 1930 reprint, New York: Arno Press, 1977.

Morini, Mario. "Leoncavallo e il suo contributo all'operetta." Palermo: Teatro Massimo, 14 March 1992. Program notes for *Reginetta delle rose*.

———. "Come è nata *Zazà*." Palermo: Teatro Massimo, 1995. Program notes.

————. Prospetto cronologico della vita e delle opere di Ruggero Leoncavallo." Palermo: Teatro Masssimo, 1995. Program notes.

Morini, Mario, Roberto Iovino, and Alberto Paloscia, eds. *Pietro Mascagni, Epistolario.* Lucca: Libreria Musicale Italiana, 1996.

Müller, Karl-Josef. *Mahler, Leben, Werke, Dokumente.* Mainz: Piper-Schott, 1998.

Nardi, Piero. *Vita di Arrigo Boito.* Verona: Mondadori, 1944.

Painter, George D. *Marcel Proust, A Biography.* London: Chatto & Windus, 1989.

Parker, Roger. "Ghosts from 'Christmas Past' nella Bohème di Leoncavallo." In Guiot and Maehder, *Atti del I° convegno internazionale di studi su Ruggero Leoncavallo,* 71–82.

Pastor, W. "Leoncavallo's *Roland von Berlin*: Uraufführung im Berliner Opernhaus." *Die Musik* 14, no. 2 (1904): 45–46.

Phillips-Matz, Mary Jane. *Verdi, A Biography.* New York: Oxford University Press, 1993.

Piccardi, Carlo. "Pierrot-Pagliaccio. La maschera tra naturalismo e simbolismo." In Guiot and Maehder, *Atti del I° convegno internazionale di studi su Ruggero Leoncavallo,* 201–45.

Pintorno, Giuseppe. *Giacomo Puccini: 276 lettere inedite.* Milan: Fondo dell'Accademia d'Arte a Montecatini Terme, 1974.

Pistone, Danièle. "Ruggero Leoncavallo e gli ambienti artistici parigini." In Guiot and Maehder, *Atti del 2° convegno internazionale di Studi su Ruggero Leoncavallo,* 41–48.

Porro, Maurizio. "I quattro volti di *Zazà* nel cinema." Palermo: Teatro Massimo, 1995. Program notes.

Prawy, Marcel. *Die Wiener Oper.* Vienna: Verlag Fritz Molden, 1969.

Rubboli, Daniele. *Ridi Pagliaccio.* Lucca: Maria Pacini Fazzi, 1985.

Ruffo, Titta. *La Mia Parabola.* Milan: Fratelli Treves Editori, 1937.

Sachs, Harvey. *Toscanini, Eine Biographie.* Munich: Piper & Co. Verlag, 1986.

Sala, Emilio. "Intorno a due 'disposizioni sceniche' della *Bohème* di Leoncavallo." In Guiot and Maehder, *Atti del I° convegno internazionale di studi su Ruggero Leoncavallo,* 117–38.

Sansone, Matteo. "Il verismo di *Fedora* e di *Zazà*." In Guiot and Maehder, *Atti del I° convegno internazionale di studi su Ruggero Leoncavallo,* 163–80.

————. "Patriottismo in musica: Il *Mameli* di Leoncavallo." In Guiot and Maehder, *Atti atti del 3° convegno internazionale di studi su Ruggero Leoncavallo,* 99–112.

————. "The verismo of Ruggero Leoncavallo; a source study of *Pagliacci*." *ML*20 (1989): 342–62.

Schickling, Dieter. *Giacomo Puccini.* Stuttgart: Deutsche Verlags Anstalt, 1989.

Seligman, Vincent. *Puccini among Friends.* London: Macmillan & Co, Ltd., 1938.

Stivender, David. *Mascagni: An Autobiography Compiled, Edited, and Translated from Original Sources.* New York: Pro/Am Music Resources, 1988.

Streicher, Johannes. "Del Settecento riscritto. Intorno al metateatro dei *Pagliacci*." In Guiot and Maehder, *Atti del 2° convegno internazionale di Studi su Ruggero Leoncavallo,* 89–102.

Tabanelli, N. "La Causa Ricordi-Leoncavallo." *Rivista Musicale Italiana* 6 (1899): 833–54.

Vallora, Marco. "Viaggio in Librettowa." Teatro Massimo, Palermo, 14 March 1992.

Program notes for *Reginetta delle rose*.

Velly, Jean-Jacques. "Quelques aspects du traitement orchestral dans *Le Roland de Berlin*." In Guiot and Maehder, *Atti del 2° convegno internazionale di Studi su Ruggero Leoncavallo*, 167–74.

Wagner, Cosima. *Diaries 1878–1883*. New York: Harcourt Brace Jovanovich, 1980.

Weaver, William, and Simonetta Puccini, eds. *The Puccini Companion*. New York: Norton, 1994.

Wilhelm II. *Meine Vorfahren*. Berlin: Verlag für Kulturpolitik, 1929.

Wright, Lesley. "Leoncavallo, *La Bohème* and the Parisian Press." In Guiot and Maehder, *Atti atti del 3° convegno internazionale di studi su Ruggero Leoncavallo*, 165–80.

Zoppelli, Luca. "*I Medici* e Wagner." In Guiot and Maehder, *Atti del I° convegno internazionale di studi su Ruggero Leoncavallo*, 149–62.

Zurletti, Michelangelo. *Catalani*. Torino: E.D.T., 1982.

Index

About the Author

$\mathscr{K}$onrad Dryden is a frequent lecturer on verismo and has written articles for numerous international opera houses, including the Metropolitan Opera, San Francisco Opera, Rome Opera, Prague State Opera, Royal Opera Covent Garden, Wexford Festival Opera, Cologne Opera, Kiel Opera, and Deutsche Oper Berlin. His interviews, reviews, and essays have appeared in a variety of publications, including *Das Opernglas*, *The Opera Quarterly*, *Die Musikforschung*, and *CPO Records*, and his biography of Riccardo Zandonai was published by Peter Lang, Inc., in 1999. He is currently professor of music and German at the University of Maryland University College–Europe.

Dr. Dryden was born in California to a British father (descendant of poet laureate John Dryden) and a German mother (descendant of Ignaz von Rudhart, prime minister to King Otto of Bavaria and Greece). He is married to the historian Countess Florence de Peyronnet-Dryden.